Will China Democratize?

A *Journal of Democracy* Book

•

Published under the auspices of
the International Forum for Democratic Studies

Will China Democratize?

Edited by Andrew J. Nathan, Larry Diamond,
and Marc F. Plattner

The Johns Hopkins University Press
Baltimore

9 8 7 6 5 4 3 2 1

Chapters in this volume appeared in the following issues of the *Journal of Democracy*:
Prologue, Winter 1990; chapter 1, July 2007; chapters 2–4, 6, and 8, January 1998; chapters 5, 13, 14, 18, 23, 25, 27, and 28, January 2013; chapters 7, 9, 10, and 17, January 2003; chapters 11 and 12, January 2012; chapters 15, 16, and 22, July 2009; chapter 19, October 2010; chapter 20, July 2000; Appendix, January 2010. For all reproduction rights, please contact the Johns Hopkins University Press.

The Johns Hopkins University Press
2715 North Charles Street
Baltimore, Maryland 21218-4363
www.press.jhu.edu

Library of Congress Cataloging-in-Publication Data

Will China democratize? / edited by Andrew J. Nathan, Larry Diamond, Marc F. Plattner.
   pages cm. — (A journal of democracy book)
   Includes index.
   ISBN-13: 978-1-4214-1243-6 (paperback)
   ISBN-13: 978-1-4214-1244-3 (electronic)
   ISBN-10: 1-4214-1243-8 (paperback)
   ISBN-10: 1-4214-1244-6 (electronic)
   1. Democratization—China. 2. Democracy—China. 3. Political culture—China.
4. Civil rights—China. 5. Human rights—China. 6. China—Politics and government.
I. Nathan, Andrew J. (Andrew James) II. Diamond, Larry. III. Plattner, Marc F., 1945–
JQ1516.W55 2013
   320.951—dc23

                                                                        2013017638

Cover image: "China Peace," bronze by Tim Holmes, 20 inches (49 cm), 1989

A week after the Tiananmen Square massacre in Beijing in June 1989, a group of escaped Chinese dissidents joined Chinese students in the United States to form the China Information Center. Their purpose was to try to get the word back into China about what had really happened since the Chinese government was covering up the event. To help raise money they called artist/activist Tim Holmes, who created this bronze "China Peace" to commemorate the movement. Viewing the bronze from the front one can make out the written characters, which reflect the Chinese dissidents' absolute devotion to nonviolent resistance. From the side, these same shapes become a leaping figure, expressing the Chinese quest for liberty within the context of the desire of all living beings to breathe free. Sales of the sculpture were used to fund a drive to subvert the government censors and get the truth to the Chinese people by faxing a narrative of the event, complete with photos of the massacre, to random fax numbers throughout China. Over the next weeks the real news of the event spontaneously erupted from fax machines all over China in what became known as the "first fax revolution in history." More of the story and access to the art can be found at *TimHolmesStudio.com*.

CONTENTS

ACKNOWLEDGMENTS

Our most recent previous *Journal of Democracy* book, *Democracy in East Asia: A New Century* (published by the Johns Hopkins University Press in March 2013), focused primarily on East Asian countries that had some experience with at least partially democratic governance. As a result, it contained only two chapters that dealt directly with the People's Republic of China (PRC), the region's most powerful and in many ways its most influential country. Yet the PRC has probably received more attention in the *Journal of Democracy* than any other single country. This led us to consider the possibility of publishing an edited volume that would bring together many of the most important essays on China's democratic prospects that have appeared over the years in our pages. The result is the book that you now hold in your hands.

Once we made the decision to proceed with this project, we immediately thought of asking our longtime Editorial Board member Andrew J. Nathan, one of the world's most eminent scholars of Chinese politics, to join us in coediting this volume. Not only had he authored a number of our most memorable articles on China, but we had regularly turned to him for guidance whenever we decided to commission a set of articles on that country. We are most grateful that he accepted our invitation to serve as a coeditor, for he provided us with the same kind of useful insights in designing and arranging this volume as he had done when advising us about the *Journal* in the past.

We are also indebted to our colleagues at the Johns Hopkins University Press (our book editor Suzanne Flinchbaugh, as well as Bill Breichner and Carol Hamblen of the Journals Division) for all their help and encouragement in the preparation of *Will China Democratize?* Most of all, however, we thank the members of the *Journal of Democracy* staff, who balanced work on this volume with the ever-present demands of the *Journal*'s quarterly publication schedule. Managing Editor Brent Kallmer handled the layout and production with dexterity and determination. The essays published here benefited from the labors of many of the editors who have served on the *Journal* staff over its nearly two-and-a-half decades of publication, but Executive Editor Phil Costopoulos and Senior Associate Editor Tracy Brown deserve the lion's share of the credit for the clarity and style found in the pages that follow. In addition, Assistant Editor Nate Grubman provided substantial assistance in the drafting of the Introduction and ably managed the voluminous editorial correspondence during the book's planning and production phases. Finally, Dorothy Warner once again assembled the Index with her customary thoroughness and precision.

We cannot conclude without once again thanking the Lynde and Harry Bradley foundation for their steadfast support for the *Journal of Democracy*. And we are grateful to have yet another opportunity to express our appreciation to President Carl Gershman and the Board of Directors of the National Endowment for Democracy for the continuing moral and financial support that they have given to the work of the International Forum for Democratic Studies and the *Journal of Democracy*.

—Marc F. Plattner and Larry Diamond

INTRODUCTION

Andrew J. Nathan, Larry Diamond, and Marc F. Plattner

With the possible exception of the United States, no country is likely to be more important than China in determining the global fortunes of democracy in the decades ahead. This is not just because China is the most populous and among the most powerful of the world's nations, though of course its size and strength count a great deal. It is also because China under the rule of the Chinese Communist Party (CCP) has become the de facto leader of those countries that are resisting the global advance of democracy. In its domestic policies, despite having granted its people much greater personal freedom in recent decades, China has resolutely opposed political freedom and multiparty competition—it remains one of the very few countries in the world today that does not even pretend to choose its leaders by popular election. Because of the grave restrictions that it places on civil liberties and political rights, Freedom House rates it as Not Free. Thanks to its huge population, it is home to more than half of all the individuals in the world who live in this category of highly repressive countries. And its international policies, especially in multilateral forums, have been dedicated to upholding a strict doctrine of noninterference in the internal sovereignty of nations, which in practice often means defending the worst abusers of human rights.

At the same time, however, China's hostility to liberal democracy has not prevented it from achieving extraordinary economic success since it opened itself up to free markets and international trade. It currently boasts the world's second-highest Gross National Product (though it still ranks relatively low in terms of per capita income), and it has achieved an extraordinary run of high annual growth rates, on average surpassing those of any other major country. China's wealth gives it the wherewithal to put diplomatic resources and muscle behind policies aimed at holding back democracy's global advance. What is more, its remarkable economic success, achieved without the benefit of oil or other significant natural-resource exports, has made it an object of envy and admiration among many of the world's developing countries. The so-called China model—even though its precise character remains vague and the Chinese themselves do not try to push it on others—has become attractive to undemocratic regimes around the world. Whatever the model's true nature, for many of its admirers it means little more than coupling economic growth with political repression. Yet because China has grown so rapidly and is increasingly making its presence felt in many areas of the globe, the Chinese example has come to be widely perceived as an attractive alternative to democracy.

The big question, of course, is whether and for how long China can continue its record of economic growth without undertaking political reforms that would move it in a more democratic direction. This is a question that the *Journal of Democracy* has pursued since its very first issue in January 1990, which featured a group of articles reflecting on the then-recent Tiananmen Square prodemocracy movement and its repression. Since then, the *Journal* has published six sets of scholarly essays assessing the trajectory of China's political development—we call them "clusters"—in January 1990, January 1998, January 2003, July 2007, July 2009, and January 2013, as well as numerous individual articles. Compelled to choose for reasons of space from among the nearly sixty articles the *Journal* has published on China, we have selected for this book those that provide especially valuable insights into the forces that are driving political change and the possible outcomes.

Doubts about whether authoritarian rule can long endure in China alongside economic dynamism arise from two different directions. One emphasizes the ways in which economic dynamism tends to undermine authoritarian rule, and the other the ways in which authoritarian rule tends to undermine economic dynamism.

The first class of doubts draws from what is often called "modernization theory." This holds that as countries grow richer and their populations are shaped by the requirements and habits of working in a modern economy, the citizenry becomes increasingly dissatisfied with its lack of say in the political sphere. Members of the emerging middle class, who are becoming better educated and more accustomed to making independent decisions about their own lives, will at some point say no to further authoritarian rule. The classic examples of this syndrome have been seen in some of China's fast-growing East Asian neighbors, especially South Korea and Taiwan.

Henry Rowen's contribution to the *Journal* gives a classic statement of this argument. In chapter 1, Rowen argues that rising prosperity produces an educated middle class that demands freedom of speech and information, the rule of law, and personal autonomy. As GDP per capita approached $10,000 in 2006 Purchasing Power Parity terms, he predicted in his 2007 article, China would become Partly Free by Freedom House standards by 2015 and fully Free at about $14,000 per capita by 2025. It is by no means clear as this book goes to press in 2013 that China will meet this exact schedule. But the working parts of Rowen's analysis remain compelling, as continuing economic growth is producing the kinds of social change that he anticipated.

The second set of doubts about the compatibility of authoritarianism and development has less to do with the social conditions that produce democracy and more to do with the functional requirements of an advanced modern economy. Analysts in this tradition question whether China can manage an increasingly sophisticated economy without reforming its institutions of governance. Authoritarianism breeds clientelism and corruption, which drag down China's economy and threaten to do more damage in the future. At the same time, the costs of the "stability-maintenance" (*weiwen*) system, which have grown to exceed even the funds spent on external defense, place a large burden on the economy. Efforts to stifle the kinds of individual expression viewed as a danger to CCP rule will impede the creativity and innovation that are needed for an advanced economy to flourish.

Michel Oksenberg explores this logic in chapter 2. He notes that even the Chinese leaders feel constrained to talk about something they call democracy. Although theirs is not the same concept of democracy as ours, it does entail the idea that they could better manage such challenges as reforming state-owned enterprises, incorporating Hong Kong (and eventually Taiwan) into the PRC, and increasing China's international respectability by granting their citizens law-based rule, more freedom, and greater opportunities to participate. Oksenberg acknowledges that the Chinese leaders might prefer to stand pat rather than court the risks of change, but on balance he thinks it more likely that the regime will move markedly toward democratization in order to solve the growing challenges before it.

Scenarios

Rowen's and Oksenberg's essays are included in the "Scenarios" section of this volume because they address not only the dynamics that might drive democratization but also the form that democratic change might take. Other *Journal* essays over the years that suggested other possibilities for the shape of change are also included in Part I of this collection. Like Rowen and Oksenberg, other contributors try to assess China's trajectory based on the interactions between political institutions and the economy, between state and society, and among political interests within the regime. Many of the chapters in this section appeared in the *Journal* more than a decade ago, but we think that their continuing relevance justifies their inclusion here. They sketch out possible futures for China that remain plausible alternatives. The date at which each chapter was first published in the *Journal* is indicated at the close of the author biography that appears on the opening page of each chapter.

Juntao Wang expects a halting process of change that he calls in chapter 3 a "gray transformation." He thinks that competition among competing social interests and political factions will produce incremental steps toward strengthening civil society, implementing checks and balances among government agencies, promoting the spread of elections, and appealing to popular accountability as a standard of legitimacy. This vision of gradual change from within continues to animate China's rights-protection (*weiquan*) movement of lawyers, petitioners, bloggers, and journalists, and to inspire people in a wider circle of civil society organizations and religious groups who keep a low profile in order to avoid repression. They hope that the regime will become enmeshed in the logic of the institutions that it has created as safety valves to preserve its rule, such as courts, the media, and volunteer social-service groups. If the Communist Party eventually finds itself coexisting with an equally powerful civil society, China will then have become at least a partial democracy, without having gone through a dramatic moment of change. Call it a new type of transition—not breakdown, extrication, or pact, but segue.

Changes of the kind that Wang identifies are also addressed by Harry Harding in chapter 4. Harding believes that the changes have already been significant enough to have created a transition from a totalitarian type of regime to an authoritarian regime. The political system has become more technocratic, law-based, pragmatic, and open than in the past. Like Wang, Harding sees a good chance that such changes will continue, resembling the course of liberalization traveled by Taiwan in the 1960s and 1970s. If so, China might evolve into a liberal one-party system, still falling short of full-fledged Western-style democracy but containing—as Harding's analysis implies—the potential for further change.

In chapter 5, Cheng Li contributes additional insights regarding the forces that are pushing China toward democracy. Li notes a pervasive sense of political uncertainty, deriving from spectacular political scandals, resentment over the concentration of power and wealth in a small elite, and intensifying environmental, public-health, and public-safety problems. Facing spreading discontent, the ruling CCP has split into "populist" and "elitist" factions that represent different regional and social interests. Balancing and checking each other, the two factions might find their way toward political reform as a way of responding to social discontent and staving off revolution. If they fail to do so, however, Li cautions, an uprising from below is possible.

Some contributors are less optimistic than Wang, Harding, and Li about the prospects for democracy, viewing the changes they analyze not as moves toward liberalized authoritarianism and eventual democracy but as adaptive responses that an authoritarian regime deploys as it seeks to maintain power in the face of new challenges. In this vein, Robert Scalapino identifies the Chinese system as a species of "authoritarian pluralism." In the face of economic strains, corruption, massive social change, and a decline of ideology, Scalapino argues in chapter 6 that the regime will continue to limit political freedoms and maintain strong security organs, while granting greater economic and social liberties and empowering technocrats. Increasingly, nationalism will replace Maoism as the CCP's source of legitimacy. Should these strategies fail, Scalapino sees greater authoritarianism rather than democratization as the Party's recourse. As he puts it, "the road to democracy does not run through failure."

In chapter 7, Andrew Nathan calls China's system "resilient authoritarianism." As keys to the system's institutionalization, he emphasizes the ruling party's ability to carry out an orderly leadership succession, the increasingly meritocratic nature of political advancement, the gradual depoliticization of many functions of government, and the creation of institutional safety valves for the venting of social discontent. While democratization remains a possibility for the future, Nathan suggests somberly that for the time being Chinese authoritarianism might turn out to be a "viable regime form even under conditions of advanced modernization and integration with the global economy."

The most pessimistic view of the future is expressed in chapter 8 by Arthur Waldron. Like several other authors, he notes the rise of a network of bureaucrats and entrepreneurs. Waldron, however, sees this nexus not as a modernizing force but rather as a virtual mafia in which corruption lubricates the alliance between the authoritarian elite and the rising business class. This form of state-society rapprochement does not facilitate a democratic transition, because instead of rendering the ruling party more accountable to society, it coopts potential social leaders into the corrupt ruling elite. The rise of this network might break the discipline of the ruling party and bring about an end to communism, but it will more likely lead to the rise of a nationalistic, corporatist regime than to a liberal democracy. Waldron foresees a weakening of the center, giving rise to a system falling somewhere between federalism and civil war.

These guarded views have drawn some critical responses. In chapter 9, Gongqin Xiao acknowledges that China has passed through a totalitarian phase and entered a postideological or "postpolarization" phase dominated by authoritarian technocrats who are backed by a new middle class with a stake in economic growth and political stability. But he does not expect this authoritarian phase to last indefinitely. As economic growth continues and middle-class values spread, Xiao anticipates that the new bourgeoisie will come to see itself as the country's dominant political force and will push for its own empowerment through the adoption of more democratic institutions—not out of ideological commitment to democracy but out of pragmatism.

Bruce Gilley likewise argues in chapter 10 that democracy is the most likely long-term outcome, although for different reasons. Despite superficial signs of institutionalization, power in the PRC remains essentially personalistic, which leaves the regime perennially vulnerable to instability. The regularization of leadership succession, the battle against corruption, local elections—these and other areas in which the regime has seemed to be making progress—are undermined whenever powerful figures intervene to benefit themselves or their followers. The contest between institutionalization and personalism has generated cycles of consolidation and breakdown in the past, which Gilley believes will likely continue until reformers in the CCP find a way to engineer a political opening that leads toward democracy.

In chapter 11, Minxin Pei offers complementary points regarding the system's inherent weaknesses. The Chinese regime appears strong thanks to refined techniques of repression, state control of the economy, and cooptation of social elites. Yet, to Pei, an emerging set of challenges posed by the heightened expectations that accompany modernization threatens to render these strategies obsolete. Ultimately, Pei argues that internal power struggles and corruption will lead to a crisis that will open the way to democracy.

Yun-han Chu looks beyond the internal dynamics of mainland politics in chapter 12 to explore the potential influence of Taiwan on the mainland's path of political change. Taiwan's authoritarian regime in the 1970s and 1980s solved challenges similar to those faced by the mainland regime today by following a path of liberalization that led ultimately to a full transition to democracy. Taiwan's experience is a possible model for leaders in Beijing. But Chu cautions that PRC leaders have options that Taiwan's leaders did not have. Although he agrees with Rowen and others that modernization will ultimately erode the foundations of the authoritarian regime, he cautions that a well-entrenched hegemonic party can drag out the process of change for a long time. It can do so, however, only by continuing to do a skillful job of managing the economy, society, and its own internal processes, which is a difficult challenge in a country as turbulent and rapidly changing as China.

Closing out Part I, Andrew Nathan suggests in chapter 13 that a democratic breakthrough in China belongs to a class of events that are inevitable but not predictable. Strong forces are pushing China toward a change in its political system, but the timing and character of that change will depend on contingent events that are inherently unforeseeable. An economic or public-health crisis or a humiliation in foreign affairs could serve as a triggering event to mobilize hitherto passive forces to demand change. The outcome might or might not be more democratic than the present system.

Social Forces

Many contributions to the *Journal* have focused on the complex, contending social forces that make the situation in China so hard to read. The selections in Part II analyze key social forces that are exerting an influence over China's trajectory. The section leads off with a comprehensive analysis of state-society relations by Zhenhua Su, Hui Zhao, and Jingkai He. In chapter 14, the authors review the shrinking social-control capacities of the state and the growing independence of society, expressed via protests, social media, petitioning, lawsuits, and outright dissidence. The party-state's repressive apparatus remains strong, but it confronts a society that is more dissatisfied, more mobilized, and less fearful than in the past. Subsequent articles in this section assess the degree to which specific sectors present new challenges to the existing model of authoritarian control.

Many democratic transitions in history have been pushed by peasants and workers, but three essays in this section suggest that these classes will not be the drivers of regime change in China any time soon. According to Kevin O'Brien, in chapter 15, peasant protest is rising, partly because the ruling party acknowledges the legitimacy of many peasant concerns and is willing to make concessions on local issues that arouse strong peasant discontent. But O'Brien believes that peasant protest remains localized and scattered, and that a mix of local concessions and selective repression for the time being is enough to keep the Party in control. To O'Brien, the appearance of tacitly permitted protest is not a symptom of frailty. Rather, it is a confident state that allows protests it knows it can ultimately control.

In chapter 16, Ching Kwan Lee and Eli Friedman portray industrial workers as disempowered in today's China not only by the political system but by the competitive pressures of globalized commodity production. To some extent the regime has emerged as a defender of labor rights against foreign and domestic capital. It has presided over a proliferation of legislation allowing individual workers greater access to legal recourse. But Lee and Friedman warn that if the regime wanted to defend workers' rights more effectively it would have to allow them to organize, which would create a potential challenge to its own monopoly of power.

An Chen draws attention in chapter 17 to the sharp polarization in incomes and interests between the top level comprising about 5 percent of Chinese society and the mass of toilers and the poor. Increasingly, the wealthy minority has become the core of a party that bills itself as the vanguard of the working class. Despite intensifying resentment on the part of the majority, this situation is not conducive to democratization, because the wider the cleavage grows, the less available becomes the option of peaceful transition, and the more tightly the rich and powerful cling to the authoritarian system that protects their interests. As Chen puts it, "China may be trapped in a vicious circle in which political repression and the revolutionary impulse reinforce each other in a deepening class conflict that precludes a peaceful political opening."

Looking beyond China's ethnic-Han heartland, Louisa Greve asks in chapter 18 whether discontent in the geographically vast but demographically small minority regions of Tibet and Xinjiang might drive change in the political system as a whole. She concludes that this is unlikely, because the Han majority has little understanding of the sources of Tibetan and Uyghur discontent. The filtered news that the Chinese public receives about the minority regions feeds the impression that the central government is benevolent and resistance is subversive. Rather than weakening the regime, the threat of an unraveling initiated by the tug of restive minorities has strengthened the regime's legitimacy in the eyes of those who would lose in such a scenario.

Unlike the lower economic classes and ethnic minorities, other social forces pose sharper challenges to the system. In chapter 19, Richard Madsen analyzes the explosive growth of religious practice, much of it outside the sphere of the five officially authorized forms of religion. Although the state is scrambling to keep some form of control by tolerating additional forms of religious activity that can be seen as consistent with the officially sponsored revival of Chinese culture, Madsen argues that religion is inherently uncontrollable and will pose a growing challenge to the regime's attempt to dominate popular values.

The intellectuals have always been a prime source of ideas and leadership for change in China. In chapter 20, Liu Junning notes a revival of liberal values both in this class and in ordinary people's daily life. He believes that individual freedom, property rights, the rule of law, and constitutionalism are values rooted in the market system and in the free-flowing information environment of the Internet. To Liu, the contradiction between official ideology and reality cannot endure. The political system will have to find some way to accommodate itself to these values. In chapter 21, Andrew Nathan describes a range of proposals that were made by reformers inside and dissidents outside the CCP in the 1990s for reforms that would limit the power of the ruling party based on principles already written into the Chinese constitution.

Jean-Phillipe Béja portrays in chapter 22 the dissident community at home and abroad. Following Tiananmen, the regime tried to bolster its legitimacy by coopting previously contentious groups such as the intelligentsia. Yet other groups have since emerged to oppose the regime, including young people, intellectuals, and those influenced by them, not to mention relatives of the victims of the 1989 crackdown. Although scattered and poorly organized, the dissident community endures despite repression and exile and continues to articulate a variety of alternative visions for Chinese society. These visions exert an influence through personal contacts and via new media of communication.

In chapter 23, Tiancheng Wang addresses a debate among intellectuals about whether gradual change would be better for China than a sudden breakthrough to democracy. Proposals for gradual change that have been popular among many Chinese intellectuals at home and abroad rely either on inching toward the implementation of certain constitutional provisions, or on pushing for democratization within the CCP before seeking to democratize that party's relations with society. While gradual transitions are often considered to be less risky than breakthrough transitions, Wang notes that the period between liberalization and democratization can be fraught with peril. The slower the transition, he argues, the greater the odds that China will "disintegrate." He calls for a rapid transition to democracy that would start with national elections.

The Internet—a force in China since the mid-1990s—is the subject of three articles in the collection. In chapter 24, Xiao Qiang describes the role of the Web as a new political zone that the regime seeks to control but in his view cannot tame. Whether officials like it or not, the Internet serves as a vehicle for China's citizens to communicate, mobilize, influence other media, and put pressure on government. In chapter 25, Xiao Qiang and Perry Link discuss some of the ways in which antiregime sentiment is circulated and crystalized on the Internet despite the best efforts of censors. According to these authors, the emerging Web discourse reveals changes in the way citizens see their relationship with the state.

In chapter 26, however, Rebecca MacKinnon explores ways in which the Internet may help to prolong rather than erode authoritarian rule. Citizens may be able to vent their views on blogs and websites, but the party-state's propaganda organs also spread regime-favorable messages in well-funded profusion. Moreover, MacKinnon argues, the venting of discontent can bolster the regime's legitimacy, while the authorities surveil the flow of communication and selectively repress those that they believe present a real threat.

Another locus of contending forces in Chinese society is the stability-maintenance system. In chapter 27, Carl Minzner points out that the government has pulled back on legal reform, choosing instead to consolidate certain authoritarian features of the court system. But in the absence of an independent and neutral system of courts, he argues, social pressures will continue to build which could present a threat to the regime. If the retreat from legal reform continues, Minzner warns that China "will not simply tip into transition, but rather plummet into cataclysm."

In chapter 28, Xi Chen shows that the courts are part of a larger *weiwen* apparatus that includes the propaganda and security agencies. Together they use surveillance, censorship, and coercion to manage the social problems that continuously emerge in a rapidly changing society. The system veers between rewarding and repressing disruptive forms of social protest. The problem is that either response by the authorities tends to delegitimize the system and generate more protest. As a result, the system expands, becoming increasingly expensive and counterproductive. Even though a more liberal, rule-based system of managing social conflict would be more stable and effective, Xi argues that the very process of transition to such a system would threaten the regime's survival.

Voices of Change

Democracy is by no means the only possible future for China in the near, medium, or even long term. Yet, running through all the essays in this volume is the sense that the current system inevitably *must* change.

We open and close the book with documents by leading Chinese thinkers that express this sense of hope and anxiety. In a 1986 essay translated and reprinted in the *Journal*'s inaugural issue in January 1990,
the late Fang Lizhi argued that the universal Chinese dream of modernization can be achieved only via democratization. His words helped to
inspire many who were active in the democratic movement that spread
throughout the country before the CCP regime violently crushed it in
Tiananmen Square in June 1989. The straightforward insights that he
articulated continue to inspire many today.

The book ends with two essays by the Nobel laureate Liu Xiaobo,
who is currently serving an eleven-year prison term for his role in drafting and circulating Charter 08, a document modeled on Czechoslovakia's Charter 77 that calls for democracy and respect for human rights.
His first essay summarizes many of the themes debated by our contributors. It sketches both the imposing strength of the regime and the fundamental changes that are emerging in society. As Liu notes, "official
suppression and civil resistance exist side-by-side at the same time."
The second essay notes that the regime itself has recognized the need for
change by issuing a call to build democratic politics in China. Yet the
official statement that he quotes goes on to list a series of reasons why
China cannot have real democracy—conditions are not ripe, the Party is
indispensable, the choice of regime is final.

Liu acknowledges the power of repression, propaganda, and economic growth to generate a "slavish mentality" that makes people view authoritarian rule as safer and even as more natural than freedom. Yet the
"imperial bestowing of favors" cannot long suffice for a mature people,
which the Chinese surely are. The human desire for dignity persists.
For Liu, "The nonviolent rights-defense movement need not pursue a
grand goal of complete transformation. Instead, it is committed to putting freedom into practice in everyday life through initiation of ideas,
expression of opinions, and rights-defense actions." He counsels reliance "on a continuously growing civil society to reform a regime that
lacks legitimacy."

Although the voice of Liu Xiaobo is silenced for now, the process of
change from below that he favors has not stopped. Liu quotes a beautiful line from the Tang Dynasty poet Bai Juyi (C.E. 772–846): "Wildfire
never quite destroys them—They grow again in the spring wind." But
upon this evocation of hope Liu offers a melancholy gloss: "This eternal, celebrated verse is . . . decidedly not an apt description of people
who have the courage to stand up straight and tall, but rather an exquisite portrayal of our countrymen accustomed to kneeling ever so gracefully." On this point, we think Liu has it wrong. What seems to keep
growing back in China from the hard soil of repression are the seedlings
of freedom that have been kept alive at great cost by people like Fang
Lizhi and Liu himself.

Prologue

PEERING OVER THE GREAT WALL

Fang Lizhi

*The distinguished physicist **Fang Lizhi** (1936–2012) emerged in the 1980s as China's most eloquent advocate of democracy and academic freedom. In an intellectual climate long constrained by Party ortho-doxy and self-censorship, his candor in criticizing Chinese communism was legendary. A popular speaker among Chinese students, Fang was charged by the Communist leadership with inciting the demonstrations that shook many of the country's universities in the winter of 1986–87. He was stripped of Party membership and his post as vice-president of the University of Science and Technology in Hefei. In the wake of the June 1989 crackdown, he sought asylum at the American Embassy in Beijing, remaining there until June 1990, when he was allowed to leave the country. In November 1989, Fang received the Robert F. Ken-nedy Human Rights Award for his contributions to the struggle for hu-man rights. The following text, which originally appeared in the Winter 1990 issue of the* Journal of Democracy, *is based on a speech entitled "Democracy, Reform, and Modernization," given by Fang at Tongji University in Shanghai on 18 November 1986. It was translated by James H. Williams of the University of California, Berkeley.*

Our goal at present is the thorough modernization of China. We all have a compelling sense of the need for this. There is a widespread feeling of dissatisfaction with the status quo among people in all walks of life. We in science and academia feel extremely strongly about this. Modernization has been one of our country's main goals ever since the Gang of Four was overthrown ten years ago, but we are just beginning to understand what it really means. At first we were aware primarily of grave shortcomings in our economy, our produc-tivity, our science, and our technology, and knew that modernization was needed in these areas. But now we understand our situation much better. We realize that grave shortcomings exist not only in our "ma-terial civilization" but also in our "spiritual civilization"—our culture, our moral standards, our political institutions—and that these also require modernization.

The question we face at present is: What kind of modernization is required? It seems obvious to me that we need total modernization, not just modernization in a few areas. People are busily comparing Chinese and Western culture—politics, economics, science, technology, education, the whole gamut—and there is a lot of argument over this subject. The central issue is whether we want "complete Westernization" or "partial Westernization." Should we continue to uphold the century-old banner of "using Western methods for practical applications but maintaining Chinese values for the essence," or is there some other "cardinal principle" on which we must stand fast? This debate certainly did not begin in this decade. Insightful people a century ago realized that China had to modernize. Some wanted partial modernization, others wanted complete modernization. This debate continues unabated today.

Personally, I stand with the "complete Westernizers." What this means to me is complete openness, a lifting of restrictions in every sphere. It means that we acknowledge that if we look at our culture in its entirety, it lags far behind the world's advanced cultures—not in any one specific area but across the board. To respond to such a situation we need openness in every sphere, not the establishment of a priori barriers. Attempting at all costs to preserve some inviolable "essence" of our society before actually coming to grips with the outside world makes no sense at all to me. Nor, again, am I inventing these ideas. A century ago people said essentially the same thing: open China up and run head on into the world tide, confronting the world's advanced cultures in every area—politics, economics, science, technology, education, and so on. When this happens, what is good will remain and what is not so good will be swept away. This situation has not changed.

Why are we so backward? Let us take a clear look at the facts of history. China has been undergoing revolution for a long time, but despite all the changes in this century, we are still very backward. This is especially true since Liberation, these decades of the socialist revolution that we all know firsthand as students and workers. Speaking quite dispassionately, I have to judge this era a failure. This is not just my opinion by any means; many of our leaders are also admitting as much, saying that the whole socialist movement is floundering. Since the end of World War II, socialism has by and large been a failure in socialist countries. There is no getting around this. As far as I am concerned, the last 30-odd years in China have been a failure in essentially every aspect of economic and political life.

Of course, some will say that China is a big, poor country, and therefore that progress is hard to come by. Indeed, overpopulation, our huge geographical area, and preexisting poverty do contribute to our problems. This being the case, some say, we have not done badly to get to where we are today. But these factors alone really do not account for the situation. For every one of them you can find a factual counterexample, a refuting instance. For example, population. While our population is the world's largest in terms of absolute numbers, our population density is not. I checked on the figures and found that China has about 750 persons per square kilometer of arable land, while Japan has about twice that, some 1,500 persons per square kilometer. Why has Japan succeeded while China has not? Our starting places were not that different. I have spent some time in Japan, and I know that after the war their economy was nearly at the same level as ours. Why have we not prospered like Japan? Overpopulation alone does not explain this.

Similarly, some argue that China has done well to attain its present level of development when you consider its prior poverty. Yet this does not completely wash either. Some very clear comparisons involving other socialist countries make the problem with this argument very clear. For instance, there is the contrast between the two Germanies, and even more starkly, between the two Berlins. I visited East and West Berlin for two days, and the visit made a profound impression on me. On the West Berlin side there are no guard posts. When people from West Berlin want to go East, there are few formalities; we bought tourist tickets and a single guard at the nearly deserted border crossing languidly waved us across. In West Berlin there was an extraordinary abundance of material goods. Then we crossed into East Berlin, which did not seem too bad at first, as the architecture is magnificent; East Berlin contains the former governmental center of Berlin, with beautiful buildings such as the Reichstag and the museums. But there was little on display in the shop windows, and the people seemed quite somber. They were unwilling to have much to do with you. Crossing from West to East, it went very smoothly on the East Berlin side, with a lone female official checking to see if our passports were legal. But on our return, it was announced that everyone had to get off the bus one at a time to be checked out. Our group of Chinese was exempt from inspection, but they did search the bus inside and out, checking to see if anyone was trying to escape by hiding underneath it. Now why should a good society fear that its people are going to run away? If you are so good, people will try to get in, not out, for heaven's sake! This is very simple logic.

My intention in telling this story is not to condemn the East Germans. As scientists, however, the first fact that we have to acknowledge is where we have failed. If we want things to improve, we must start by having the courage to admit our failures. And the socialist system in China over the last 30-odd years has been exactly that, a failure. This is the real situation we face. No one says it, or at least no one says it frankly enough, but the fact is that in terms of its actual accomplishments, orthodox socialism from Marx and Lenin to Stalin and Mao Zedong has been a failure.

We need to take a careful look at why socialism has failed. Socialist thought was very appealing when it first appeared, and there are admirable things about it. But we have to ask two things about the way it has been put into practice: Are the things being done in its name really socialism? Moreover, do they make any sense? We have to take a fresh look at these questions, and the first step in that process is to free our minds from the narrow confines of orthodox Marxism. . . .

The Swedish Approach

It is widely acknowledged now that socialism of the Lenin-Stalin variety faces grave problems and is in serious need of reform. But is the whole socialist movement in the same boat? No, in fact, it is not. The socialist movement, from the inception of socialist thought on down to Marx, from the Paris Commune to the October Revolution and beyond, has included many diverse streams. There have been a number of different approaches to socialism, some of which make a great deal of sense. . . .

For example, this past July, I went to a conference in Sweden. People there call Sweden a socialist country. And, indeed, why not? One way of defining socialism is as a system of public ownership, and another is as a system in which the disparity between rich and poor is small. Sweden meets both these criteria: more than half of all ownership is public, and the gap between rich and poor is small. . . . Moreover, Sweden's gross national product is very high, about US$19,000 per capita. China cannot begin to compare to this. Sweden's social welfare far surpasses our own; they are the archetypal welfare state. They care for their citizens essentially from cradle to grave.

In ideological terms, they also profess to follow Marx—though not Lenin, which makes a big difference. . . . Why has Sweden been so successful? The Swedish Social Democratic Party broke with Lenin at the Second International. Lenin opposed the Second International and called the Social Democrats traitors. We have stood by Lenin ever since, holding that nothing accomplished by these "renegades" is worth discussing. But I say we need to look around at what the rest of the world is doing, whether they are renegades or not, and see how they deal with their problems. Is not practice the real test of truth? We need to see what kind of progress other nations have made and how it compares to the socialist ideal. Have they fallen behind, or have they in fact surpassed us? If their societies are actually more stable and advanced than ours, we should admit it.

Sweden was once a poor country, no richer than the Soviet Union. But, as some Swedes told me, while China and the Soviet Union were busy implementing the dictatorship of the proletariat and destroying the bourgeois class, Sweden was traveling a different path. They acknowledged the existence of classes and class conflict, but sought to reconcile these conflicts through compromise and social harmony. After 50 years of this, Sweden also eliminated a class, but it was not the bourgeoisie—it was the proletariat. The bulk of their population joined the middle class. This was their way of eliminating a class, by turning the proletariat into a true middle class. Does the Swedish experience have anything to offer us? I am a physicist and my true interest is in the distant realm of cosmology, but I know that there is something very substantial and worth studying in the Swedish example. Unfortunately, we remain wedded to archaic beliefs and thus continue to see things in a very perverse light.

Much that is wrong in socialism comes from subscribing to outdated ideas with little basis in either theory or reality. Yet we never change because we have lived with these notions so long that we are no longer aware of them. I do this myself. I used to think that many of our problems were simply the way things are, the natural order. But going abroad has changed my perspective drastically. Socialism has been a failure, especially in China. There are many reasons for this, but there is no doubt that a great deal of what goes on here is neither progressive nor socialist. It is backward and feudalistic in the extreme.

Understanding Democracy

Now I want to discuss democracy. Our understanding of the concept of democracy is so inadequate that we cannot really even discuss it. With our thinking so hobbled by old dogmas, it is no wonder we do not achieve democracy in practice. Not long ago it was constantly said that calling for democracy was equivalent to wanting things to be "loosened up." In fact the word democracy is quite clear, and it is poles apart in meaning from "loosening up." If you want to understand democracy, look at how people understand it in the developed countries, compare it to how people understand it here, and then decide for yourself who is right and who is wrong.

I think that the key to understanding democracy is first to recognize the rights of each individual. Democracy comes from below. Every individual possesses certain rights, or to use what is indeed a very sensitive expression in China, everyone has "human rights." We seldom dare to utter the words "human rights," but actually human rights are very basic. What are these human rights? That everyone from birth has a right to live, the right to existence. From birth I have a right to think. Of course, I have a brain; a person with a severe mental handicap may not be capable of possessing this right. I want to learn, and I have the right to an education. I have the right to find a mate; and so forth. This is what human rights are. In China we talk about human rights as if they were something fearful, a terrible scourge. In reality they are very commonplace and basic, and everyone ought to acknowledge them.

But we are starting to look at the history of humankind a little differently. We are beginning to see "liberty, equality, and fratemity" as a positive spiritual legacy. Over the last 30 years it seemed that every one of these good words—liberty, equality, fraternity, democracy, human rights—was labeled bourgeois by our propaganda. What on earth did that leave for us? Did we really oppose all of these things? If anything, we should outdo bourgeois society and surpass their performance in human rights, not try to deny that human rights exist!

Democracy is based on recognizing the rights of every single individual. Naturally, not everyone wants the same thing and therefore the desires of different individuals have to be mediated through some sort of democratic process to form a society, a nation, a collectivity. But it is only on a foundation that recognizes the humanity and the rights of each person that you will build democracy. In China, however, when we talk about "furthering democracy," it refers to your superiors "furthering democracy" for you. This is a mistaken concept. This is not democracy.

The concept of "loosening up" is even worse. If you think about it, what it implies is that we are tied up very tightly right now, but if we stay put they will loosen the rope a little bit and give us more room to run around; it used to be one foot, now they will make it five feet. This is a completely top-down approach. Democracy is first and foremost the rights of individuals, and it is individuals who must struggle for them. Expressions like "furthering democracy" and "loosening up" would have you think that democracy can be bestowed upon us by those in charge. Nothing could be further from the truth.

The newspaper often refers to National People's Congress (NPC) representatives coming for an "inspection" tour. At times we ourselves speak sloppily, talking about "inspections." Think about it: Why should a visit from an NPC representative be called an inspection? We have become accustomed to talking this way, but it could not be more mistaken. These people are our elected representatives, who supposedly listen to us and speak on our behalf at the People's Congress, so why should their visit be called an inspection? Simply to use the word "inspection" reveals contempt for democracy. But the fact is that our NPC representatives hardly represent our opinions; I do not even know who my representative is.

Why bother with this comparison? At one time I thought that it was perfectly natural for big officials from the NPC to come "inspect" us. But during the first half of this year I was at Princeton's Institute for Advanced Studies, in New Jersey, doing research in cosmology. While I was there I received a mailing from our local member of the United States Congress, explaining what Congress had been up to lately and what he had been doing during the session. He wrote quite a bit about his voting record, explaining what he had voted for and against. He spoke about his achievements in office, how he had gone on the record for this or that, and why he had done so. In short, he was "reporting" to us. Although I was only a temporary resident, he had sent me this material, showing respect for anyone living in his district. He wanted us to know where he stood on the issues and to see if we agreed with him; if not, we could raise our concerns and he could turn around and express them in Congress. Despite representing a "false democracy," this man was clearly accounting for his actions. Now what about our "true democracy"? I have never, ever received any document telling me what issues my representative talked about, or how he or she voted at the NPC. I have never known what my representative supported or opposed, or what his accomplishments in office were. And the next time I have to go to cast my vote for this person, I will still be totally in the dark. Our "true democracy" had better get on the ball so that it can do better than their "false democracy"! I lived in China a long time without being aware of these problems. But when I went abroad and was finally able to see for myself, the contrast was glaringly obvious.

In democratic countries, democracy begins with the individual. I am the master and the government is responsible to me. Citizens of democracies believe that the people maintain the government, paying taxes in return for services—running schools and hospitals, administering the city, providing for the public welfare. . . . A government depends on the taxpayers for support and therefore *has to* be responsible to its citizens. This is what people think in a democratic society. Here in China, we think the opposite way. If the government does something commendable, people say, "Oh, isn't the government great for providing us with public transportation." But this is really something it *ought* to be doing in exchange for our tax money. . . . You have to make the economic relationship clear—who is paying for whom—because setting this straight leads to a democratic mentality. Yet China is so feudalistic that we always expect superiors to give orders and inferiors to follow them. What our "spiritual civilization" lacks above all else is the spirit of democracy. If you want reform, we need more changes in our political institutions than I have time to talk about here, but the most crucial thing of all is having a democratic spirit and outlook.

An experience I had in France exemplified the democratic spirit. Western Europe is now experiencing a lot of terrorist activity and people are worried about it; there is strong public opinion in favor of a crackdown against terrorism. A Chinese graduate student in France told me that a recent wave of violence there, including airport bombings, had led to proposed legislation requiring citizens who witness acts of violence or suspicious activities to report them to the police immediately. This seems natural to us in China: raise the alarm and get the whole country up in arms. Therefore, I assumed that passing such a law was just what the French should do. But the student, to my great surprise, told me that after this bill was proposed, the National Assembly discussed it for a while and then voted it down. Why? They obviously did not reject it because they approve of terrorism. Their reasoning was that such a law would create informers, and that the appearance of informers is the worst thing that could happen to a democratic society. People have human dignity and a right to privacy. The French Assembly refused to allow people to be subject to casual suspicion.

In China, if I suspect that you might do something bad, I will just run over and "make a report," and never think twice about it. In fact, such behavior is praised for demonstrating "a high sense of alertness" and "an elevated class consciousness." But it runs completely counter to democracy, and what it demonstrates is a total lack of understanding about basic human rights—that people should not be subject to casual suspicion or forced to live under constant terror. But in China people seem to have always lived in terror, afraid of someone reporting them even when they did nothing wrong. If it seems as if I might be doing something wrong, whether I am or not, you will rush right out and report me. Such an atmosphere of terror is not an environment in which democracy can take root. When I heard this story about France, I finally grasped this concept for the first time, and could see how backward my own ideas were. I had lived in China so long that I became accustomed to the idea that informing on people is normal. But the French felt that the existence of informers would endanger a democracy. It is things like this that make us see what a democracy is all about.

Knowledge and Power

Let me say a few things more. In democratic societies, science and democracy—and most of us here are scientists—run parallel. Democracy is concerned with ideas about humanity, and science is concerned with nature. One of the distinguishing features of universities is the role of knowledge; we do research, we create new knowledge, we apply it to developing new products, and so forth. In this kind of work, within the sphere of science and the intellect, we make our own judgments based on our own criteria. This is characteristic of a university. In Western society, universities are independent from the government in this sense: while the money to run the school is provided by the government, the basic decisions—on curricula, research topics, criteria for judging research findings, the value of different kinds of research—are made by the schools themselves on the basis of values intrinsic to the academic community, and not by the government. At the same time, good universities in the West are also independent of big business. A main characteristic of universities, then, is that the intellectual realm is independent and has its own values.

This is an essential guarantee of democracy. Only when you believe that you know something independently are you really free from relying on authorities outside the intellectual domain, such as the government.

Unfortunately, it is not this way in China. I have discussed this with educators. In the past, especially during the 17 years from the Great Leap Forward in 1959 to the end of the Cultural Revolution in 1976, our universities were mainly engaged in producing tools, not in educating human beings. Education was concerned not with helping people become critical thinkers, but with producing docile instruments to be used by others. Chinese intellectuals need to insist on thinking for themselves and using their own judgment, but I am afraid that even now we have not grasped this lesson.

In physics, for example, you would assume that the evaluation of physicists is what matters in deciding the merits of their colleagues' research. But in China, the work of physicists has long been subject to the evaluation of officials who know nothing about physics, and we are ecstatic if they deign to say good things about us. This leads to a "docile tool" mentality that is still a major problem. It is even worse in the social sciences. We physicists naturally check out the latest "philosophical" writings in order to keep ourselves out of hot water, but much of the writing of philosophers and social scientists in this country is little more than recapitulation of the latest official pronouncements. If our leaders were experts in philosophy—or experts in something—their words might cany some weight as academic authorities. But if they are not philosophers, what is the value of quoting them? It is worthless and it does not prove a thing, but it is there because we need the sanction of political authority before we dare to do anything.

The opposite relationship obtains in the West. At Princeton I met some Chinese economists. They delved into the subject as they pleased and explored whatever areas they saw fit, without any interference. But contrary to our situation, when the American government was making policy, it requested the opinions of these academics; the government wanted to know if they had obtained any relevant results on which to base policy. What a far cry from our situation—officials needing the sanction of college professors to give them credibility! This is what I mean by intellectual independence. Knowledge must have independence from power, state power included. If knowledge is subservient to power, it is worthless. . . .

We have our own independent values. If you know some physics, then we can have a debate; we are more than willing to do that. But if you do not know physics, then get out of the damned way! This is the kind of spirit you must have to safeguard democracy. When it comes to our areas of knowledge, we must think for ourselves and exercise our own judgment about what is right and wrong, and about truth, goodness, and beauty as well. We must refuse to cater to power. Only then will Chinese intellectuals be transformed into genuine intellectuals and will our country have a chance to modernize and attain genuine democracy.

I

Scenarios

1

WHEN WILL
THE CHINESE PEOPLE BE FREE?

Henry S. Rowen

Henry S. Rowen *is director emeritus of the Asia-Pacific Research Center at the Freeman Spogli Institute for International Studies and professor emeritus in the Graduate School of Business at Stanford University. He is also a senior fellow at the Hoover Institution on War, Revolution, and Peace. This essay originally appeared in the July 2007 issue of the* Journal of Democracy.

Little more than a decade ago, my answer to the question posed by this essay's title was the year 2015.[1] My assessment, published in the Fall 1996 issue of *The National Interest,* began by observing that all countries (leaving aside states that make nearly all their money from oil exports) which had attained a Gross Domestic Product per capita (GDPpc) of at least US$8,000 per year (as measured by the Purchasing-Power Parity or PPP standard for the year 1995) stood no worse than Partly Free in the ratings of political rights and civil liberties published annually by Freedom House (FH).

As China's economy was growing at a rate that promised to carry it to a level near or beyond that GDPpc benchmark by 2015, I reasoned that this, the world's largest country, was a good bet to move into the Partly Free category as well. Since then, China has remained deep in Not Free territory even though its civil-liberties score has improved a bit—from an absolutely abysmal 7 to a still-sorry 6 on the 7-point FH scale—while its political-rights score has remained stuck at the worst level.

Yet today, as I survey matters from a point slightly more than midway between 1996 and 2015, I stand by my main conclusion: China will in the short term continue to warrant a Not Free classification, but by 2015 it should edge into the Partly Free category. Indeed, I will go further and predict that, should China's economy and the educational attainments of its population continue to grow as they have in recent years, the more than one-sixth of the world's people who live in China will by 2025 be citizens of a country correctly classed as belonging to the Free nations of the earth.

In order to flesh out my analysis, I shall examine four questions. The first asks about the prospects for sustained economic growth. The second inquires into what recent scholarship tells us about the nexus between economic development and political freedom. The third estimates when a relatively free China is likely to emerge. And the fourth ponders the implications for war and peace that are likely to flow from this momentous change.

Let us take the question of the economy first. China's per-capita growth over the last decade has averaged a highly impressive 8.5 percent annually (reaching a GDPpc of $6,000 in 2006 international-PPP dollars).[2] Serious challenges lie ahead, yet given China's competent economic-policy makers, a supportable projection is an average per-capita growth rate of 7 percent a year, enough to raise GDPpc to $10,000 PPP by 2015. After that, slower workforce expansion (a product of changing demographics) plus China's expected approach toward convergence with the world's leading developed economies suggest that the growth rate will climb less steeply. Annual growth of 5 percent in GDPpc starting in 2015 will bring China to roughly $14,000 PPP (in 2006 dollars) by 2025, or about where Argentina is today.

Short-term disruptions would do little to disturb this projection. There was such a hitch after the Tiananmen Square massacre in 1989, but the growth rate subsequently recovered so robustly that the slow period was soon offset with no lasting economic effects. The prospect for sustained growth over at least the next decade appears strong.

Does Prosperity Breed Liberty?

The next question to be explored is the relation between economic development and democratic freedom. There are three possibilities: 1) Development might lead to democracy; 2) democracy might foster development; or 3) there might be a common cause driving both.

My 1996 projection was based on the first direction. This is the hypothesis, associated with Seymour Martin Lipset, that only a society with educated, wealthy people can resist the appeal of demagogues.[3] Stable democracy presupposes a certain level of accumulated human, social, and physical capital. A related view is that institutions which promote limited government (particularly via constraints placed on executive power) support growth.[4]

Education promotes growth, and might also independently promote political pluralization by reducing the costs of political action in support of relatively democratic regimes.[5] Schooling makes democratic revolutions against dictatorships more probable and successful antidemocratic coups less probable. After analyzing more than a hundred countries,

Robert J. Barro found that higher incomes and higher levels of (primary) education predict higher freedoms.[6] He also found significant time lags between the appearance of a factor positive for electoral rights and its expression in politics. He interpreted such lags as tokens of inertia in institutions affected by changes in economic and social variables, and noted that after about two decades "the level of democracy is nearly fully determined by the economic and social variables."[7] This observation helps one to understand why a rapidly growing country such as China has a freedom rating today well below the level that its current income would predict.

Adam Przeworski and his coauthors also find that levels of economic development best predict the incidence of various types of political regimes. To explain this, however, they point to the superior survival capacity of wealthier democracies rather than to transitions from dictatorship to democracy at higher levels of wealth. The higher the level of income that a given country enjoys, these researchers note, the better are the odds that a democratic regime in that country will endure. They estimate the probability that a democracy will die in a country where annual GDPpc is $6,000 (in 2006 PPP dollars) as close to zero. In contrast, Carles Boix and Susan Stokes attribute transitions to democracy in wealthier countries to incomes becoming more equally distributed as development progresses: "[T]he rich find a democratic tax structure to be less expensive for them as their country gets wealthier and they are more willing to countenance democratization."[8]

The second possibility is realized if the rules of electoral democracy turn out to be better on average for development than are those of dictatorships. Democracies tend to foster governmental transparency and the production of public goods while placing some limits on what rulers can steal. Yet a democracy with a populist bent can insist on economically damaging schemes for redistributing income and wealth. Barro and Przeworski are among those who find that democracy does not lead directly to higher growth. According to Torsten Persson and Guido Tabellini, the evidence that democratizations yield economic growth is weak. They also write that "democracy" is too blunt a concept and that institutional details matter greatly.[9] The theoretical picture remains unclear and the literature is divided.

The third possibility, that democracy and development have a common cause, finds support from Daron Acemoglu and his coauthors, who argue that "though income and democracy are positively correlated, there is no evidence of a causal effect. Instead . . . historical factors appear to have shaped the divergent political and economic development paths of various societies, leading to the positive association between democracy and economic performance."[10] These scholars see political and economic development paths as interwoven. Some countries embarked on development paths associated with democracy and economic growth, while others followed paths based on dictatorship, repression, and more limited growth.

Might there be a regional, specifically Sinitic, effect involving the polities influenced by Chinese civilization? These also include Japan, the two Koreas, Vietnam, Singapore, and Taiwan. Today they present a mixed picture. Japan, South Korea, and Taiwan are rated Free; Singapore is Partly Free; and North Korea, Vietnam, and China are Not Free. Nonetheless, the paths carved out by Japan, South Korea, and Taiwan show that Western-style democracy can take root in Sinitic societies.

Education is crucial, and here China does not impress. In 2000, the country's entire over-25 population had only an average of 5.74 years of schooling (between all developing countries at 4.89 years and the East Asia and Pacific country average of 6.50 years).[11] Yet large educational-improvement efforts are underway, especially in rural areas and the rapidly expanding postsecondary sector. My projection is that by 2025 the average Chinese person over 25 will have had almost eight years of formal schooling.

Between 1999 and 2005, postsecondary admissions tripled, reaching five million during the latter year. Currently China has about twenty million people with higher degrees; by 2020 there will be more than a hundred million. Although there are problems of educational quality and jobs, China's rising educational indicators bode well for both economic development and democracy.

What conclusion should we draw from the scholarship so far on democracy and development? I think it is that growth-friendly policies, if consistently pursued (historically determined institutions may prevent this), lead to the accumulation of human and physical capital and the rise of limited government. Autocratic regimes in economically growing countries can delay but not ultimately stop this from happening.

China's so-far slight improvement in the FH rankings has been in the Civil Liberties category, where it has gone from a 7 (the absolute worst score) to a 6. Looking behind the FH numbers, we can identify several factors that have led to a substantial growth in personal liberties and promise more freedom to come.

The first is that a modern economy is simply not compatible with the Leninist requirement of comprehensive party and state control over society. The Chinese Communist Party (CCP) has faced a hard choice: Maintain control and risk economic stagnation and political disaffection, or let go and risk eventually losing dominance. The CCP has chosen to pull back in several domains. Most notably, it allows markets to function. It also has accorded certain legal institutions and media outlets a degree of autonomy. The CCP has become Marxist-Leninist in name only. In reality, it seeks to rule a system that might be called party-state capitalism, setting broad rules while leaving much authority to local

Party figures and various private actors. Central authorities can intervene, but they ration their energies.

One might think that a party which promotes markets, has formally enrolled "capitalists," and has allowed the state sector's share of the economy to shrink has lost any plausible claim to be called communist or socialist. Phrases such as "capitalism with Chinese characteristics" and "democratic socialism" do not disguise the reality of the CCP's massive but mostly unacknowledged ideological shift. Not that there is much nostalgia for socialism—or even a Confucian contempt for profit: In a 2005 survey of twenty countries, China featured the highest share of respondents (74 percent) who agreed with the proposition that the best economic system is "the free-market economy."[12]

The regime's legitimacy seems to rest on three main pillars: 1) It has brought social order after a century and a half of upheavals;[13] 2) people's incomes are growing rapidly (even if the growth is unevenly distributed); and 3) Chinese enjoy a sense that the Beijing government is restoring China to its rightful place of prominence in the world.

Surveys show that confidence in the government is high, and people seem satisfied with the way that "democracy" is unfolding.[14] Yet sources of discontent such as corruption, environmental damage, and sharp income inequality remain. In a departure from Chinese tradition, there is a developing attitude that individuals have rights.

Local elections, along with the aforementioned rise of certain relatively autonomous legal and media institutions, are helping to expand personal liberties and may have the potential to transform Chinese society.

Legal Institutions, Social Groups, and the Media

Legal reform began in 1979 when the CCP under its leader Deng Xiaoping decided that a modern economy required clear, predictable rules rather than obscure, arbitrary decisions. Although China remains a long way from being under the rule of law, the country has made considerable progress.[15] The main questions have to do with the extent of legal institutions' de facto independence today and the advances they might make tomorrow, together with the closely related issue of which, if any, claims to authority the Party will choose to defend to the end.

Almost three decades after Deng started the reform process, the National People's Congress (NPC) has passed many laws—determined by the State Council—and established a nationwide judiciary. Laws now provide for judicial review of the acts of state agents, compensation for damages from unlawful state actions, protection for people subject to noncriminal administrative sanctions, and rights to counsel and procedures for the conduct of criminal trials. Business transactions increasingly conform to legal rules. Important international commitments flow from China's membership in the World Trade Organization.

Many laws are ambiguous and contradictory, giving the Party ample opportunities to maintain its authority while also allowing changes to occur. Thus the Organic Law on Villager Committees recognizes the authority of the elected village head but requires committee conformance with "state policies" (thereby allowing the local Party secretary to overrule the locally elected leader). One consequence of these ambiguities is that local officials often are able to pick or interpret the laws that they prefer to follow.

With the number of lawyers at 150,000 and climbing, more people are seeking legal representation. The 4.3 million civil cases that China's courts heard in 2004 marked a 30 percent increase over the 1999 figure. People are suing not only one another but also state officials and enterprises with links to the Party-state establishment. Such suits can serve the Party-state's overall goal of "curbing administrative wrongdoing."[16]

The legal system remains firmly under CCP control. Party members often determine court decisions, officials press judges to throw out suits over property rights, and citizens' legal rights to counsel are ignored when the Party or local officials have already decided the case. Yet the system is evolving. The Supreme People's Court has begun to make interpretations and decisions—a role contrary to communist dogma. An anticorruption guideline dating from 2000 requires judges to stand aside from civil cases if they have taken money or gifts from a litigant. Judges are also banned from taking lucrative positions at law firms until at least two years after leaving the bench.

Many shocking abuses of the law occur. Nonetheless, a better-educated population and a more complex economy demand the rise of improved legal institutions. Rural unrest and pervasive corruption pressure leaders to take more steps toward the rule of law even if this means having to relax the Party's control over society. Thus developments in the legal arena, halting though they are, signal something positive about China's economic and political future.

Any Leninist regime must be suspicious of organizations—particularly social organizations cutting across class or regional lines—that it does not control. So far, the groups most worrisome to the powers that be have been religious in nature, such as the Falun Gong meditation movement. Nongovernmental organizations (NGOs) in general have been proliferating. More than 280,000 were officially registered as of 2005; unofficial estimates put the number of unregistered NGOs as high as two million. The regime monitors their activities, but accords them de facto leeway because of the benefits they bring. Many seek improvements in health, education, environmental protection, and services for the disabled, all to the sound of government toleration or even approval. By contrast, groups that focus on human rights and cultivate foreign ties have suffered increasing official harassment over the past two years.

The jailing of journalists, the closing of newspapers, and the censoring of websites reveal the CCP's determination to limit information and the independent organizing that it may spur. Nonetheless, information access and the ease of communication have both been on the rise. The media enjoy the freest hand they have had over their own content since 1949.[17]

The last three decades have seen the appearance of many new magazines and newspapers as well as talk radio, the Internet, and cell phones. The media cover a far wider range of topics than earlier, including official malfeasance and social problems as well as everyday concerns. More than a hundred million Chinese enjoy Internet access, and 450 million people—more than a third of the population—use cell phones. The government was able to block news of the Severe Acute Respiratory Syndrome (SARS) outbreak in late 2002 and early 2003—risking a global pandemic—but with half a billion text messages now beaming back and forth daily, the censors' task is hard and growing harder. What the regime ought to fear more than the spread of "unpatriotic" messages is the usefulness of devices such as the cheap, ubiquitous cell phone in organizing protests, exposing cover-ups, and even exacerbating situations that sometimes become riotous.

A conflict of goals besets the CCP. It wants economic information to flow freely, and the media can help to ferret out local corruption. Yet communications with any political coloration worry the Party greatly. The imperatives pull in opposite directions, giving rise to cycles of relaxation (the late 1980s before Tiananmen) and repression (the years after Tiananmen as well as the period since 2004). Backslidings toward restriction are almost certainly in store from time to time. Yet the underlying choice to accept markets is boosting people's access to information and their ability to reach each other, even if the right to free speech has yet to be recognized.

Village Elections Today, Township Elections Tomorrow?

The 1988 Organic Law on Villager Committees required that they be popularly elected and charged with responsibility and hence authority in such areas as fiscal management, land allocation, and education. By the mid-1990s, 90 percent of committee heads held their posts by virtue of the ballot. The degree to which elections are fair, open, and competitive varies. Such requirements as direct nomination by individuals, multiple candidates, secret ballots, public counting of all votes, immediate announcement of results, and regular recall procedures are not always followed, and the CCP's influence can decide outcomes.

As people come to enjoy more personal freedom, demand a larger say in matters that touch them directly, and feel fewer inhibitions about manifesting their discontents, the governance problems facing the CCP mount. If denied regular ways of dealing with their grievances and desires, people will increasingly choose irregular ways. The CCP might decide that the best way to fend off disorder is to empower people more. Township elections could be next.

The authorities in Beijing keep track of what they call "mass incidents." In 1995, about ten thousand were reported; a decade later the official figure had increased almost ninefold. Grievances are not in short supply. Although rural incomes have slowly grown, health and educational services have deteriorated in many places and the income gap between city and countryside is growing. The urban-rural Gini coefficient went from 0.28 in 1991 to 0.46 in 2000. (A higher number means less equal; it is 0.30 on average in Europe and 0.45 in the United States.) Income differences have also widened within urban areas, symbolized by reports of (dollar) billionaires.

Although taxes on peasants have been abolished, local officials still find ways to cheat them, often by colluding with developers to seize peasant lands with little compensation. With legal channels clogged and inadequate, mass protests become vehicles for voicing discontent and seeking change. The police report that many protests have elaborate organizations, complete with designated leaders, "public spokespersons," "activists," and "underground core groups." The protesters typically steer away from anything that looks like a direct challenge to Party authority, preferring to cite rights listed in party documents, laws, State Council regulations, and speeches by CCP leaders. Protests also tend to be carefully limited to local matters.

Informal protocols have evolved. The resisters seek redress by publicizing local officials' violations of national laws and norms. Local officials sometimes ignore the protesters or go through endless procedures without fixing the problems. If demonstrations persist or get too large, authorities may call in the police, arrest ringleaders, and then provide some compensation to the protesters. One scholar claims that "the state has made a conscious decision not to use its full coercive power to stop demonstrations. The airing of peasant grievances has become an accepted part of local politics. Workers and peasants now take to the streets feeling that it is now within bounds."[18]

Here as elsewhere, the government faces cross-pressures. Protests help to reveal the locations of abusive (and hence trouble-creating) local officials in need of removal, but an authoritarian party-state can hardly welcome frequent spontaneous demonstrations. The regime's solution so far has been to spend more on infrastructure, pollution control, health care, and education in rural areas while also campaigning against troublemakers, with a focus on abusive and corrupt officials. Whether such efforts will contain the problem, however, remains unclear.

One should not assume that wildcat protests in the countryside mean the regime is seriously threatened. People know the role of protests—and of leaders sometimes encouraging them—in their history. Yet while such unrest is not a sign that the Party is tottering, neither is it a sign of Party legitimacy.

More wealth means more freedom. People have assets, more choices among goods, and a greater ability to decide where to work, live, and travel. Private ownership of housing, automobiles, and businesses is becoming widespread in China, and many small enterprises have gone from state to private hands.

Not so long ago, a typical city-dweller depended directly on the state for schooling, health care, and housing. Reforms reduced these services but made many more goods available. And there are better jobs. The labor market is not fully free, and there is unemployment, including among new university graduates, but one of a citizen's major life choices—work—is no longer dictated by government.

A residency permit, long needed to gain access to state-enterprise jobs as well as housing, education, and various subsidies, is less vital than before. Economic liberalization, labor surpluses in the modernizing agricultural sector, and the shrinking of the state sector have led more than a hundred million people without permits to move to cities. There they often lack services but stay on anyway, evidently preferring freer urban air to the straitened life prospects that faced them in the countryside.

As literacy, urbanization, and mass-media exposure rise, modernizing societies experience characteristic shifts in values. The grip of tradition and hierarchy loosens as women begin working outside the home, the nuclear family replaces the extended one, marriage becomes more an individual choice than a family decision, and women bear children later in life. Such changes are occurring in China. Alex Inkeles writes that although not everything is changing, least of all the Chinese commitment to filial piety, "[m]any fundamental values are being challenged and reformulated, basic human relationships are redefined and reordered, and numerous traditional ways of thinking and behaving are undergoing a great transformation."[19] Overall, investigators find the rejection of values that have long been near the core of Chinese culture to be "nothing short of phenomenal."[20]

One interpretation of the above is that civil liberties have outrun political rights. The state might seek to close this gap by taking away people's recently acquired personal liberties, but such a course would cause so much trouble that officials are unlikely to pursue it. The gap might also portend coming political instability. Here, what matters is that coming events not interfere with long-term growth in education and income. One can, of course, postulate long-lasting political instability, or slower long-term growth, but my projection assumes that neither of these will happen.

China's long-term prospects for achieving a stable form of liberal-democratic government will in all likelihood be best if the liberal part comes first as a groundwork for the democratic part. For that groundwork to be securely laid, education needs to continue spreading and improving, property rights need to receive increasing protection, transparent legal and financial institutions need to grow along with a robust private sector, personal liberties need to keep expanding, and income distribution needs to avoid extremes of inequality. The general idea, as Persson and Tabellini put it, is that "the sequence of reforms is crucial; countries liberalizing their economies before extending political rights do better."[21]

Former U.S. secretary of state George Schultz once related to me how Deng Xiaoping addressed the matter in July 1988, when the two men were discussing Mikhail Gorbachev's reforms in the Soviet Union: "He's got it backwards," said Deng. "He opened up the political system without a clue about the economy. The result is chaos. I did it the other way around, starting in agriculture and small businesses, where opening up worked, so now I have a demand for more of what succeeds." When Schultz asked when political opening would occur, Deng said: "That will come later and will start small, just as in the economy. You have to be patient but you have to get the sequence right."

Scholar He Baogang suggests that the CCP might become the seedbed of a multiparty system, or at least its functional equivalent.[22] The CCP is home to factions that represent different interests, it holds internal contests for posts, and it is increasingly eager to monitor its members' performance, all of which might help to limit its tendencies toward tyranny and corruption. Taking another tack, Gang Lin argues that democracy (at least within the Party), rather than arising as a side-effect of ruling-party splits, could become a tool in the CCP's campaign to prop up its own authority.[23]

How will events unfold? No one can convincingly claim to know. There are many possible paths—rough, smooth, or in-between—that can lead to democracy. One way to gauge the route that may lie before China would be to estimate how freedoms might evolve as the country works its way through the lag between rapidly changing socioeconomic realities and the political modes and orders that come under pressure to keep up despite the drag exerted by the force of institutional inertia.

Robert J. Barro's model generates quantitative predictions for electoral rights (corresponding to FH's "Political Rghts" category). He found that the level of democracy, so measured, that is present in a given earlier period allows one to forecast the level of democracy found in a later period, albeit with decreasing certainty as the interval between periods widens. Barro also found several social variables to be predictors of democracy. These rising (in the case of China) variables include GDPpc and the educational level of the populace. Another positive predictor

TABLE—PREDICTIONS FOR CHINA'S FUTURE

Year	Per Capita GDP (2006 PPP)	Average Years of Schooling (>25)	Predicted Electoral Rights	Predicted Freedom House Rating
2010	$8,500	6.3	22	Not Free
2015	$10,000	6.7	43	Partly Free
2020	$11,800	7.2	61	Partly Free
2025	$14,000	7.7	76	Free

of democracy is a shrinking gap between the proportions of males and females who have been to primary school. Thus the extent of democracy in a country converges gradually toward a (moving) target determined by the social variables.

On a scale of zero to a hundred, entering my predicted social inputs (economic and educational inputs plus others) yields the predictions about electoral rights shown in the Table above for successive five-year periods to 2025. For 2010, China is still Not Free but by 2015 it edges into the Partly Free category and gets into the Free one by 2025. Evidence from around the world suggests that over almost two decades, a well-educated people whose average income is rising toward a figure of perhaps $14,000 (PPP) by 2025 will almost certainly see its freedoms—including its electoral freedoms—expand. In 2005, every country in the world (oil states excepted) with GDPpc topping $8,000 (PPP) was at least Partly Free; indeed, all ranked as Free except the tiny island city-state of Singapore.[24]

And yet—several things could go wrong. I have mentioned some of them.[25] The Barro parameters are based on the experiences of many countries and China is but one. In any case, I do not argue that China will ever be a Sweden or New Zealand; its democracy will probably have some "Chinese characteristics." Nearby there is Taiwan, whose democratization took almost forty years to complete beginning with local elections in the early 1950s; counting the same number of years from China's 1988 Organic Law on Villager Committees yields about 2025. The technocratic authoritarianism of Singapore offers a model that some CCP leaders must prefer to Taiwan's. Or Chinese politicians might come up with a novel political arrangement that falls short of true liberal democracy but nonetheless offers the Chinese people more liberty and a bigger say in how they are ruled than they currently enjoy.

Implications for Peace

I observed in 1996 that a democratic China in a region with many democracies would be good for peace because democracies do not fight each other (which does not imply that democracies are inherently peaceable).

Yet all is not necessarily well. Edward D. Mansfield and Jack Snyder find that countries making the transition from authoritarian to democratic governance are more likely to start foreign broils than are consolidated democracies because internal contests for power can cause a faction to identify, or to conjure up, a foreign enemy as a means of rallying mass support.[26] Mansfield and Snyder hold that this is most likely where elections are held in countries with a weak sense of nationhood, a shaky rule of law, feeble bureaucracies, poor civilian control of the military, a winner-take-all attitude among contending parties, and few safeguards for press freedom. This leads them to recommend that, where possible, elections should come on the heels and not ahead of institution-building, with a competent central government and legal system needed most urgently of all.

If these premises are correct, China's prospects are not bad. The Chinese today possess a strong sense of nationhood, a legal system that is moving in the right direction, a military that seems firmly under civilian control, increased professionalism in many organizations, and nothing like the shadow of "premature" elections on the horizon. Other positives for peace are China's high trade-to-GDP ratio and membership in several international organizations.

On the negative side, the country's experience with competing political parties was brief and long ago, and it turned out poorly. Corruption is pervasive, and the Communist Party shows no sign of a being ready to put up with having to run against anyone, much less lose to them. Most worrisome of all is the flashpoint for nationalist conflagration that sits just off China's coast on the other side of the Taiwan Strait.

To Beijing, Taiwan is but a renegade province, and the use of force against it would count not as a foreign war but as a domestic police action. If the disaster of an armed conflict between Beijing and Taipei (whose supporters are Japan and the United States) can be averted long enough for the mainland to become a democracy, the prospect of a peaceful solution will gather strength. Indeed, a more democratic mainland China is probably necessary for a peaceful resolution of this dispute. Yet a power struggle within China that drove some faction or factions to rouse popular nationalist sentiment could be one way in which rising political pluralism might lead to big trouble. Another way would be for Taiwan to declare itself an independent country.

Should the hazards that come with transition be skirted, the democratic-peace thesis leads to a prediction that relations between China on the one hand and Japan and the United States on the other will remain pacific. Nonetheless, China's burgeoning economic and military clout will have consequences. In twenty years, the PRC's annual defense budget might exceed $200 billion, and its military forces will have high-technology weapons. Its power will cause many small states to align themselves with Beijing like iron filings near a powerful magnet. There would remain the chance that China could use force against nondemocracies, but a China that navigates the transition to democracy without taking up the sword should on the whole improve the prospects for peace in the region and beyond.

Returning to the four questions posed at the beginning of this essay: 1) The economy looks likely to stay on a high growth path, albeit slowing as China's demography changes and its economy's performance converges on that of the world leaders. It is not immune to serious disruption. 2) Seymour Martin Lipset's hypothesis that development leads to freedoms is better supported than any current rival explanation. 3) By 2015, there is a good chance that China will have made its way into Freedom House's middling or Partly Free group, with a ranking as Free following by 2025. 4) Although the period of transition to free government could hold dangers, a democratic China will be a China that is less likely to fight with its democratic neighbors.

Sometimes events move fast. As late as the mid-1980s, few even among the experts anticipated that the Soviet Union would soon be gone. I am not suggesting that the CCP will be gone in one or two decades, but I do think that if it survives, it will be because it has learned to adapt and adjust to a much transformed—meaning a much freer—political landscape.

NOTES

I owe thanks to many people, especially Robert Barro, Tricia Bolle, Peter Lorentzen, Alex Inkeles, John Lewis, Stanley Lubman, and Andrew Walder, none of whom bears any responsibility for the results.

1. Henry S. Rowen, "The Short March: China's Road to Democracy," *National Interest* 45 (Fall 1996): 61–70.

2. The widely used *CIA World Factbook* (*www.cia.gov/cia/publications/factbook/index. html*) estimates China's GDPpc for 2006 as $7,600 rather than the $6,000 figure that I deem more accurate. Estimating PPP values is an imperfect art and the *Factbook* value seems too high for a country whose exchange-rate GDPpc is only $1,900 per annum. This last number, based on data from China's National Statistical Bureau, is much less controversial than the PPP figure.

3. Seymour Martin Lipset, "Some Social Requisites of Democracy: Economic Development and Political Legitimacy," *American Political Science Review* 53 (March 1959): 69–105.

4. Edward L. Glaeser et al., "Do Institutions Cause Growth?" National Bureau of Economic Research Working Paper No. 10568, 2004.

5. Edward L. Glaeser, Giacomo Ponzetto, and Andrei Shleifer, "Why Does Democracy Need Education?" National Bureau of Economic Research Working Paper No. 12128, 2006.

6. Robert J. Barro, "Determinants of Democracy," *Journal of Political Economy* 107 (December 1999): S158–83.

7. Robert J. Barro, "Rule of Law, Democracy, and Economic Performance," *2000 Index of Economic Freedom* (Washington, D.C.: Heritage Foundation, 2000).

8. Adam Przeworski et al., *Democracy and Development: Political Institutions and Material Well-Being in the World, 1950–1990* (Cambridge: Cambridge University Press, 2000); Carles Boix and Susan C. Stokes, "Endogenous Democratization," *World Politics* 55 (July 2003): 517–49.

9. Torsten Persson and Guido Tabellini, "Democracy and Development: The Devil in the Details," National Bureau of Economic Research Working Paper No. 11993, 2006.

10. Daron Acemoglu, Simon Johnson, and James A. Robinson, "The Colonial Origins of Comparative Development: An Empirical Investigation," *American Economic Review* 91 (December 2001): 1369–1401.

11. Robert J. Barro and Jong-Wha Lee, "International Data on Educational Attainment: Updates and Implications," *Oxford Economic Papers* 53 (2001): 541–63.

12. See *www.globescan.com/news_archives/pipa_market.html*.

13. When asked in a 2003 Roper Survey where stability ranked as a social value, Chinese ranked it second. Its average ranking by other nations' citizens was twenty-third. Joshua Cooper Ramo, "The Beijing Consensus," at *http://fpc.org.uk/publications/123*.

14. Zhengxu Wang, "Before the Emergence of Critical Citizens: Economic Development and Political Trust in China," *International Review of Sociology* 15 (March 2005): 155–71.

15. "[T]he progress in legal reform since the end of the Mao era has been unprecedented in Chinese history, as reflected in the passage of a large number of new laws, the increasing use of the courts to resolve economic disputes, social and state-society conflicts, the development of a professional legal community, and improvements in judicial procedures. . . . Chinese courts have assumed an indispensable role in resolving economic, social and, to a limited extent—political—conflicts." Minxin Pei, "Statement to the Senate Foreign Relations Committee, June 7, 2005," at *http://www.foreign.senate.gov/imo/media/doc/PeiTestimony050607.pdf*.

16. Benjamin L. Liebman, "Watchdog or Demagogue? The Media in the Chinese Legal System," *Columbia Law Review* 105 (January 2005): 64.

17. Liebman, "Watchdog or Demagogue?" 56.

18. Jean Oi, "Bending Without Breaking: The Adaptability of Chinese Political Institutions," in Nicholas C. Hope, Dennis Tao Yang, and Mu Yang Li, eds., *How Far Across the River? Chinese Policy Reform at the Millennium* (Stanford: Stanford University Press, 2003), 450–68.

19. Alex Inkeles, "The Generalist Meets the China Specialist," in *One World Emerging? Convergence and Divergence in Industrial Societies* (Boulder, Colo.: Westview, 1998), 96–113.

20. Goodwin C. Chu and Yanan Ju, *The Great Wall in Ruins: Communication and Cultural Change in China* (Albany: State University of New York Press, 1993).

21. Persson and Tabellini, "Democracy and Development," 2.

22. He Baogang, "Intra-Party Democracy: A Revisionist Perspective from Below," in Kjeld Erik Broedsgaard and Yongnian Zheng, eds., *The Chinese Communist Party in a New Era: Renewal and Reform* (London: Routledge, 2005), 192–209.

23. Gang Lin, "Ideology and Political Institutions for a New Era," in Gang Lin and Xiaobo Hu, eds., *China After Jiang* (Stanford: Stanford University Press, 2003).

24. The 2006 coup in Thailand has caused that country to drop from Free all the way to Not Free in the FH rankings. Thailand's 2006 PPP level of $9,100 makes this a rare event. Russia, where per-capita income was $12,100 PPP in 2006, was recently downgraded from Partly Free to Not Free. Yet Russia earns more than 60 percent of its export revenues from oil and natural gas, which puts it in the (politically unfortunate) category of petroleum states and hence outside the relevant comparison set for this essay.

25. Assuming a future growth rate 1 percentage point lower than in the case shown in the text would put China in the Partly Free rather than the Free FH category as of 2025.

26. Edward D. Mansfield and Jack Snyder, *Electing to Fight: Why Emerging Democracies Go to War* (Cambridge: MIT Press, 2005). For critiques of this line of thinking, see Michael McFaul, "Are New Democracies War-Prone?" *Journal of Democracy* 18 (April 2007): 160–67; and John R. Oneal, Bruce Russett, and Michael L. Berbaum, "Causes of Peace: Democracy, Interdependence, and International Organizations, 1885–1992," *International Studies Quarterly* 47 (September 2003): 371–93.

2

CONFRONTING
A CLASSIC DILEMMA

Michel Oksenberg

Michel Oksenberg (1938–2001) was instrumental in the normalization of U.S.–China relations in the late 1970s while serving on the National Security Council under President Jimmy Carter. From 1995 to 2001, he was a senior fellow of the Asia/Pacific Research Center at Stanford University. He served as president of the East-West Center in Honolulu, Hawaii, from 1992 to 1995, and taught at the University of Michigan from 1973 to 1992. He was coeditor of Making China Policy: Lessons from the Bush and Clinton Administrations *(2001) and* Policy Making in China: Leaders, Structures, and Processes *(1998). This essay originally appeared in the January 1998 issue of the* Journal of Democracy.

Since the brutal suppression of student demonstrations in June 1989, China scholars have waged a vigorous debate about the prospects for a democratic transition in the People's Republic of China (PRC). Roughly speaking, three views exist. The first stresses the strengths and resiliency of the existing authoritarian arrangements. The second emphasizes their weaknesses. The third focuses less on the toughness or fragility of the current political system, and looks instead at the long-term democratizing implications of economic and social change.

The first school argues that China's institutional arrangements are deeply embedded in society, and are yielding sufficient economic resources and coercive capabilities to keep the communist elite in power indefinitely. This elite is determined to maintain its power through authoritarian rule. The regime's performance, as reflected in high economic growth and the avoidance of a Soviet-style social and political collapse, garners it a required minimum of support from relevant sectors of society. Institutional developments such as village elections and the strengthening of the National People's Congress, which are often cited as evidence of democratization, are still in an incipient stage. They face considerable opposition and an uncertain future, and it is too early to say whether they will lead to democracy.

Moreover, these promising developments have not prevented the regime from increasing its capacity to suppress dissent and quell unrest through expanded surveillance and the strengthening of the People's Armed Police.

The trends of the past two decades point less toward democracy than toward the rise of a corrupt "soft" authoritarianism not unlike that found in Suharto's Indonesia or Park Chung Hee's South Korea. Only a calamity severe enough to divide and paralyze the top leadership and rouse widespread social unrest could fundamentally threaten the regime. And any such collapse would more likely unleash widespread violence and chaos, followed by the reimposition of authoritarian rule, than bring about democracy.

Adherents of this first view also find little support for democracy in Chinese political thought, whether traditional or contemporary. They typically believe that the 1989 demonstrations were not fundamentally democratic in nature, and furnished little evidence of an emerging civil society. Finally, these analysts tend to think that the Chinese dissident community will have little influence over China's future.

The second opinion claims that: 1) the Chinese Communist Party (CCP) is moribund; 2) the central state is losing power relative to provincial and local political units; 3) the regime is losing popular support; 4) the armed forces may no longer be willing to carry out a crackdown like that of 1989; and 5) growing corruption is corroding the regime's legitimacy and effectiveness. Proponents of this view find evidence of some of the same dynamics that destroyed communism in the former Soviet bloc. They also look upon the 1989 demonstrations as indicating a popular yearning for democracy and a potential for the formation of a civil society. They find support for democracy in traditional Chinese political thought, and even more so in the recent work of Chinese political thinkers who hail from Hong Kong and Taiwan but have influence on the mainland as well. Such analysts usually believe that political dissidents, whether living abroad or imprisoned in China, are likely to play an important role in the years ahead.

The third set of analysts finds encouragement in China's openness to the outside world and the country's dramatic move away from socialist planning and the command economy. These analysts point to the inevitable political consequences of economic growth, the communications revolution, and the emergence of a more diverse society and an urban middle class. They tend to see in China the same economic and sociological processes that have led to democracy elsewhere in East and Southeast Asia. They stress the importance of a range of recent reforms, including village elections; the strengthening of people's assemblies at all levels of the hierarchy; the formation of government-licensed nongovernmental organizations; the development of a legal system; the expansion of the media and the beginnings of investigative journalism; and the leadership's acceptance of a species of interest-based politics (even if most interests are pursued by and through agencies of the state). Some claim that the market economy toward which China is supposedly moving will give the individual more power vis-à-vis the state and necessitate the adoption of democracy and the rule of law. While these analysts caution that change may well occur slowly (perhaps taking as many as 15 or 20 years), they remain confident that the process of China's transformation is inevitable and under way.

The best analysts of the contemporary scene weave these seemingly conflicting perspectives into a coherent whole. They recognize that all these perspectives yield cogent insights. China's political structures do indeed seem firm and deeply rooted. At the same time, certain key aspects of the system do appear vulnerable to rapid disintegration. Finally, profound underlying economic, technological, and social changes are clearly propelling China into a new political era.

New Factors at Work

As the debate has unfolded, China itself has changed. The prospects of a speedy regime collapse, which seemed sizeable in 1989, have since diminished. Yet incremental changes continue. In particular, the growing autonomy of Chinese society vis-à-vis the state and the rapid pace of economic transformation are making it increasingly likely that the current political system will not be able to persist unaltered. The question increasingly seems to be about the scope of the transition. Will it be limited, producing a more durable, predictable, and humane authoritarian regime that rules through law yet excludes real democracy? Or will it go farther, to the point where leaders are selected through competitive, universal-suffrage elections and officials operate not merely *through* but *under* law? And can a transition from "soft" authoritarianism to some form of democracy occur gradually and peacefully, as it did in Taiwan or South Korea, or will there be widespread violence and economic hardship, as we have seen in Yugoslavia or the former Soviet Union? Finally, one might even ask if some other, unanticipated type of political transformation will be the one that actually occurs.

Such questions are being debated not only by China specialists outside of China, but even (if very quietly) by nondissident intellectuals within China—in itself evidence both of the uncertainty that haunts China's political future and of the serious possibility that a democratic transition might be in store. Several developments in the past two years have not only increased the likelihood of the latter, but also hint that it might occur more rapidly than most observers expect. These developments include an important evolution in the thinking of the leaders; an increased probability of social unrest that will demand a high-level strategic (rather than tactical) response; the influence of Hong Kong and Taiwan on mainland politics; and the consequences of the Chinese leadership's involvement in world affairs.

Most important, the nature of political discourse is changing. China's leaders are mentioning political participation and democracy in more serious fashion than at any time since the mid-1950s. Mao Zedong wrote about China's "New Democracy," but that was before he proclaimed the founding of the People's Republic. Following his ascent to power, he spoke primarily in Leninist terms about "the dictatorship of the proletariat" or "democratic centralism." Deng Xiaoping did not even tolerate explorations of democratic theory, much less reveal any interest in it.

More recently, however, China's leaders have begun to talk about their country's eventual evolution into a democracy. At the Fifteenth Congress of the CCP in September 1997, General Secretary Jiang Zemin stated explicitly that by the middle of the twenty-first century, "China will have become a prosperous, strong, democratic, and culturally advanced socialist country." Jiang avoided specifics, gave no explanation of what he meant by "democratic," and made clear elsewhere in the same speech that he was committed to preserving the supremacy of the CCP at all costs. In his many meetings with visiting Americans, Jiang has not denigrated democracy as a form of government, but rather avers that China, still plagued by poverty and a poorly educated populace, currently lacks the capacity to sustain it. To some Americans, Jiang has explicitly stated that nations pursue different paths of development due to their diverse cultures and historical experiences, but will converge in their social and organizational forms.

Let there be no illusion: Jiang gives no evidence of being a closet liberal democrat, and has shown himself willing and able to suppress dissent. Yet whatever his intentions, Jiang has helped to make "democracy" a word of acceptable currency among China's leaders and its populace. Nor is this rhetoric limited to Jiang. Officials of the CCP, especially at the lower levels, often admit that they must move in the direction of increased political participation, although it is not clear that their understanding of the term "democracy" resembles the meaning cherished by most Americans. In short, in the 1990s, China's elite political culture has begun to change. Democracy has begun to be enshrined as an ultimate goal for China, and it is just a matter of time before discussions begin over the features of "socialist democracy with Chinese characteristics" and the methods that the nation should use to move toward this goal. Once such a debate begins, it will assume a life of its own and accelerate the process of change.

The second major development accelerating the pace of political change will be the consequences of the reform of state-owned enterprises (SOEs). The pressure to embark upon this very difficult reform has become intense. Subsidies for inefficient SOEs are absorbing large shares of both the government budget and available bank credit, draining the state's coffers and plaguing the financial system with bad debt. This misallocation of investment retards national economic development. Yet letting these firms go under, in the absence of an effective social security system, will spark worker discontent and protest. As Elizabeth Perry has shown, the Chinese working classes have long exhibited a considerable propensity for various forms of labor unrest. Perry persuasively contends that worker movements have had a much more significant impact on the evolution of Chinese politics than most observers realize. Already there have been signs of spontaneous unrest and organization in response to wage cuts and job losses at SOEs around the country.[1]

In the past, such activity usually would have led to crackdowns, possibly accompanied by tactical efforts to redress some worker grievances. But an alternative response to an increasingly restive society could be for the leaders in Beijing to increase the number of democratically elected local officials, with the idea of letting them bear the brunt of popular discontent. Thus responsibility for managing SOE reform would be shifted away from the center, while opportunities for local-level political participation would increase. There are three indications that the top leaders are thinking precisely along these lines. First, Jiang's Fifteenth Party Congress report explicitly mentioned the need to make officials at the grassroots more accountable through elections. Second, the SOEs slated for privatization are the ones run not by the central government, but rather by local governments. Finally, plans are under way to experiment with extending direct, competitive elections to county-level people's assemblies as well as urban wards and neighborhoods.

The likely increase in social unrest will confront China's leaders with the classic dilemma that other authoritarian regimes have faced: whether to repress dissent, or to seek to bolster the regime's legitimacy and support by broadening opportunities for political participation. Following Robert Dahl, we may anticipate that the leaders' calculations will be governed by an assessment of the relative costs, benefits, and risks to them of each course of action. If the unrest is widespread but not so massive as to threaten communist rule, the leaders might opt for an orderly and accelerated expansion of democratizing reform, especially if such changes also come to be seen as offering one way to curtail corruption, which now concerns rulers and public alike. Such an admittedly difficult decision would be eased by some confidence that a more open political system would not challenge the dominance of the CCP, and a recognition that suppression would be costly. That is, the leaders would calculate that communist rule, political stability, and honest government would be enhanced rather than weakened by a process of democratization. One can now envision circumstances in which a majority of the Politburo would support such a conclusion.

In a development that most analysts have not yet taken into account, Hong Kong's reversion to PRC sovereignty and Taiwan's transition to democracy will accelerate the process of change. No longer can it be claimed that Chinese culture is somehow incompatible with democracy. Taiwan's March 1996 presidential election, in which incumbent Lee Teng-hui triumphed over vigorous opponents and won majority support in an electorate of 14 million people, was without precedent in four thousand years of Chinese history. Taiwan's experience shows that a Chinese populace can indeed participate effectively in electoral politics extended well beyond the local community. Moreover, Hong Kong will be under pressure to achieve the stated goal of directly electing, through universal suffrage, all 60 members of its Legislative Council. If that city continues to thrive under freedom and democracy, many Chinese will naturally conclude that these principles can enhance the quality of rule on the mainland as well.

Furthermore, the tens of thousands of Hong Kong and Taiwan citizens working throughout the mainland, and the many PRC citizens temporarily residing in Hong Kong will affect the mainland's political culture. The massive flow of people among these three parts of China will probably increase the yearnings on the mainland for greater freedom and political participation. In addition, a firm and credible commitment to democratization on the part of the PRC leadership would facilitate a peaceful resolution of the Taiwan issue.

Finally, the involvement of China's leaders in world affairs will have a cumulative effect on their approach to governance at home. Paradoxes now abound. Chinese leaders traveling abroad will take questions from foreign audiences, but will not allow any such thing in China. They give speeches at foreign universities and nongovernmental organizations, while protesters demonstrate outside, but are unwilling to subject themselves to such discipline at home. They go to international gatherings where they are among the few (or sometimes even the only) leaders who have not had to win the votes of their citizens. How does this anomalous situation affect the self-perception of China's leaders? Will they begin to pay an unacceptable political, economic, or psychological price for it? Will they eventually feel impelled to seek the same kind of mandate that leaders of other countries enjoy? In short, will their craving for stature, respect, and equality in international affairs become an increasing consideration in the years ahead?

Obstacles to Democratization

Naturally, enormous political obstacles deter China's leaders from explicitly embarking upon the process of democratization. An acknowledgment that major mistakes were made in the crushing of the 1989 demonstrations is probably a prerequisite for the adoption of such a bold political course, and the current leaders—many of whom were at least indirectly involved in the crackdown—are reluctant to revisit that event. A reappraisal of the June 1989 tragedy would necessitate finding a scapegoat for it, and none is readily available. And a reappraisal would vindicate and thereby rehabilitate deposed General Secretary Zhao Zi-yang and his supporters, a very divisive move. Moreover, powerful conservatives among the leaders, including officials of the military and security apparatus, would no doubt oppose an explicit commitment to democratization, fearing political instability and a loss of power by the CCP. The strength of these conservative forces is evident in the leaders' reluctance to resurrect the slogan of a decade ago—"separate the Party and government"—which falls far short of democratization but which would entail constraints on the CCP's authority. In addition, the party would surely face stiff competition at the ballot box in Tibet and Xinjiang, complicating Han Chinese rule in those regions. An openly competitive political system could also invite efforts by Taiwan and the United States to intervene in Chinese domestic politics. It might produce the same chaotic consequences as in Russia. Finally, the organization and conduct of fair elections would be a gargantuan undertaking. China has roughly two thousand counties, each with a population ranging from a third of a million to a million or more. Many are comparable in size to small republics such as Haiti, Nicaragua, or El Salvador—to name three countries where the difficulties surrounding the introduction of elections proved to be considerable.

To conclude, several factors are propelling China toward a speedier democratic transition than most analysts think likely. Yet cautious forecasts seem realistic in light of the obstacles to a swift transformation. Nonetheless, for the reasons already noted, China's leaders are likely to find introducing democracy at lower levels of the system and firmly committing themselves to the attainment of full democracy over a protracted period to be an increasingly attractive option. The commitment would have to be accompanied by a realistic plan for maintaining Communist Party dominance, and by a strategy for ensuring that the use of elections expands only gradually, while the ancillary institutions necessary to the maintenance of a vibrant democracy are put in place.

The logic of the situation is compelling. Such a course would contribute to China's stability, increase the international respect accorded to China's leaders, enhance their power, and improve the governance of China. China's leaders may come to the same conclusion—provided they are not pressured to do so—at an earlier date than most outside observers now think possible. On the other hand, history is replete with authoritarian rulers who, out of fear or habit, proved unwilling to adjust to new realities and then lost power; with leaders who bravely sought to undertake democratic reforms and then failed; and with dictators who hung on for years or even decades, often bringing their societies stability and growth while confounding outside observers' predictions of the early demise of their system.

NOTES

1. Elizabeth Perry, *Shanghai on Strike: The Politics of Chinese Labor* (Stanford, Calif.: Stanford University Press, 1993); "Shanghai's Strike Wave of 1957," *China Quarterly* 137 (March 1994): 1–27; "Labor's Battle for Political Space," in Deborah Davis et al., eds., *Urban Spaces in Contemporary China* (New York: Cambridge University Press, 1995), 302–26; and (with Li Xun), *Proletarian Power: Shanghai in the Cultural Revolution* (Boulder, Colo.: Westview, 1997).

3

A "GRAY" TRANSFORMATION

Juntao Wang

Juntao Wang *received his doctorate in political science from Columbia University in 2006, and is currently chief editor of* Public Intellectual, *a Chinese quarterly based in Taiwan. A longtime democratic activist and early member of the "Democracy Wall" movement in the late 1970s, he was arrested by Chinese authorities during the crackdown that followed the Tiananmen Square massacre in 1989. After serving five years of a thirteen-year sentence, he was released on medical parole and exiled to the United States in April 1994. This essay originally appeared in the January 1998 issue of the* Journal of Democracy.

The changes that China has been undergoing over the last 20 years, as well as the country's rise to world-power status, lend urgency to questions about the possibility of democratization in China. Will China become democratic? If so, how will the process take place? If not, what will happen? Can a nondemocratic China remain politically stable?

On the first question, most Western observers believe that China will democratize, although they do not expect this to happen anytime soon. Some expect a peaceful evolution, guided by a self-consciously reformist government and promoted by business interests, whose influence is growing rapidly. Still others, however, see little if any prospect of democratization, and fear that China will descend into chaos once people decide that they can no longer put up with the communist dictatorship. Within China itself, on the other hand, the prevailing view among intellectuals close to the regime is that the country will remain stable if the government maintains a tight grip on power as fundamental economic and social changes proceed. Those who take this view fear that if the state does try to conduct political reform, the process will surge out of control and bring chaos.

Although China seems to be coming to a crossroads of some sort, it is difficult to predict exactly what lies in store. Yet we can predict certain possible outcomes, and describe the conditions under which each is most likely to occur. In essence, the possibilities are three: recrudescent dictatorship, chaos, and democratization. The first I would rate as distinctly possible, the second as unlikely, and the third as most likely of all.

Over the past ten years, China has changed its communist ideology, but kept the dictatorial regime that went with it. Nonetheless, economic reforms, sweeping social changes, and rising official corruption have all helped greatly to weaken the state's actual control. The full-blown dictatorship of a single all-powerful leader may have passed away for good with the death of Deng Xiaoping. His successor Jiang Zemin is relatively weak in terms of personal connections and credibility, has no cohesive social class or set of interests behind him, and enjoys only a rather limited degree of power and legitimacy. Indeed, Jiang has no shortage of potential challengers, and must act carefully in order to ensure his political survival. On a broader level, few Chinese want the old order back, and the state itself is pushing political, legal, and administrative reforms with an eye to giving itself more flexibility and efficacy under the new conditions.

Since the mid-1980s, many Chinese intellectuals have been discussing the possibility of the emergence of a collective dictatorship in the post-Deng era. Their argument is that a small group of leaders, recognizing a common interest in the maintenance of order, would cooperate to achieve a balance of power among themselves, thus promoting stability. In an era of drastic change, however, it will be very difficult to establish or preserve a diverse yet stable and united leadership group. The prerequisites are missing. Twenty years of reform, corruption, and power struggles have destroyed the supremacy of communism as an ideology and weakened the party's political machine. Furthermore, China is not the closed society it once was. The public is able to get news and information from outside official channels, even though open discussion of some issues is still prohibited.

Although no signs of a return to full-blown dictatorship are currently in evidence, such a development is not utterly impossible. Political reform has yet to become systematic or institutionalized. The party-state may be weak due to inefficiency, but in principle its power remains unlimited. If certain conditions arise, Jiang Zemin may receive a chance to set up a personal dictatorship. The Fifteenth Party Congress, held in September 1997, leaves one with two strong impressions: 1) Although Jiang has no clear vision of how to promote China's progress, he is skilled at accumulating power. He readily and adroitly broke promises and played the "dirty game" of party infighting in order to outmaneuver his rivals. 2) In the minds of China's ruling elites, dislike and distrust of Jiang take a backseat to fear of political turmoil; hence their willingness to tolerate Jiang's actions to consolidate his personal power. If Jiang seeks popular support for the reestablishment of absolute dictatorship, there are at least three strains of political opinion that he might try to exploit.

The first is egalitarianism. Market-oriented economic reform, including de facto privatization, has not proceeded by means of a fair, competitive process. Instead, it has been riddled by corruption and as such is intensely resented by most Chinese. Although democracy offers good prospects for containing corruption and guaranteeing governmental fairness, most Chinese want to see the government take severe actions against corruption immediately. In recent cases, anticorruption measures taken in violation of legal procedure have nonetheless won widespread public support. If Jiang can gain a reputation as a corruption fighter, he could gain grassroots support for a renewed personal dictatorship.

Should there be a serious economic downturn, moreover, people will clamor for a recentralized government capable of carrying out social-welfare functions. The Beijing government has recently announced plans to reform the state-owned enterprise sector; about 40 million workers are expected to lose their jobs. In the 1930s, economic crisis created conditions in which some unstable democratic regimes could be and were overthrown. It would take far less to reverse the uncertain process of democratic reform in China.

A second worrisome strain of opinion is authoritarianism. In the long span of Chinese history, the formal authorities have always enjoyed a certain legitimacy, as long as they do not behave too egregiously. The contemporary elites, who are very concerned about chaos, include not only government officials but many intellectuals and a majority of businesspeople as well. Contrary to the expectations of many Western analysts, China's businesspeople are not interested in democratization. They want a government that they can depend on to keep order, take their bribes, and guarantee their privileges. Democratization would open up opportunities for all people and jeopardize their special status.

The third strain of opinion that might provide support to dictatorship is nationalism, which in recent years has been on the upswing in China. There seem to be three reasons for this rise in nationalist sentiment. First, many Chinese, citing conflicts over trade and security issues as evidence, believe that the West opposes a powerful China. (Interestingly, few Chinese seem to count Western criticism of China over human rights as such evidence unless it is linked to some economic dispute.) Second is the historical memory of the ethnic and regional separatism that followed the collapse of the last imperial dynasty in 1912. With that in mind, most Chinese support a strong national government as a check to such centrifugal tendencies. Third are the territorial disputes that currently set China against some of her neighbors and naturally encourage nationalism. In its search for a new source of legitimacy to fill the vacuum left behind by the collapse of communist ideology, the government finds nationalism a handy recourse. Certain Chinese intellectuals, moreover, tend to view nationalism as an important precondition for modernization.

Despite China's many problems, large-scale chaos should not be expected. The elites are too anxious to maintain stability, and economic development is filling the legitimacy gap. Even regionalists pursuing economic development demand a large national market. A professionalized bureaucratic class is forming, and is proving itself skillful at handling trouble. Most Chinese live in the relatively better developed regions, and thus have little incentive to oppose the government.

What Path Toward Democratization?

Few Western students of China see democratization as much of a near-term probability. Ordinary Chinese, they reason, care little about politics, while the elites are cautious and stability-minded. The Chinese people, these experts point out, are eager to pursue economic prosperity and are tolerant of official political repression. The government's police actions, meanwhile, have stymied opposition movements within China, and opposition groups outside of China, beset with their own internal problems, are in decline.

This conventional wisdom notwithstanding, my opinion is that democratization is the most likely outcome in today's China. The key problem is the question raised near the beginning of this essay: How will this process take place? If we expect a typical democratic revolution—I call it "clear" democratization—in which people self-consciously pursue democratic and liberal ideals, overthrow a dictatorial regime, and then in an incandescent civic moment design a constitution replete with checks and balances, multiparty political competition, free elections, and guarantees of basic civil and political rights, then we will be disappointed. What we can expect to see instead is a "hazy" or "gray" democratization. The basic idea behind this expectation is that both the people and the elites are self-interested, eager to maximize their own power and serve their own interests. As they jostle and compete with one another, it will become apparent that none can control the others completely. Thus they may be driven to agree upon rules to regulate the political process. The separation of powers, open competition among diverse factions, a more responsible administration, and elections may all emerge in this way. Although piecemeal and unsystematic at first, such practices can become institutionalized as time goes by.

Over the last 20 years, China has been a country of just such piecemeal change, most of it economic. Looking at the period since June 1989, can we see any evidence that a political process of gradual, "gray" democratization has been at work? In fact, at least four such signs of progress exist.

The first sign is the rapid growth of civil society. The share of China's national wealth controlled by nonstate actors now nearly equals, and may even exceed, the share controlled by the state. In addition, the nonstate sector is growing much faster than the state sector, which means more wealth will be available to support the expansion of civil society. Organizations formally independent of the state (yet controlled by the elite) are becoming prominent in the fields of education, culture, publishing, and law.

The second sign is the continuing phenomenon of institutional conflicts within the regime, which may mark the beginning of the separation of powers. At the highest levels, political leaders are agreeing on certain rules to help settle disputes among themselves. (While Jiang Zemin's maneuvering at the Fifteenth Party Congress was carried out with disregard for the rules, the effects of his actions remain unclear.) In elite circles generally, appeals to the rule of law are coming to dominate debate, and professional bureaucrats are taking over more and more important jobs.

Third, the practice of holding free elections is spreading. For now, voting is found mostly in nonpolitical organizations and at the lower levels of government. Yet elections are coming to play ever more important roles in middle-ranking and higher-level political settings. Indeed, recent elections for delegates to both the Party Congress and the National People's Congress (China's central legislature) have seen outcomes that deviated from the ones that the leaders thought they had arranged beforehand.

The fourth sign is the changing nature of political legitimacy in China today. The Tiananmen Square massacre and the subsequent crackdown destroyed the communist regime's ideological legitimacy. The state needs a new and more reliable ideal upon which to base its claim to rule. In the contemporary world, there is no other choice but democracy.

The "gray democratization" scenario has nothing fanciful about it. It focuses on what is really happening in China, and is premised on the reliable idea that people have an incentive to seek their own interests. They also need some deliberative rules, of course. At present, the Chinese are showing dissatisfaction with massive government control and autocratic leadership, but have not as yet drawn a connection between this discontent and the idea of democracy. They support the rule of law, which promises to place appropriate limits on the state and political leaders. This, and not democracy as such, best represents mainstream political thinking in China today.

Given that democratization is a game in which all Chinese groups will have to contribute to creating new rules, what then is the particular role of those groups and individuals in China who are already self-conscious democrats? I think that principled democrats are essential in "gray" democratizations, for two reasons. First, although democratization is guided by self-interest, it presupposes the existence of morals and ideals that ground and regulate the process. Democracy, in other words, requires not only the pursuit of self-interest, but the sincere acceptance of rules which limit that pursuit. It requires, moreover, deliberate intellectual as well as moral effort. Democrats in any given time and place must gauge the problem presented by a particular constellation of interests and find a solution consistent with democratic ideals and principles. Since democratization is only one among several competing alternatives, the absence or failure of such efforts will make it probable that a solution other than democracy will be adopted.

Second, democrats can act as a catalyst, initiating important events that open up more free political space, change actual institutions, and create new "rules of the game." Such efforts are not the natural first choice of people who pursue their own immediate interest first, who base their choices on marginal cost-benefit calculations, and who are likely to remain "free riders" while idealists pull the bandwagon of reform.

The final lesson to be drawn from the "gray democratization" scenario is that Chinese democrats need to reorient their strategy. They must show how democratic principles and ideals can resolve the problem of clashing interests. If they do not, the mainstream of Chinese politics will leave them aside, and democracy itself will lose out to one of its competitors. Chinese democrats must also join more fully in the real life of Chinese society, seeking opportunities to open more space for free activity, to initiate institutional changes, and to create new rules of the game. China's democrats must resist the dangerous temptation to become an isolated and self-satisfied group whose high ideals lead it to shun actual politics as immoral.

4

THE HALTING ADVANCE OF PLURALISM

Harry Harding

Harry Harding, *Dean of the Frank Batten School of Leadership and Public Policy at the University of Virginia, is also a vice-chairman of the Asia Foundation and a director of the National Committee on U.S.-China Relations. He is the author of* China's Second Revolution: Reform After Mao *(1987),* A Fragile Relationship: The United States and China Since 1972 *(1992), and* The India-China Relationship: What the United States Needs to Know, *edited with Francine R. Frankel (2004). This essay originally appeared in the January 1998 issue of the* Journal of Democracy.

Early in 1997, it seemed possible that the People's Republic of China (PRC) might be on the verge of accelerated political reform. In several speeches during the spring, President Jiang Zemin called for further restructuring of the country's political system. Zhao Ziyang, the former Party general secretary who had fallen from power during the Tiananmen Square crisis, reportedly asked the Chinese Communist Party (CCP) for a favorable reassessment of the massive popular protests of 1989. Some intellectuals, sensing a more hospitable climate for political reform, submitted petitions calling for direct elections of provincial and national leaders, the freedom to demonstrate, the right to strike, and the rehabilitation of Zhao Ziyang.

In the end, however, the Fifteenth Party Congress meeting in September 1997 did little to fulfill those expectations. Jiang Zemin's political report announced neither new measures for political restructuring nor an acceleration of ongoing political reforms. Instead, spokesmen emphasized that the CCP would not adopt Western models of democracy, or revise its assessment of Tiananmen.

Moreover, the chairman of China's national legislature, Qiao Shi, was completely removed from the central party leadership, losing both his position in the Politburo and his seat on the Central Committee. Qiao was said to be not only a rival of Jiang Zemin, but also a proponent of more rapid and thoroughgoing political reform. If those reports are accurate, Qiao became the third major leader in the post-Mao era—following Hu Yaobang and Zhao Ziyang—to lose power for endorsing political liberalization.

These developments reinforced the conventional wisdom that China is a "market-Leninist" society that is pursuing economic reform while resisting political change. In fact, this cliché oversimplifies a much more complex reality. Although the Fifteenth Party Congress made no dramatic new decisions on China's political reform, it also did nothing to reverse some important developments that have been slowly but steadily transforming the character of Chinese politics over the past two decades:

• The principal objective of the CCP is now to promote economic modernization, not to foster continual class struggle, as was the case during the Maoist era.
• Official doctrine no longer motivates many citizens. The legitimacy of the political system therefore depends largely on economic performance, supplemented by a growing popular nationalism. Nor does doctrine guide many policy decisions in today's China. The most important areas where ideology is still invoked are to defend CCP leadership in politics and state ownership of major industry.
• The governing elite is more technocratic and more civilian in character. More and more officials have college educations, albeit primarily as engineers. Fewer and fewer seats in the Politburo and the Central Committee, let alone in the State Council, are occupied by the military.
• Alternative policy options are formulated by the bureaucracy, with some input from specialists in research institutions and universities. The options generally reflect a preference for cautious, pragmatic, and incremental approaches to policy reform, rather than utopian efforts to promote radical change.
• The legal system is steadily developing. Not only does the state govern through the adoption and implementation of laws and regulations, but those laws are beginning to constrain state behavior. Even the highest officials are subject to limited terms of office. Citizens are suing the state for malfeasance. Courts are occasionally overturning the recommendations of state prosecutors.
• Meaningful elections are becoming common in rural areas. For the first time, elections are being held to executive positions on village councils as well as to legislative bodies at higher levels. In many places, these elections appear to be more competitive, and the process of nomination less tightly controlled by the party, than was originally anticipated.
• Legislatures have become more active, particularly at the provincial and national levels. Legislatures meet on more regular schedules,

and the National People's Congress has a more elaborate committee and staff structure. Occasionally, legislatures reject party nominees to executive positions, and delay or modify proposed legislation. But legislators at higher levels are still nominees of the party, and are still indirectly elected.

• China has experienced a considerable growth of nongovernmental organizations (NGOs), particularly professional associations and social service organizations. But virtually all NGOs require some kind of official sponsorship, and NGOs can engage in overt political advocacy only at great risk. Independent trade unions and religious organizations are particularly subject to suppression.

• Prepublication censorship of the press is far less common, there is considerable freedom to write on nonpolitical issues, and private discussion of political issues is far less constrained than before. But freedom of speech and protest on political matters remains tightly restricted.

All this adds up to a fundamental transformation of Chinese politics. By any reasonable definition, China is no longer a totalitarian system. The role of both the party and official communist ideology within the political system has been substantially reduced. An increasing range of activity is outside the scope of central economic planning, ideological constraint, or political control.

But Chinese citizens cannot yet freely express their political beliefs publicly, nor openly challenge the official ideology. Moreover, although China now has considerable pluralism in economic organizations, truly independent social and political institutions are still prohibited. Thus China can best be categorized as an authoritarian system, and still of a relatively "hard" variety.

A Parallel with Taiwan?

If this is a capsule description of China's political system today, where it is likely to go from here? It is true that China is not following the same path as much of the former Soviet Union or Central and Eastern Europe toward rapid political democratization and thoroughgoing economic privatization. Instead, it is taking a different course—one that more closely resembles that traveled by Taiwan in the 1960s and 1970s. Now, as then, we see a more technocratic government, whose highest priority is economic modernization, and whose legitimacy depends on success in that regard; a society freer of administrative and ideological controls; the emergence of a middle class of intellectuals, professionals, entrepreneurs, and managers, many of whom have had the opportunity to travel or receive education abroad; and a ruling party that is losing its ability to penetrate society or to determine the details of government policy.

One optimistic, yet highly plausible, assessment is therefore that over the next ten years mainland China will continue to evolve in ways similar to Taiwan. The state would still be known as the PRC (just as Taiwan is still known as the Republic of China), and the CCP would still be the ruling party (just as the Kuomintang, or KMT, has retained power in Taiwan for years after political reform). But under this scenario, China's political system would be characterized by even greater political and social freedom; incipient social and political pluralism, albeit still within limits; and a more responsive and accountable political system, although not yet a genuinely democratic one.

Several conditions must be met, however, for this optimistic scenario to unfold. It will require steady pressure from society on behalf of further political reform, the willingness of a far-sighted leadership to endorse political change, and the ability of the government to manage the contradictions of modernization such that the more open and pluralistic institutions are not swamped by demands from below. A blend of pressure and encouragement from the international community would also help. Unfortunately, it is not clear that these conditions will be satisfied as fully in mainland China as they have been across the Taiwan Strait.

Consider first the political elite. The political report presented by Jiang Zemin to the Fifteenth Party Congress can be seen as reflecting the party's present consensus on this issue. The elite seems to recognize that China needs a better educated, more efficient civil service in order to promote modernization. It must root out corruption in order to maintain legitimacy. The country needs a stronger legal system to provide greater predictability in administration. It also requires some degree of grassroots democracy to give local government the authority to mobilize the financial resources needed to promote rural development. But that same elite also believes that China needs order and stability, particularly at a time when it must implement some painful and potentially controversial economic reforms. It must therefore place limits on independent expression and independent organization.

Some members of the political elite may see the need for even further political reform. It was Deng Xiaoping, after all, who pioneered the call for the fuller separation of party from government—a program that the CCP adopted in 1987, but never fully implemented. And three of Deng's lieutenants—Hu Yaobang, Zhao Ziyang, and Qiao Shi—appear to have supported further political reforms, particularly in the areas of freer speech, a freer press, and more powerful legislatures. In each case, however, this line of thinking alienated them from the mainstream of the party, and ultimately contributed to their political downfall.

Indeed, unlike the Kuomintang, the Chinese Communist Party does not have a programmatic or ideological commitment to full democratization. On the contrary, it insists on maintaining the leadership of the party and a privileged place for Marxism-Leninism for the indefinite future. To that end, it rejects what it regards as "Western" models of democracy, and calls vaguely for "socialist democracy with Chinese characteristics." This may change when younger generations come to power, but until then the willingness of the CCP to undertake political reform will be distinctly limited.

The degree to which Chinese society will press the elite for political reform is also open to question. On the one hand, neither the CCP nor its ideology appears to enjoy much legitimacy in the eyes of either rural or urban Chinese. Ordinary Chinese mistrust the official press, and resent the widespread corruption among their political elites. They believe that their country needs further political reform to supplement its economic modernization. Those who have studied or lived abroad may have considerable direct experience with democratic institutions overseas. The urban protests of 1989 show how explosive these demands can become.

Yet there are also countervailing factors that support more cautious forecasts of China's political future. The emerging economic elite—a major potential force for political change—has a much more symbiotic relationship with the party and government than was the case on Taiwan. Moreover, while some intellectuals see democracy as a way of ensuring the accountability of the political system—and some even see it as a way of enhancing China's international prestige—others believe that some kind of neo-authoritarianism will be more effective in pursuing China's quest for wealth, power, and stability. Relatively few Chinese regard democratic institutions as ends in themselves; instead, they support whatever political system can govern their country best.

Even Chinese who advocate political reform may have a different definition of democracy than is common in the West. Many Chinese appear to favor a freer press, a more effective legal system, and somewhat more active legislatures, but are uncertain about the desirability of truly competitive elections and independent political organizations, at least at China's present levels of educational attainment and economic development. Some proreform intellectuals thus predict that China will develop and maintain a political system with institutions very different from those in the West.

Moreover, mainland China's social and economic problems are vastly more complex than Taiwan's. Most of China's provinces have a population larger than Taiwan. The country faces daunting obstacles to continued rapid growth: shortages of arable land and potable water; bottlenecks in the energy, agriculture, and education sectors; increasing problems of air, water, and soil pollution; huge quantities of surplus labor; and a steadily aging population.

Solving these problems will require substantial financial resources. Yet despite China's high savings rates, strong export performance, and massive foreign-exchange reserves, its banking system verges on insolvency, and its fiscal system extracts woefully small tax revenues relative to GDP. To deal with these problems responsibly through more stringent financial discipline will almost certainly mean lower growth and higher rates of unemployment; to deal with them irresponsibly through lax fiscal and lending policies could mean higher inflation, followed by economic collapse.

These dilemmas are so serious that they could conceivably derail any efforts at further political liberalization in China. The grievances produced by any combination of slower growth, higher unemployment, and more severe inflation could easily overwhelm the country's political institutions, leading either to political repression or to political decay.

Finally, the international environment may be less decisive for China than it was for Taiwan. The international community has so much at stake in its relations with China that it cannot focus solely on issues of human rights and democratization. Chinese who have been educated or who have lived abroad are a much lower proportion of the total population than was true in smaller Asian societies. Many Chinese resent overt foreign pressure, even if they may agree with the objectives that the foreigners are trying to promote. And, above all, as a major power, China has much greater ability to resist foreign pressure than did smaller societies such as South Korea or Taiwan, which are heavily dependent on American good will.

The Next Decade

Thus while continued political evolution toward greater liberalization and pluralism remains a very plausible scenario for mainland China, this process may well advance more slowly and less thoroughly than it has on Taiwan. Over the next ten years, some aspects of political reform are more probable than others. In particular, the political trends of the last two decades could well continue:

• The government's role in the economy and in society will decline significantly. Fewer enterprises will be owned by the state, and economic policy will be further liberalized. The role of various kinds of NGOs would expand. China would thus increasingly fit the description already being used by some Chinese analysts: a "large society" with a "small state."

• The political and administrative elites of the country will become increasingly well-educated. More and more will hold degrees from foreign institutions. The selection and promotion of administrative officials will become more meritocratic, although corruption will probably remain a serious problem.

• A more highly developed legal system and more active legislatures will provide a more powerful check on administrative power.

• The press will become much freer to report political news and to censure local officials, although it will still lack the ability to challenge fundamental national policies or to criticize national leaders.

• Competitive elections for both legislative and executive positions will spread up the administrative hierarchy in rural areas and into the cities. The emergence of an unorganized nonparty opposition is not inconceivable.

It is far less probable that direct elections for leaders at provincial and national levels, autonomous political organizations, or opposition political parties will emerge.

Furthermore, even this limited kind of political change is by no means inevitable. It is possible that the trends toward political liberalization and pluralization could be halted or even reversed, particularly if the country's socioeconomic problems mounted. In such a case, China could witness an even "harder" authoritarian system, with tighter controls over social and political life. Or its political system could lose coherence, with instability and unrest becoming the norm.

In short, China in the year 2008 is likely still to call itself the People's Republic and to be governed by the Chinese Communist Party. There is a good chance—but no guarantee—that its political system will be more open, more rational, more responsive, and more accountable than it is today. On balance, however, the prospects for full Western-style democratization are very limited.

5

TOP-LEVEL REFORM
OR BOTTOM-UP REVOLUTION?

Cheng Li

Cheng Li *is director of research and senior fellow of the John L. Thornton China Center at the Brookings Institution. His books include* The Political Mapping of China's Tobacco Industry and Anti-Smoking Campaign *(2012) and* The Road to Zhongnanhai *(2012, in Chinese). This essay originally appeared in the January 2013 issue of the* Journal of Democracy.

The People's Republic of China (PRC) has been troubled of late by widespread social unrest, slowing economic growth, and rampant official corruption as revealed by the Bo Xilai scandal. Less obvious to the outside world, however, have been the two sharply contrasting and controversial perspectives on the country's near- to medium-term future that are now locked in mutual contention. These two rival scenarios reflect fundamentally different assessments of the socioeconomic situation and likely political trajectory of the world's most populous country.

The first scenario envisions an abrupt bottom-up revolution. This assessment has recently generated much heated intellectual and political debate in the PRC. In December 2011, the thirty-year-old best-selling author Han Han (China's most popular blogger whose site has registered well over 580 million hits) posted a now-famous essay titled "On Revolution."[1] Although Han argues that "revolution is hardly a good option for China," his intriguing view of the choice between reform and revolution has pointedly reflected—and greatly enhanced—the public awareness of the risk of revolution in the country.

Additionally, one of the most popular books in PRC intellectual circles today is the Chinese translation of Alexis de Tocqueville's 1856 classic *The Old Regime and the Revolution*. One frequently quoted passage is Tocqueville's argument that revolutions usually occur not when the old regime resists change, but rather when it begins to attempt reform only to find expectations outstripping any possible rate of improvement.

The second scenario is reform from above, which Chinese Communist

Party (CCP) elites often refer to as "top-level reform" or the "top-level design of reform" (*gaige de dingceng sheji*). The latter term was first heard at a top CCP leadership meeting in October 2010.[2] It is related to the leaders' newfound understanding that China is now in "deep water" with regard to reform, and can no longer afford to "cross the river by feeling the stones," as the Chinese expression goes. Improvised reform, in short, needs to give way to a more methodical and more profound set of changes. Moreover, with so many of China's present-day socioeconomic problems growing out of impasses and obstacles within the political system, basic political reform will have to be part of the agenda as well.

According to those who call for top-level reform, China needs better coordination between socioeconomic policy and political development, along with structural changes that are more coherent. The older, bottom-up approach that stresses grassroots elections must yield, they say, to a new roadmap that includes intra-CCP elections to choose national-level Party leaders, enhanced institutional checks and balances, and judicial reform.[3]

It is critically important for foreign analysts to grasp the ongoing Chinese discourse in three key areas: 1) the impact of the Bo Xilai crisis on China's political trajectory, 2) possible triggers for sociopolitical uprisings and initiatives, and 3) institutional safeguards with which the CCP leadership may open the way to systemic change. Foreign analysts need to rethink the thesis of "authoritarian resilience," a predominant view in overseas studies of Chinese politics which argues that Chinese authoritarianism is "resilient" or "strong."[4] This view underestimates both the inherent vulnerability in the one-party system and the growing resentment that the public feels over CCP leaders' enormous power and wealth.

1) Bo Xilai and the Illusion of CCP Meritocracy. In 2012, the Bo Xilai affair put the political system's deep flaws on display. Although the CCP has been guilty of political repression and grave mistakes during its long rule, its senior leaders have generally not been known for gangland-style murders. But now Bo's wife has been convicted of plotting the murder of a British business associate; and Bo's former lieutenant, the police chief of Chongqing, has also been found guilty of abusing his power. The public is left wondering: What expectations of impunity moved Bo, well known as Party chief of Chongqing and a rising star in top CCP ranks, to engage in the misdeeds alleged on his long charge sheet? How could this iron-fisted leader, most famous for cracking down on organized crime in Chongqing, have been running the city's police force in a lawless and at times outright criminal fashion?

The current CCP leadership dismisses these incidents as "isolated and exceptional," but many PRC intellectuals argue that rampant official corruption, especially when involving relatives of senior Party leaders, exemplifies an especially decadent form of crony capitalism that of late has become more the rule than the exception.[5] In addition to the Bo scandal, another separate and pending corruption case—one that involves former top officials of the Railways Ministry taking bribes totaling several billion U.S. dollars—has vividly shown the public that national-level elite corruption is occurring at a scale never seen before.[6]

One of the official charges against Bo is that "he made erroneous decisions in the promotion of personnel, resulting in serious consequences." Chinese critics find this charge particularly ironic, asking why those who promoted Bo should not also be held accountable for their own even greater "erroneous decisions." In a dramatic and astonishing way, the Bo imbroglio belies the notion—so central to the authoritarian-resilience thesis—that the CCP elite is in any way a meritocracy. In the eyes of the Chinese public, the current method of selecting PRC leaders—with its nepotism, patron-client ties, "black-box" manipulation by political heavyweights, fake academic credentials, and even the use of bribes to "purchase office" (*maiguan*)—looks to be based on anything *but* merit.[7] The legitimacy of the CCP leadership as a whole is now in doubt. Bo's trial (expected to occur sometime in 2013) may turn into a trial of the CCP's monopoly on power, which made Bo's decade of abusing his authority possible in the first place.

It should be noted that Bo still has a significant number of supporters in China. His strongly nationalist views, his tendency to use violence to resolve socioeconomic conflicts, his pronounced hatred of the rich, and his reputation as a leader who can get things done are traits that resonate deeply with some groups in Chinese society. Furthermore, unless China profoundly changes its method of governance, demagogues even more brazen and despicable than Bo may well arise in the future.

2) A Bottom-Up Revolution in the Making? The CCP legitimacy crisis that the Bo incident has sparked is, of course, not the only factor that could lead to a sociopolitical uprising. After more than two decades of remarkably rapid economic growth, China has recently experienced a slowdown. This downturn is not only born of political bottlenecks, but will further reveal flaws in the PRC's authoritarian system and thus become a trigger for political crises. The growing oligarchic power of state-owned enterprises, especially gigantic flagship companies, is widely viewed as driving massive corruption, crowding out private investment, shrinking the middle class, and stalling the innovation that China must achieve if it is to make the transition from an export-led economy to one oriented toward consumption and innovation.

The sense of political uncertainty—and fear of socioeconomic and other disasters—is on the rise in China. Many worry about environmental degradation, public-health hazards, and all manner of public-safety problems. Anxiety and discontent touch all socioeconomic classes. The large flow of capital leaving China in recent years is a signal that the elites themselves lack confidence in the country's political stability. According to a 2011 report by Global Financial Integrity (GFI), from 2000 to 2009 China's illegal capital outflow was the world's highest at US$2.7 trillion.[8] The latest GFI report, released in October 2012, showed that cumulative illicit financial flows from China totaled a massive $3.8 trillion for the period from 2000 to 2011.[9]

Middle-class anger at government policies has become increasingly evident in recent years. An unemployment rate of about 20 percent among recent college graduates (who usually come from middle-class families and are presumed to be members of China's future middle class) should send an alarming signal to the Chinese government. Given how hard it is to get a small-business loan, the opaque and poorly regulated nature of the Chinese stock market, and the general lack of investment opportunities, middle-class savings have flowed heavily into real estate. The nightmare of a bursting property bubble is a real possibility: Some regions are dotted with massive but tenantless areas of new construction known as "ghost cities." A study conducted by the Beijing Municipal Security Bureau revealed that there are 3.8 million vacant housing units in the capital alone.[10]

Lower down the social scale, the manual-labor shortage that has hit some coastal cities in recent years reflects the growing awareness of individual rights among "vulnerable social groups." Migrant workers especially will move from job to job seeking better pay. Yet China's urbanization policy is noticeably unaccommodating to migrants. Such workers resent seeing middle-class families with multiple homes and corrupt officials or rich entrepreneurs who buy costly villas for their mistresses.

Given the CCP elite's interest in preserving its own grip on power, it is no surprise that the police have become more powerful, with an influence over socioeconomic policy that matches their bigger budgets. The total sum spent on "maintaining social stability" now exceeds the amount spent on national defense.[11] The growing power of the police has also created a vicious circle in which the more fiercely the police suppress unrest, the more violent and widespread it grows. With all the sources of social resentment, possible triggering factors, and disturbing trends, one should not be too quick to disregard the scenario of a bottom-up revolution.

3) Will Intra-Party Democracy Work? Given the ominous portent of the Bo Xilai crisis and its airing of the CCP's dirty laundry, as well as many other sources and triggering factors for bottom-up revolution, what are the prospects that the CCP leadership will act to save itself by undertaking systemic political reform? Does the Party have a chance?

Since the era of Deng Xiaoping (and especially in the last ten years), a few institutional reforms designed to promote intra-CCP democracy have been gradually put into place. Authorities and the state-run media often speak of "intra-Party democracy" as a byword for institutionalized checks and balances within the CCP. In September 2009, the Fourth Plenary Session of the Seventeenth Central Committee called for promoting democracy within the Party and characterized intra-Party democracy as the "lifeblood" of the Party and the principal determinant of whether the CCP would be able to maintain its position of primacy in the future.

It is understandable that CCP leaders and their advisors are inclined to pursue democratic experiments within the Party, or in other words, to carry out political reform in a way that is incremental and manageable. The CCP is the world's largest ruling party, consisting of 4 million grassroots branches and 83 million members. In the absence of any organized opposition, one can hardly expect China to suddenly adopt a multiparty political system. Under these circumstances, a form of intra-Party democracy—one characterized by elite competition, balance of power among factions, and links to distinct interest groups in Chinese society—may well be a more realistic way to promote democracy in the country.

The path to democracy varies from nation to nation, and depends largely on a country's historical and sociopolitical circumstances. Chinese leaders and public intellectuals have every right to argue that the PRC's version of democracy will, and should, have its own distinct (or even unique) features. After all, the democratic regimes that one finds in India, Indonesia, the United Kingdom, and the United States are distinct from one another in significant ways. Moreover, it is even possible for a democracy—Japan is an example, as is Mexico—to undergo lengthy stretches of one-party government without losing the right to be called a democracy. A dynamic interplay of checks and balances among ruling-party factions is often a key to this achievement.

In China today, intra-CCP democracy is more than just rhetoric. A number of important institutional developments have already changed the way that China's political elite does business. Holders of top posts in both the Party and the state now serve terms capped at five years, and no official may serve more than two terms. Leaders above a certain level cannot exceed a set age limit. For example, all CCP Central Committee members who were born before 1940 retired from that body at the 2007 Party Congress. Similarly, all Central Committee members who were born before 1944 retired from that body at the 2012 Party Congress. The CCP has endorsed a method known as the "more candidates than seats election" (cha'e xuanju) in order to choose members of the Central Committee and other higher bodies. These rules and norms not only spawn a sense of consistency and fairness in the selection of leaders, but also speed up turnover within the elite.[12]

Such experiments in intra-Party democracy, however, have made lit-

tle progress since 2009. The scope and scale of intra-Party competition
have not increased much over the past two decades. Despite promises to
the contrary, top posts at various levels are still not filled by means of
multicandidate elections.

Yet it remains important that the CCP leadership is now structured
around two informal coalitions or factions that check and balance each
other. This is not the kind of institutionalized system by which, say, the
U.S. government's executive, legislative, and judicial branches check
and balance one another. But it does represent a major departure from
the strongman traditions of the Mao and Deng eras, and it is reshaping
the inner workings of high-level intra-Party politics in China.

The two groups can be labeled the "populist coalition," led by outgoing president Hu Jintao, and the "elitist coalition," which emerged during
the Jiang Zemin era and is currently led by Jiang's top protégés. At the
Eighteenth Party Congress in November 2012, Xi Jinping from the elitist
faction became the secretary-general of the Party, and Li Keqiang from
the populist faction was designated to become China's premier. This division of power is sometimes referred to as the "one party, two coalitions"
political mechanism.

These two coalitions represent different socioeconomic and geographical constituencies. Most of the top leaders in the elitist coalition,
for instance, are "princelings" from families of veteran revolutionaries
and high-ranking officials. These princelings often began their careers
in rich and economically well-developed coastal cities. The elitist coalition usually represents the interests of China's entrepreneurs.

Most of the populist coalition's leading figures, by contrast, come
from less-privileged families. They also tend to have accumulated much
of their leadership experience in less-developed inland provinces. Many
of these leaders began their respective climbs up the political ladder via
leadership in the Chinese Communist Youth League (CCYL) and are
known as the *tuanpai* (League faction). The populists often voice the
concerns of vulnerable social groups such as farmers, migrant workers,
and the urban poor.

Leaders of these two competing factions differ in expertise, credentials, and experiences. Yet they understand that they must find common
ground in order to coexist and govern effectively, especially in times of
crisis—and now is such a time. A factional leader such as the princeling
Bo Xilai may fall due to scandal, but the factions themselves are too
strong to be dismantled.

The rise of a subdued form of Chinese "bipartisanship" within the
leadership may still not be enough to save the CCP, however. Cutting
deals, sharing power, and arriving at compromises can be hard. Moreover, the presence of more candidates than there are seats to fill naturally creates a sense of winners and losers. Nor are contentious issues
lacking: There are serious disputes brewing over how best to distrib-

ute national resources, the optimal methods for fighting corruption, the establishment of a public healthcare system, the construction of more affordable housing in the cities, and the reform of finance and of rural landownership. Can a consensus on these matters wide and strong enough to support effective governance be formed? The question remains an open one.

China's much-needed political reform may be delayed due to the strong resistance from some conservative leaders and vested interest groups such as state-monopolized large firms. Public demand for a more competitive, more institutionalized, more transparent political system will, however, only become stronger. Factional competition and cooperation in the top leadership may be all the more consequential because they are in accord with what important new stabilizing forces—none of which existed in 1989—desire for China. Along with a larger middle class, the country has a more assertive legal profession that argues for constitutionalism and strong measures to curb corruption and abuses of power. The media, too, are more commercialized and influential, and social media have achieved a level of pervasiveness that no one could have imagined only a few years ago.

Various other interest groups, including foreign business lobbies, have become more numerous. Most important, there is a widespread perception that China, its current economic problems notwithstanding, is on the rise rather than the decline. All these factors should enhance public confidence that a political transformation could go well and point in the direction of a freer and more open China.

The competitive dynamics within the collective CCP leadership, meanwhile, should have the effects of making lobbying more transparent, factional politics more legitimate, rules and laws more respected, elections more genuine, and elites more accountable and representative. Could the CCP itself split formally into elitist and populist camps? It is not difficult to imagine this happening. In the best case, the split will be more incremental than traumatic, violence will be absent or minimal, and the example of elections and competition within the CCP will, via a classic "demonstration effect," promote the cause of general elections for the whole country.

Over the next decade or so, the Middle Kingdom's future will hinge on the dynamic between the fear of revolution and the hope for political reform. The threat of revolution from below may push the elite to pursue incremental yet bold political reform. Should reform fail, however, revolt may well be the upshot. And the unfolding drama, wherever it leads, will undoubtedly have profound ramifications far beyond China's borders.

NOTES

1. "On Revolution" was one of the three articles of Han Han's series, which he wrote on the eve of 2012; the other two were "On Democracy" and "On Freedom." *http://blog.*

sina.com.cn/s/article_archive_1191258123_201112_1.html. For more discussion, see Eric Abrahamsen, "Han Han's U-Turn?" *International Herald Tribune*, 26 January 2012, available at *http://latitude.blogs.nytimes.com/2012/01/26/blogger-han-han-controversy-on-democracy-in-china.*

2. Zou Dongtao, Zhou Tianyong, Chi Fulin, and Li Zhichang, "Dingceng she-ji—Gaige fanglie de yige zhongda fazhan" [Top-level design: Reform's important strategic development], *Beijing ribao* [Beijing daily], 24 January 2011, available at *http://theory.people.com.cn/GB/13796713.html.*

3. Liu Junxiang, "Jingying minzhu—Zhongguo dingceng zhenggai xiwang" [Elite democracy: The hope of China's top-level political reform], *Wenzhai* [Digest], 22 October 2012, available at *www.21ccom.net/articles/zgyj/xzmj/article_2012102269487.html.*

4. David Shambaugh, for example, observed that the CCP is a "reasonably strong and resilient institution." *China's Communist Party: Atrophy and Adaptation* (Washington, D.C.: Woodrow Wilson Center Press, 2008), 176. See also Andrew J. Nathan, "China's Changing of the Guard: Authoritarian Resilience," *Journal of Democracy* 14 (January 2003): 6–17; and Alice Miller, "Institutionalization and the Changing Dynamics of Chinese Leadership Politics," in Cheng Li, ed., *China's Changing Political Landscape: Prospects for Democracy* (Washington, D.C.: Brookings Institution Press, 2008), 61–79.

5. In March 2012, for example, Renmin University political scientist Zhang Ming launched a strong critique of widespread official corruption. It would take the foreign media another few months to begin tracing the "family trees" of crony capitalism among the Chinese leadership. See Zhang Ming, "Zhongguo xiang he chuqu?" [Whither China?], *Ershiyi shiji* [Twenty-first century], 3 March 2012. For the CCP authorities' effort to make the Bo case "isolated and exceptional," see Sina News, 25 May 2012, available at *http://news.sina.com.hk/news/1617/3/1/2673095/1.html.*

6. See Evan Osnos, "Boss Rail: The Disaster That Exposed the Underside of the Boom," *New Yorker*, 22 October 2012, available at *www.newyorker.com/reporting/2012/10/22/121022fa_fact_osnos#ixzz2Abq3Okl1.*

7. See Minxin Pei, "The Myth of Chinese Meritocracy," *Project Syndicate*, 14 May 2012, available at *www.project-syndicate.org/commentary/the-myth-of-chinese-meritocracy.*

8. *Shijie ribao* [World journal], 20 April 2012, A4.

9. Dev Kar and Sarah Freitas, "Illicit Financial Flows from China and the Role of Trade Misinvoicing," Global Financial Integrity, Washington, D.C., October 2012, iv.

10. Jia Lynn Yang, "As China's Growth Lags, Fears of a Popping Sound," *Washington Post*, 3 October 2012, A16.

11. In 2009, the regime spent 532 billion yuan to defend against foreign threats, and 514 billion to keep domestic order. In 2012, the figures were 670 billion yuan for the military and 702 billion for "stability maintenance." See "Kanshou Chen Guangcheng" [Watching Chen Guangcheng], *Shijie ribao* [World journal], 3 May 2012, A4.

12. On these political experiments, see Cheng Li, "Leadership Transition in the CPC: Promising Progress and Potential Problems," *China: An International Journal* 10 (August 2012): 23–33.

6

CURRENT TRENDS
AND FUTURE PROSPECTS

Robert A. Scalapino

Robert A. Scalapino (1919–2011) was a founding member and the first chairman of the National Committee on United States–China Relations. From 1977 until his retirement in 1990, he was Robson Research Professor of Government at the University of California, Berkeley. He served on the boards of directors of many organizations, including the Council on Foreign Relations, the Asia Foundation, the Atlantic Council, and the Pacific Forum of the Center for Strategic and International Studies. Among his many publications was The Last Leninists: The Uncertain Future of Asia's Communist States *(1992). This essay originally appeared in the January 1998 issue of the* Journal of Democracy.

Firm predictions about the future of China are hazardous. Many variables, both domestic and international, can influence events, and few of them can be predicted with any certainty. Nonetheless, those who have undertaken a study of this society have the obligation to assign certain "probabilities" and "improbabilities" to various future scenarios, reassessing the situation at frequent intervals.

At the height of the Cultural Revolution in the 1960s, it was legitimate to ask whether China could avoid an implosion that would rip the nation apart. This period, however, demonstrated anew the fact that Chinese society can live with a high degree of tension and chaos, perhaps in part because its nuclear units remain relatively cohesive.

There is no evidence at present to suggest that the People's Republic of China (PRC) will be dismembered or undergo drastic regime change in the foreseeable future. It is true that the process of decentralization has been an important political trend since the onset of reform 20 years ago under the late Deng Xiaoping. Dynamic regions like Guangdong Province on the southeastern coast have rushed forward economically—in this case, interacting with Hong Kong to form a so-called Natural Economic Territory. A few years ago, central control of macroeconomic policy seemed threatened, and Vice Premier Zhu Rongji was given the difficult assignment of strengthening it. But regions enjoying full autonomy, whether economic or political, are a fiction in today's China.

It is also correct to note that in regions where there have been security problems, such as Xinjiang or Tibet, the military plays a very significant political role. Moreover, key military figures always have representation at the top level of central Chinese Communist Party (CCP) and governmental structures.

The China of the 1990s, however, is not the China of the 1920s and 1930s. While the military may on occasion act as a pressure group, and on certain issues may speak with a commanding voice, the evidence suggests that the Communist Party's leadership and the supremacy of civilian authority are overwhelmingly accepted. Equally important, appointment power at all key levels remains in the hands of central authorities, and frequent rotation can ensure that no power enclaves can be built up within the officer corps.

Drawing Up a Balance Sheet

If neither disintegration nor drastic regime change seems to be in the offing, what is the most likely scenario for the twenty-first century? It can be summed up as follows: China will be a major power with major problems. To draw up a balance sheet of the PRC's accomplishments and difficulties is to underline that statement. Few developing nations can point to the kinds of economic gains that China has made in recent years: productivity increases of more than 10 percent a year; hefty foreign-currency reserves bolstered by surging exports; rising foreign investment bringing advanced technology; and controlled inflation.

Yet daunting economic problems remain. Banking and financial institutions are in serious disarray due to uncollectible loans. State-owned enterprises account for two-fifths of China's industrial ouput, yet fully half of these enterprises are operating at a loss. Unemployed or underemployed rural dwellers have been migrating to the cities in massive numbers, seeking opportunity but facing many strains and hardships in the nearer term. Corruption is widespread, and there is a growing gap in living standards between the fast-developing east and the more static western provinces.

China's leaders recognize these problems, and are trying to come to grips with them. Both the resolve that these leaders have shown and the successes that they have achieved have been variable. Clearly, solutions will not come quickly or easily. Well into the next century, this most massive of all human societies will be searching for the best economic policies. Yet while the negative side of the economic ledger will cause downturns at times and may breed unrest in some sectors, the positive side is likely to be sufficiently strong to propel China into the ranks of major powers. China's economy will influence the entire region, for which it will represent both an opportunity and a source of competition.

On the political front also, a carefully drawn balance sheet is necessary. Here, stability and citizen satisfaction are the chief desiderata. On the positive side, the critical transition from an older to a younger generation of leaders appears to be going reasonably well. China currently enjoys more stability—with less coercion—than it has had in most periods of its past. Today's leaders are better educated, more technologically inclined, and more experienced as administrators than their predecessors. No single individual, however, has the kind of power that Mao and Deng had at their respective zeniths. Of crucial importance, therefore, is the question of whether collective leadership can work, or whether recurrent factional struggles at the center will disrupt the body politic.

It is too early to answer this question definitively. Collective leadership runs against the traditional grain of Chinese political culture. The need up to now has been for someone at the top of the pyramid who can symbolize supreme power. Yet given the diversity and growing specialization that are the inevitable handmaidens of development, adjustments are essential. A compromise may be to make one individual first among equals. This is what has been done with Jiang Zemin: when Deng died in 1996, Jiang became known as "the core" of the party. The fortunes of Jiang—and in all likelihood, those coming after him, too—will hinge on his abilities as an administrator and coordinator, together with the wisdom of the policies that he and his colleagues select.

There is also a strong need at present to institutionalize a federal system for China. The formal and systematic allocation of power among center, region, province, and locality would represent a significant advance over the current method of depending on personalities to sort out the lines of authority. All continental-sized societies need such a system, with the precise allocations frequently reviewed and, when necessary, adjusted.

While the problem of leadership and that of structure are important, neither poses a real threat to the regime, at least at present. As long as its policies—especially its economic policies—are mostly successful, China should be able to 1) make the adjustment from charismatic to technocratic rule, and 2) manage the ever-shifting balance of power among central, regional, and local levels of government.

More serious is the ideological decline that has accompanied China's new materialist age. Despite the ardent efforts of its leaders, appeals to support Marxism-Leninism, adhere to the thought of Mao, or heed the words of Deng have produced limited results. Few, even among CCP cadres, remain true to the classical socialist values.

At the grassroots, the main trend is not hostility but political indifference. There is lively expression of specific grievances, to be sure—for example, among farmers plagued by multiple taxes. In general, however, political activism is at a low ebb and political concerns have low priority.

Thus nationalism—always deeply embedded in China's communist movement—has been surging. In part, this is the result of a conscious policy of cultivation by the elite, which is anxious to find the most effective means of stimulating loyalty and support. China's five thousand years of "glorious history" are now celebrated. Confucius has been revived. Sun Yat-sen is accorded full honors. Even socialism must have "Chinese characteristics."

It remains to be seen whether nationalism can do the work once assigned to Marxism-Leninism-Maoism, especially with relation to the *esprit de corps* and morale of party cadres and military personnel. Yet it has played such a role with reasonable effectiveness in other societies. Again, economic success may be the crucial factor.

People outside China, meanwhile, will naturally be anxious to see whether Chinese nationalism takes its place on the world stage in a relatively benign or an obtrusively militant form. In all likelihood, there will be a lengthy contest between xenophobic, exclusivist elements and leaders who realize that internationalism—of the market rather than the Marxist type—is vital to China's future.

Meanwhile, certain developments have occurred that encourage those whose commitment is to greater political openness. In recent times, freedom of speech has increased appreciably, although the freedoms to write and to assemble remain constrained. Further, village elections enable the citizen to have some choice of local officials, albeit generally only after a prior CCP screening of candidates. In the National People's Congress, moreover, debate on certain issues has been more extensive and more open than in the past. In addition, figures from outside the CCP have been appointed to important posts or had greater attention accorded to their views.

Toward Authoritarian Pluralism

Is China, then, *en route* to democracy? In my view, any answer to this question must be given with great caution. The most basic political trend in China today is the gradual transformation of Leninism into authoritarian pluralism, not democracy. Authoritarian pluralism can be defined as a system wherein political life remains under the unchallenged control of a dominant-party or single-party regime; strict limits are placed on liberty (albeit with some circumstantial variations possible); and military or national security organs keep a close eye on things. At the same time, however, an authoritarian-pluralist system typically has a civil society apart from the state. The various branches of this society enjoy a certain degree of autonomy, and thus are able to express diverse interests. Finally, the economy is mixed, with the market playing an ever more important role.

Authoritarian-pluralism has been widely utilized in developing East Asian societies, partly because it accords with their political culture, but more importantly, because it is a means of maintaining stability in the midst of rapid growth and the huge socioeconomic changes that it brings. South Korea and Taiwan had authoritarian-pluralist regimes until quite recently, when they began their decade-old experiments with democracy. Such regimes are still found today in Indonesia, Singapore, and arguably, Malaysia, with Burma possibly in the early stages of a shift from crude military dictatorship toward a more sophisticated authoritarian pluralism.

The key question for China is whether its emerging authoritarian-pluralist system will later evolve into a democracy. Democracy has three essentials: genuine, regularized political choice for the citizenry; the requisite freedoms to make that choice meaningful; and the rule of law. No government is perfect, but to be called a democracy, a system must meet these criteria to a reasonable degree.

As noted above, one may legitimately speak of a softening of authoritarianism in contemporary China. But democracy as I have defined it is a distant prospect. For example, while some progress toward developing a legal system has been made, Chinese politics, especially at the informal level, is still overwhelmingly governed not by legality but by reciprocity: "You do this for me, and I'll do that for you." Political choice continues to take a back seat to party dictatorship. And freedom is less a matter of liberty under law than of ignoring the rules and getting away with it.

A central obstacle to democracy in China is, and will remain, the country's sheer scale. Can 1.2 billion people (there may be 1.6 billion before the middle of the next century), representing diverse subcultures and spread over a vast territory, be permitted to choose their top leaders, enjoy the full range of freedoms, and accept law as their ultimate guide? It can be argued that India represents a society similar in scale and diversity that has defied numerous obstacles in order to preserve democracy over the fifty years since its independence. Yet the political culture of modern India—or at least of its elite—was deeply influenced by a lengthy period of British tutelage. And Indian democracy, make no mistake, was imposed from the top down. Will China's elite opt for such a course? There are no such signs on the horizon.

In my opinion, what we will most likely see in Chinese politics is the continued slippage of Leninism and the firm implantation of authoritarian-pluralism. A single party—the Communist Party—will retain dominance, with other parties and political forces shaped and controlled by this fact. Both the party and the government will be strongly elitist, but the nature of the elite will continue to be altered, as noted earlier, with specialists and technocrats playing ever more important roles.

While some progress in the direction of greater political openness may well continue, many segments of Chinese society, including the intellectuals, feel deeply worried about the possibility of chaos. Stability has a strong appeal. Moreover, Chinese authorities will continue to defend their regime by insisting that the most meaningful freedoms for their people lie in the economic and social realm—a better livelihood, better education, and more social services. This will not be acceptable to exponents of democracy, but it will have considerable appeal nonetheless.

Hopes for a long-term evolution to genuine democracy may well hinge on two factors: the continued success of domestic economic development, with the major problems outlined earlier being either solved or alleviated; and an international scene marked by a low level of perceived threat, with well-developed mechanisms for dialogue and negotiation in place. The prospect that either of these conditions will come to full fruition over the course of the next decade is exceedingly slight.

Should critical policies fail, or should serious factional power struggles ensue, the upshot almost certainly will be more rather than less authoritarianism, with a strong military presence evident in governance. The road to democracy does not run through failure.

We should take encouragement from the trends that are now under way. Even if the achievement of democracy is a distant prospect, the lowering of ideological barriers to dialogue has already occurred. Furthermore, communication at the nonofficial level of conferences, educational exchanges, and business meetings is more open than ever. In these forums, Chinese citizens and foreigners sometimes frankly exchange views on a wide range of subjects. And cultures, including the Chinese, are proving to be porous, with extraordinary diversity accompanying successive stages of modernization. In sum, the prospects are for a more open and diverse society, capable of interacting with others on a broader front, but with its authoritarian features still clearly in evidence.

7

AUTHORITARIAN RESILIENCE

Andrew J. Nathan

Andrew J. Nathan is Class of 1919 Professor of Political Science at Columbia University and a member of the Editorial Board of the Journal of Democracy. *His most recent book is* China's Search for Security *(coauthored with Andrew Scobell, 2012). This essay originally appeared in the January 2003 issue of the* Journal of Democracy.

After the Tiananmen crisis in June, 1989, many observers thought that the rule of the Chinese Communist Party (CCP) would collapse. Instead, the regime brought inflation under control, restarted economic growth, expanded foreign trade, and increased its absorption of foreign direct investment. It restored normal relations with the G-7 countries that had imposed sanctions, resumed the exchange of summits with the United States, presided over the retrocession of Hong Kong to Chinese sovereignty, and won the right to hold the 2008 Olympics in Beijing. It arrested or exiled political dissidents, crushed the fledgling China Democratic Party, and seems to have largely suppressed the Falun Gong spiritual movement.

Many China specialists and democracy theorists—myself among them—expected the regime to fall to democratization's "third wave."[1] Instead, the regime has reconsolidated itself.[2] Regime theory holds that authoritarian systems are inherently fragile because of weak legitimacy, overreliance on coercion, overcentralization of decision making, and the predominance of personal power over institutional norms. This particular authoritarian system, however, has proven resilient.

The causes of its resilience are complex. But many of them can be summed up in the concept of institutionalization—understood either in the currently fashionable sense of behavior that is constrained by formal and informal rules, or in the older sense summarized by Samuel P. Huntington as consisting of the adaptability, complexity, autonomy, and coherence of state organizations.[3] This article focuses on four aspects of the CCP regime's institutionalization: 1) the increasingly norm-bound nature of its succession politics; 2) the increase in meritocratic as opposed to factional considerations in the promotion of political elites; 3) the differentiation and functional specialization of institutions within the regime; and 4) the establishment of institutions for political participation and appeal that strengthen the CCP's legitimacy among the public at large. While these developments do not guarantee that the regime will be able to solve all the challenges that it faces, they do caution against too-hasty arguments that it cannot adapt and survive.

Norm-Bound Succession Politics

As this article is published, the Chinese regime is in the middle of a historic demonstration of institutional stability: its peaceful, orderly transition from the so-called third generation of leadership, headed by Jiang Zemin, to the fourth, headed by Hu Jintao. Few authoritarian regimes—be they communist, fascist, corporatist, or personalist—have managed to conduct orderly, peaceful, timely, and stable successions. Instead, the moment of transfer has almost always been a moment of crisis—breaking out ahead of or behind the nominal schedule, involving purges or arrests, factionalism, sometimes violence, and opening the door to the chaotic intrusion into the political process of the masses or the military. China's current succession displays attributes of institutionalization unusual in the history of authoritarianism and unprecedented in the history of the PRC. It is the most orderly, peaceful, deliberate, and rule-bound succession in the history of modern China outside of the recent institutionalization of electoral democracy in Taiwan.[4]

Hu Jintao, the new general secretary of the CCP as of the Sixteenth Party Congress in November 2002, has held the position of successor-apparent for ten years. Four of the other eight top-ranking appointments (Wu Bangguo, Wen Jiabao, Zeng Qinghong, and Luo Gan) had been decided a year or two in advance. The remaining four members of the Politburo Standing Committee (PBSC) were simply elevated from the outgoing Politburo. Barring a major crisis, the transition will continue to an orderly conclusion in March 2003, leading to the election of Hu Jintao as state president and chairman of the Central Military Commission, Wu Bangguo as chair of the National People's Congress (NPC), and Wen Jiabao as premier. Outgoing officials President Jiang Zemin, NPC Chair Li Peng, and Premier Zhu Rongji will leave their state offices, having already left their Party offices in the fall, and will cease to have any direct role in politics.

It takes some historical perspective to appreciate this outcome for the achievement that it is. During the Mao years, Party congresses and National People's Congresses seldom met, and when they did it was rarely on schedule. There have never before been effective terms of office or age limits for persons holding the rank of "central leader"; Mao and Deng each exercised supreme authority until the end of his life. Nor has there ever been an orderly assumption of office by a designated successor: Mao purged Liu Shaoqi, the president of the PRC, by having Red Guards seize him and put him in prison, where he died. Mao's officially designated successor, Lin Biao, allegedly tried to seize power from Mao, was discovered, and died in a plane crash while fleeing. Mao appointed Hua Guofeng as his successor simply by stating that Hua was his choice. Hua was removed from office at Deng Xiaoping's behest before Hua's term of office was over. Deng removed from power both of his own chosen successors, Hu Yaobang and Zhao Ziyang. Deng and the other elders overrode the Politburo in 1989 to impose Jiang Zemin as successor to the Party leadership.

Measured against these historical precedents, the current succession displays many firsts, all indicative of institutionalization:

• Jiang Zemin survived his full allotted time in office. He was installed as general secretary in 1989, and was reelected in 1992 and 1997, serving two-and-a-half terms (he assumed the Central Military Commission chairmanship in 1989 and the state presidency in 1992). His patron, Deng, did not remove him from office (although Deng considered doing so in 1992). Although Jiang was called to the top post in Beijing over the heads of Li Peng and Li Ruihuan, and had at times adversarial relations with both of them, neither tried to replace him. In consolidating his authority, Jiang engineered the fall from power of Yang Shangkun in 1992 and Qiao Shi in 1997, but neither of these men tried to unseat him.

• Jiang did not stay in office past the time when, according to the rules, he should have left office. In 1997, the Politburo established by consensus a new, informal rule that senior leaders should not be reappointed to another term after they reach the age of 70. When this rule was established, Jiang was 71, but he had himself declared a one-time exception to it, promising to retire in 2002. This promise, along with the fact that he would be 76 in 2002, were the main reasons why no serious consideration was given to his remaining in office, even though there was much speculation in the international press that he was trying to stay. The age-70 rule will also make it necessary for Jiang to retire from the post of Central Military Commission chairman, a post for which there have never been either term or age limits, and to which the 1997 decision did not explicitly apply. Jiang's third post, the state presidency, is limited by the Constitution to two terms, which he has already served.

• Jiang Zemin was the first leader in the history of the People's Republic of China (PRC) not to select his own successor. Mao chose several successors for himself (Liu Shaoqi, Lin Biao, and Hua Guofeng). So did Deng (Hu Yaobang, Zhao Ziyang, and Jiang Zemin). By contrast, Deng Xiaoping made Hu Jintao the PBSC's youngest member in 1992, and for the entire ten years of Hu's incumbency as informal successor-designate, Jiang Zemin did not challenge Hu's position. The incoming premier, Wen Jiabao, was recommended by Zhu Rongji over Jiang's choices, Wu Bangguo and Li Changchun.

• The retired elders (consisting after 1997 of Wan Li, Qiao Shi, Song

Ping, Liu Huaqing, and several others) did not attempt to intervene in the succession or, indeed, in any decision. The right of three earlier elders (Deng Xiaoping, Chen Yun, and Li Xiannian) to intervene had been established by a secret Politburo resolution in 1987 and was reinforced by Deng's chairmanship of the Central Military Commission. This right was exercised to decisive effect during the 1989 Tiananmen crisis.[5] In 1997, Deng Xiaoping, the last of the three elders, died. A new group of elders was created by the retirements of Qiao Shi and others from the PBSC. The 1987 Politburo resolution was not renewed for them, nor did any of them sit on the CMC. These new elders received intra-Party documents and occasionally expressed their views,[6] but they did not attend Politburo meetings or exercise any decision-making power.

• The military exercised no influence over the succession. Although some senior military officers spoke in favor of Jiang's staying on in the position of CMC chair, they were ignored. They expressed no views on any other issue relating to the transfer of power. The succession of uniformed officers within the CMC echoes that in the civilian hierarchy: Senior officers associated with Jiang Zemin and over the age of 70—Fu Quanyou and Yu Yongbo—have retired, to be replaced by a younger generation of officers. Following a tradition set in place in 1997, no uniformed officer was elected to the PBSC; the military representatives in Party Center were seated in the Politburo.

• The selection of the new Politburo was made by consensus within the old Politburo. The process was, to be sure, dominated by the senior members, and each of them tried and succeeded in placing associates in the successor body. But these factional considerations were played out within limits imposed by the need for a leadership consensus. None of the top leaders—Jiang, Li Peng, or Zhu Rongji—was powerful enough to force a nominee on his colleagues against their wills.

Never before in PRC history has there been a succession whose arrangements were fixed this far in advance, remained so stable to the end, and whose results so unambiguously transferred power from one generation of leaders to another. It is not that factions no longer exist, but that their powers are now in a state of mutual balance and that they have all learned a thing or two from the PRC's history. Political factions today have neither the power nor, perhaps more importantly, the will to upset rules that have been painfully arrived at. The absence of anyone with supreme power to upset these rules helps make them self-reinforcing.

Meritocracy Modifies Factionalism

Factional considerations played a role in the succession process. But they were constrained by a twenty-year process of meritocratic winnowing that limited the list of candidates who could be considered in the final jockeying for position. Certainly, except for the period of the Cultural Revolution (1966–76), there have always been both meritocratic and factional elements in promotions within the Chinese party-state. But until now, even at the most meritocratic times, the major criteria for promotion at the top were the ability to shift with changing political lines and personal loyalty to the top leader—first Mao Zedong, then Deng Xiaoping. While those among the new leading group are ideologically alert and politically savvy, and have mostly allied themselves with one senior leader or another, they rose to the top predominantly because of administrative skill, technical knowledge, educational background, and Party, rather than personal loyalty.

The start of this process was Deng Xiaoping's 1980 instruction to senior Party leaders to undertake a "four-way transformation" *(sihua)* of the cadre corps by finding and promoting cadres around the age of 40 who were "revolutionary, younger, more educated, and more technically specialized" *(geminghua, nianqinghua, zhishihua, zhuanyehua)*. In this way, Hu Jintao was promoted several levels by the CCP first secretary of Gansu Province, where he was then working; Wu Bangguo was promoted to party secretary of Shanghai's science and technology commission; and Wen Jiabao became deputy head of the provincial geology bureau in Gansu. The story was more or less the same for each member of the new Politburo.

In 1983, the CCP's Organization Department created a list of the most promising cadres of the "four transformations" generation, which it turned to whenever it needed to recommend a younger cadre for a post carrying ministerial rank. Hu Jintao was selected from this list to become Party secretary of Guizhou, Wen Jiabao to become deputy head of the powerful Central Party Office, and so on. The same cadre-rejuvenation policy led Deng to order that someone younger than 50 be appointed to the Fourteenth Politburo Standing Committee in 1992. That choice fell upon Hu Jintao, so that his current accession to the position of General Secretary marks the orderly working out of the same process set in motion twenty years earlier.

Five of the nine members of today's new PBSC were members or alternate members of the Central Committee in 1982. This indicates the deliberateness and regularity of the succession process. The need to select PBSC members from the relatively small pool of candidates who survived the twenty-year selection process constrained the way in which factionalism worked between 2000 and 2002. Jiang Zemin could make the case for Zeng Qinghong or Zeng Peiyan, Li Peng for Luo Gan, and Zhu Rongji for Wen Jiabao, only on the basis of each person's excellent performance over the course of two decades in technically and administratively challenging jobs, and not because of symbolic importance (for example, Mao's promotion of Chen Yonggui) or ideological correctness (Mao's promotion of the so-called Gang of Four).

A norm of staff neutrality has become to some degree accepted at high levels within the Party Center, the State Council, and the Central Military Commission, so that the careers of rising stars have been relatively unperturbed by factional turmoil at the top. When Zhao Ziyang was purged in 1989, a few of his associates were immediately purged, but most of them were gradually moved into secondary bureaucratic posts over the course of the next couple of years. Some even continued to advance in their careers. Wen Jiabao, for example, served eight consecutive years as director of the powerful Party Central Office under three different general secretaries (Hu Yaobang, Zhao Ziyang, and Jiang Zemin). In contrast to the old spoils-like practices in which a leader's purge led quickly to the rooting-out of his followers several levels down the political system, the new system limits the damage that factional strife does to the orderly careers of the rising generation of leaders.

The product of this less factionalized, more regularized process is a competent leadership group that has high morale; that is politically balanced in representing different factions in the Party; that lacks one or two dominant figures, and is thus structurally constrained to make decisions collectively; and that is probably as collegial as any political leadership can be, because all the members came to the top through the same process, which they all view as having been broadly fair.[7]

Whether this event sets the template for future successions remains uncertain, but the chances of that happening are increased insofar as the current succession entrenches—as it does—rules that have elite support (for example, the age-70 rule), historical depth (the rules governing the meritocratic promotion system), and structural reinforcement from the informal political structure of balanced factional power.

Institutional Differentiation Within the Regime

At the high point of political reform in 1987, Zhao Ziyang proposed the "separation of Party and government" and the "separation of Party and enterprise." With Zhao's fall from power in 1989, these ideas were abandoned. Yet in the intervening 14 years, much of what he proposed has happened by evolution, as the separation of responsibilities and spheres of authority—which Max Weber saw as definitive characteristics of the modern state—has gradually increased. What belongs to a given agency to handle is usually handled by that agency not only without interference, but with a growing sense that interference would be illegitimate.

One group of specialists, located in the Party Center, manages ideology, mobilization, and propaganda (in the outgoing regime, it included people like Jiang Zemin, Li Ruihuan, Hu Jintao, and Zeng Qinghong). Another group, located in the State Council, makes economic policy (including Premier Zhu Rongji, vice-premiers Wen Jiabao and Wu Bangguo, most State Council members, and most provincial governors and

Party secretaries). Provincial-level governors and Party secretaries have an increasingly wide scope to set local policy in such areas as education, health, welfare, the environment, foreign investment, and economic development. Many large state enterprises have now been removed from state ownership or placed under joint state-private ownership. Enterprise-management decisions are made on predominantly economic rather than political bases. State Council members, provincial-level officials, and enterprise managers are selected increasingly for their policy-relevant expertise. And economic policy makers at all levels suffer less and less frequently from intervention by the ideology-and-mobilization specialists.

The NPC has become progressively more autonomous, initiating legislation and actively reviewing and altering the proposals for legislation presented to it.[8] The police and courts remain highly politicized, but in the case of the courts, at least, a norm of judicial independence has been declared (in the 1994 Judges' Law and elsewhere) and judges are applying it more often in economic and criminal cases that are not sensitive enough to draw interference from Party authorities.

The military is still a "Party army," but it has also become smaller, more technically competent, and more professional. The officers being promoted to the CMC in the current succession are, as a group, distinguished more for their professional accomplishments and less for their political loyalties than was the case with previous CMC cohorts.[9] Calls have come, apparently from the younger members of the officer corps, to make the army a nonpartisan national force without the obligation to defend a particular ruling party. And although the incoming leader, Hu Jintao, has rejected these calls, the fact that they were voiced at all is a sign of a growing professional ethos within military ranks.[10]

All Chinese media are owned (at least formally, and for the most part actually) by Party and state agencies. But the media have become more commercialized and therefore less politicized. A handful of important outlets remain under variously direct control by the Party's propaganda department—for instance, *People's Daily,* the New China News Agency, China Central Television, provincial-level Party newspapers, the army newspaper, and so on. But to some extent, these media—and even more so, other newspapers, magazines, and radio or television stations around the country—fight for market share by covering movie and pop stars, sports, and scandals. In the political domain, they often push the envelope of what the regime considers off-limits by investigating stories about local corruption and abuses of power.

To be sure, the Chinese regime is still a party-state, in which the Party penetrates all other institutions and makes policy for all realms of action. And it is still a centralized, unitary system in which power at lower levels derives from grants by the center. But neither the top leader nor the central Party organs interfere as much in the work of other agencies as was the case under

Mao and (less so) Deng. Ideological considerations have only marginal, if any, influence on most policy decisions. And staff members are promoted increasingly on the basis of their professional expertise in a relevant area.

All of this is partly to say, as has often been said before, that the regime is pragmatic. But behind the attitude of pragmatism lie increased institutional complexity, autonomy, and coherence—attributes that according to Huntington's theory should equip the regime to adapt more successfully to the challenges it faces.

Input Institutions and Political Legitimacy

One of the puzzles of the post-Tiananmen period has been the regime's apparent ability to rehabilitate its legitimacy (defined as the public's belief that the regime is lawful and should be obeyed) from the low point of 1989, when vast, nationwide prodemocracy demonstrations revealed the disaffection of a large segment of the urban population.

General theories of authoritarian regimes, along with empirical impressions of the current situation in China, might lead one to expect that the regime would now be decidedly low on legitimacy: Although authoritarian regimes often enjoy high legitimacy when they come to power, that legitimacy usually deteriorates for want of democratic procedures to cultivate ongoing consent. In the case of contemporary China, the regime's ideology is bankrupt. The transition from a socialist to a quasi-market economy has created a great deal of social unrest. And the regime relies heavily on coercion to repress political and religious dissent.

Direct evidence about attitudes, however, shows the contrary. In a 1993 nationwide random-sample survey conducted by Tianjian Shi, 94.1 percent of respondents agreed or strongly agreed with the statement that, "We should trust and obey the government, for in the last analysis it serves our interests." A 2002 survey by Shi found high percentages of respondents who answered similarly regarding both the central and local governments.[11] There is much other evidence from both quantitative and qualitative studies to suggest that expressions of dissatisfaction, including widely reported worker and peasant demonstrations, are usually directed at lower-level authorities, while the regime as a whole continues to enjoy high levels of acceptance.

A number of explanations can be offered for this pattern. Among them:

• Most people's living standards have risen during two decades of economic growth.

• The Party has coopted elites by offering Party membership to able persons from all walks of life and by granting the informal protection of property rights to private entrepreneurs. This new direction in Party policy has been given ideological grounding in Jiang Zemin's theory of the "Three Represents," which says that the Party should represent advanced productive forces, advanced culture, and the basic interests of all the Chinese working people—that is, that it should stand for the middle classes as much as or more than the workers and peasants.

• The Chinese display relatively high interpersonal trust, an attitude that precedes and fosters regime legitimacy.[12]

• The Chinese population favors stability and fears political disorder. By pointing to the example of postcommunist chaos in Russia, the CCP has persuaded most Chinese, including intellectuals—from whom criticism might be particularly expected—that political reform is dangerous to their welfare.

• Thanks to the success of political repression, there is no organized alternative to the regime.

• Coercive repression—in 1989 and after—may itself have generated legitimacy by persuading the public that the regime's grip on power is unshakeable. Effective repression may generate only resigned obedience at first, but to maintain cognitive consonance, citizens who have no choice but to obey a regime may come to evaluate its performance and responsiveness (themselves components of legitimacy) relatively highly.[13] In seeking psychological coherence, citizens may convince themselves that their acceptance of the regime is voluntary—precisely because of, not despite, the fact that they have no alternative.

All these explanations may have value. Here, though, I would like to develop another explanation, more directly related to this essay's theme of institutionalization: The regime has developed a series of input institutions (that is, institutions that people can use to apprise the state of their concerns) that allow Chinese to believe that they have some influence on policy decisions and personnel choices at the local level.

The most thorough account of these institutions is Tianjian Shi's *Political Participation in Beijing,* which, although researched before 1989, describes institutions that are still in place. According to Shi, Chinese participate at the local and work-unit levels in a variety of ways. These include voting, assisting candidates in local-level elections, and lobbying unit leaders. Participation is frequent, and activism is correlated with a sense of political efficacy (defined as an individual's belief that he or she is capable of having some effect on the political system). Shi's argument is supported by the work of Melanie Manion, who has shown that in localities with competitive village elections, leaders' policy positions are closer to those of their constituents than in villages with noncompetitive voting.[14]

In addition to the institutions discussed by Shi and Manion, there are at least four other sets of input institutions that may help to create regime legitimacy at the mass level:

• The Administrative Litigation Act of 1989 allows citizens to sue government agencies for alleged violations of government policy. According to Minxin Pei, the number of suits stood in 1999 at 98,600. The success rate (determined by court victories plus favorable settlements) has ranged from 27 percent to around 40 percent. In at least one province, government financial support is now offered through a legal aid program to enable poor citizens to take advantage of the program.[15]

• Party and government agencies maintain offices for citizen complaints—letters-and-visits departments *(xinfangju)*—which can be delivered in person or by letter. Little research has been done on this process, but the offices are common and their ability to deal with individual citizen complaints may be considerable.

• As people's congresses at all levels have grown more independent—along with people's political consultative conferences, United Front structures that meet at each level just prior to the meeting of the people's congress—they have become an increasingly important channel by which citizen complaints may be aired through representatives.

• As the mass media have become more independent and market-driven, so too have they increasingly positioned themselves as tribunes of the people, exposing complaints against wrong-doing by local-level officials.

These channels of demand- and complaint-making have two common features. One is that they encourage individual rather than group-based inputs, the latter of which are viewed as threatening by the regime. The other is that they focus complaints against specific local-level agencies or officials, diffusing possible aggression against the Chinese party-state generally. Accordingly, they enable citizens to pursue grievances without creating the potential to threaten the regime as a whole.

An Authoritarian Transition?

Despite the institutionalization of orderly succession processes, meritocratic promotions, bureaucratic differentiation, and channels of mass participation and appeal, the regime still faces massive challenges to its survival. This essay does not attempt to predict whether the regime will surmount them. What we can say on available evidence is that the regime is not supine, weak, or bereft of policy options. In contrast with the Soviet and Eastern European ruling groups in the late 1980s and early 1990s, the new Chinese leaders do not feel that they are at the end of history. The policy-statement excerpts contained in their investigation reports show that these leaders think they can solve China's problems.[16] They intend to fight corruption; reform the state-owned enterprises; ameliorate the lot of the peasants; improve the environment; comply with World Trade Organization rules while using transitional privileges to ease China's entry into full compliance; suppress political opposition; meet the challenge of U.S. containment; and, above all, stay in power and direct China's modernization. The argument that democratization, freedom, and human rights would lead to a truer kind of stability—as convincing as it may be to the democrats of the world—holds no appeal for these men.

The theoretical implications of China's authoritarian resilience are complex. For the last half-century, scholars have debated whether totalitarian regimes can adapt to modernity. The implications of the Chinese case for this discussion are two: First, in order to adapt and survive, the regime has had to do many of the things predicted by Talcott Parsons and those who elaborated his theory: The regime has had to 1) abandon utopian ideology and charismatic styles of leadership; 2) empower a technocratic elite; 3) introduce bureaucratic regularization, complexity, and specialization; and 4) reduce control over private speech and action. Second, contrary to the Parsonian prediction, these adaptations have not led to regime change. In Richard Lowenthal's terms, the regime has moved "from utopia to development."[17] But the Party has been able to do all these things without triggering a transition to democracy.

Although such a transition might still lie somewhere in the future, the experience of the past two decades suggests that it is not inevitable. Under conditions that elsewhere have led to democratic transition, China has made a transition instead from totalitarianism to a classic authoritarian regime, and one that appears increasingly stable.

Of course, neither society-centered nor actor-centered theories of democratic transition predict any particular outcome to be inevitable in any particular time frame. The Chinese case may, accordingly, merely reinforce the lesson that the outcome depends on politicians and their will to power. Alternatively, it may end up reminding us that democratic transition can take a long time. But it may also suggest a more disturbing possibility: that authoritarianism is a viable regime form even under conditions of advanced modernization and integration with the global economy.

NOTES

1. As an example, see the multi-author symposium on Chinese democracy in *Journal of Democracy* 9 (January 1998).

2. In other words, to adapt a concept from democratic consolidation theory, the CCP has once again made itself the only game in town and is in the process of carrying out a successful transfer of power.

3. Samuel P. Huntington, *Political Order in Changing Societies* (New Haven: Yale University Press, 1968), 12–24.

4. The factual base for this discussion is contained in Andrew J. Nathan and Bruce Gilley, *China's New Rulers: The Secret Files* (New York: New York Review Books, 2002), and is summarized in two articles in the *New York Review of Books,* 26 September and 10 October 2002. These publications are in turn based on Zong Hairen, *Disidai* (The Fourth Generation) (Carle Place, N.Y.: Mirror Books, 2002). Zong Hairen's account of the new

generation of Chinese leaders is based on material contained in internal investigation reports on candidates for the new Politburo compiled by the Chinese Communist Party's Organization Department.

5. *The Tiananmen Papers: The Chinese Leadership's Decision to Use Force Against Their Own People—In Their Own Words,* Zhang Liang, comp., Andrew J. Nathan and Perry Link, eds. (New York: PublicAffairs Books, 2001), 102, n. 1, and passim.

6. Zong Hairen, *Zhu Rongji zai 1999* (Zhu Rongji in 1999) (Carle Place, N.Y.: Mingjing Chubanshe, 2001); English translation edited by Andrew J. Nathan in *Chinese Law and Government* (January–February and March–April 2002).

7. Like any meritocratic process, of course, this one had elements of contingency. Hu Jintao's career is a good example, in particular his 1992 selection from among four candidates as the representative of the Fourth Generation to join the PBSC.

8. Michael Dowdle, "The Constitutional Development and Operations of the National People's Congress," *Columbia Journal of Asian Law* 12 (Spring 1997): 1–125.

9. *Disidai,* ch. 11.

10. *Disidai,* ch. 1.

11. The 1993 survey was conducted for the project on "Political Culture and Political Participation in Mainland China, Taiwan, and Hong Kong." The 2002 survey was conducted for the project on "East Asia Barometer: Comparative Survey of Democratization and Value Changes." Data courtesy of Tianjian Shi.

12. Ronald Inglehart, *Modernization and Postmodernization: Cultural, Economic, and Political Change in 43 Societies* (Princeton: Princeton University Press, 1997), 173, n. 2. Also Tianjian Shi, "Cultural Impacts on Political Trust: A Comparision of Mainland China and Taiwan," *Comparative Politics* 33 (July 2001): 401–19.

13. On components of legitimacy, see M. Stephen Weatherford, "Measuring Political Legitimacy," *American Political Science Review* 86 (March 1992): 149–66. The relationship I am proposing between successful coercion and legitimacy is hypothetical; so far as I know it has not been empirically established.

14. Tianjian Shi, *Political Participation in Beijing* (Cambridge: Harvard University Press, 1997); Melanie Manion, "The Electoral Connection in the Chinese Countryside," *American Political Science Review* 90 (December 1996): 736–48.

15. Minxin Pei, "Citizens v. Mandarins: Administrative Litigation in China," *China Quarterly* (December 1997): 832–62, and personal communication. On legal aid, see *Disidai,* ch. 7; the province is Guangdong.

16. See Andrew J. Nathan and Bruce Gilley, *New Rulers,* chs. 7, 8.

17. Talcott Parsons, *The Social System* (New York: Free Press, 1951), 525–35; Richard Lowenthal, "Development vs. Utopia in Communist Policy," in Chalmers Johnson, ed., *Change in Communist Systems* (Stanford: Stanford University Press, 1970), 33–116.

8

THE END OF COMMUNISM

Arthur Waldron

Arthur Waldron *is Joseph H. Lauder Professor of International Relations at the University of Pennsylvania and vice-president of the International Assessment and Strategy Center, a nonprofit research organization in Arlington, Virginia. He is editor, most recently, of* China in Africa *(2008). This essay originally appeared in the January 1998 issue of the* Journal of Democracy.

I would dearly like to affirm that China will be a fully democratic state in ten years' time, but in all honesty I see that possibility as very small. What I do believe is that the next ten years will see extensive change and perhaps turbulence in China without leading, by the period's end, to any conclusive resolution of fundamental issues of governance. I expect a mixed governmental system, still in flux, in which the powers of regions and localities will be greater than they are today, and the center weaker. I expect communism to have disappeared even as rhetoric, with nationalism taking its place. Extremes of wealth and poverty will be greater than today; so will the differences in degrees of liberty between regions. I hope, and expect, that on balance this system will be considerably more open than what exists now, but do not discount the real possibility of a corporatist China, run on antidemocratic lines by an alliance of political authoritarians, big business, and elements of the military.

Will there still be a People's Republic of China governed by the Chinese Communist Party in ten years? My bet is "no." To start with the name, "People's Republic" is less widely used today than it was even a decade ago. Chinese stamps, for example, regularly bear only the name "China"; that usage is followed as well in ordinary speech, political demonstrations, and international organizations. The reason? These days "China" has a far stronger ring of legitimacy and historical continuity about it than does the rusty "People's Republic," with its East European, Soviet, and other archaic associations. One saw in Beijing, shortly after the fall of communism in the West, embassy nameplates with the words "Democratic People's" blacked out, leaving only "Republic of" whatever. Mao Zedong himself reflected from time to time that calling the new regime "People's Republic" had been a mistake; it would have been better to stick with the "Republic" that China had been since 1912.

Much the same can be said of the Chinese Communist Party. Substantial efforts are currently being made to recruit the best and the brightest of China's youth into the Party, and to coopt influential figures, from Hong Kong, for example. Special scholarships in "Marxism" have been created at the Chinese Academy of Social Sciences in an effort to attract bright scholars into a field they currently shun. But such actions serve only to underline the fact that communism's fundamentals—the theory of class struggle, the alliance with the former socialist states, and an antidemocratic policy—now lack the power to persuade or to inspire. World communism depended upon genuine conviction and dedication, on the genuine belief that communist doctrine explained and predicted things, which led to the willingness to die for it. Many early communists sincerely believed that they were truly creating a better world, in which oppression and poverty would be abolished, and true freedom and dignity would be established for all. They were mistaken, but they were not hypocrites like those in China's leadership today, who call for honesty and simplicity while salting away hundreds of millions of corruptly obtained dollars in foreign bank accounts. Without such animating beliefs, the Party becomes no more than a cover for opportunists; the name may persist, as the Chinese say, but the reality will be gone, *mingcun shiwang*.

At this point, the conventional wisdom responds roughly as follows: "Yes, you are right about Chinese communism, but you fail to see that a new political system is growing inside the shell of the old. You must recognize that the Party has transformed itself into a modernizing elite, with its hands on the existing institutions and levers of power, and is still recruiting the best and the brightest. Furthermore, nationalism has already displaced communism as an ideology. When ordinary Chinese see the red flag, they think 'China,' not 'communist.' The present system is changing, and gaining strength and legitimacy from the reform process."

This view has a lot of adherents across the political spectrum, so let me say why I disagree.

First, those who affirm that the Party is modernizing and changing tend to make two contradictory arguments simultaneously. The first is that real reform is under way: The Party has dozens of study groups at work on topics ranging from privatization to the legal system to local and county elections. As those reports are acted upon, they maintain, the Party itself will become the leading agent of change. The second argument, which cuts against the first, is that the current elite is very strong and absolutely unwilling to concede real authority to anyone else: It has control of the military and police, of a vast hoard of foreign exchange, and of the media, and it will crush dissent ruthlessly. In other words, we are told that the Party is simultaneously undermining and defending its own position—which may in fact be true, but if so cannot lead to stability. Furthermore, people who make this argument tend not to know their Party. They imagine it is full of educated, idealistic people, when in fact it is more like a mafia or underworld organization, bound by narrow personal interests and loyalties maintained by money and force. As such, it is less and less appealing to ordinary Chinese.

Instead of creating improbable scenarios in which Leninist socialists build democratic, free-market economies, perhaps we should come at the question the way a serious Marxist would. China's current system is simply inadequate to the challenges it is creating for itself. China's prosperity already depends on the workings of a free market, but without the rule of law such an economy cannot function beyond a very low level. The communist regime is already too weak to impose its will by force alone, but it has no other tool to sway the people. Without some sense of participation and justice, people will not accept political outcomes such as unemployment that harm their interests. Efficiency in government and resource allocation will be the key to China's effectiveness in the world market, but without good information, no authority can make appropriate decisions. As the late Jean Pasqualini, a former political prisoner in China, memorably put it when asked what was needed to fix China, the only answer is "changement de régime." China requires a new government, for reasons that are not only moral but practical.

Today pressure is building for *real change*, and real change is, by definition, *rarely incremental*. There is no such thing as a gradual and imperceptible transition from lawlessness to legality or from authoritarianism to democracy. There is no asymptotic approach to freedom, with democracy being the limit reached at infinity. History is usually fits and starts, big bangs, upheavals, the new displacing the old.

Patterns of Change

Therefore, China *must* change. The only question is whether change will come from above or below. I believe that the pattern will be sequential, with an attempt at change from above starting the process, but then stalling and being superseded by action at the local and regional level that goes farther than was intended. Power will pass from the Party to the intellectual, military, and business elites, with the urban populations as a swing factor. I expect foreign reactions to this process to tilt it, marginally, in a democratic direction.

The pattern that emerged in the USSR is instructive. Marxism got history exactly backward: Marx believed that with each step up on the historical ladder, from slavery to feudalism to capitalism and so on, the

number of "contradictions" was reduced, until with industrialism a ho-
mogenous "working class" was created that had a single and uniform
set of interests. The "dictatorship of the proletariat" was thus imagined
to be rather simple to implement, just by doing what the vast and overwhelming majority of the population wanted. In reality, however, historical development moved in the opposite direction. Primitive or agrarian
societies were fairly easy to rule, but with industrialization interests became more complex, and ever more intricate mechanisms were required
to reconcile diverse interests fairly. Hence the development of law, and
of democracy.

In the USSR, Gorbachev faced a situation in which an infinity of
opposing interests had been created under "socialism." These mostly
had little to do with politics, instead involving things like relationships
between factories and differing interests regarding resource uses, prices,
and the like. Once those differences were recognized, and not simply
squashed by fiat, the entire system became riven with conflict. To resolve the disputes required objective mechanisms with fixed procedures.
But once such mechanisms were in place, *the Party could have no role*—
for it was forbidden, by definition, to meddle in the workings of those
objective mechanisms. This Gorbachev could not accept. He wanted the
Party still to rule, not simply to reign, so he refused to establish the
objective mechanisms. When chaos developed, he was soon reduced to
calling on people to support the Party for reasons of "stability"—but he
found few followers.

China will face precisely the same problem in the coming years. The
numerous disagreements and conflicts of interest that pervade the society are already coming to the fore—and being resolved by gangsterism,
corruption, and arbitrary force in a totally unsatisfactory way. Some are
ameliorated temporarily by vast infusions of foreign money, or by log-
rolling among elites, but as in the USSR, these conflicts can be solved
fundamentally only by fair due process, which by definition denies the
Party any role.

To this argument, conventional wisdom has been able to respond (until recently) with the two magic words "economic development." And
indeed, almost anything has seemed possible during China's most recent period of rapid growth. People—the Chinese above all—seemed to
forget that it is precisely rapid growth and rising living standards, the
proverbial "revolution of rising expectations," that dissolves dictatorships. They also seem to have imagined that double-digit growth rates
could continue indefinitely. They forgot that markets go down as well as
up, and that the social displacements caused by economic change have
historically led to major political change as well. As old livelihoods and
neighborhoods are destroyed; as new careers empower some while unemployment marginalizes others; as old political status hierarchies are
destroyed and new ones, based on wealth, take their place; as corruption

and environmental degradation alarm and alienate large portions of the population, society inevitably becomes turbulent.

This turbulence was contained as long as elders like Deng Xiaoping survived and economic growth continued—although, it should be recalled, the successful containment of turbulence involved having soldiers murder defenseless civilians, while the subsequent economic recovery was boosted by massive infusions of foreign funds. The past several years, however, have seen the old guard pass on. A dramatic increase has occurred in low-level conflicts between the people and the authorities: industrial strikes and farmers' protests have become common.

The center's reaction has been not to crush these disorders—as a true dictatorship would—but rather to assuage them with money. Such a process can continue only as long as the money holds out.

It will not hold out indefinitely. Although sections of China's economy are very strong, the central government has control of a diminishing portion of resources and runs a chronic deficit. State industries are kept afloat only by vast loans that have cumulatively rendered the banking system insolvent. Foreign investment and growth in exports have kept funds flowing in, but these are now likely to slow. With the devaluation of other Asian currencies, the renminbi is less competitive than it was. But a Chinese devaluation will wreak havoc in the region, and reduce foreign-currency inflows. Economic margins are tightening, which means that waste and misallocation of resources are exacting serious political costs.

As the Center Weakens

One can therefore expect some initiatives from the center to reform the economy and to ameliorate the living conditions of ordinary people. A reexamination of the Tiananmen massacre and the release of some dissidents may also follow. Fiscal health will require the imposition of major taxes on enterprises, wealth, and income. These actions will be limited, because the hard-liners in the Party will not permit root-and-branch reform. Reexamination of Tiananmen will be popular; imposition of taxes will be poison. But the attempt at such measures will clearly signal that even the Party center recognizes that change is essential.

Three groups will increase in prominence as a result of these initiatives. The first will be the brain trust of the current regime: the professoriate, the members of the Academy of Sciences, and the like. Chinese have traditionally trusted the educated, but distrusted professional politicians. The second group will be the local security officials throughout the country. As the center starts the process of reform, its pattern will vary from place to place according to the ability of the local civilian elites to persuade the security people. The third will be the wealthy, especially those with foreign connections.

As the center weakens, administration in the regions will increasingly fall to authorities composed of alliances of these groups. Large popular assemblies will also play a role at the center, in the provinces, and in the localities. Politics will became far more freewheeling and independent than it is today, although no single mechanism (such as voting) will be used to decide issues.

I expect lines of cleavage to be cultural and linguistic: the Mandarin-speaking north; the area around Shanghai; the Hong Kong-Canton region; Taiwan and Fujian; and the deep-inland region of Sichuan and the southwest. China is so large and diverse today that Chinese nationalism is not a strong force for cohesion, but regional and linguistic identities are strong. The Shanghainese have a strong sense of themselves; so too do the Cantonese, and others. This linguistic, cultural, and regional affinity can provide cohesion in the face of challenges or economic downturns. They will not mean that China permanently divides, but rather that it begins to operate on the principle of subsidiarity, as understood in Europe.

Some areas will become relatively free and rather enlightened. I can imagine the area near Hong Kong, or greater Shanghai, or Fujian in informal collaboration with (a still entirely autonomous) Taiwan producing a highly efficient regional regime, along Singaporean or Hong Kong lines, with substantial attention to individual rights and electoral processes, and with relatively clean government. By the same token, some areas may become gangster kingdoms, with local dictators or *capos*. Other areas will become chaotic and dangerous. Beijing will diminish in importance as it loses its preeminent administrative role (it has never been a major economic center); it will become a city of embassies, garrisons, bureaucrats, and international organizations, probably far more tightly regimented than areas further south.

At the same time, workers and urban populations will begin to engage in political action in ways that the three elite groups cannot entirely control. We may expect strikes and demonstrations, particularly in major regional cities with substantial numbers of factories and institutions of higher education, and connections to the rest of the country and the world. In some places, repression will be attempted; elsewhere, clever negotiation and economic benefits will prevent violence.

This loosely amalgamated China will be functional in many respects, but it will not be neat. For its political classes the most pressing issue will be "unification," and to this end consultations will be carried on endlessly, with meetings, conventions, statements, and the like as the central government attempts to reassert more control over the regions, while the regions try to entrench their autonomy and regularize their connections to the center. Hong Kong will become the effective capital of the south and Shanghai the capital of the center; Beijing will remain the capital of the north. The result, if all goes well, will be the "federalism" that Chinese reformers have long advocated. If things go badly, there will be civil war.

This unwieldy and politically volatile China will be very different from the country that we have known since 1949. But it has good historical precedent. The end of the Qing Dynasty in 1912 followed a pattern whereby local elites took over local power—handling it rather well, until power struggles at the top and invasion by Japan brought chaos and disaster. Local elites are far better prepared today than they were in 1912.

New regimes usually build on their predecessors: France's republican system, for example, still displays many characteristics of the monarchy. But communism, because it imposes itself and refuses to absorb or make use of genuinely indigenous traits, usually leaves behind very little that is usable—witness the ruins of the former East German and Soviet regimes. The same will be true for China. Communist economics misallocated resources; communist social policy destroyed genuine society; communist governance smothered the development of real political parties. The end of communism, therefore, will mean (as it has in Europe and in Russia) building a bridge back to the precommunist past, taking up where it left off, and moving forward.

Out of this flux I can envision two outcomes: one democratic or semidemocratic, and the other corporatist or authoritarian. The first would obviously be preferable for many reasons: it would permit further economic development and individual freedom. But the second will appeal strongly to those who fear chaos *(luan)*. The two approaches will struggle, with the center attempting to implement the second while regions increasingly practice the first. Nationalism will be a wild card, as authorities attempt to turn popular support away from democracy by evoking xenophobia regarding imperialism and international markets.

Here, I suspect, international reaction will be critical. The world community will not tolerate an authoritarian solution, I believe. Criticism will be endless and will lead to economic sanctions. Hong Kong will strongly oppose authoritarianism, and the whole of southeastern China could follow. Meanwhile, international economists will attempt to persuade the new authoritarians of the center to play Pinochet and not Peron, so as to put viable economic structures in place. That in turn will smooth the way toward institutional change.

Such a process of change unfolded the last time an entrenched dictatorship fell in China—when the Qing emperor abdicated in 1912. The outcome then was civil war and a new tyranny. Today I can only hope that a combination of internal and external factors will channel the coming transition in China toward the construction of a more fair and open system, one that can survive amid the complexity of the contemporary world.

9

THE RISE OF THE TECHNOCRATS

Gongqin Xiao

Gongqin Xiao is professor of history at the Shanghai Normal University. He is the author of Good-bye to Political Romanticism *(2001),* Collected Works of Gongqin Xiao *(1995), and* The Dilemma of Confucian Culture *(1986). He has published several influential articles on Chinese politics in* Strategy and Management, *China's leading policy journal. This essay originally appeared in the January 2003 issue of the* Journal of Democracy.

Since reform began in the early 1980s, China has had opposing political camps of reformists and leftists. The reformists were democratically inclined students, intellectuals, and Chinese Communist Party (CCP) members who wanted to promote political participation, human rights, and freedom, including economic freedom. The reformists' ideas resonated favorably with the Chinese public, seemed in line with the larger global trend toward democracy known as the "third wave," and by the late 1980s were stirring intense activism among college students.

The mainstays of the leftist[1] camp were CCP bureaucrats who insisted on adherence to traditional communist ideology. Leftists took as their ideal the bureaucratic system of Maoist China in the 1950s, and demanded preservation of the CCP's power, privileges, and strong grip on social life.

For two decades or so, these camps engaged in a struggle in which the future of the world's largest country was seemingly at stake. Among the leftists' most powerful weapons was their authority to interpret the official ideology. They also tended to have substantial political experience, effective networks, and skill at elite-level bureaucratic politics. Some of them were patronized by Deng Xiaoping, to whom they portrayed themselves as defenders of the CCP's interests. Reformists competed with leftists for Deng's favor, arguing that the latter in fact opposed many of Deng's own policies. The story of the fight between these two factions has in many ways been the story of Chinese politics since 1978.

Where has it led? The possible outcomes are as follows:

1) Reformists sweep the board and eventually bring about the total collapse of the old totalitarian system. The chain of events that Mikhail Gorbachev's reforms started in the former Soviet Union is an example.

2) Leftists win decisively and stop or even reverse the reform process.

3) The two opposing camps battle to a draw and become opposing parties in a budding pluralistic society.

4) Both camps get pushed aside by a third force of market-friendly, authoritarian technocrats who determine the future of China.

The fourth possibility is the one that actually seems to be happening. The reformists can date their marginalization to the Tiananmen Square massacre of 4 June 1989 and the crackdown that followed it. The leftists' influence began to wane three years later, when Deng used an inspection tour of Southern China as an occasion to denounce them for opposing his reforms. Since the end of the 1990s, State President Jiang Zemin and the technocratic authoritarianism that he represents have dominated the political scene and carried China into a "postpolarization" era in which reformists and leftists alike find themselves relegated to the sidelines.

Marginalizing Ideology

The events of spring 1989 represented the culmination of the reformist-leftist conflict that had been brewing since the early 1980s. After the shootings in Tiananmen Square on June 4, the leftists knocked the reformists out of the political game. In time, however, the leftists would find themselves outmaneuvered by the rising technocrats under Jiang (then the CCP chief in Shanghai), who replaced Zhao Ziyang as CCP general secretary on 24 June 1989. In the tense atmosphere of China after Tiananmen, the new technocrats' air of moderation and competence made them seem like an important force for stability and greatly strengthened their hand.

The crackdown years of the early 1990s were a time of burgeoning leftist influence. The leftists aimed to restore the supremacy of traditional communist ideology and negate Deng's policy of "reform and opening." Deng neatly parried them in his "South China speech" of 1992. Deng implicitly recognized that in the wake of Tiananmen most liberal intellectuals had embraced a politically cautious and quiescent "moderation," meaning that a leftist counterweight against them was no longer needed. In his South China speech, therefore, he invoked his personal authority to call for an emphasis on "opposing the leftist ideology" and to demand an end to debate about whether his "reform and opening" policy was "capitalistic" or "socialistic," thereby silencing the leftists who then controlled the regime's media and propaganda organs.

By the mid-1990s, the gerontocrats of the revolutionary generation had largely passed from the scene, robbing the left of its key political patrons.

Meanwhile, Deng's market-based reforms and the massive changes that they brought had captured the imaginations of a whole generation of young people and deprived the leftists of successors to whom they could pass on their ideology. Having lost their protectors among the old and their replacements among the young, the leftists faced their twilight just as the new century dawned.

The New Middle Force

The decade of growth that followed Deng's South China speech led to the emergence of a new middle social stratum composed mainly of government technocrats, private entrepreneurs, university professors, lawyers, white-collar employees of companies backed by foreign capital, journalists in the state-owned media, and so on. The stake that these people held in the booming economy hardly made them adventurous political reformists. On the contrary, they worried that too much political change too fast would cause social upheavals and endanger their material interests. Wanting neither a return to socialism nor a leap into the uncertain future of radical political change, they gravitated to the pragmatic authoritarianism of the new technocrats, perhaps comforting themselves with the belief that economic development would eventually lead to democracy and the rule of law. Whatever their motives, they formed the main power base for Jiang and his new technocrats. For intellectuals, too, the South China speech was a watershed. Marginalized politically after Tiananmen, they learned from Deng that their knowledge and mental skills were special types of nonmaterial capital that could be employed for material gains.

The drastic changes that the 1990s witnessed in Eastern Europe and the former Soviet Union and the tremendous costs and side effects of economic "shock therapy" there also prompted Chinese intellectuals to shift toward moderation. Meanwhile, the declining salience of ideology and the sharpening competition for jobs turned college students away from politics. The spread of markets and with them commercial values promoted a new materialism that displaced many deeply rooted convictions both left and right.

By now, the middle social stratum that emerged from the market economy has grown into a middle class whose willingness to support political authoritarianism is contingent on its understanding of the historical phase through which it believes that China is now passing. As economic growth continues and middle-class values continue to spread, this expanding new bourgeoisie will come to see itself as the country's dominant political force, and to identify the adoption of democratic processes and institutions as keys to its own empowerment. In the end, this class will form the social engine driving China's democratization as middle-class citizens impose ever more stringent tests of legitimacy on their government.

As I have already suggested, this likely trajectory sets China apart from the former Soviet world. China's recent history of reform and opening, mounting conflict between leftists and reformists, and the subsequent elbowing-aside of both by technocratic authoritarians is markedly different from the Soviet Union's journey from polarization to revolution to collapse.

The depolarization process that began in China in the early 1990s enabled the country to avoid the "explosion of political participation" frequently witnessed in totalitarian countries that are heading toward transition. Such explosions of participation should be regarded as "exceptional" side effects of the highly charged ideological character of totalitarian systems. If for no other reason than the desire to survive, people living under totalitarian systems tend to be deeply concerned about and sensitive to political affairs, and are used to seeing heavy emphasis placed on state-generated campaigns of ideological propaganda and sociopolitical mobilization. In the typical developing-world authoritarian society, by contrast, the populace generally views politics with indifference. A socialist mammoth like the former Soviet Union—or China—is just the sort of place where one would expect to see rapidly expanding political participation as reform gathers steam. What happened in the Soviet world between the fall of the Berlin Wall in November 1989 and the failed hard-liners' putsch of August 1991, and what happened in China during the months leading up to the Tiananmen confrontation were typical examples of this. Each period was a time of ideological polarization leading ultimately to crisis. In China since 1989, however, the transition from totalitarianism to authoritarianism has seen the "abnormal" political sensitivity of the 1980s give way to the more "normal" political indifference characteristic of the 1990s.

Depolarization has also left the new technocrats, now liberated from entanglement in ideological squabbles, free to make more or less independent decisions based on functional rationality and cost-effectiveness as they seek pragmatic ways to handle various problems arising from modernization. The "Three Represents" slogan that Jiang Zemin announced after firming up his bourgeois-technocratic power base draws on this same confidence in functional rationality.

History provides grounds for hope that depolarization will help move Chinese society toward true pluralism. Multiple interest groups formed on the basis of a market-based division of labor are mutually dependent and will find it a matter of shared interest to agree on a set of rules for the game. Depolarization and the decline of ideological militance make it all the more likely that this process of calculation and accommodation will occur.

At the same time, we must acknowledge that depolarization can have adverse effects too. First, the disappearance of external critics and challengers may mean that official corruption will increase as effective monitoring wanes, and that government leaders will find it easier to tighten social control without fear of provoking strong reactions. With the emergence of a liberal middle stratum, however, the values of new political technocrats are likely to change with time and thus to limit this authoritarian tendency. Then too, the existence of ideologically polarized groups at least implies a concern with ideals, while people in the postpolarization society are preoccupied with material desires. In such a society, politics revolves around narrow competitions for economic advantage amid the jostling of diverse interests, and broader ethical concerns are pushed to the sidelines.

Authoritarianism Rising

What impact is depolarization likely to have on China's political structure? Since Deng launched his reforms, China has gone through two distinct periods. The first began with the Eleventh Party Congress in 1978 and ended just over a decade later when soldiers attacked the unarmed student demonstrators in Tiananmen Square. This was the age of the "socialist-totalitarian New Deal." Its hallmark was the political center's use of the socialist-totalitarian organizational apparatus and structures of legitimacy to institute new policies that were themselves meant to ease totalitarian restrictions. Communist ideology continued to dominate social life and there was no real pluralism, although intellectuals enjoyed an environment of "policy freedom."

The second period, beginning in the mid-1990s, was the time of post-totalitarian technocratic authoritarianism. Unlike their predecessors who tried to achieve utopian goals through political action guided by egalitarian dogma, the new technocrats who consolidated their rule in the late 1990s were intent on achieving pragmatic modernization, albeit often through compulsory policies. Behind the push for modernization and markets lay the hand of the ruling strongman (first Deng, then Jiang), while limited pluralism became a regular feature of social life and ideology was pushed aside.

In contrast to their authoritarian counterparts elsewhere in East Asia or in Latin America, China's new rulers had at their disposal a totalitarian state apparatus and all the control over society that implies. While totalitarian means and institutions remained in place, however, the goal was not to enforce communist egalitarianism but rather to speed the transition to a market economy. The totalitarian state machinery was kept because of its functional value, while communist ideology hung on as a kind of ceremonial protocol honored more in the breach than in the observance.

China today is governed by a type of regime that we might call "technocratic authoritarianism" or—overlooking the oxymoron—"limited totalitarianism." Under such a system, ideological politics gradually loses its appeal and ideology itself, which used to be the main determinant of social goals, is neutralized and hollowed out. Ideology's only function now is to serve as a deterrent against possible political challenges; it no longer orients the regime toward the egalitarian goal of communism. This is the fundamental difference between totalitarianism and authoritarianism in the Chinese case.

What does all this imply about the prospects for meaningful movement toward democracy in the world's largest country? There are good reasons to believe that, having disencumbered themselves of totalitarian ideology, those in power will adopt a functional and more pragmatic approach to democracy—not out of any commitment to democratic ideals, of course, but simply for reasons of expediency. In assessing the necessity and timing of democratic reform, they will probably be guided by the following four criteria:

• *Usefulness*. Can a democratic or quasi-democratic innovation effectively replace some dysfunctional element of the existing system and thereby improve governability?

• *Safety* (or *Controllability*). How risky will a given democratic innovation prove? Will it lead to challenges against the existing political order and the power of the ruling class? Can the measure be expanded, limited, or dropped as circumstances dictate?

• *Feasibility*. Will the proposed democratic innovation work within the existing system and without causing structural conflict?

• *Legitimacy*. Can the new measure be justified according to Marxist principles in a manner convincing enough to preclude challenges from the marginalized left?

Although the rulers' use of the above criteria will limit democratic innovation and thereby fail to appease the public's demand for reform, it remains likely that the rulers—pressed by the growing middle class—will nonetheless allow at least some steps toward government by consent. Still, no one should be under the illusion that in the depolarized but still authoritarian China which has been taking shape, movement toward democracy will take anything less than enormous persistence. The democratic idea has just emerged on the horizon, and is still a very long way away. But it is no mirage, and chances are that the country will keep gradually drawing closer to it.

NOTE

1. Before Deng's reforms began in 1978, the official political trend was characterized as the "leftist" line. Those who have continued to identify with such thinking have become known as the "leftist conservative force." The school of thought that has advocated freedom and opening up to the outside world has been dubbed "rightist" in both official and popular parlance, and is also known as the "progressive" camp. To simplify matters, I will generally refer to these two opposed groups as "leftists" and "reformists," respectively.

10

THE LIMITS OF AUTHORITARIAN RESILIENCE

Bruce Gilley

Bruce Gilley is associate professor of political science at Portland State University. He is the author of The Right to Rule: How States Win and Lose Legitimacy *(2009) and* China's Democratic Future: How It Will Happen and Where It Will Lead *(2004). This essay originally appeared in the January 2003 issue of the* Journal of Democracy.

The success of the recent leadership transition in the Chinese Communist Party (CCP) might be interpreted as evidence that China's authoritarian regime is historically unique. More than a decade after the collapse of the Soviet Union and the communist orders of Eastern Europe, the CCP not only remains in power but has installed a younger, better-educated, even more confident set of successors at its head. And the CCP's Sixteenth Party Congress in November 2002 marked the first smooth leadership transition in a communist regime not to have involved the death or purging of the outgoing leader.

Authoritarian regimes have been traditionally understood by political theorists as being terminally weak at their core, due to the absence of any of the checks on power that the rule of law, the separation of powers, or popular contestability would afford. The view is that the inherent weakness of these regimes will inevitably become more pronounced as the relative balance of resources shifts over time away from the state and toward autonomous social forces, often as a result of such forms of development as economic growth or international opening. At these stages of development, it is generally believed, authoritarian regimes find themselves suffering from what might be called "the logic of concentrated power"—that is, the tendency for power to concentrate in the hands of a few individuals or personalistic factions and to be fatally misused by them, with results that typically include misgovernment, a deterioration of legitimacy, corruption, and weak norms of conduct among governing elites.[1]

But China—whose people represent roughly half of that part of the world's population which is not allowed to choose its leaders though

democratic elections—has so far defied the traditional model. Some have
attempted to account for this in terms of a fundamental reconsolidation
of the CCP's house following the nadir of the Party's legitimacy after
the 1989 Tiananmen protests. The CCP, these observers argue, appears
to have effectively solved the democracy deficit without democracy by
putting in place mechanisms that have mitigated, or possibly eliminated,
the traditional weaknesses of authoritarian regimes. Andrew Nathan nicely
sums up the evidence for such mechanisms under the rubric of "regime
institutionalization."

I think that this characterization is mistaken, a point I will argue below
in reference to three features of authoritarian regimes that have historically been among the most difficult to institutionalize: 1) the process of
elite promotions; 2) the maintenance of elite functional responsibility;
and 3) popular participation.

Certainly by comparison to the bedlam of the Mao Zedong era, the
People's Republic of China (PRC) is today a fairly institutionalized state.
But relative to the actual needs of contemporary Chinese society, the
PRC falls conspicuously short: Any given feature of a political system
can be said to be "institutionalized" only when it is both consistent with
a state's normative ideals and effectively implemented. By these standards, the evidence of PRC institutionalization remains faint. Nor does
it seem likely that such institutionalization will eventually strengthen.
Indeed, since 1949, there have been discernable cycles of consolidation
and breakdown in China: The limits of regime institutionalization have
been reached before and, in response, the "logic of concentrated power"
has reasserted itself. Something similar is likely to happen again and, in
due course, weaken the institutionalization apparent at the CCP's recent
Sixteenth Party Congress.

Present Institutionalization

Samuel P. Huntington characterizes political institutionalization as the
process by which a given feature of a political system acquires the traits
of "adaptability, complexity, autonomy, and coherence." The feature in
question may be a process, an institution, or a rule. When institutionalization is achieved throughout a political system, Huntington says, it
produces government which is "effective, authoritative, [and] legitimate."[2]

Although this definition suffices to explain a government's effectiveness or authoritativeness, Huntington has almost certainly misconceived
the particular nature of the problem of legitimacy in an authoritarian
context: He fails to grasp that for any of the above mentioned features of
a political system to be legitimate, it must be consistent with an overarching normative view of the state. (This condition, it should be emphasized,
is easy to take for granted in a pluralistic state.) If a given feature lacks
a broad normative justification, then that feature will undermine the le-

gitimacy of the state itself. This sort of "normative coherence" is distinct from the sort of coherence that Huntington postulates, which consists in a functional understanding among insiders, not a consensus within the society at large.

So, political institutionalization has both *efficacy-enhancing* and *normatively cohering* elements that must obtain in order for a given feature to be institutionalized. By way of negative example, the mass round-ups involved in the Chinese regime's frequent recourse to "Strike Hard" anticrime campaigns have been remarkably "effective" in yielding more convictions, but the violations of due process that the campaigns involve have flatly contradicted the state's commitment to developing the rule of law.

The best evidence on elite promotions comes from a remarkable Chinese-language book entitled *Disidai* (The Fourth Generation) that credibly claims to be based on the internal CCP dossiers from the 2002 leadership transition.[3] The information contained in this book confutes the appearance of an institutionalized promotion process. It shows that the ease of the handover had more to do with the powerful legacy of patriarch Deng Xiaoping than it did with institutionalization. It was Deng who chose Hu Jintao to be the designated heir in 1992, removing the single most contentious succession-related issue from the political arena. Deng and Hu's patron Song Ping also remained healthy long enough to ensure that Hu's succession was assured. Accordingly, the Sixteenth Congress appears to be more of a fortuitous byproduct than a systemic outcome.

In particular, *Disidai* shows that:

• In 1997, as a tactic for ousting his liberal rival Qiao Shi, Jiang Zemin proposed a rule that no person aged 70 or over should be appointed to the Politburo. Jiang, 71 at the time, excused himself from the rule, though he pledged to obey it at the Sixteenth Congress of 2002. Yet from 2001 until the Congress, Jiang allowed a number of military leaders, Party scholars, and close aides to float the idea of his breaching the rule again and remaining in office. This effort failed. He did, however, succeed in purging another liberal, Li Ruihuan, 68, on the ad hoc grounds that he had served on the standing committee since 1989. These challenges to the rule, which remains unwritten and imprecise, have raised widespread questions about its durability.

• Only three top leaders—Jiang Zemin, Li Peng, and Zhu Rongji—dominated the selection of the new leadership (with retired Party elders Bo Yibo and Song Ping playing influential roles behind the scenes). This concentration of influence ran contrary to the formal rule that such decisions should be made by the entire 21-member Politburo, and so represents a failure of the PRC to implement the kind of "collective leadership" that, might mitigate the dangers of centralized power in a communist regime.

• Personal loyalties mattered far more than individual merit. Seven of the nine new members of the Politburo Standing Committee (PBSC)—

Hu Jintao, Zeng Qinghong, Luo Gan, Wu Bangguo, Jia Qinglin, Huang Ju, and Li Changchun—were chosen based on factional loyalties and despite their known shortcomings as officials.[4] Only Wen Jiabao and Wu Guanzheng were selected principally on merit. In a pluralistic political system, the appointment of officials based on personal loyalty is both normatively acceptable and easily implemented, because the officials doing the appointing are themselves elected or appointed by those who are. But since the CCP is China's uncontested power holder, it is constrained to espousing a normative ideal of strictly merit-based appointments at every level. Yet this ideal is not effectively implemented, and so transparently bad appointments are liable to prompt dissent and protest.

• Normal promotion rules in the CCP hierarchy have been disregarded when inconvenient for the Party's senior leadership. This was the case for all three of the leading "fifth-generation" cadres due to take over the PBSC in 2012. Li Keqiang was confirmed as Communist Youth League general secretary in 1993 despite failing to win so much as an alternate seat on the Central Committee at the Fourteenth Party Congress of 1992. Bo Xilai was brought to the Fifteenth Congress of 1997 as a "specially invited delegate" after failing to win election as a delegate from his local Party membership. And Xi Jinping was appointed to the Central Committee at the Fifteenth Congress after failing to win election from Congress delegates.

On the question of elite functional specialization, *Disidai* presents the first glimpse at the vast number of contending bureaucratic battles that beset elite politics in China. While PBSC members have traditionally been assigned particular portfolios (economic matters, internal security, foreign affairs, and so on), these divisions remain subject to chronic evasion or disregard—meaning that the "autonomy" required for political institutionalization in the Huntington sense remains abrogated in many important policy spheres.

The breakdown of elite specialization is manifest in several functional areas:

• *Economic issues:* The delegation of economic issues to the premier can be reversed where PBSC members differ. So, for example, in 1999 Jiang Zemin virtually seized the state-enterprise portfolio from Premier Zhu Rongji by convening a conference of state-enterprise officials from four major regions.

• *Personnel and organization:* The importance of this portfolio for factional maneuvering makes it a frequent bone of contention. Between 1993 and 1997, the dominant figure on personnel and organizational issues was Jiang's aide Zeng Qinghong, who was not even a Politburo member at the time. Over this period, the PBSC member formally in charge of these issues, Hu Jintao, accepted the infringement in order to preserve his future succession.

• *Anticorruption:* The processing of high-level corruption cases in the Party remains a matter of political expediency, a smokescreen for factional battles at the top—meaning that the PBSC member in charge of anticorruption efforts is a mere administrator of cases chosen for political reasons. This has become a matter of popular knowledge, for which reason even the apparently genuine prosecution of a high-level corruption case means a step backward as much as a step forward for the legitimacy of the Party.

One feature below the elite level that has a strong potentiality for mitigating the doleful effects of concentrated power in authoritarian regimes is political participation: A democracy deficit can be at least partially offset by a "participation surplus." As evidence of growing institutionalization at the subelite level, scholars have cited village elections, popular petitioning, and the role of local legislatures. Yet in none of these cases are the two criteria of institutionalization—efficacy and coherence—met. To take a few well-known examples:

• Village elections have undeniably proved effective in improving the governance of China's nearly one-million villages and establishing the authority of the state in rural areas. But they lack normative coherence: Within a one-party state, political competition must be kept under tight control. At the same time, maintaining that control sometimes means that the Party must subvert the very rules of competition which it has established—for example, by contravening its own policies in village elections, invalidating unacceptable election results, or surreptitiously implanting Party control in maverick villages. The introduction of elections may have been a tactic on the part of some central-government officials to sneak democracy in the back door, but such sneaking can only go so far before it starts to apply acute pressure on the governing normative ideal that the Party alone should hold political power.

• Local and national legislatures suffer from the same kind of normative incoherence in their attempts to assert their role in "supervising" government work. Since the Chinese party-state does not accept the idea of devolved political power, these legislatures are invariably weak. In those rare instances where they manage, for example, to reject a law, a nominee for office, or a government report, there is almost comical confusion about what to do. Unlike in village elections, where devolved administrative powers are permitted at least to be effective, China's parliaments remain so tightly controlled by the Party that for the most part they fail the effectiveness test as well.

• There is also the system of popular petitioning *(xinfang)*, which may be said to comply with a pervasive normative idea: that people should be allowed to raise suggestions to help the Party with its work. In 2000, a new State Bureau of Letters and Visits was established as a subministry body. Yet the handling of popular petitions remains highly erratic, since the process ultimately depends not on the regular exercise of devolved power but rather the selective acceptance of supervision by the Party itself.

So the evidence of institutionalization appears at present to be decidedly limited. Institutionalization does not consist merely in the absence of bedlam; it entails the positive presence of efficacy and normative coherence. The CCP has moved, then, from political tumult to an ad hoc peace; but it has gone no further. As a result, the problems traditionally associated with nondemocratic regimes—illegitimacy, misgovernment, corruption, and elite instability—remain legion in China. Corruption alone is estimated to amount to the equivalent of anywhere from 10 to 20 percent of GDP. Elite instability has been clearly manifest in the factional and ideological battles that have characterized the Jiang years, including the purging of no fewer than six Politburo members. All this suggests that China's attempts at institutionalization have largely failed.

Future Institutionalization

Perhaps a more pertinent question is what the future will bring. Will the norms so weakly institutionalized in the Chinese state become stronger, or break down? That is, can we look forward to a period of "creeping democratization" that overcomes the ineffectiveness and incoherence of the current system?

All democratic consolidations begin with changes that are, by definition, not yet embedded, and which may be characterized as a *modus vivendi* among the relevant players. Only with time do these changes come to be embedded, come to be seen generally as worthy for their own sake, and so become norms. But there is always the opposite possibility as well, one which I believe is more likely in China's case: that these new processes will break down as a result of "the logic of concentrated power."

On the question of elite promotion, for example, it is certainly easy to imagine that the age-70 rule will become more institutionalized over time. And yet it takes just one or two dissenters to spoil the bargain, as was seen in the Sixteenth Congress succession battle. At the Seventeenth Party Congress in 2007, hard-liner Luo Gan will be over 70, while Zeng Qinghong, a rival to Hu, will be 68. Both represent powerful factions. And when ultimate power is at stake, the maintenance of norms is precarious—as authoritarian regimes around the world have demonstrated time and again. The more jealously held power is, the more volatile such norms tend to be.

Likewise, merit-based promotions have surely helped bring a greater number of capable people into higher office. But at the local level, the promotion process commonly turns on bribery, while at the elite level, the process is still determined by the vagaries of political factions. Changing these patterns would require substantial latitude for monitoring by an uncensored media, anticorruption efficacy, or political devolution, none of which the CCP appears likely to take up. Changing wider patterns of corruption would require similar, and similarly unlikely, developments.

When it comes to village elections, Party leaders will be apt to meet any signs of efficacy on the part of elected village heads with alarm. The emergence of such elected officials, as a group unsusceptible to coop- tation or subversion, will inevitably raise the question of whether the Party should revise its norms in favor of sharing political power—which was the path followed by the strong authoritarian regimes of Taiwan, South Korea, and Thailand. But a "voluntary withdrawal" of this kind is unlikely in the case of a weak regime like the CCP's.[5] A more likely course is that the Party will continue to subvert village elections as new political groups begin to compete with more and more success. As Paul Brooker has noted, authoritarian regimes that introduce real local elections "may eventually face the problem of having to find a not too blatantly undemocratic way to hobble a party that is competing too successfully with the official party."[6]

This dilemma also helps to explain why, despite its repeated promises, the CCP has not yet endorsed the expansion of direct executive elections beyond the village level. Scattered experiments in electing township governors have been criticized by the Party leadership, for instance, even though they have been popularly embraced in those places, largely in response to an ongoing crisis of township governance.

As for people's congresses, certainly they have improved governance in many areas. But usually they have done so by seizing power against the wishes of the Party. Where they have improved regime legitimacy, it is only because their members have been fully coopted by the Party: They can improve governance or improve regime control, but cannot do both.

In each case—township elections or People's Congresses—the Party is forced to choose between efficacy and coherence. It almost always chooses the latter.

Cycles and Breakdown

Many have written of the cycles of politics in the PRC since 1949. While personal and historical contingencies tend to explain the specific timings of these cycles, the underlying dynamic that has led to a break- down after each consolidation is precisely the "logic of concentrated power": In times of political crisis, dysfunction, or succession, any power that has been carefully devolved for the improvement of governance and elite political stability is quickly reined back in. In general, one can see four distinct cycles since 1949:

• Consolidation Phase One (1949–1956): the establishment of the PRC.
• Breakdown Phase One (1956–61): from the Anti-Rightist Movement to the Great Leap Famine.
• Consolidation Phase Two (1961–66): recovery from famine.

- Breakdown Phase Two (1966–76): Cultural Revolution.
- Consolidation Phase Three (1976–86): reestablishment and expansion of government and Party institutions and laws.
- Breakdown Phase Three (1986–94): rise of student protest movements which reflect elite splits on reforms; reimposition of rule by Party elders.
- Consolidation Phase Four (since 1994): death of Party elders and expansion of rule of law and government professionalization; entry into the World Trade Organization.

A cursory analysis of the literature on these cycles suggests that scholars of Chinese politics have been all too prone to interpret them at each stage as linear change. In 1978, for example—at the beginning of what I term Consolidation Phase Three—an article appeared entitled "Modernization and Succession Politics in China" which, while offering some warnings of uncertainty about the future, made many of the arguments being made now, in the period of the Sixteenth Congress.[7] The literature after 1989, by contrast, tended heavily to emphasize continued regime breakdown.

There is certainly much to be said for tracing the ups and downs of particular phases and comparing them to earlier ones. The danger lies in believing that those phases are irreversible, which CCP history in particular and authoritarian-regime theory in general suggests they are not. Suharto's Indonesia may be the best counterexample—a regime that fell from power just as it had seemingly bucked the trend and consolidated itself through new forms of institutionalization in the mid-1990s, appearing "solid and highly efficient."[8]

If we should have been looking more vigilantly for signs of consolidation after 1989, we should be looking more vigilantly for signs of breakdown now, at the cusp of what would be Breakdown Phase Four in the schema above. Such signs might include the appearance of a more-or-less open split among PBSC members on a key policy issue such as Taiwan or local elections; the reappearance of retired leaders like Jiang or Li Peng in public; or the loss of power by a Politburo member over a functional area such as internal security.

Where a new phase of breakdown might lead is beyond the scope of this paper. But a word of caution by way of conclusion: Institutional breakdown does not portend collapse. The strength of China's coercive apparatus—six million police officers and soldiers—along with the weakness of civil society ensure that the CCP will not fall or be pushed from power. Tragedy in the form of political purges and social repression has been a more typical result of breakdown phases in the PRC.

At the same time, there is an alternative consequence that might rescue China from these political cycles: a democratic breakthrough. Institutional breakdown provides opportunities—often on account of attendant crises of governance—for reformist elites to engineer an extrication of the regime with promises of political opening, which is the first step toward democracy. Ironically then, China's best democratic hope may lie in the very contradictions that make its current institutionalization so troubled.

NOTES

1. The expression "the logic of concentrated power" refers to Robert Dahl's invocation of the "logic of equality"—the drive toward widespread participation and responsible political power that Dahl sees as inexorably resulting from a starting assumption of political equality among members of a society. See Dahl's *On Democracy* (New Haven: Yale University Press, 1998), 10.

2. Samuel P. Huntington, *Political Order in Changing Societies* (New Haven: Yale University Press, 1968), 12, 2.

3. Zong Hairen, *Disidai* (The Fourth Generation) (New York: Mirror Books, 2002). It is the basis of an English-language book I coauthored with Andrew Nathan, *China's New Rulers: The Secret Files* (New York: New York Review of Books, 2002). We address the authenticity of *Disidai* at length in the introduction to our book.

4. These shortcomings are explicitly acknowledged in official Party documents. See Andrew Nathan and Bruce Gilley, *China's New Rulers*—for Hu Jintao, 68; for Wu Bangguo, 102; for Luo Gan, 110; and for Li Changchun, 114.

5. I provide a sustained treatment of the likely course of democratic breakthrough in *China's Democratic Future: How It Will Happen and Where It Will Lead* (New York: Columbia University Press, 2004).

6. Paul Brooker, *Non-Democratic Regimes: Theory, Government and Politics* (Basingstoke, England: Macmillan, 2000), 115.

7. Kenneth Lieberthal in *Journal of International Affairs* 32 (Fall 1978): 239–54. The article noted the "startling results" of post-Mao consolidation resulting from the "strong . . . cohesion" of the leadership and its drive to "reinvest the party with its previous authority and competence." It did, however, warn that it was "too early to say" whether the process was irreversible.

8. R. William Liddle, "Indonesia: Suharto's Tightening Grip," *Journal of Democracy* 7 (October 1996): 70. Cited in Larry Diamond, *Developing Democracy: Toward Consolidation* (Baltimore: Johns Hopkins University Press, 1999), 262.

11

IS CCP RULE FRAGILE
OR RESILIENT?

Minxin Pei

Minxin Pei *is the Tom and Margot Pritzker '72 Professor of Government and director of the Keck Center for International and Strategic Studies at Claremont McKenna College. He is the author, most recently, of* China's Trapped Transition: The Limits of Developmental Autocracy *(2006). This essay originally appeared in the January 2012 issue of the* Journal of Democracy.

The continuing survival of authoritarian regimes around the world and the apparent resilience of such regimes in several major countries, particularly China and Russia, have attracted enormous scholarly interest in recent years.[1] Analysts have put forward various theories to explain the success and durability of these regimes. Some theories focus on authoritarians' capacity to learn from mistakes (their own as well as those made by other authoritarians) and adapt accordingly. Others center around an observed correlation between high natural-resource rents and regime survival. Still others identify the repressive capacity of authoritarian regimes as the key to their durability, while a final group of explanations pays special attention to the capacity of authoritarian regimes to institutionalize their rule.

These theories may provide tantalizing explanations for the endurance of authoritarian regimes, but they suffer from one common weakness: They are ad hoc and inductive. Moreover, they have a selection-bias problem resulting from small sample sizes (limited by the number of surviving autocracies). As a result, when supposedly invulnerable autocracies crumble in the face of mass protest and popular uprising, the explanations of authoritarian resilience largely break down. The series of popular revolts in 2011 that toppled autocracies in Tunisia and Egypt, triggered a civil war in Libya, and sparked prolonged and bloody anti-regime protests in Syria and Yemen provide a humbling lesson for those who had viewed those regimes as "robust" and "resilient."

In terms of authoritarian resilience, the People's Republic of China

(PRC) stands out as exemplary. Not only did the ruling Chinese Communist Party (CCP) survive the turbulent spring of 1989, when millions of protesters nationwide nearly toppled its rule and it put down demonstrations in Beijing's Tiananmen Square with dramatic violence, but it has since thrived. The ruling elites coalesced around a new strategy that joined the promotion of rapid (mostly export-led) economic growth to the preservation of one-party rule through selective political repression. The rapid growth of the Chinese economy in the post-Tiananmen era has lent the CCP popular legitimacy and the resources to defend its political monopoly. The Party has demonstrated remarkable tactical sophistication, a knack for adaptation, and a capacity for asserting control. It has succeeded in maintaining unity within the elite cadres, resisted the global tide of democratization, and prevented the revolution in communications technologies from undermining its grip on the flow of information. It has also manipulated nationalism to bolster its support among the young and better educated, eliminated any form of organized opposition, and contained social unrest through a combination of carrots and sticks.

The CCP's ability to consolidate authoritarian rule even as a wave of democratic openings swept much of the world after 1989 raises several important questions. Does the Chinese case validate any of the theories of authoritarian resilience advanced by scholars who specialize in the study of other regions? What are the explanations for authoritarian resilience in China, and what evidence supports them? Are these explanations theoretically robust? Is authoritarian resilience in China a passing phenomenon, or is it something more durable?

Explaining Authoritarian Resilience

Theories of authoritarian survival all share a common feature: They turn theories of democratic transition upside down. Specifically, they attempt either to identify the *absence* of factors normally favorable to democratic transition or to pinpoint the *presence* of unfavorable factors associated with the prevention of democratic transition. Among all these explanations, three stand out.

The first focuses on matters of political economy. Generally speaking, authoritarian regimes that are dependent on natural-resource rents tend to be more durable. Such regimes are able to buy off the population with high welfare spending and low taxation. Resource-based rents also allow autocratic regimes to escape political accountability and maintain a strong repressive apparatus. Authoritarian regimes with significant control over economic resources, such as state-owned enterprises, have greater survival capabilities because such control allows rulers to keep their key supporters loyal through patronage and to reassert their influence over the economy.

The capacity to adapt to new social and political challenges is a second variable associated with authoritarian resilience. For example, a number of authoritarian regimes have managed to stay in power by manipulating elections. The long-ruling one-party regimes in Malaysia and Singapore stand out for the sophistication of their political institutions. During its 71-year reign, Mexico's Institutional Revolutionary Party (PRI) was said to have maintained a "perfect dictatorship" featuring highly developed political institutions that managed leadership succession and generated popular support.[2] Resilient authoritarian regimes adapt by learning to differentiate between the types of public goods that they provide. More sophisticated autocracies typically supply welfare-enhancing public goods such as economic growth but limit "coordination goods" such as the freedom of information and association, in order to reduce the opposition's ability to organize.[3]

The third explanation concerns the balance of power between the regime and opposition. Despite its obvious importance, the role of repression in the survival of autocracies has received surprisingly little attention. Yet a simple and persuasive explanation for authoritarians' longevity is that they are ready, willing, and able to use the coercive power necessary to suppress any societal challenge. More than anything else, it is effective repression that has sustained the Middle East's autocracies.[4] As long as this balance of power favors autocratic regimes, their survival is guaranteed by the application of repression. Of course, if the military refuses support, as happened in Tunisia and Egypt in early 2011, the balance of power shifts decisively and the regime is doomed.

In the Chinese context, the discussion about authoritarian resilience has centered around three themes—regime institutionalization, organizational learning and adaptation, and organizational and administrative capacity. Regime institutionalization—the process through which important norms and rules of the game are formulated and enforced—is thought by some to be the key to the CCP regime's durability. Since 1989, the CCP supposedly has greatly improved the procedures governing political succession, defined functional responsibilities, and promoted elites on the basis of merit. These and other measures, according to Andrew Nathan, have greatly increased the degree of institutionalization within the CCP, enabling it to survive and succeed.[5] In Steve Tsang's view, the post-Tiananmen regime has evolved into a distinct and more resilient form of Leninist rule by adopting a mixture of survival strategies that focus on governance reforms (to preempt public demands for democratization), greater capacity for responding to public opinion, pragmatic economic management (considerations of socialist ideology take a back seat to the need for growth), and appeals to nationalism. Tsang calls this "consultative Leninism."[6]

Those who stress the second theme—organizational learning and adaptation—note that authoritarian elites are motivated by an urge to survive and can draw useful lessons from the demise or collapse of their counterparts in other parts of the world. As a result, a regime may adopt new policies that contribute to its longevity and power. David Shambaugh argues that the collapse of the USSR taught the CCP valuable lessons, leading it to implement effective policy responses to post–Cold War challenges both at home and abroad.[7]

The third theme stresses that, compared to other developing-world autocracies, China's organizational and administrative capacity is exceptional. Since 1989, the CCP has undertaken further measures to strengthen the capacity of the Chinese state in revenue collection and regulatory enforcement. By building state capacity, the CCP has made itself more resilient.[8]

These explanations of the Chinese regime's durability leave several important questions unanswered. For example, is regime survival the same thing as regime resilience? Scholars studying the persistence of authoritarian rule in China rarely make a conceptual distinction between the two. Yet the mere fact of regime survival does not necessarily indicate regime resilience; survival is an empirical measurement, whereas resilience is a subjective concept. Thus authoritarian regimes that survive are not necessarily resilient.

If it lacks strong opposition or employs brutal repression, even a decrepit autocracy—that is, one without a high degree of institutionalization or performance-based legitimacy—may hang on for a long time. It would, for example, be a definitional stretch to label the personalistic dictatorship of Zimbabwe's elderly Robert Mugabe a "resilient autocracy." What, after all, constitutes the resilience of a regime? Longevity is perhaps the most-used criterion, and by that standard, the regimes of Burma, Cuba, and North Korea would be considered resilient. But because the word "resilience" implies inherent strengths and the capacity to endure and overcome adversity, regime survival reflects only one aspect of resilience, not others. In fact, these regimes appear to live under perpetual siege and in a permanent state of crisis and insecurity, making it hard to call them resilient. Even for the more successful authoritarian regimes—China and, to a lesser extent, Russia—their degree of resilience is debatable. In the case of China, for example, the CCP faces daily instances of defiance and disturbances, ranging from hundreds of local protests to accidents and disasters caused by corruption and incompetence. It is forced to devote massive resources to maintaining domestic order.

Authoritarian resilience, however defined, may result from tried-and-true survival tactics rather than the adoption of innovative political strategies. Although many studies have focused on autocrats' use of semicompetitive elections to legitimize their power and on authoritarian regimes' successful management of succession and promotion of regime elites,[9] the more critical variables are economic patronage, political cooptation, and ruthlessly effective repression. For all their current success and perceived strengths, authoritarian regimes have not been able to address effectively the systemic and well-known weaknesses that imperil their long-term survival and limit their policy choices in responding to public demands. Such weaknesses include political illegitimacy; endemic corruption caused by lack of political accountability and misalignment of interests between the regime and its agents; political exclusion of the middle class; and predatory state policies that victimize and alienate disadvantaged social groups. As long as such systemic weaknesses persist under authoritarian rule, autocracy is unlikely to remain resilient.

To be sure, some authoritarian regimes have helped their survival chances by improving internal rules governing succession and promotion, learning useful lessons from the success or failures of other authoritarian regimes, strengthening the administrative capacity of the state, and managing to restrict the provision of coordination goods. Such autocracies are undeniably more sophisticated in institutional and tactical terms than garden-variety dictatorships in developing countries. But an explanation of the survival of "resilient" authoritarian regimes must take into account the additional factors that enable them to maintain power and the underlying forces that threaten their long-term survival. Such a comprehensive analytical approach is likely to yield more useful insights into the political dynamics of regime survival and demise in contemporary autocracies.

In particular, we should consider simpler and more straightforward explanations for the survival of authoritarian regimes—economic performance, for example. Everything else being equal, empirical research shows that authoritarian regimes that manage to perform well economically tend to survive longer.[10] Obviously, autocracies gain political legitimacy if the standard of living rises as a result of sustained economic growth. Autocratic regimes can use the resulting rents to coopt the middle class and redistribute the benefits from growth among the ruling elites, thus avoiding internecine struggles over a more or less fixed set of spoils. Sustained economic growth in an authoritarian regime also allows ruling elites to finance and maintain an extensive repressive apparatus to suppress political opposition.

Another straightforward explanation is that the greater the range of a regime's survival strategies—the more diversified its "portfolio" of methods for staying in power—the more likely it is to endure. Force alone may sustain some authoritarian regimes, but heavy use of repression can be costly. Moreover, large military and internal-security forces will consume resources that might otherwise be spent on nonrepressive survival strategies such as cooptation and patronage. Highly repressive regimes are also unlikely to instill confidence in private entrepreneurs or to create business opportunities for them. Robert Barro has found that heavy repression depresses economic growth, while moderate repression may have a positive impact.[11] In autocracies that rely solely on repression, economic performance tends to be abysmal, sowing the seeds of social discontent and sapping regime legitimacy.

Even if a regime's economic performance has been satisfactory and its survival strategies and tactics sophisticated, it must still contend with autocracy's inherent flaws—the absence of procedural legitimacy, a narrow base of social support, gross misalignment of interests between the regime and its agents, and systemic and pervasive corruption—all of which threaten its long-term durability. Thus, perceived authoritarian resilience is, in all likelihood, a temporary phenomenon that conceals fatal weaknesses.

The Keys to CCP Survival

The three keys to the CCP's survival are refined repression, economic statism, and political cooptation. Proponents of the authoritarian-resilience theory have downplayed or overlooked their role. Although autocracies may use other, sometimes more sophisticated, means of keeping power, the most important is the use of violence against political opposition. No autocracy has survived without in some way resorting to repression. The difference between more successful autocracies and less successful ones lies mainly in how they use repression. The more successful autocracies do so more selectively, efficiently, and effectively while the less successful ones typically repress opposition in cruder, more wasteful, and less productive ways.

Since the early 1990s, China has shifted toward "smart repression." The CCP has narrowed the scope and shifted the focus of its repressive actions. While the CCP continues to restrict people's political freedoms and civil rights, it has almost completely withdrawn from their private lives and stopped meddling in lifestyle issues. At the same time, the regime has drawn a clear line against organized political opposition, which is not tolerated in any form.

Selective repression, such as brutally suppressing the quasi-spiritual group the Falun Gong or targeting leading dissidents, avoids antagonizing the majority of the population while achieving the objectives of political decapitation and preventing organized opposition from emerging. This approach also conserves the regime's repressive resources and utilizes them more efficiently. The CCP regime has become more selective in its application of harsh crackdowns both because it learned lessons from the 1989 experience and because of the party-state's institutional decentralization. China's multiple levels of authority allow the regime to avoid either using excessive repression or making needless concessions in dealing with popular resistance.[12]

The regime's repressive tactics have also grown more sophisticated, even as the Party remains ruthless in defending its political monopoly. It now favors a less brutal approach, forcing top dissidents into exile abroad, for example, rather than sentencing them to long prison terms. Routine harassment of human-rights activists and political dissidents has taken on softer forms: Inviting them to have tea with the police is a favorite tactic. The regime's methods for dealing with rising social unrest have likewise become more sophisticated. Confronted with hundreds of collective protests and riots each day, the party-state has shown a considerable capacity to deploy highly effective measures such as quickly arresting and jailing protest leaders to decapitate local unrest, disperse crowds, and pacify the masses.[13]

The regime's efforts at manipulating public opinion have also become more complex—a mix of harsh censorship and campaigning for popular support. Rather than simply relying on old-fashioned ideological indoctrination, the CCP's propaganda department has, in recent years, learned to influence the social agenda by showcasing the Party's success in addressing social issues such as rising housing prices and declining access to healthcare. Although this approach has not been entirely successful, it is a telling example of the CCP's growing tactical sophistication.

Through its massive investment in manpower, technology, and training, the CCP has greatly improved the operational capabilities of its already well-funded, well-equipped, and well-trained security forces. The CCP has dealt with the emergence of new threats, such as information and communication technologies, with relatively effective countermeasures that include both regulatory restrictions and technological fixes. In this manner, the regime has contained the political impact of the information revolution, although it has had to adopt new tactics in order to do so. Instead of losing its grip on the flow of information, the CCP's propaganda operations have grown more sophisticated, helping to guard the CCP's political hegemony.

The Party's operational capabilities with regard to emergency management have also improved during the last decade. In 2003, with the SARS outbreak, China faced its first major public-health crisis since the end of the Cultural Revolution. The government's initial response was incompetent and ineffective. After replacing key leaders, however, the regime quickly turned the situation around. Natural disasters, major accidents, protests, and the like are frequent in China. Because of better emergency response, however, such periodic shocks have not inflicted serious damage on CCP control.

The CCP fully understands the inseparable link between political survival and control over the country's economic resources. Without its ability to hand out economic rents, the Party would surely lose the loyalty of its supporters and its ability to retain power. Thus the CCP keeps extensive and tight control over China's state-owned enterprises so that it can dole out political patronage.[14] This means that the Party

is inherently incapable of implementing market-oriented reforms beyond a certain point, since they will ultimately undermine its political
base. China's stalled economic reform in recent years has vindicated
this view. Indeed, the Party has not only publicly announced its intention of retaining state control of key economic sectors such as finance,
energy, telecom services, and transportation, but has also successfully
defended these monopolies or oligopolies from domestic and international competition. State-owned firms dominate these industries, while
private firms and foreign competitors are kept out. Such policies have
slowed the pace of privatization but have enabled the state to remain the
country's most powerful economic actor.

Even after three decades of economic reform, firms owned or controlled by the party-state account for close to 40 percent of China's
GDP. The regime's domination of the economy rose to a new level after
the government used aggressive fiscal and monetary policies to maintain
high rates of growth following the 2008 global economic crisis. With a
fiscal-stimulus package of nearly US$700 billion and $2 trillion in new
bank loans, the Chinese state further strengthened state-owned enterprises at the expense of the private sector.[15]

While the economic-efficiency losses caused by the state's continuing and deep involvement in the economy are huge, the political benefits
of this strategy are clear. The Party retains the power to appoint top
officials in state-owned firms and the capacity to distribute lucrative
economic rents to its key constituents (bureaucrats and businessmen
with ties to the ruling elites). For members of these groups, the Communist Party's patronage pays. One study shows that politically connected
firms often have higher offering prices when their stocks are listed on
China's equity markets.[16] Economic patronage thus serves a dual function: It is both a critical instrument for influencing economic activities
and a source of incentives to secure and maintain the backing of the
regime's key political supporters.

In addition to keeping a strong hand on the levers of the economy,
authoritarian regimes can help to extend their lives by expanding their
social bases. Since the early 1990s, the CCP has been working successfully to do just that, building an elite alliance through cooptation. El-
evating the political status of the intelligentsia and the professional class
and improving their material benefits—while simultaneously using regulations and sanctions to penalize and deter intellectuals who dare to
challenge the regime—are the most important elements of this strategy.

The Party has systematically campaigned to recruit the intelligentsia
and professionals into its fold and to award them important technocratic
appointments. This effort has succeeded both in raising the CCP's technocratic capacity and in extending its base into the intelligentsia, an
elite social group that was at odds with the Party in the 1980s over the
issue of political reform.[17] The much-publicized effort to recruit private

entrepreneurs into the Party has done less to expand its social base, since the majority of private owners of nonagricultural firms were already Party members who had used their power to convert state-owned assets into private property. Nevertheless, numerous studies have concluded that the CCP has been relatively successful in coopting private entrepreneurs. Some scholars have even called Chinese private entrepreneurs "allies of the state."[18] One case study finds that local officials who are supportive of the private sector have proven to be more effective in incorporating private businesspeople into local power structures.[19]

The CCP's strategy of political cooptation has been unexpectedly successful, leading some observers to argue that China's emerging middle class mainly favors the status quo. In addition to pacifying the middle class, the CCP has managed to transform its own membership base. During the Mao era, it was predominantly a party of peasants and workers; now it is a party of elites. According to official figures released in 2010, roughly 10 percent of the Party's 78 million members at the end of 2009 were workers and 20 percent were farmers. The remaining 70 percent were bureaucrats, managers, retired officials, professionals, college students, and intellectuals. Particularly noteworthy is the high proportion of well-educated individuals in the CCP—36 percent were either college graduates or had received some college education, and 15 percent were management, technical, and professional personnel and college students.[20] By comparison, less than 8 percent of China's total population is college-educated. In short, political cooptation has turned the Party into an elite-based alliance. The incorporation of key social elites into an authoritarian regime generates significant political benefits for the rulers. Among other things, it denies potential opposition groups access to social elites and makes it much harder for lower-status groups to organize and become effective political forces.

Behind the Façade of Authoritarian Strength

There is a sharp and intriguing discrepancy between how strong autocracies seem to outsiders and how insecure the rulers themselves feel. Autocrats are constantly on guard against forces that pose even the slightest threat to their rule, expending tremendous resources and taking excessively harsh and repressive measures in the process. But if authoritarian regimes really were so strong, then such costly measures motivated by insecurity would be self-defeating and counterproductive: They would be unnecessary and, by wasting a regime's scarce resources, would undermine its long-term survival. So why is there this discrepancy? The answer is quite simple: The authoritarian strength that outsiders perceive is merely an illusion. Insiders—the authoritarians themselves—possess information about the regime's weaknesses that outsiders know little about. These weaknesses make authoritarians feel insecure and prompt them to act accordingly.

The resilience of China's authoritarian regime may be a temporary phenomenon, fated to succumb eventually to autocracy's institutional and systemic defects. These defects are inherent features of autocratic systems and therefore uncorrectable. Thus the measures that the CCP has taken since the early 1990s to strengthen its rule (regardless of how effective they may have been) merely serve to offset somewhat the deleterious effects that these flaws have on regime survival. In the long run, China's authoritarian regime is likely to lose its resilience.

Ironically, an authoritarian regime's short-term success can imperil its long-term survival and effectiveness. Success, defined in terms of suppressing political opposition and defending a political monopoly, makes it more likely that authoritarians, unrestrained by political opposition, free media, and the rule of law, will engage in looting and theft, inevitably weakening the regime's capacity for survival.

Authoritarian regimes tend to breed corruption for a variety of reasons. A principal cause is the relatively short time horizon of autocrats, whose hold on power is tenuous, uncertain, and insecure. Even where the rules of succession and promotion have improved, as they have in China, such improvement is only relative to the previous state of affairs. Succession at the top remains opaque and unpredictable in China. Although the top leadership has managed to reach compromises through bargaining, thereby avoiding destabilizing power struggles, succession politics continues to be mired in intrigue and factionalism. In the case of promotion, the only objective rule appears to be an age requirement; all the other factors that are supposedly merit-based can be gamed. The fact that many officials resort to bribery to gain promotions indicates that personal favoritism continues to play an important role in internal Party promotions.[21]

All this renders uncertain the political future of members of the CCP hierarchy and thus encourages predatory behavior. There is evidence that corruption has worsened in China in recent years despite periodic anticorruption campaigns launched by the CCP.[22] More important, because of the deep and extensive involvement of the Chinese party-state in the economy, the combination of motives (driven by uncertainty) and opportunity (access to economic rents) can create an ideal environment for regime insiders to engage in collusion, looting, and theft.

Corruption endangers the long-term survival of authoritarian regimes in several ways. It can hinder economic growth, thus reducing the regime's political legitimacy and capacity to underwrite a costly patronage system and maintain its repressive apparatus. Corruption also contributes to rising inequality by benefiting a small number of well-connected elites at the expense of public welfare, thus further fueling antiregime sentiments and social tensions. Corruption creates a high-risk environment, making it difficult to enforce regulations governing the workplace, food and drugs, traffic, and environmental safety, thereby increasing the risks of accidents and disasters and the likelihood of mismanaged government responses to them.[23]

The Limits of Political Cooptation

By nature, autocracies are exclusionary political coalitions. Although the incorporation of social elites can generate short-term benefits for rulers, it is a costly and ultimately unsustainable strategy because the modernization process produces social elites at a faster rate than authoritarian rulers can coopt them. Eventually, the regime will be unable to afford to coopt so many social elites, thus creating a potential pool of opposition leaders.

A key test of the CCP's capacity for coopting new social elites is the employment of college graduates. Since the late 1990s, college and university enrollment in China has shot upward. In 1997, Chinese tertiary educational institutions admitted a million new students; in 2009, they admitted 6.4 million. The number of college graduates soared in the same period. In 1997, students graduating from college numbered 829,000; in 2009, that figure was 5.3 million.[24]

For all its focus on coopting social elites, however, the CCP has been able to recruit into its own ranks only a small percentage of China's college graduates. In 2009, the CCP recruited 919,000 new members with a college degree (roughly 30 percent of the Party's annual new recruits).[25] In other words, so far the CCP has been able to absorb each year only about a fifth of the net increase in the college-educated population. This implies that the CCP leaves out the vast majority of newly minted college graduates. Because Party membership confers enormous material benefits, college graduates who are rejected by the CCP are bound to be frustrated politically and socially.[26] Because of the difficulty that graduates of second- and third-tier colleges have experienced in finding employment in recent years, the prospect that this group will form an antiregime force has become ever more likely.[27]

The long-term effectiveness of political cooptation is also limited by the questionable loyalty of those social elites being targeted for recruitment into the Party and its patronage system. To the extent that these individuals join the Party or support its policies chiefly out of pecuniary interests, the CCP may not be able to count on their loyalty if its ability to satisfy their material interests declines, due to poor economic performance or constraints on the state's fiscal capacity. In a crisis, when these opportunistic supporters might be called on to risk their lives or property to defend the Party, it is doubtful that a majority would stick with a regime in danger of collapse.

For the most part, however, authoritarian regimes adapt and make adjustments in times of crisis. The CCP adopted many of its regime-strengthening measures in response to the challenges posed by the Tiananmen crisis in 1989 and the collapse of European communism that followed soon thereafter. These measures have largely been effective in addressing the challenges stemming from these twin crises: reviving the country's stagnant economy through greater liberalization and opening to the outside world; ending international isolation; placating the intelligentsia; and boosting the confidence of the business community. But the measures that helped to keep the regime in power during the tumults of the late twentieth century are not necessarily working as well in the postcrisis era.

Activist Opposition

Today, after two decades of rapid economic growth, China's political landscape and socioeconomic environment have radically changed. New threats to the CCP's hold on power have emerged, while the dangers of the early 1990s—the threats that the Party's current adaptive survival strategies were designed to meet—have disappeared or dissipated. The Chinese government no longer faces international isolation or a mass antiregime movement led by the intelligentsia.

Instead, the CCP regime now faces an entirely new set of challenges. Rapid economic growth has greatly expanded China's middle class. Although most members of that middle class have remained politically acquiescent, some have become more active in civic affairs, such as environmental protection and charity work. While regime repression has effectively destroyed the political-dissident community, opposition to the regime has taken more innovative forms. Activists today challenge the CCP on issues that can connect them with ordinary people—labor rights, forced evictions, land disputes, environmental protection, and public health. The CCP's single-minded focus on GDP growth has led to a systemic degradation of the Chinese state's capacity for providing such essential public goods as health care, education, and environmental protection. Rising official corruption and an unbalanced economic-development strategy that has depressed the growth of household income and consumption have also fueled a rapid increase in income inequality.

Most of the countermeasures that the Party has taken since Tiananmen are ill suited to dealing with these issues. If the CCP is to address these challenges effectively, it will have to abandon many key components of its post-Tiananmen strategy. Economically, it needs to find a different development model that is less investment-intensive and socially costly. Politically, it may have to replace repression and cooptation with some form of political liberalization to gain a broader base of social support. But the leadership of the Hu Jintao administration has shown no sign that the Party is ready or willing to embrace such fundamental policy shifts. This means that the CCP is now at risk of falling into the trap of "adaptive ossification"—applying an outdated adaptive strategy that no longer works. The result can be, ironically, an accumulation of tensions and risks during the period of perceived authoritarian resilience. Just when the party-state has come to be viewed as resourceful and supremely skilled at hanging on, it may in fact have entered a time of stagnation and dwindling dynamism.

Is the PRC's authoritarianism resilient or decaying? The answer to this question will depend on whether the CCP's post-Tiananmen strategy of relying on economic growth and political repression continues to prove effective despite social and economic conditions that have changed drastically during the past two decades. Proponents of the resilience school are expecting the CCP's adaptive capacity to be equal to the challenges that lie ahead. Skeptics, meanwhile, are pointing to the institutional flaws inherent in any autocracy and expressing doubt that the CCP will manage to frame and implement a substantially different survival strategy that can help it to maintain its political monopoly and gain new sources of legitimacy.

I side with the skeptics in rejecting the argument that the post-1989 regime has made itself resilient through fundamental institutional and policy innovations. Instead, the principal reasons for the CCP's survival since Tiananmen have been robust economic performance and consistent political repression. Although it is true that the CCP may have improved its political tactics, its survival for the last two decades would have been unthinkable without these two critical factors—economic performance and political repression.

In the future, economic performance and political repression may remain important factors for the CCP's survival, but their contribution is likely to decline for several reasons. First, the deleterious effects of authoritarian decay will offset the positive impact of economic growth. Second, political repression is likely to be less effective in defending the regime's political monopoly, as opposition groups and figures equipped with novel methods and technologies will acquire greater capabilities to challenge and delegitimize CCP rule. Finally, the probability of splits in Party ranks will rise as the CCP's fortunes fall and the choices confronting it become harder. Ironically, those at the top of the Party's hierarchy may prove the least firmly bound to it, whether by ideological commitment or political loyalty. As regime decay sets in and "crises of order" begin to increase in frequency and severity, top players within the party-state itself will be tempted to exploit the opportunities thereby presented for boosting their own power and advantages. Open factionalism will not be far behind. Splits within the rulers' highest inner councils, we should recall, are typically a prime condition for democratic transition.

NOTES

1. For representative works on the theme of resilient authoritarianism, see Olga Kryshtanovskaya and Stephen White, "The Sovietization of Russian Politics," *Post-Soviet Affairs* 25 (October 2009): 283–309; Andrew Nathan, "China's Changing of the Guard: Authoritarian Resilience," *Journal of Democracy* 14 (January 2003): 6–17; Marsha Pripstein Posusney, "Enduring Authoritarianism: Middle East Lessons for Contemporary Theory," *Comparative Politics* 36 (January 2004): 127–38; Eva Bellin, "The Robustness of Authoritarianism in the Middle East: Exceptionalism in Comparative Perspective," *Comparative Politics* 36 (January 2004): 139–57; Jason Brownlee, "Low Tide after the Third Wave: Exploring Politics under Authoritarianism," *Comparative Politics* 34 (July 2002): 477–98; Bruce Bueno de Mesquita and Alastair Smith, "Political Survival and Endogenous Institutional Change," *Comparative Political Studies* 42 (February 2009): 167–97.

2. Chappell Lawson, "Mexico's Unfinished Transition: Democratization and Authoritarian Enclaves in Mexico," *Mexican Studies* 16 (Summer 2000): 267–87.

3. Bruce Bueno de Mesquita and George W. Downs, "Development and Democracy," *Foreign Affairs* 84 (September–October 2005): 77–86.

4. See Bellin, "Robustness of Authoritarianism in the Middle East"; and Louay Abdulbaki, "Democracy and the Re-Consolidation of Authoritarian Rule in Egypt," *Contemporary Arab Affairs* 1 (July 2008): 445–63.

5. Nathan, "Authoritarian Resilience."

6. Steve Tsang, "Consultative Leninism: China's New Political Framework," *Journal of Contemporary China* 18 (November 2009): 865–80.

7. David Shambaugh, *China's Communist Party: Atrophy and Adaptation* (Berkeley: University of California Press, 2008).

8. Dali Yang, *Remaking the Chinese Leviathan: Market Transition and the Politics of Governance in China* (Stanford: Stanford University Press, 2004).

9. See Steven Levitsky and Lucan A. Way, "Elections Without Democracy: The Rise of Competitive Authoritarianism," *Journal of Democracy* 13 (April 2002): 51–65.

10. Adam Przeworski et al., *Democracy and Development: Political Institutions and Well-Being in the World, 1950–1990* (New York: Cambridge University Press, 2000).

11. Robert J. Barro, "Democracy and Growth," *Journal of Economic Growth* 1 (March 1996): 1–27.

12. Yongshun Cai, "Power Structure and Regime Resilience: Contentious Politics in China," *British Journal of Political Science* 38 (July 2008): 411–32.

13. See Murray Scot Tanner, "Chinese Government Responses to Rising Social Unrest," Testimony presented to the U.S.-China Economic and Security Review Commission, 14 April 2005.

14. See Richard McGregor, *The Party: The Secret World of China's Communist Rulers* (New York: Harper, 2010).

15. Barry Naughton, "China's Economic Policy Today: The New State Activism," *Eurasian Geography and Economics* 52 (May–June 2011): 313–29.

16. Bill Francis, Iftekhar Hasan, and Xian Sun, "Political Connections and the Process

of Going Public: Evidence from China," *Journal of International Money and Finance* 28 (June 2009): 696–719.

17. Cheng Li, "The Chinese Communist Party: Recruiting and Controlling the New Elites," *Journal of Current Chinese Affairs* 38, no. 3 (2009): 13–33.

18. Jie Chen and Bruce J. Dickson, *Allies of the State: China's Private Entrepreneurs and Democratic Change* (Cambridge: Harvard University Press, 2010).

19. Björn Alpermann, "'Wrapped up in Cotton Wool': Political Integration of Private Entrepreneurs in Rural China," *China Journal* 56 (July 2006): 33–61.

20. Xinhua News Agency, 28 June 2010.

21. The practice of paying bribes for appointments and promotions is widespread in China. See Yan Sun, "Cadre Recruitment and Corruption: What Goes Wrong?" *Crime, Law and Social Change* 49 (January 2008): 61–79; Jiangnan Zhu, "Why Are Offices for Sale in China? A Case Study of the Office-Selling Chain in Heilongjiang Province," *Asian Survey* 48 (July–August 2008): 558–79.

22. Andrew Wedeman, "Anticorruption Campaigns and the Intensification of Corruption in China," *Journal of Contemporary China* 14 (February 2005): 93–116.

23. For a survey of the consequences of corruption in China, see Yan Sun, *Corruption and Market in Contemporary China* (Ithaca: Cornell University Press, 2004).

24. *Statistical Yearbook of China* (Beijing: Zhongguo tongjinianjian chubanshe, 2010), 756–57.

25. Xinhua News Agency, 28 June 2010.

26. For a study of the privileges enjoyed by CCP members, see Bruce J. Dickson and Maria Rost Rublee, "Membership Has Its Privileges: The Socioeconomic Characteristics of Communist Party Members in Urban China," *Comparative Political Studies* 33 (February 2000): 87–112.

27. A 2009 online survey of 21,057 new college graduates found that only half had found jobs. In 2007 and 2008, the percentage was 56 and 52 percent respectively; see *http://edu.QQ.com,* 30 July 2009.

12

THE TAIWAN FACTOR

Yun-han Chu

Yun-han Chu *is Distinguished Research Fellow at the Institute of Political Science at Academia Sinica (Taipei) and professor of political science at National Taiwan University. He is coeditor (with Tse-Kang Leng) of* Dynamics of Local Governance in China during the Reform Era *(2010). This essay originally appeared in the January 2012 issue of the* Journal of Democracy.

If the People's Republic of China (PRC) moves toward democracy, it is likely to be in no small part due to the influence of the Republic of China (ROC or Taiwan). This influence comes not only from the direct impact of Taiwanese political and social actors in promoting change, but also from Taiwan's being the first and only democracy yet to be installed in a culturally Chinese society. In addition to demonstrating the compatibility of democracy and Chinese culture, Taiwan's successful democratic transition illustrates a possible exit strategy that the Chinese Communist Party (CCP) could follow if it seeks to move away from one-party authoritarianism. It is very uncertain, of course, whether China will take this path, as the CCP is also subject to a wide range of other influences and pressures that might push it in an altogether different direction.

Geographically separated from mainland China by the Taiwan Strait, the island of Taiwan has been politically separate since the end of the Chinese Civil War in 1949, when the Nationalist Party, or Kuomintang (KMT), retreated to the island. In 1987, Beijing and Taipei lifted the mutual ban on travel and trade. Since then, the trickle of cross-Strait economic and cultural exchange has become a massive flow. By 2003, mainland China had overtaken the United States as Taiwan's most important trading partner. In 2010, Taiwanese travelers made more than six-million visits to mainland China, and there are now close to a million Taiwanese expatriates living and working in the PRC. Taiwanese companies and businessmen have invested more than US$150 billion in mainland China and have reinvested the bulk of their profits to expand their operations. With more than 70,000 business projects across the mainland, Taiwanese firms have penetrated into China's remotest corners.

The geographic proximity and cultural affinity between the two Chinese societies, along with increased economic exchange and social contacts, make Taiwan a plausible social and political model for the PRC. While most PRC residents learn about Taiwan via state-controlled and government-censored news media, many urban dwellers access Taiwan-based news and entertainment programs via satellite TV and the Internet. Some PRC-based websites copy and paste articles from Taiwan's leading newspapers, thereby circumventing the ban on those papers' sites. The reach of Taiwan-based mass media and popular culture has been intensively felt not only in the PRC's urban centers, but throughout Chinese-language cyberspace. During 2011, two of the top three media stars with the most "followers" (almost nine million) on Sina Weibo (China's version of Twitter) were from Taiwan.[1]

Taiwanese political commentators, political comedians, and talk-show hosts have become household names in China. Some of Taiwan's best-known social critics have blogs that attract large numbers of Internet users ("netizens") from mainland China. The PRC's urban middle class closely follows and discusses all the major twists and turns in Taiwanese politics. When mainland Chinese visitors come to Taiwan for the first time, they often stay up late into the night, glued to the television, watching political talk shows and satires. On the evening of Taiwan's 2008 presidential election, an estimated 200 million mainland Chinese viewers watched the ballot counting via satellite TV or the Internet. One of the hottest online discussion topics in mainland China today is about the implications of major political events in Taiwan.

Just as Taiwan's mass media have been instrumental in spreading news about Taiwan's democratic experience, many Taiwan-based social actors have contributed to China's political liberalization with information, ideas, and practical knowledge. Taiwanese NGOs working on a broad range of social issues—from the environment to consumer rights to assisting battered wives—have developed extensive networks with like-minded organizations throughout China. For instance, Taiwan-based religious groups have played a key role in reviving the traditional religions, in particular Buddhism and Taoism, on the mainland, paving the way for official recognition of the legitimacy of Buddhism by the PRC.[2] Other NGOs, meanwhile, have helped to spread the ideas and practices of civic action. In 2007, the Tzu Chi Foundation, Taiwan's largest Buddhist charitable organization, became the first overseas religious organization officially to be registered in the PRC, and it has developed the most extensive private charity network to date in mainland China.

Taiwanese entrepreneurs have also helped to lead the social transformation that has been taking place in China over the last two decades. In addition to being investors, employers, and providers of modern managerial know-how and access to international markets, they have played a significant role in shaping local governance, especially in the areas of regional planning and industrial development. There are hundreds of Taiwanese chambers of commerce across China, and they engage with local governments on a range of policy issues. Taiwanese experts and businessmen have helped to develop industrial, science, and trade zones in many provinces, including Fujian, Guangdong, Hubei, Jiangsu, and Shanghai. Taiwanese advisors and entrepreneurs have transformed Kunshan, a rural town in Jiangsu, into the world's premier production center for computer and telecommunications equipment, and all medium-sized Chinese cities aspiring to become high-tech hubs now emulate the "Kunshan model."

Taiwan has also become a critical source of know-how for developing a modern law-bound state, a prerequisite for liberal constitutionalism. PRC experts and bureaucrats have carefully scrutinized every aspect of Taiwan's legal system. Because Taiwan's legal system is based on German code law rather than on Anglo-Saxon common law, it has had greater influence than that of Hong Kong on the revamping of China's legal system. Taiwanese legal scholarship has been the greatest overseas source of ideas in China's recent efforts to overhaul its civil and criminal codes, litigation and bankruptcy procedures, and regulatory frameworks. Lee & Li, one of Taiwan's leading law firms, collaborates closely with two top Chinese law schools—Tsinghua University Law School and Zhejiang University Law School—holding a joint graduate seminar on business and law each year and sending its senior partners to both schools as guest lecturers.

Cross-Strait exchange and cooperation between academics and professionals have also increased in recent years—most notably, in the fields of finance and banking, public administration, management science, local governance, and survey research. Many former Taiwanese government officials and scholars specializing in public administration have helped the senior cadres of various Chinese ministries to better understand the mechanisms of internal control and horizontal accountability that are built into Taiwan's state bureaucracy in such areas as budgeting, auditing, administrative procedures, and civil-service exams. When the PRC's Ministry of Civil Affairs revised the rules and procedures for China's local elections, officials looked to Taiwan's election laws and procedures and sought the input of Taiwanese experts.

Taiwan's government has played only a limited role in fostering the cross-Strait engagement. In fact, under presidents Lee Teng-hui (1988–2000) and Chen Shui-bian (2000–2008), the Taiwanese government created a number of obstacles to cross-Strait exchange that impeded Taiwan-based social actors from unleashing their full potential in China. The 2008 presidential election, won by the KMT's Ma Ying-jeou, ushered in a new era of cross-Strait rapprochement. Recognizing the importance of Taiwan's soft power yet knowing that conventional public diplomacy could provoke China into taking countervailing measures, President Ma's government has refrained from taking an explicit role in coordinating cross-Strait cultural exchange. Spontaneous private initiatives enjoy more room for maneuver, as they are seemingly less offensive, intrusive, and threatening.

Similar Challenges

The leaders of the CCP have closely observed and drawn lessons from Taiwan's democratic transition and particularly from the collapse of the KMT's hegemony after its electoral debacle in 2000.[3] Many in the Party elite see strong parallels between the fate of the KMT and the possible future of the CCP. The genesis and early organizational development of the two parties were not only strikingly similar but also intimately intertwined.[4] Both emerged in the early twentieth century with the aims of rebuilding state and society out of the ashes of imperial China and saving the nation from predatory imperialist powers. Each adopted a Leninist configuration—clandestine, organized by cells, vanguard-led, presumably mass-based, and committed to the principle of democratic centralism. With self-proclaimed (and competing) historical missions—a nationalist one for the KMT and a socialist one for the CCP—both parties superimposed themselves onto the state and society, achieving institutional hegemony.

After 1949, the KMT evolved quite differently than did its communist rival. Nonetheless, the one-party authoritarian regime installed by the KMT on Taiwan conformed to many of the organizational and operational characteristics of classic Leninist parties in terms of the centralization of power in the paramount leader, the symbiosis between party and state, and the way in which the party-state penetrated society.[5] Moreover, for more than thirty years the KMT (much like the CCP) organized the society that it governed, structured the political arena in which it operated, and articulated a worldview that lent substance and coherence to its political domination.[6]

The postwar KMT regime differed in key ways from its Marxist-Leninist counterparts, however. First, the KMT was closely linked to the West ideologically, as well as through a security alliance and an economic partnership. Second, the party recognized private-property rights, supported a market economy, and partially institutionalized the rule of law. Third, the KMT attracted the support of a distinctive development coalition based on the country's export-led industrialization. Paradoxically, since China opened up to the West in the late 1970s and embarked on a path of market-oriented reform, the CCP has similarly deviated from the classic Leninist model. With its epic transition from totalitarianism to developmental authoritarianism, the CCP has drawn closer to the KMT's political trajectory.

After presiding over more than three decades of rapid economic growth and social transformation, the CCP now faces a set of five major political challenges to its hegemony similar to those faced by the KMT in the late 1970s and early 1980s. Taiwan's ruling party responded to these challenges with a series of strategic and institutional adjustments that might have appeared incremental or even cosmetic, but were in fact quite consequential. The first challenge was how to replace a bankrupt guiding ideology and discredited revolutionary mandate with a new foundation for regime legitimacy. The second-generation KMT leadership under Chiang Ching-kuo (CCK), the son of founding president Chiang Kai-shek and president himself from 1978 to 1988, shelved the mission of "recovering the mainland and reunifying China" and replaced it with "building up Taiwan" and "shared affluence" (*junfu*). The leadership worked to realize this new vision through ambitious projects for modernizing the island's infrastructure and upgrading its industrial sector. The KMT regime also boosted its legitimacy by adopting a populism anchored in a compassionate, approachable, and public-spirited leadership that exemplified the Confucian virtues of unselfishness, frugality, and self-discipline.

In recent years, the PRC has adopted similar approaches for tackling this first challenge. President Jiang Zemin's (1993–2003) vision of the "well-off society" (*xiaokang shehui*) and his successor Hu Jintao's call for a "harmonious society" and for China's "peaceful rise" represent the CCP's latest efforts to redefine the regime's *raison d'être* in a way that will resonate with a majority of the people. Other parallels to the Taiwanese approach include President Hu's adopting the populist motto of the "New Three People's Principles" (*sange weimin*),[7] and PRC premier Wen Jiabao's amiable leadership style, which is strikingly similar to that of CCK, who often visited villagers and workers and immediately rushed to areas devastated by natural disasters.

The second challenge faced by the KMT and later by the CCP was how to reestablish the party's social foundation as new social forces emerged outside its organizational scope. The KMT's second-generation leadership tried to transform it from a vanguard into a catchall party and from a revolutionary to a ruling party. The KMT vigorously recruited new members not just from its old constituencies (including mainlanders, the military, public-sector employees, teachers, and members of farmers' and fishermen's associations), but also from the expanding entrepreneurial, professional, and urban middle classes that had benefited from the state's export-led industrialization strategy. More specifically, CCK tried to rejuvenate the party's old and fading membership with younger technocrats, foreign-educated scholars, and talented native Taiwanese groomed through the party's academy. At its peak in the mid-1980s, party member-ship reached almost 18 percent of the entire adult male population.

In 2004, the CCP leadership decided to broaden its party base, just as the KMT had a few decades earlier. With a new guiding principle known as the "Three Represents," enshrined in the PRC's constitution that year, the CCP cast its lot with the beneficiaries of its economic reform. No longer a vanguard party of the "three revolutionary classes" (peasants, workers, and soldiers), the Party now claims to represent advanced pro-ductive forces, advanced culture, and the fundamental interests of the great majority of the Chinese people (the "Three Represents"). While this effort to coopt private business owners, intellectuals, and profes-sionals is often derided as window dressing, it reflects the Party's ef-forts to adapt itself to the changed economic and social environment in China.[8]

Dealing with a More Plural Society

The third challenge was how to safeguard the party's monopoly on organized social life from the encroachment of autonomous social movements and bottom-up civic organizations. As early as the 1950s, the KMT party apparatus had incorporated business and professional associations, labor unions, farmers, state employees, journalists, the intelligentsia, students, and other targeted groups into state-sponsored corporatist organizations. During the 1960s and 1970s, these organiza-tions functioned as private-sector arms of both the state bureaucracy and the party. But with the growing importance of private enterprise, the KMT had to formally recognize the economic might of the private sector. Beginning in the early 1980s, the existing business associations became functional conduits for soliciting policy input and coordinat-ing industrial policy. In particular, representatives from the "big three" national organizations—the Federation of Industry, the Federation of Commerce, and the blue-ribbon National Council of Industry and Com-merce—were elevated to the party's top echelon and granted member-ship on the KMT Central Standing Committee.

The KMT leadership adopted a two-pronged approach for dealing with the emergence of autonomous labor and environmental move-ments, consumer-rights groups, and other public-interest advocacy organizations outside the existing corporatist structure. First, it en-acted the Civic Organization Law (1989) to register and regulate these voluntary groups. And second, it elevated the bureaucracies in charge of labor affairs, the environment, and consumer protection to minis-try-level agencies and selectively coopted moderate leaders of social movements into the new ministries' advisory bodies. As the legal space and mobilizing power of grassroots NGOs expanded, the reach of the party-state into associational life necessarily receded.

The CCP today is reigning over a society undergoing epochal transformation, and as state-society relations evolve, the level of the state's
control over its citizens declines. All kinds of new actors, especially
foreign-trained professionals, have emerged in key areas such as the
state bureaucracy, the export sector, and higher education. This has
transformed the ruling establishment and created a more plural society,
along with new forms of political discourse and political participation.
It has also necessitated new legal, regulatory, and market structures.
In order to absorb newcomers into the Party and government, the CCP
has had to introduce new organizational rules—largely merit-based or
market-based—that have replaced the old hierarchical structure of the
socialist command economy.[9]

The CCP regime is also dealing with waves of social protest. Beneath the veneer of rapid economic growth and political stability, there
are myriad simmering social grievances against the government. These
stem from the widening gap between rich and poor, legal discrimination
against uprooted migrants from the countryside, corruption and abuse of
power by local officials, land expropriation without proper compensation, and environmental degradation. Like the KMT in the early 1980s,
CCP leaders have shown adaptability, and at times even tolerance, in
dealing with popular protest. The regime has adjusted its national fiscal priorities in order to mitigate the negative consequences of uneven
development, has improved the state's administrative and regulatory
capacities to deal with emerging social problems and market failures,
and has instructed local authorities to handle incidents of social unrest
carefully in order to prevent them from escalating.

The CCP regime must also contend with an explosion of associational life in China.[10] Grassroots NGOs, which typically evade regulation by
declining to comply with difficult registration procedures, have proliferated, posing a significant challenge to the party-state's once-omnipres-
ent control over organizational space. Likewise, an increasing number
of underground religious sects and even organized criminal gangs have
undermined the state's governance capacity. Nevertheless, the regime
has had some success in maintaining ties with certain key constituencies
(workers, youth, women, businessmen, scientists and engineers, and literary and art circles)—by reinvigorating existing mass organizations.
At the same time, the Party has put other segments of society, such as
underground religious movements, dissident intellectuals, human-rights
lawyers, and independent labor movements, on a tighter leash.

The most notable development is the rapid expansion of intermediary
organizations between the state and the private sector. With the Party's
approval, business and industrial associations such as the All-China
Federation of Industry and Commerce were established alongside their
government-agency counterparts and formally assimilated into the hierarchy of state-sanctioned organizations. Both private and state-owned

enterprises have become involved in a tug of war with government agencies and with each other to gain policy advantages, often setting the agenda, providing alternative options, and pressing for favored outcomes.

The fourth challenge that has confronted both the KMT and the CCP is how to contain and harness the rise of demand-driven mass media and alternative sources of information that compete with official organs. During the 1970s and early 1980s, the KMT still imposed rigorous censorship over mass media, films, and publications. It stopped issuing new licenses for newspapers and restricted the maximum number of pages that newspapers were allowed to publish. Nevertheless, the growing demand for independent news and critical opinion steadily eroded the KMT's monopoly on the supply of information and ideas. Party-owned newspapers gradually lost readers to KMT-affiliated but privately owned newspapers, which often evaded monitoring agencies in order to gain wider circulation. Independent publishers constantly played hide-and-seek games with law enforcement and found ways to turn decent profits off reprints of banned books and magazines. Despite granting some leeway to independent print media, however, the KMT still kept a tight grip on radio and television and managed to foster a broad consensus supporting orderly and incremental political change.

Similarly, the CCP today is grappling with the political consequences of the rapid commercialization and internationalization of the media in China, and like the KMT it fiercely guards its ownership of electronic media. The CCP faces a much greater challenge than did the KMT of the late twentieth century, however, as the CCP's policing power has been overwhelmed by the explosion of online social media. In December 1997, China had about 670,000 Internet users; by December 2010, this number had shot up to 457 million. As Guobin Yang put it, "[T]his communication revolution is a social revolution because the ordinary people assume an unprecedented role as agents of change."[11] Every day a torrential flow of information and opinion passes through cyberspace, as billions of messages are transmitted wirelessly. In its attempts to police China's netizens, the regime is fighting an impossible battle against time and technological innovation.

The fifth major challenge to the one-party state in both Taiwan and China has been how to deal with contending economic interests and with the rising popular demand for political representation and participation engendered by socioeconomic modernization. Of all the institutional adjustments that the KMT leadership introduced during the 1970s and early 1980s, none had a greater impact than allowing limited popular elections for national representative bodies. Under the pretext of a protracted civil war, the KMT had suspended national elections for almost a quarter-century and extended indefinitely the tenure of incumbent representatives elected on the mainland in 1948. A series of devastating diplomatic setbacks in the early 1970s compelled the KMT to introduce a limited electoral opening in 1972, which was then expanded in 1980 and again in 1989. Each time, more seats in the Legislative Yuan and the National Assembly were decided by popular election.

This historic opening did not seem risky at the time. After all, the KMT had developed a proven formula for controlling limited popular elections at the local level: The party had introduced elections at the township, city, and county levels as early as 1950 and for the Taiwan Provincial Assembly as early as 1954, seeking to incorporate the native Taiwanese elite into the party-building process and provide the authoritarian system with a modicum of democratic legitimacy. At the grassroots level, the KMT incorporated existing patron-client networks into the party structure. Within each administrative district below the provincial level, the KMT kept at least two competing local factions striving for public offices and rents. The fierce competition among these factions effectively blocked the entrance of opposition candidates into local elections. On top of this, the central leadership could enjoy an overall electoral victory that was delivered by disparate local factions. Thus for almost three decades, the KMT faced a weak and unorganized opposition consisting primarily of defiant local factions that had no national political ambitions and posed little threat to the KMT's dominant position.

Yet the gradual opening of the national representative bodies set in motion the regime's demise, as Taiwan's socioeconomic development had already made the island ripe for a democratic opening. In the second half of the 1970s, a loose coalition formed of anti-KMT independent candidates with national political aims, which came to be known as *dangwai* (literally "outside the party"). *Dangwai* candidates used the electoral process to foster popular aspirations for democratic reform and a separate Taiwanese identity. Emboldened by their electoral success in the 1977 provincial-assembly and county-magistrate elections, the *dangwai* coalition steadily moved closer to becoming a quasi-party, and in 1986 finally founded the Democratic Progressive Party (DPP) in open defiance of martial law.

Chiang Ching-kuo's decision to tolerate the formation of the DPP and his announcement a week later that he intended to lift martial law and many other longtime political bans essentially sealed the fate of the authoritarian regime. This incumbent-initiated political liberalization was intended to be the first part of a guided transition, or "democratization in installments."[12] With a multistage constitutional-reform process, the KMT managed to ensure an orderly sequencing of democratic openings and to extend the transition period to almost a decade. It was able to do so in part because the DPP lacked the capacity to impose its reform schedule and agenda on the incumbent regime. The KMT's socioeconomic-development program had been broadly based, and the party had already locked in the support of key constituencies, thereby limiting the range of mobilization and confrontation strategies available to the opposition.

As a result, the KMT was able to engineer a transition from a one-party authoritarian regime to "a one-party-dominant regime" (a system best exemplified by Liberal Democratic Party rule in Japan), making Taiwan perhaps the only case among the third-wave democracies in which a quasi-Leninist party not only survived an authoritarian breakdown but turned the crisis to its advantage. Had a political cleavage over national identity not emerged and led to an intraparty split, the KMT might possibly have kept power for much longer after the democratic transition.

The CCP leadership today recognizes that China's rapid socioeconomic transformation has already brought about a growing demand for accountability, representation, and participation. It feels compelled to lower the barriers for various kinds of stakeholders to join the policy-making process and to make the system more responsive to the increasingly diverse demands of Chinese society.[13] Before long, China's urban sector will demand further political opening. Taiwan's "democratization in installments" could be a useful model for the next generation of CCP leaders, who will be under increasing pressure to find a viable exit strategy. The island's experiences have demonstrated that it is possible for a hegemonic party to engineer a peaceful and gradual transition away from one-party authoritarianism on the basis of a successful record of economic modernization.

Although there are numerous parallels between the rocky political terrain that the second-generation KMT leaders encountered during the late 1970s and early 1980s and the delicate political situation that the CCP leadership finds itself in today, the strategic options available to the two sets of incumbent elites are not identical. Much more than the Chinese party-state, the KMT regime was severely constrained by three structural vulnerabilities. First, the KMT was vulnerable to the influence and pressure of foreign actors. Taiwan had been highly dependent on the United States for access to markets, security guarantees, and meaningful participation in international organizations such as Asia-Pacific Economic Cooperation and the World Trade Organization. Before its transition, Taiwan had been a relatively small and strategically insecure society that needed to democratize in order to regain international legitimacy and maintain the support of its most vital ally, whereas the PRC today is a rising global power and a strategic rival to the United States.[14]

Second, the ideological foundation of the KMT's postwar authoritarian order was intrinsically shaky, anchored as it was on the disputed claim that the ROC government remained the sole legitimate government representing the whole of China. The mainlander-dominated KMT leadership had been fighting an uphill battle—defending its extraconstitutional arrangements (martial law) amid a global wave of democratization, insisting on the "One China" principle when almost all major nations had shifted their diplomatic recognition to the PRC, and upholding a Chinese identity in opposition to an emerging Taiwanese identity. Toward the second half of the 1980s, it became increasingly difficult for the KMT to deny the necessity of redistributing power from the mainlander elite to native-Taiwanese citizens through democratic means.

Third, the KMT was constrained by its own ideological and institutional commitments. The ROC's 1947 Constitution embraced democratic norms and upheld the right to dissent and to open political contestation, at least in principle. The KMT had defended Taiwan's postwar authoritarian arrangements on the grounds that the country was under imminent military threat from its communist rival across the Strait. Authoritarian rule was founded on a system of extraconstitutional legal arrangements and emergency decrees that replaced or superseded many important provisions in the 1947 Constitution. The cross-Strait détente of the early 1980s began to soften the people's siege mentality, however, and undermined the regime's rationale for maintaining a state of emergency. It became increasingly difficult and costly for the KMT to suppress the popular demand for returning to constitutional "normality." Yet the KMT remained strong because of its ability to engineer electoral dominance and because it had a unified political coalition behind its development strategy, which had impressively addressed issues both of growth and equality. Therefore, the option of peacefully transforming authoritarian rule was readily available.

The CCP's Freedom of Action

The structural conditions that Hu Jintao's generation inherited are in many respects less stringent than those of Taiwan two decades ago. First of all, the CCP regime is unencumbered by the kind of ideological or institutional commitments that had constrained the KMT. The CCP has committed itself to the development of "socialist democracy," not Western-style liberal democracy. The Party's monopoly on power is still enshrined in the PRC's constitution, which precludes public contestation for power. In addition, while Chinese nationalism turned out to be a liability for the KMT elite, it remains the CCP's most valuable political asset. Hu Jintao's vision of China's peaceful rise, which addresses the popular yearning for China's preeminence on the world stage, serves as an important pillar of legitimacy for the regime.

Furthermore, in terms of ideology, Western ideas and values have yet to establish themselves, especially in the face of two strong ideological counterweights: First, the CCP's socialist legacy has been reinvigorated by the so-called New Leftists, who are critical of neoliberal economics, characterize U.S. democracy as a plutocracy, and advocate a stronger role for the state in addressing inequality, regional disparities, and the rampant corruption and injustice brought on by privatization. Second, there has been a resurgence, with the support of the regime, of Chinese cultural identity, philosophy, and worldviews—notably, Confucianism, which is presented as a compelling alternative to Western liberalism as the country retreats from communism.[15]

Of all the world's transitional societies, China—due to both its size and its history of anti-imperialist struggle—is the least susceptible to the sway of the United States or any of the industrialized democracies. On the contrary, China enjoys a growing strategic and economic capacity for creating a more hospitable external environment, especially within its own orbit of political and economic influence in Asia. Moreover, the world today is vastly different than the one in which Taiwan began its transition. The global tidal wave of democratization has receded, giving way in the developing world to what Larry Diamond has dubbed a "democratic recession."[16] Even the advanced Western democracies, long admired by China's liberal-minded intellectual elite, are steadily losing their attractiveness as the European fiscal crisis deepens and the political paralysis that has gripped Washington since 2008 lingers.

At the same time, the limited electoral pluralism that the CCP has allowed at the local level has not yet reached the critical point where it could set in motion the self-propelling dynamics of institutional evolution that Taiwan experienced. Yes, village elections have become a normal feature of grassroots political life, and they represent an important step forward in China's quest for a more accountable political system. But the impact of village-level democracy within an overarching authoritarian environment is limited.[17]

The local and national People's Congresses—the representative bodies that are entrusted with the formal power to enact laws, pass the budget, and elect top executive officials at all levels of government—are perhaps more promising. The pluralization of economic interests and deepening social stratification in China have already had an impact on elections for the local People's Congresses, as well as on the role that their deputies have played in setting policy priorities and drafting laws and regulations. China's emerging business-owning and professional class, however, is not yet the kind of autonomous social force that incubated Taiwan's political opposition, however. China's economic structure today is far more state-centric and state-dominated than was Taiwan's twenty years ago. China's state-owned enterprises still occupy the commanding heights of the economy, and most private firms rely on state actors to ease the resource constraints of China's regulated markets. In addition, state involvement in decision making at the firm level, especially in the areas of corporate governance, labor relations, and finance, remains a core feature of China's state-guided capitalism. Furthermore, a majority of private capital holders are inextricably linked to the agents and institutions of the party-state.[18] As a result, for the foreseeable future the CCP will still be able to exert its supremacy over the local and national People's Congresses and keep today's limited political pluralism in check.

There are two starkly different lessons to be drawn from Taiwan's transition experience with regard to China's democratic future. On the one hand, the eventual demise of the KMT's one-party regime suggests that developmental authoritarianism, despite its organizational capacity and adaptability, will eventually become the victim of its own success. A highly resilient developmental authoritarian regime may find ways to slow or mitigate the corrosive effect of rapid socioeconomic modernization on its political hegemony, but there is no way to stop it.

On the other hand, a well-entrenched hegemonic party such as the CCP can drag out the process of gradual political liberalization over a long period of time. This is likely to be even truer for the CCP than it was for the KMT, as China is far more powerful than was Taiwan and is thus operating in a less restrictive external environment. If the CCP can avoid an irreparable intraparty split (which often results from power struggles over succession under authoritarianism), sustain the momentum of economic growth, and adequately address China's growing regional disparities and economic polarization, it is not inconceivable that the CCP could retain its hegemonic status in China for quite a while yet.

In order to do so, the Party would have to adopt the right balance of coercion and materialist payoffs, along with a blend of populism and nationalism; it must rebuild the state's governing capacity and adapt the existing representative institutions and consultative mechanisms to accommodate an increasingly complex economy and pluralistic society; it will have to combine eclecticism and pragmatism in dealing with socioeconomic issues; and it must selectively coopt emerging social forces and constantly replenish its pool of talent. This was largely how the second-generation KMT leaders stretched out Taiwan's political-liberalization process and concomitant authoritarian weakening over almost two decades (from the early 1970s to the late 1980s) amid rapid socioeconomic change and a deterioration of its international standing.

No matter how the CCP elite sizes up its strategic options, Taiwan's democratic trajectory still constitutes a crucial and illuminating social experiment in the eyes of mainland Chinese citizens. Competing interpretations of Taiwan's democratic experience will continue to shape the parameters of public discourse on the mainland as the intellectual debate over China's political future gains momentum.

At the same time, Taiwan-based political, economic, and social actors are potentially powerful catalysts for democratic change in China. Taiwan's transformative power lies not just in its experience with economic modernization, social pluralism, and democratic development, but also in its "Chinese-ness." The people of Taiwan in their daily lives have preserved and practiced Chinese social customs; dietary habits; conceptions about the body and health; notions of life, death, fate, and the supernatural; and family-based ethics. The elements of modernity embodied in the Taiwanese model are inspirational, while the island's shared linguistic and cultural heritage with China makes Taiwan's way of life relevant, comprehensible, and accessible. On Taiwan, modernity and tradition have combined to form a vibrant and constantly evolving society.

The improvement in cross-Strait relations since March 2008 has accelerated the flow of exchange and deepened social ties between the two sides. As more and more mainland Chinese visitors and exchange students set foot on the island for the first time, Taiwan's influence on the PRC grows. If the island is to have a real impact on the mainland, however, it must first improve the overall quality of its young democracy and make its citizens proud of their political system. Over the long run, Taiwan can maximize its political leverage if its next generation of leaders is willing to engage with China about the long-term prospect of a reunified political community founded on democratic principles and rules. The tail can wag the dog only if the tail is still attached to the dog.

Maximizing the island's soft power of democracy is the best and perhaps the only strategy available to Taiwan for protecting its long-term interests. Doing so will enhance the ROC's capacity to steer the future course of cross-Strait relations despite the growing imbalance between the two sides in hard power. This strategy will also allow Taiwan to become a significant and constructive player in East Asia and on the world stage. If Taiwan fails to seize this critical opportunity, it risks becoming increasingly vulnerable, irrelevant, and marginalized.

NOTES

1. The two TV stars are Xiao (Junior) S and Tsai Kang-yung.

2. Taiwan-based Buddhist organizations were the principal sponsors of the inaugural meeting of the World Forum on Buddhism. This meeting, which was endorsed by the Chinese government and held in Hangzhou in 2006, was widely regarded as a watershed event.

3. In fact, following Taiwan's historic power rotation in 2000, the CCP's Central Party School (CPS) commissioned a special research project to determine what lessons the Party should draw from the KMT-directed political opening and its eventual fall from power. I was invited by the China Reform Forum, an offshoot of the CPS, to give a presentation in front of the CPS's vice-president and senior research staff about what caused the KMT's eventual fall from power.

4. Bruce J. Dickson, *Democratization in China and Taiwan: The Adaptability of Leninist Parties* (New York: Oxford University Press, 1997), ch. 1.

5. For the quasi-Leninist features of the postwar KMT, see Yun-han Chu, *Crafting Democracy in Taiwan* (Taipei: Institute for National Policy Research, 1992), ch. 2, and Tun-jen Cheng, "Democratizing the Quasi-Leninist Regime in Taiwan," *World Politics* 41 (July 1989): 471–99.

6. Yun-han Chu, "The Legacy of One-Party Hegemony in Taiwan," in Larry Diamond and Richard Gunther, eds., *Political Parties and Democracy* (Baltimore: Johns Hopkins University Press, 2001), 266–98.

7. On 18 March 2003, a day after assuming the presidency, Hu Jintao proposed the "New Three People's Principles" (*xin sanmin zhuyi* or *sange weimin*): to use the power for the people (*quan weimin shuoyong*), to link the sentiments to the people (*qing weimin shuoji*), and to pursue the interest of the people (*li weimin shoumo*).

8. Bruce J. Dickson, "Dilemmas for Party Adaptation: the CCP's Strategies for Survival," in Peter Hays Gries and Stanley Rosen, eds., *State and Society in 21st-Century China: Crisis, Contention, and Legitimation* (London: RoutledgeCurzon, 2004), 141–58.

9. Edward S. Steinfeld, "China's Other Revolution," *Boston Review*, July–August 2011.

10. Shaoguang Wang and Jianyu He, "Associational Revolution in China: Mapping the Landscapes," *Korea Observer* 35 (Autumn 2004): 485–533.

11. Guobin Yang, *The Power of the Internet in China: Citizen Activism Online* (New York: Columbia University Press, 2009).

12. This concept was coined by Masahiro Wakabayashi in *Taiwan—Bunretsu kokka to minshuka* [Taiwan: democratization in a divided country] (Tokyo: University of Tokyo Press, 1992), 17.

13. Andrew Mertha, "'Fragmented Authoritarianism 2.0': Political Pluralization in the Chinese Policy Process," *China Quarterly* 200 (December 2009): 995–1012.

14. Larry Diamond, "Why China's Democratic Transition Will Differ from Taiwan's," in Bruce Gilley and Larry Diamond, eds., *Political Change in China: Comparisons with Taiwan* (Boulder, Colo.: Lynne Rienner, 2008).

15. Daniel Bell, *China's New Confucianism: Politics and Everyday Life in a Changing Society* (Princeton: Princeton University Press, 2008).

16. Larry Diamond, "The Democratic Rollback: The Resurgence of the Predatory State," *Foreign Affairs* 87 (March–April 2008): 36–48.

17. Thomas P. Bernstein, "Village Democracy and Its Limits," *Asien* 99 (April 2006): 29–41.

18. Christopher A. McNally and Teresa Wright, "Sources of Social Support for China's Current Political Order: The 'Thick Embeddedness' of Private Capital Holders," *Communist and Post-Communist Studies* 43 (June 2010): 189–98.

13

FORESEEING
THE UNFORESEEABLE

Andrew J. Nathan

Andrew J. Nathan *is Class of 1919 Professor of Political Science at Columbia University and a member of the Editorial Board of the* Journal of Democracy. *His most recent book is* China's Search for Security *(coauthored with Andrew Scobell, 2012). This essay originally appeared in the January 2013 issue of the* Journal of Democracy.

The consensus is stronger than at any time since the 1989 Tiananmen crisis that the resilience of the authoritarian regime in the People's Republic of China (PRC) is approaching its limits. To be sure, this feeling in part reflects the fevered atmosphere that surrounded the PRC's once-per-decade leadership succession at the Eighteenth Party Congress of November 2012. But according to some of the best-informed observers, deep changes have been taking place that will eventually have major consequences.[1]

Regime transitions belong to that paradoxical class of events which are inevitable but not predictable. Other examples are bank runs, currency inflations, strikes, migrations, riots, and revolutions. In retrospect, such events are explainable, even overdetermined. In prospect, however, their timing and character are impossible to anticipate. Such events seem to come closer and closer but do not occur, even when all the conditions are ripe—until suddenly they do.

In analyzing what may sooner or later happen in China, it is helpful to review what we know about the dynamics of such events. Theories of "threshold models," "revolutionary bandwagons," and "informational cascades" share a logic that runs as follows:[2] Imagine that the forces arrayed against change are dominant—change fails to occur. Now imagine that the balance of forces shifts until the forces favoring and opposing change are closely balanced—a stalemate results. Suppose again, however, that the balance shifts further, so that the forces in favor of change are stronger than those against it—and yet, nothing happens.

Why is this so? Because no actor knows for sure that the balance has actually tipped. People may speculate that it has, and some may gamble by taking action. But—and this is especially likely to be so under the kinds of conditions created by authoritarianism—the information that people need to make an informed choice about whether to come out in favor of change is hidden. Quoting Václav Havel's parable of the greengrocer who hangs a proregime slogan in his shop window "because everyone does it, and because . . . if he were to refuse, there could be trouble," Timur Kuran calls this phenomenon "preference falsification." A majority, even a vast one, may want change. But when each actor weighs the benefits of stepping forth against the danger of being punished for doing so, most stay silent.

Until, that is, a triggering event occurs. Theory does not tell us what this event has to be, or why it has the magic capability to unleash change when other, similar events do not. But whatever it is, the trigger moves a new group of citizens, still a minority, to reveal publicly their dissatisfaction with the status quo.

At this point, theorists ask us to imagine that the ratio between the desire for change and the fear of repression is unevenly distributed across the population. The dissidents and "troublemakers" who always act out regardless of consequences have ideals that are greater than their fears. But they are a constant. What starts a cascade is the first group of ordinary citizens whose distaste for the status quo suddenly overwhelms their fear, or whose fear becomes less. Once that group has acted out, the group with the next largest desire-to-fear ratio perceives that support for change is more widely shared than they knew, and repression more costly and less likely. This shifts their desire-to-fear ratio enough for them to join the movement. This in turn affects the desire-to-fear ratio of those belonging to the next most fearful group, who also join.

In this way, an "informational cascade" occurs, as each shift in the publicly available information about the public mood alters the calculation of the next group. As Kuran puts it in his analysis of how the East European communist regimes collapsed in 1989, "seemingly unshakable regimes saw public sentiment turn against them with astonishing rapidity, as tiny oppositions mushroomed into crushing majorities."[3]

Something like this happened in China in 1989. The desire for change was strong and widespread, but people were afraid. Then a small group of students knelt before the Great Hall of the People on Beijing's Tiananmen Square to demand democratic reforms in the spirit of the recently deceased liberal leader Hu Yaobang. The regime failed to repress them promptly, sending a signal of indecision, and more students—the group with the next-strongest desire for change and a reduced fear of repression—came to the Square. When they in turn were not quickly punished, much of Beijing joined the demonstrations, followed by the citizens of more than three-hundred other cities around the country.

No one knows why one "collective incident" and not another is capable of sparking a cascade. Perhaps the outbreaks that have been occurring ever more frequently in China have been too small and too local. Perhaps the regime has responded too deftly with a mix of punishments and concessions.

Moreover, the PRC is not East Germany. It is not the client of a hated foreign power, but a rising state proud of its prospects. Its economy is growing faster, not more slowly, than those of its neighbors.

Three other contrasts are important. First, citizens' access to information about what other people think is not as occluded in China today as it was in the East Germany of the 1980s. The rise of the Internet and social media—as well as a more sophisticated government propaganda strategy that floods citizens with harmless information and allows a limited level of grumbling for tension relief—has allowed citizens to know a fair amount about one another's desire for change. Everyone knows about the problems of corruption, land grabs, environmental pollution, and the polarization of wealth. Citizens are widely aware that the regime itself says the political system needs to be reformed.[4] Paradoxically, however, information overload may actually *weaken* the prospects of an informational cascade, because relatively routine outbreaks of protest send a less dramatic triggering signal than would be the case where protests are more rigorously suppressed. The kind of message the regime censors especially strictly is the type that proposes a concrete blueprint for change, such as the one found in Charter 08.[5] The difficulty that people have in envisioning an alternative to CCP rule is one of the greatest obstacles to voicing a demand for change.

Second, on the repressive side of the equation, the police in China are more numerous, better funded, more technologically advanced, and more skillful in the arts of repression than in other authoritarian regimes.[6] They seem so far to have kept up—even if the race is a tight one—with the rise of the Internet and new social media, censoring messages that they view as threatening, posting messages that support the regime, and punishing messengers whom they consider particularly dangerous, such as Liu Xiaobo and Ai Weiwei. So while people may know more about one another's desire for change than they do in the classic cascade model, they also have a frightening picture of the regime's capacity and willingness to repress critics.

Third, the PRC regime as it stands today is more adaptive than other authoritarian regimes. The leadership proactively addresses the most neuralgic sources of popular dissatisfaction by making health and retirement insurance available, attacking corruption,[7] cracking down on the worst polluters, and increasing the appearance of transparency and accountability with devices such as e-government, opinion surveys, and limited-scope elections. The regime likes to *talk* about making itself more democratic, installing the rule of law, and promoting human rights. The apparent goal is to build a form of one-party rule that people will accept as responsive and legitimate. The PRC's rulers look to Singapore for an example of how that sort of thing can be done, even though conditions in that tiny and wealthy city-state are different from conditions in China.

Even if the East German scenario is unlikely to apply in its specifics, the general threshold model still might. Perhaps the key variable in the cascade model of political change is fear, and that seems to be diminishing. As it does so, the chances increase that the desire for change will find wide expression.

For change to happen, there will need to be a breakthrough moment. Do we feel that moment coming? We can imagine many possible triggers, including the bursting of the bubble economy, violent confrontations with local demonstrators, a protracted power struggle within the regime, or a natural disaster or public-health crisis that exposes scandalous incompetence or corruption. Even though the regime has recently survived several such scenarios (the Sichuan earthquake, the Western financial crisis, the tainted-milk scandal of 2008; the Wenzhou train collision of 2011; and the Bo Xilai incident of 2012), the occurrence of another could, unpredictably, lead to a different outcome. Perhaps the power-deflationary event to which this particular regime is most vulnerable is a foreign humiliation. That is one good reason why the PRC has been relatively cautious in its foreign relations—even, I would argue, as it ramps up its assertion of territorial claims in the South China and East China Seas.

No one, however, is able to say for sure whether, when, and how change will come. From where we sit, on the unpredictable side of what may turn out to be an inevitable event, fundamental change in fact continues to look unlikely. Small farmers are unhappy, but they live scattered across the countryside and far from the center of power. Worker unrest has increased, but it focuses on enterprises, not the government. Intellectuals are weak as a class, divided, and unable to spark resistance. Civil society is growing in scale and potential assertiveness, but remains under effective government surveillance and unable to form national linkages. Independent entrepreneurs have ideas and means, and show increasing initiative, but their stake in stability makes them cautious. The broad middle class sees through the regime but is busy enjoying itself. National minorities such as the Uyghurs, Tibetans, and Mongolians live on the periphery of a vast continental landmass and are culturally and socially cut off from the much larger Han Chinese majority. When it comes to defecting from the existing order, each group seems likely to look at the others and pipe up with a hearty "After you!"

So too with forces within the regime. The elite is evidently divided, to judge from the story of Bo Xilai, the high-flying, charismatic Chongqing Communist Party boss and political rising star who was undone by a scandal involving murder and corruption. Yet the damage from this embarrassing case has apparently been contained. The Party's privileges remain intact. The military and security forces seem willing to keep doing their jobs. Local-level officials, who shoulder the impossible task of mediating between state and society, might have the most to gain from a change of system. Yet if they ever tried to link up with one another to form a bloc powerful enough to effect change, the risks that they would face would be staggering. This is not 1911, when power was dispersed, the center was weak, and the premodern state of the information and military technologies then prevalent in China kept central authorities from intervening strongly in the localities.

And yet, the expectation of dramatic change persists. The very anticipation of such change, even if it is unfounded, imparts a particular type of "meta-instability" to the Chinese system today. There is a sense of impermanence that we do not find in mature political systems—no matter how troubled in other ways—whose members operate on the assumption, wise or not, that their system is lasting.

Change, if and when it happens, will not necessarily come in a form that we envision or that Chinese actors prefer. Some Chinese form of democracy is one possible outcome, but since there is no well-developed opposition movement (as there was in Taiwan before its democratic transition in the late 1980s), the prodemocracy forces would have to come from inside the ruling Communist Party. A Chinese Vladimir Putin might emerge to reconsolidate authoritarian or semiauthoritarian institutions. A crisis might even galvanize a shift from social dissatisfaction to social support for the current regime. Or China might descend into disorder, a scenario that no prodemocracy activist, Chinese or foreign, wants. What one can say, however, as we wait for history to deliver its answer, is that more and more people believe some kind of change is coming.

NOTES

1. For another excellent analysis along such lines, see Yu Liu and Dingding Chen, "Why China Will Democratize," *Washington Quarterly* 35 (Winter 2012): 41–63.

2. Seminal statements are Mark Granovetter, "Threshold Models of Collective Behavior," *American Journal of Sociology* 83 (May 1978): 1420–43; Timur Kuran, "Now Out of Never: The Element of Surprise in the East European Revolution of 1989," *World Politics* 44 (October 1991): 7–48; Susanne Lohmann, "The Dynamics of Informational Cascades: The Monday Demonstrations in Leipzig, East Germany, 1989–91," *World Politics* 47 (October 1994): 42–101.

3. Kuran, "Now Out of Never," 13.

4. On this point, among many sources, see Cheng Li, "The End of the CCP's Resilient Authoritarianism? A Tripartite Assessment of Shifting Power in China," *China Quarterly* 211 (September 2012): 599–602.

5. Jean-Philippe Béja, Fu Hualing, and Eva Pils, eds., *Liu Xiaobo, Charter 08, and the Challenges of Political Reform in China* (Hong Kong: Hong Kong University Press, 2012).

6. Xu Youyu and Hua Ze, eds., *Caoyu jingcha* [Close encounters with the Chinese PSB (Public Security Bureau)] (Hong Kong: Kaifang chubanshe, 2012).

7. Andrew Wedeman, *Double Paradox: Rapid Growth and Rising Corruption in China* (Ithaca: Cornell University Press, 2012).

II

Social Forces

14

AUTHORITARIANISM AND CONTESTATION

Zhenhua Su, Hui Zhao, and Jingkai He

Zhenhua Su is associate professor of government in the College of Public Administration, Zhejiang University, China. *Hui Zhao* is a columnist whose work appears frequently in the Chinese media. *Jingkai He* is a graduate student in government at Harvard University. This essay originally appeared in the January 2013 issue of the Journal of Democracy.

After the Chinese Communist Party (CCP) regime suppressed the Tiananmen Square protests in 1989, there emerged two starkly contrasting views regarding China's future. One held that the horrific methods the government had used in cracking down would wreck public confidence in the regime and split the CCP, probably causing it to fall swiftly from power. The other view asserted that 1989 and the purges that followed it had so completely flattened the opposition that the forces of contention in Chinese society would never rise again.

The truth lay somewhere in between. The CCP would not split or collapse, and indeed came out of 1989 in a strong position, having dealt oppositionists a massive setback. Not only had the protesters been put down, but the rapid sustained growth that began with the economic opening of 1992 gave the authoritarian regime a cushion as people focused on material gain rather than politics and the CCP drew more professionals, intellectuals, businesspeople, and other elites into its ranks. Economic growth, moreover, gave the party-state more resources to spend on both welfare and its many agencies of social surveillance and control. In these ways, the CCP displayed itself as a model of what Andrew J. Nathan has called "authoritarian resilience."[1]

Yet the opposition, however far down it may have been pushed by the weight of repression, never allowed itself to be fully quelled. In 1998, within a decade of Tiananmen, prodemocracy activists would try to form a party. The regime crushed them in short order, but within two years dissident intellectuals began giving protest a voice by means of online petitions. These efforts scored their most famous achievement in December 2008, when Charter 08 (*www.charter08.com*) was released. After the arrest of its leading sponsor, literary critic and later Nobel Peace Prize laureate Liu Xiaobo, more people joined. So the opposition is far from dead, even if it remains weak.

At the same time, what the regime calls "mass incidents" have been on the rise. Well-known episodes include the 2008 riots over police misconduct in Weng'an; the unrest that followed the exposure of CCP corruption in Shishou in 2009; and a months-long protest of vote-rigging, local corruption, and land seizures in Wukan during 2011 and 2012. These cases show that the hold the authorities' have on society is not as strong as is often thought. Public demonstrations with unmistakably political overtones have also drawn wide attention. These have included the successful 2007 protests against the building of a chemical plant in Xiamen; the 2009 rallies against a proposed waste-burning plant in Guangzhou; demonstrations aimed at Peking University psychologist Sun Dongdong for his support of the notion that people who petition officials are usually mentally ill and may merit detention; and gatherings outside courthouses during high-profile trials of figures such as Liu Xiaobo, the muckraking social activist Tan Zuoren, tainted-milk whistleblower Zhao Lianhai, and three Fujian Province "netizens" who had posted online evidence that police had raped and murdered a young girl. Additionally, small-scale and limited acts of "ordinary resistance" have been on the upswing since the 1990s,[2] as have land disputes and protests against forced demolitions.[3]

Examples such as these suggest that, despite the appearance of tight regime control, the forces of contention are alive and well more than two decades after Tiananmen. Although no dissident political movement capable of openly defying state repression has so far appeared, it seems fair to say that the regime's ability to hold society down is growing weaker.

The CCP has ruled China continuously since 1949 by maintaining conformity within its own ranks, staying in charge of key resources, absorbing nascent elites, and efficiently controlling society. The Tiananmen protests of 1989 had been set in train eleven years earlier, when China emerged from two years of turbulence following the 1976 death of Mao Zedong. In 1978, Deng Xiaoping began a shift from a holistic ideology of total control to a more relaxed stance meant to foster economic growth and social development. Although conditions were still far from ideal, civil society began to flourish and to cultivate the capacity for protest and opposition that eventually materialized in Beijing's Tiananmen Square at the end of the 1980s.

As bloody and thorough as the 1989 crackdown was, it did not completely reverse the process of social opening that the party-state had initiated. Deng's famous tour of southern China in 1992 marked the post-

Tiananmen CCP's return to the course that the Party had set back in the 1980s of trying to blend increased openness with continued control. On the one hand, the CCP still owned the key resources, actively absorbed rising credentialed elites, dominated (or tried to dominate) society, and revealed that it could adapt to new situations. On the other hand, wealth flowed into and from the private sector in ways that both required and allowed ever more people to leave behind their collective work units and communes. The new and more market-friendly economic arrangements spurred huge demands for mobile and technically skilled professionals and freelance workers. Their mode of living could no longer be the closely watched and even barracks-like existence that for decades had been associated with the PRC. The basic change has been this: The individual is no longer under the complete control of a state whose dominance has been eroding in a least four ways:

1) The coherence, ideological and otherwise, of the ruling elite is weakening. This elite can now be better described as a mix of interests rather than a unity. The CCP now features within its ranks a variety of ideas and interests that would stun Chairman Mao. Some are simply expressions of localism. The PRC's revenue-sharing system, adopted in 1994, divides tax proceeds between the center and the provinces. This naturally gives the latter more leeway to make their own decisions on various matters—and at times to passively reject unwelcome decisions coming from Beijing. Moreover, certain of the central government's resource-management arms (including the agencies in charge of electricity, telecommunications, and petroleum) have effectively monopolized their sectors as state-owned enterprises (SOEs) and begun pursuing their own interests. Lastly, the party-state bureaucracy is no longer informed by Marxism, Maoism, or any other "-ism" except careerism. Corruption is widespread, and many officials focus on nothing but the acquisition of wealth and social status. Certainly few concern themselves with upholding the law or disinterestedly serving the public.

2) The share of China's economic and social resources under direct CCP control has been shrinking year by year since 1978. It is true that since 2003 the state—despite widespread criticism—has expanded at the expense of the private sector, but not by enough to reverse the overall trend. The CCP regime has long relied on economic performance to bolster its legitimacy, but the SOEs, though richly supplied with resources, are all too often low-productivity operations that depend for survival on fiscal subsidies, massive loans from state banks, and monopolistic pricing. They contribute little to the PRC's bottom line, and indeed have forced a reliance on foreign and private capital to a degree that has curtailed the state's discretionary powers and even softened its iron fist. Then too, the state's control of social resources may not match its control of economic resources. For instance, the *China Statistical Yearbook* for

2008 notes that in 2007, SOEs controlled 44.8 percent of the national capital but employed only 21.8 percent of China's urban population.

3) The CCP is losing its capacity to absorb rising new social elites. The CCP cannot survive as China's sole ruling force unless it brings newly important social groups (such as educated professionals) into its ranks. Its main way of doing this has been to give people jobs. But that avenue is closing. The institutions that are under CCP control—party and state administrations, SOEs, and the bureaucracies that oversee culture, education, scientific research, and health services, for example—are already overstaffed. Each year, very few fresh college graduates manage to become civil servants. Nor is this to say that everyone wants a job with the party-state: As the market-based economy has grown, more members of elite groups (especially if they are younger) have preferred to seek lucrative work in the private sector.

4) The CCP can no longer control society the way it used to. Prior to the 1978 reforms, the vast majority of China's populace lived and worked under the direct control of communes, labor units, or village and neighborhood committees. Social control in that era relied heavily on decrees from the CCP leadership. As the old systems governing residence and employment have loosened, more people have slipped outside the orbit of direct Party control. In recent decades, hundreds of millions of China's 1.2 billion citizens have left the permanent addresses under which they are registered in order to live and toil elsewhere. The party-state's watertight control of society has been a thing of the past since the late 1980s; the post-Tiananmen crackdown could not and did not restore it.

The Limits of "Stability Maintenance"

In the organization-chart sense, social control in the PRC before 1978 was the duty of law-enforcement agencies and other armed forces maintained by the state; various departments of government and the CCP (the Ministry of Culture, the Communist Party propaganda office, and so on); and mass organizations or committees for workers, women, young people, and neighborhood or village residents. But what really held it together was the party-state's domination of politics, the economy, society, and culture, along with a harsh household-registration system that segregated city and country dwellers and prevented citizens from moving around freely.

Deng's reforms allowed society to make major gains vis-à-vis the state, and have left only the skeleton of the classic social-control system still standing. Social control currently, therefore, has gone from wholesale to retail: It is a matter of the CCP regime focusing special attention on particular individuals and organizations deemed threats to stability. The arms of the party-state dedicated to "stability maintenance" (*weiwen*) aim to "nip all factors of instability in the bud." This means controlling (if need be through police repression) the activities of dissidents; helping local governments to "manage" (which sometimes means block) citizens' petitions;[4] and making sure that officials at all levels are held accountable for doing their part to maintain stability.

Most stability-maintenance measures are taken after the fact, and consist, in effect, of punishments for various transgressions. Authorities will at times take before-the-fact or "precautionary" measures if the need seems urgent, even though under the party-state's own laws meting out punishment for acts that have not yet been committed is clearly illegal. Advocates of the authoritarian-resilience thesis like to point out that since 1989 the regime has not shied away from using heavy-handed precautionary measures to enforce stability. Among its other problems, however, this whole effort is very expensive: In 2009, China spent almost as much on domestic-order maintenance as it did on military defense.[5]

The violent post-Tiananmen crackdown plunged China into a miasma of fear, and many people abandoned any idea of facing the regime in a posture of contention. Almost a quarter-century later, that paralyzing fear has faded. Today, no one under 24—or in other words, about 513 million of China's 1.3 billion people—has any memory of 1989. Ironically, the regime's own efforts to stifle discussion of what happened during and shortly after that year—like its efforts to throw a veil of silence over its more recent crackdowns on movements such as Falun Gong—have helped to dispel fear by dispelling memory. Less memory means less fear, and less fear means more contention.

Another problem for the CCP regime is that precautionary enforcement conflicts with the rule of law, which the regime has been trying to promote. In recent years, precautions against dissidents and petition groups have included violence, illegal searches and imprisonment, house arrest, stalking, and summoning for interrogations, often in blatant violation of current Chinese law. Such steps have been known to backfire, moreover, by rallying public sympathy to the side of their targets. The lack of underlying legal justification, meanwhile, has left security officials feeling so anxious that in many cases they do little more than go through the motions of bringing the state's weight to bear against the forces of contention. The police nowadays, for instance, not uncommonly "invite" activists whom they are watching to drop by headquarters to "drink tea"—a process meant to show that potential troublemakers have been noted, scrutinized, and warned by the state. Nowadays, many netizens enjoy posting online about their own "tea drinking" experiences, treating their receipt of such an "invitation" from authorities as an honor and a point of pride. Thus has a measure meant to intimidate become instead an incentive for activism.

As the number of citizens engaging in contentions grows, even punishment is failing to achieve its anticipated effect. People know that pen-
alties are mainly reserved for high-profile leaders such as Liu Xiaobo,
Guo Feixiong, and Hu Jia.[6] Followers face much less risk, and there are
supportive social networks to assist those who do run seriously afoul
of the authorities. Even more than "drinking tea," being singled out for
actual repression has become an honor and even a means to accumulate
political capital, so more people are willing to chance it.

Just two years after the government's 2006 repression of hunger-
strike protesters came the even larger and more influential Charter 08
movement. The regime sentenced its most famous member, Liu Xiaobo,
to eleven years in jail, but the forces of contention showed no sign of
stalling. In 2011 and early 2012, dozens of people tried to visit the blind
lawyer and rights defender Chen Guangcheng (since exiled) during his
house arrest in Shandong Province. All would-be visitors—including
the actor Christian Bale, who made world news by filming himself being
confronted by plainclothes security agents—met with official harassment and in some cases physical attacks. No one actually got through
the cordon to meet with Chen before he left China in May 2012, but
people refused to be intimidated and kept trying. The whole episode
underlines the limits of state repression and hence of the authoritarian-
resilience thesis.

But exposing the limits of what repression can do is not the same
as forming an organized political opposition capable of systematically
confronting the regime. What are the prospects that such an opposition
will emerge?

New Society, New Forces

As one would expect given China's status as a modernizing, urban-
izing country with a dynamic economy based on markets and strong involvement in globalization, the country has become a place where conditions favor the emergence of organized groups devoted to contending
against an authoritarian state. The forces of contention are gathering and
beginning to point themselves in the direction of political protest. The
signs of the times are clear:

1) The public is gradually putting aside political apathy and fear.
For a time after the repression of 1989 and the turn to markets and
limited openness in the early 1990s, political indifference and a pre-
occupation with moneymaking prevailed throughout Chinese society.
But in recent years, rights-consciousness has risen as citizens become
increasingly discontented with the actions of an exploitative state, be
they direct (forcible housing demolitions) or indirect (growing income
inequality, rampant corruption, and environmental pollution).[7] People
want to know how the government is affecting them, including wheth-

er it is effectively administering public services and honestly providing promised benefits.

The CCP's own promotion of nationalist feelings has focused people on politics. Those born in the 1980s and 1990s have reached adulthood without memories of personal political trauma or a fearsome state bureaucracy holding sway over them.

2) There are now market-based media outlets to provide an alternative to the old state-run media. In the 1990s, the old wall of prohibition around news, commentary, and social communication in general began to crack. Once completely banned, media not run by the state now serve a more diverse society with a growing appetite for all things cultural, recreational, and informational. Although censorship continues, profit-seeking "marketized media" organs (state-owned but not tightly state-run) increasingly adapt their content to the tastes, preferences, and values of the public. Opinion columnists and commentators often examine local officials, national policies, and various social phenomena with critical eyes. There is live television news and in-depth coverage of current issues, including matters that the authorities would prefer to see undiscussed. Burgeoning Internet use likewise spurs portions of the "marketized media"—staffed by people who do not identify with the institutions of the party-state but think of themselves as independent professionals—to grow bolder in presenting controversial viewpoints and reports. China's "marketized media" outlets still belong to the state, but they nonetheless provide a more open platform for speech that departs from the official line. Count them as another reason why the CCP regime has less control than it used to over what Chinese people are reading, thinking, and saying.

3) The rule of law and the defense of rights are growing in prestige and prominence. After 1978, the CCP's market-friendly reforms led to the disintegration of the communes and the system of "official affiliations" that once placed most of the populace under direct state control. In the 1990s, hundreds of millions of migrating workers and businesspeople further cemented such change. Economic development has produced whole new social classes in the form of tens of millions of entrepreneurs, small-business owners, freelancers, and white-collar workers. The state's original direct-control system could not keep up. The CCP regime has had little choice but to turn to the rule of law as one of its main methods for managing society and as a major supplement to authoritarian tactics. Thus promotion of law-based rule became official state policy in the late 1990s.

For the party-state, the strengthening of the rule of law is a two-edged sword. It aids in the task of social control, but it also sets up protections for common people that the authorities are not used to worrying about. In pursuit of rapid economic growth, the Chinese state often seizes key resources at below-market prices and suppresses

stakeholder groups that might object. The ranks of the discontented
are not small. They include laid-off SOE workers who receive scanty
one-time severance payments based on their seniority; peasants whose
land is seized without adequate compensation; property owners rendered homeless when the government flattens their houses to make
way for a railway or a dam; and the like.[8] Abuses of power by all levels
of government, as well as the state's repression of religious groups,
have prompted large numbers of people to join the ranks of *shangfang*
(petition and appeal) movements. In response to having their interests
trampled, promised benefits taken away, and voices stifled, people
have been turning to new methods of "rightful resistance,"[9] making
use of the current legal system as well as more traditional measures
such as personal letters of petition. The new term *weiquan* (rights defense) has grown out of this movement.[10]

The rights-defense movement expresses itself in the form of individuals' appeals on behalf of their personal interests, but taken as a
whole it involves impressive numbers of citizens who span various
social classes and speak for a wide array of concerns. The movement has not only given birth to a legal group dedicated to defending
rights, but has turned ordinary people who were once concerned only
with their own narrow interests into activists who will fight to defend
rights more generally. Intellectuals, activists from nongovernmental
organizations, and media types have also become involved.

True, there is as yet no single unified rights-defense organization,
but many *weiquan* "micro-ecologies" have germinated and are showing potential. The typical rights-defense micro-ecology brings together petitioners with lawyers (who often work for free), journalists, and
NGO activists. Political dissidents can appear among petitioners, as
can members of influential elites, whose presence is a particular boon
to mobilization. In these loose groups, members reach consensus on
values and typically do much of their communicating and mobilizing via interpersonal networks and the Internet. In recent years, the
"gatherings" held to protest Sun Dongdong's speeches or to draw attention to the legal plight of the three Fujian Province netizens have
displayed the micro-ecological systems' growing capacity for organizing and mobilizing dissent.

*4) Despite the CCP's harsh control efforts, political dissidence en-
dures.* The Tiananmen crackdown created a group of dissidents who
have kept the flame burning for almost a quarter-century now. Some
intellectuals have joined their ranks through self-reflection, as have others who have found themselves on the wrong side of an abusive state
and wish to see past injustices righted and future injustices prevented.
The Internet has inspired people to become dissidents or at least to sym-
pathize with dissidents. Then there are those on the receiving end of the
CCP's religious persecution. All these dissidents lack identifiable orga-

nizations, but they make political claims. They keep in constant contact with one another and stay involved in public affairs and rights-defense activities. When incidents occur, they issue public position statements. They make the case for reforms of various kinds and sponsor movements such as Charter 08. Dissidents are not vast in number, but some can boast of elite credentials and some even possess charismatic leadership qualities. Liu Xiaobo's Nobel Peace Prize has brought them intense international interest and attention. The regime regards political dissidents as the most formidable opposition force it faces, and has tightened its control by subjecting many active dissidents to special monitoring and inspection.

5) Second-generation migrant workers now form a more restive labor force. Labor movements are not new in China. Ching Kwan Lee's work on Chinese labor protest before 2000 suggests that the rise of labor movements is caused by worker resentment of state cadres, managers, and capitalists, and facilitated by new political and institutional spaces conducive to expressions of personal interests and resentment.[11] Since 2009, major strikes at Honda plants and a series of worker suicides at the massive Foxconn Electronics complex in Guangdong Province near Hong Kong have drawn considerable public scrutiny.

The labor force—and with it labor activism—today is dominated by second-generation internal-migrant workers born in the 1980s and 1990s. They have higher expectations regarding individual rights than their parents had. They work not only to feed their families, but to live fulfilling lives. They grew up in cities, but officially still count as rural residents and so often are left out of civic welfare programs and pension arrangements. They live at the harsh intersection where the conditions required for China's continued rapid economic growth and global competitiveness—ample amounts of low-paid, high-productivity labor—meet dreams of a better life. The realities of long hours working for meager pay in difficult and even dangerous conditions will continually fuel the Chinese labor movement. The impetus for this movement is not political, but as stability-prizing local governments put heavy pressure on restive workers, the conflicts are turning from matters of employee versus employer to showdowns that pit workers squarely against the authoritarian CCP regime.

A Network of Contention Emerges

Under current authoritarian conditions, overt contentious activities remain scattered. But various contentious forces have managed to stay connected both online and on the ground, thereby establishing a contentious network with explicitly political views. Within this network, contention is no longer about the concerns merely of individuals or single groups, but draws on the extended network for support. Contemporary

contention in Chinese society displays the following unique characteristics:

*1) Coalitions are built via the Internet and interpersonal mobiliza-
tion.* The Internet, introduced to the Chinese public in the late 1990s,
now has more than 400 million Chinese users. It has multiplied opportunities for expression free of *ex ante* censorship, and has blunted the
regime's use of ostracism and social isolation against citizens deemed
to be "dangerous." The freedom of the online world has emboldened the
"marketized media" to engage in freer reportage and comment as well.
In the last ten years, the Internet has become the cutting-edge platform
for news and information, the medium for the most incisive and auda-
cious speech, and also the most effective tool for mobilization. Since
2009, the tools of choice for talking about and mobilizing contention
have been Twitter and Sina Weibo (a microblogging service similar to
Twitter), neither of which the state has so far been able to censor effectively in real time.

Political dissidents, rights defenders, and other social activists have
been going online to communicate in real time since 2000, when politicized online signature movements began to proliferate.[12] Statements are
drafted and spread online; anyone can sign, either directly or by sending
information to managed emails for listing. The topics at first were particular incidents, but now all kinds of politically restricted subjects are
raised. In 2004, an appeal for accountability in the matter of the 1989
Tiananmen crackdown drew more than a hundred intellectuals to affix
their online signatures. Four years later came Charter 08, which drew
thousands of signatures and made worldwide headlines, timed as it was
to fall within the same year as the Beijing Olympics.

In China as elsewhere, many people communicate and become ac-
quainted online, and these interactions can have a political cast. Those
active in the causes of dissent and organized contention like to bond, as
the online acronym goes, IRL ("in real life") as well, and do so through
meals, seminars, lectures, and other *weiguan* (crowd gatherings). In
April and August 2010, artist and activist Ai Weiwei hosted dinners
in Hangzhou and Shanghai, respectively. The first drew nearly three-
hundred people and the second drew a thousand. More than half were
petitioners. In 2009, activists from all over China organized "tours" of
Hubei Province's Badong County out of concern over possible state
manipulation of a local murder case in which the victim was an official. (With formal rallies and demonstrations normally banned, activists
opted to go as tourists.) This was the first instance of a collective act of
contention organized entirely by netizens.

Anxious not to let the freedom of the Internet grow unchecked, the
regime has adopted measures such as the infamous Great Firewall of
China to prevent activists from accessing sensitive material that could
be used to promote political and religious dissidence. Widely available

proxy software, however, allows many to "climb over the wall" and view blocked content. Most Chinese netizens may not be actively circumventing censorship on a regular basis, but they receive much freer access to expression and information online than has ever been possible before. The Internet has made the regime's desire to control what its citizens may learn or say impossible to fulfill.

Through their daily doings and online interactions, as well as through shared participation in specific rights-defense movements, contentious activists become well known to one another. Circles of acquaintance expand, groups grow, and collective actions become easier to mobilize through personal networks. Influential cases include the 16 April 2010 gathering,[13] the 16 June 2010 gathering,[14] and the May 2009 seminar organized by nineteen intellectuals in memory of the twentieth anniversary of the 4 June 1989 movement.

Study of the professional and regional backgrounds of Charter 08 signatories reveals that people from many walks of life are willing to openly express their political opinions and bear the consequences. The signers came together through various interpersonal networks with clear and relatively similar political claims and identities—an indicator that a network of social contention is emerging to challenge authoritarianism in China.

2) The forces of contention are becoming less reactive and more proactive. Rapid economic growth and the rise of markets have brought increased income inequality. Many citizens feel exploited in both relative and absolute terms, and a growing number resent the government. The CCP has not been able to alleviate their discontent, and the resentment grows seemingly unchecked. Flare-ups occur in the form of widely covered incidents such as the ones mentioned earlier that took place at Shishou, Weng'an, and Wukan. These protests involved many people whose personal interests were not directly at stake. They were involving themselves proactively by identifying with and supporting movements whose principles they affirmed.

3) A strong economy is not enough to stop contention from breaking out. The CCP regime has overseen some of the world's most impressive rates of economic growth during the past several decades, but none of that translates into political legitimacy.[15] For one thing, even in the area of economics alone, the CCP must keep outdoing itself: No matter how rapidly growth occurs, people's demands and expectations will outstrip it. Yet woe to the regime should economic progress stall: Discontent aimed directly at the government would quickly escalate until it gave rise to a massive proactive contention that the forces of order would find themselves hard-pressed to contain.

4) Defense of economic rights leads to political contention. Contentions focused on the defense of rights often begin when economic interests are violated, and generally aim to influence local governments. But when the petition route fails and appeals to the rule of law do not avail, rights defenders must change tactics and turn to the cause of political reform if they wish to safeguard their economic rights. Meanwhile, proactive contentions making direct political claims are also growing under the influence of Charter 08 and the 16 April 2010 gathering.

The authoritarian regime that rules China has nearly exhausted all the stability-maintenance measures at its command. The measures themselves are declining in effectiveness yet rising in cost. Collective contentions continue to increase as the forces of contention coalesce. The government can manage small-scale social movements led by middle-class urbanites, but beyond that it is mostly at sea and unable to adapt its response mechanisms to deal with large-scale contentions.

The Politics of Contention

We do not pretend to own a crystal ball and will venture no firm prediction as to whether China is likely to become democratic or not. Yet we do propose that the key to understanding China's near-term political future is to grasp the dynamic between the authoritarian state and civil society. The regime has been successful so far at using direct control to stunt the growth of opposition groups. Yet as the regime's control weakens while emerging networks of contention become stronger, how will the dynamic evolve?

First and foremost, the state's continuing will and ability to wield the stick of repression remain the most important factors. Activists can be (and have been) willing to stand against the regime's punishments and deterrents, but the scale and intensity of repression matter. The recent upheavals in the Arab world have made the CCP highly alert to the danger of possible democratic diffusion effects. The security apparatus is more thoroughly institutionalized, and its organization and practices have been overhauled to improve coordination among its various departments. Were the regime to opt for more selective and severe repressive tools (as in some cases it already has), dissidents could face higher hurdles as they seek to organize contentions.

With adequate funds and an increasingly sophisticated network of security officials, China does not seem to suffer from any lack of means to enforce repression. Yet the regime's resolve to repress may become complicated by the increasing political prominence of the security apparatus. In 2002, the CCP placed the PRC's Ministry of Public Security (China's national police) under a member of the CCP Politburo. One seat on the powerful Politburo Standing Committee had also been assigned to the national head of internal security (the secretary of the CCP's Central Commission for Political and Legal Affairs). At the local level, police chiefs have received higher administrative ranks and in many cases head the entire local security apparatus.

Has the increased political power that security cadres now enjoy, not to mention the concentration of so much authority in the hands of the police, made the "strongmen" the most potent force within the ruling party? The fall amid scandal in 2012 of Bo Xilai, a powerful Politburo member from Chongqing whose trademark policy, or so he claimed, was using that city's police force to fight organized crime, may hint that his fellow CCP higher-ups are now worried about keeping the state-security establishment under control. Before the opening of the Eighteenth Party Congress in early November 2012, most local governments rearranged their internal lines of authority so that senior judicial-branch officials (procurators-general and court presidents) now stand on the same level as the police chief.

In the newly formed CCP leadership, chosen at the Eighteenth Party Congress in November 2012, the rank of internal-security leader has been demoted to general Politburo-member status (instead of going to a member of the Politburo's more elite Standing Committee). Moreover, the Central Party Secretariat, the political body in charge of coordinating CCP affairs, now includes no figure from the security sector. This should have the effect of making the security apparatus—placed as it now is under a larger array of decision makers—less arbitrary and less likely to launch bouts of violent repression.

Last but not least, the emerging network of contention will play its own role, despite the state's strong repressive machine. This network's importance lies in its decentralization and "flatness." The popularity of Sina Weibo has made it even easier for citizens to form contentious groups and otherwise spontaneously organize themselves. Leaders matter less since people no longer need political entrepreneurs to mobilize and connect them; the contention networks (whether online or interpersonal) can do that. This means that the state will not be able to shut down contentious networks by striking at a handful of central figures. Ordinary members (in a sense, everyone in a flat network is an "ordinary" member) will remain aware of and available for contentions, and arresting a few people will not change that. Without obvious targets for repression that it can single out, the security apparatus will be of less use. Or so it would seem, at any rate. The authoritarian regime that rules China has shown itself highly adaptable in the past, and perhaps its police officials will come up with new ways to adapt to the flat-network and speed-of-Twitter problems as well.

The relationship between the CCP regime and China's networks devoted to democratic contention will continue to be a high-powered standoff. The state apparatus is slipping a bit but still strong, while civil society groups have limited power but greater organizational flexibility and the will to make persistent political demands. When resilient authoritarian state meets resilient contention network, who will rise most effectively to the challenge: a new party-state leadership or an ever-evolving and dynamic Chinese society?

NOTES

The authors thank Dingxin Zhao and Dali Yang of the University of Chicago for many valuable insights. They also thank Yu Xunda of Zhejiang University for reviewing and commenting on earlier drafts. Zhenhua Su recognizes the University of Chicago Political Science Department for aiding him in the revision of an earlier version of this essay when he was a visiting scholar in 2010–11.

1. Andrew J. Nathan, "China's Changing of the Guard: Authoritarian Resilience," *Journal of Democracy* 14 (January 2003): 6–17.

2. Thomas Lum, *Problems of Democratization in China* (New York: Garland, 2000); Merle Goldman, *From Comrade to Citizen: The Struggle for Political Rights in China* (Cambridge: Harvard University Press, 2005).

3. Yongshun Cai, "Civil Resistance and Rule of Law in China: The Defense of Home-owners' Rights," in Elizabeth J. Perry and Merle Goldman, eds., *Grassroots Political Reform in Contemporary China* (Cambridge: Harvard University Press, 2007), 174–95.

4. Petitioning is the administrative system for hearing complaints and grievances from individuals in China. Under the system, the State Bureau for Letters and Calls and its local branches are commissioned to receive letters, calls, and visits from individuals or groups bearing suggestions, complaints, or grievances. Staffers are then supposed to forward these appeals to the appropriate departments and monitor the progress that is being made to settle them, which progress the staffers are then supposed to report to the filing parties. The Letters and Calls Bureau is often the last legal resort that people have to resolve their conflicts with the government, and it has attracted tens of millions of active petitioners.

5. *Shehui Kexu Bao*, 27 May 2010.

6. Guo Feixiong is a social activist who regularly offers legal assistance to rights-defending petitioners. He was detained and tortured from 2006 to 2007, and in November of the latter year received a five-year jail term. Hu Jia is a Chinese activist and dissident who has focused on the Chinese democracy movement, environmentalism, and HIV/AIDS prevention. Hu was detained after Christmas 2007 and sentenced to three-and-a-half years in jail the following spring.

7. Merle Goldman, *From Comrade to Citizen.*

8. David Zweig, "To the Courts or to the Barricades? Can New Political Institutions Manage Rural Conflict?" in Elizabeth J. Perry and Mark Selden, eds., *Chinese Society: Change, Conflict and Resistance,* 2nd ed. (London: RoutledgeCurzon, 2003), 132.

9. Kevin J. O'Brien and Lianjiang Li, *Rightful Resistance in Rural China* (Cambridge: Cambridge University Press, 2006).

10. Jean-Philippe Béja, "China Since Tiananmen: The Massacre's Long Shadow," *Journal of Democracy* 20 (July 2009): 5–16.

11. Ching Kwan Lee, "Pathways of Labor Insurgency," in Perry and Selden, *Chinese Society,* 71.

12. Béja, "The Massacre's Long Shadow."

13. On 16 April 2010, many contention activists from across China gathered around the courthouse of Mawei District, Fuzhou City, the capital of Fujian Province, where the three netizens were being tried. These activists gave out leaflets and peacefully demonstrated to protest the trial. The campaign drew much online coverage.

14. On 16 June 2010, rights-defending activist and lawyer Ni Yulan, who had recently been released after serving two years in jail for protesting the state's eminent-domain seizure of her house, was again detained by police while she was attending rallies with other activists. The activists on the scene, along with others mobilized via Twitter, quickly gathered around the Donghuamen police station where Ni was being detained, and confronted the police while protesting.

15. Zhao Dingxin, *Guojia Shehui Guanxi Yu Bajiu Beijing Xueyun* [State-society relations and the 1989 Beijing student movement] (Hong Kong: Chinese University of Hong Kong Press, 2010).

15

RURAL PROTEST

Kevin J. O'Brien

Kevin J. O'Brien *is Alann P. Bedford Professor of Asian Studies and Political Science at the University of California, Berkeley. His books include, with Lianjiang Li,* Rightful Resistance in Rural China *(2006), and an edited volume,* Popular Protest in China *(2008). This essay originally appeared in the July 2009 issue of the* Journal of Democracy.

China's farmers did not play a large part in the 1989 protests, except as a presumed backstop of support for the regime, which Deng Xiaoping saw fit to invoke on several occasions.[1] Since then, however, villagers have launched their share of the hundreds of "mass incidents" (*quntixing shijian*) that occur every day. Whether submitting respectful petitions detailing cadre corruption, mounting rightful resistance against illegal fees, or even engaging in violent clashes over land grabs, rural dwellers have shown a willingness to take stronger issue with the powerful than might have been expected in the repressive months following 4 June 1989.

This unrest has been triggered in part by a factor familiar to students of political contention: opportunity. Chinese villagers, like the aggrieved anywhere, respond to openings or perceived openings. At a time when the relaxation of official controls over political expression and activity has been fitful and uneven, rural folk have been among the biggest beneficiaries of loosening. Early in the reform period, the end of institutionalized "class struggle" and communes left villagers less fearful and less dependent on local leaders. More recently, marketization and increased mobility have afforded rural people more room in which to maneuver, while grassroots elections and legal reforms have provided both new abuses to protest and more safeguards against retaliation. Although many types of claims are still off-limits and Beijing remains unyielding in its hostility to Falun Gong believers, "separatists" in Tibet and Xinjiang, and anyone who would dare to organize a new political party, top leaders periodically signal that those grievances about which villagers care the most are indeed legitimate. These include concerns related to corruption, selective law enforcement, and people's livelihoods.

But political relaxation and socioeconomic change are not wholly responsible for the upsurge in rural contention. Savvy "peasant leaders" (*nongmin lingxiu*) have been quick to seize opportunities, and in some instances have expanded the size of openings, helping to nudge once-forbidden types of claims into the realm of the acceptable. Chronic resistance is thus partly a product of decisions made by skilled protest organizers who know how to shape claims, mobilize followers, orchestrate acts of defiance, and (occasionally) mount actions that transcend the borders of a single community. In the face of long odds, these activists have regularly tested the truth of the saying, "A big disturbance produces a big result, a small disturbance produces a small result, and no disturbance produces no result." While many have paid a price for their boldness—beatings, detention, and imprisonment remain common—others have continued to spearhead contention, often at the urging of community members who praise such protest leaders as "heroes" (*yingxiong*) if they persist, but decry them as "cowards" (*danxiaogui*) or even "traitors" (*pantu*) if they back down.[2]

How they are perceived by their followers and interested onlookers is critical for protest organizers. Popular support makes it easier to raise funds, aids recruitment, and can inspire villagers to act as bodyguards or engage in daring rescues when an activist is detained. In recent years, heavy-handed repression has sometimes backfired. Instead of isolating "troublemakers," it has boosted their popularity and prestige. Although intimidation, beatings, fines, confiscation of valuables, and public humiliation can swiftly end an incident and demoralize those involved, suppression also provides evidence of the costs that activists are willing to pay, and displays their public-spiritedness. Even long jail sentences may not diminish their standing, but instead generate popular acclaim, as is evident when thousands turn out for the welcome-home ceremony of a paroled protest leader.[3]

Social recognition can steel an activist's resolve and also lead to more spirited defiance. As time has passed, more activists have concluded that comparatively tame forms of contention, such as lodging complaints, are ineffective, and that forceful and attention-grabbing tactics (such as blocking a road or organizing a sit-in) are needed. Examples of confrontational tactics include outfitting pickup trucks with loudspeakers to publicize beneficial policies that have been ignored; demanding meetings with schoolmasters to press for the reversal of tuition hikes; and surrounding fee collectors as a prelude to driving them off. Whereas protest leaders in earlier years typically turned to higher-level officials in order to ask for help in cleaning up local misconduct, more are now willing to challenge powerholders directly and seek concessions on the spot.

Violence is also on the rise.[4] A number of clashes between farmers and local authorities have taken place recently over issues such as locating a power plant on village land, or refusing to allow the recall of a corrupt official. More than a few of these incidents have led to significant casualties after armed police or local toughs arrived to repress the protesters. At the same time, Yu Jianrong, a researcher at the Chinese Academy of Social Sciences, has documented the spread of unplanned, "accidental" protests that rapidly take on a life of their own. These "anger-venting" flare-ups are often touched off by essentially random sparks. Rioting last summer by tens of thousands after a girl was found dead in Weng'an County, Guizhou Province, bespeaks the growth of "accumulated grievances" and "social despair" in some locations.[5] It also suggests that underlying tensions may only grow during the current economic downturn as millions of unemployed workers return to the countryside.

But is rural China about to explode? Not likely. Most contention remains weakly organized, and cooperation across class lines is still rare—though involvement of public intellectuals and "rights-protection lawyers" (*weiquan lüshi*) in rural protest has increased. Claims tend to be circumscribed and popular action is usually small-scale and local. Even taking into account developments such as calls to privatize farmland that swept Heilongjiang, Henan, and Inner Mongolia in 2008, wide-ranging demands and long-lasting leadership are the exception, and there are few signs of the solidarity, scope, and coordination that a sustained social movement would require. Rural protest plays a role in fending off extraction, deflecting predatory behavior, and sending unpopular cadres packing, but there is little evidence that it poses an imminent threat to the regime.

That the Communist Party hierarchy tolerates so much rural contention is a sign of the Party's confidence. As with the dash of accountability offered by village elections, permitting a dollop of dissent is an element of the regime's high-wire legitimation strategy, and it reflects faith that things can be kept in hand. The authorities still have enormous powers of repression at their disposal, and they can unleash disproportionate force if they conclude that core interests are at stake. Openings can be closed instantly and new "forbidden zones" declared (or old ones enforced). Should the center begin to treat farmers' grievances like those of Tibetans or Falun Gong supporters, we will know that the leadership is shaken and perhaps even that the regime is weakening. As in Poland following the suppression of Solidarity, lack of protest can sometimes be a better indicator of a tottering regime than a great deal of protest. In today's China, pressure is building, possibly faster than it can be released, and observing rural contention and how it is handled is a good way to see how solid—or how brittle—the political system may be.

NOTES

1. See, for example, Deng's speeches of 25 April and 16 June 1989: *Deng Xiaoping Nianpu, 1975–1997* [Chronicles of Deng Xiaoping, 1975–1997] (Beijing: Zhongyang Wenxian Chubanshe, 2004), 1273; and *Selected Works of Deng Xiaoping, Vol. III, 1982–1992* (Beijing: Foreign Languages Press, 1994), 301.

2. On the demographic background and characteristics of protest leaders, see Kevin J. O'Brien and Lianjiang Li, *Rightful Resistance in Rural China* (New York: Cambridge University Press, 2006), 88–90, 135–37.

3. In parts of Hunan Province in the late 1990s, the social standing of protest leaders exceeded that of grassroots officials. Many villagers extolled activists as their protectors and would offer them free meals or welcome them like close relatives when they visited. One protest leader in Hengyang County who had enjoyed this largesse said that he was treated better than the township head, a man to whom villagers would no longer offer a cup of tea or even a seat. Interview by Lianjiang Li, 2003. For more on repression and its effect on popular support, see Lianjiang Li and Kevin J. O'Brien, "Protest Leadership in Rural China," *China Quarterly* 193 (March 2008): 17–22.

4. Zhao Shukai, "Lishixing tiaozhan: Zhongguo nongcun de chongtu yu zhili," [A historical challenge: Conflicts and governance in rural China] in Ru Xin et al., eds., *2004 Nian: Zhongguo shehui xingshi yuce yu fenxi* [2004: Forecasts and analyses of social trends in China] (Beijing: Shehui Kexue Wenxian Chubanshe, 2004), 212–23. On land disputes leading to violence and large-scale conflict as "more likely to erupt in rural versus urban areas," see Yu Jianrong, "Social Conflict in Rural China," *China Security* 3 (Spring 2007): 3, 7.

5. Yu Jianrong, "Emerging Trends in Violent Riots," *China Security* 4 (Summer 2008): 75–76.

16

THE LABOR MOVEMENT

Ching Kwan Lee and Eli Friedman

Ching Kwan Lee is professor of sociology at the University of California, Los Angeles, and author of Against the Law: Labor Protests in China's Rustbelt and Sunbelt *(2007). **Eli Friedman** is assistant professor in the department of International and Comparative Labor at Cornell University. This essay originally appeared in the July 2009 issue of the* Journal of Democracy.

The twenty years since 1989 have brought two major developments in worker activism. First, whereas workers were part of the mass uprising in the Tiananmen movement, albeit as subordinate partners to the students, labor activism since then has been almost entirely confined to the working class. While the ranks of aggrieved workers have proliferated (expanding from workers in the state-owned sector to include migrant workers) and the forms and incidents of labor activism have multiplied, there is hardly any sign of mobilization that transcends class or regional lines.

Second, we observe that a long-term decline in worker power at the point of production—power that was previously institutionalized in skill hierarchies, union representation, democratic management, permanent or long-term employment, and other conditions of service constitutive of the socialist social contract—is going on even as workers gain more power (at least on paper) outside the workplace. New labor laws have broadened workers' rights and expanded administrative and judicial channels for resolving labor conflicts. These legal and bureaucratic procedures have atomized and depoliticized labor activism even as they have engendered and intensified mobilization outside official limits.

The political and economic conditions that once enabled workers to join students in rebellion have disappeared. The bloody crackdown that began in Tiananmen Square on 4 June 1989 disheartened many reform-minded intellectuals, who have since dropped the idea that a mass movement can be a vehicle for political change. The government's decisive turn toward economic liberalization as a response to the legitimacy crisis and social discontents that underlay the Tiananmen Uprising rearranged the interests of various classes. In the 1990s, market reform began to benefit a much wider segment of the Chinese populace, most significantly the educated and the entrepreneurs, even as officials of the communist party-state continued to profit heavily from their bureaucratic positions and connections.

China's working class has become more internally varied, and different parts of it have faced different challenges as economic change has moved ahead. For instance, with a massive influx of foreign capital and expansion of the private economy came the formation of a large pool of migrant laborers who now total almost 130 million people, or roughly 10 percent of China's total population. In the mid-1990s, the "restructuring" (read: privatization and bankruptcy) of many state-owned industrial concerns, together with labor reforms that involved replacing permanent with contract employment, unleashed a decade-long spell of high unemployment. During this period, state and collective firms shed some 45 million urban workers. In the meantime, casualization of employment, a worldwide trend, proceeded apace even in core industries such as automobile manufacturing. Today, self-employed, part-time, temporary, and casual workers account for about 40 percent of the urban working population, and workers as a whole have little bargaining power. Nonetheless, anger at unpaid wages, pension arrears, plant closures, and poor working conditions has continued to give rise to labor unrest, albeit of an overwhelmingly local character.

Within the working class, the urban-rural division has persisted. Different household-registration statuses entail different provisions for workers' subsistence beyond wage employment, and thus have the effect of creating distinct interest groups within the working class. State and nonstate workers, not surprisingly, tend to take different approaches to collective action. Finally, the state's resolute use of repression against anything that smacks of labor activism across enterprises further inhibits the rise of a broad-based working-class movement.

The changing role of the official union speaks volumes about the disempowerment that China's people have suffered at work. The All China Federation of Trade Unions (ACFTU) was affected by the same ferment that swept large swaths of Chinese society during the first half of 1989. During this time, internal talk concerning greater union autonomy heated up, while some ACFTU officials met with student leaders and expressed support for independent unions.[1] Yet as happened in so many other corners of national life, the massacre of June 4 put a dramatic end to open discussions of greater liberalization within the trade unions. Since that time, no union leaders have dared to openly question the formal subordination of the ACFTU to the Chinese Communist Party (CCP). This means that in addition to protecting the rights and interests of workers, the state's goals of preserving social stability and promoting economic development have been firmly established as primary tasks of unions. As a result, the ACFTU has been limited to promoting workers' interests within a rather strict and externally defined set of legal and administrative constraints—a scenario that bespeaks a severe lack of substantive worker representation on the shop floor.

The extreme powerlessness of the Chinese worker as a direct producer is also grotesquely illustrated by the rampant problem of wage nonpayment. An authoritative national survey released by the State Council found that in 2006 less than half (48 percent) of the migrant workforce got paid regularly, while 52 percent reported regular or occasional nonpayment of wages.[2] The fact that wage collection for migrant workers became the subject of Premier Wen Jiabao's personal crusade in 2004 threw into sharp relief the lack of institutional protections for workers. China's labor standards have plunged to new depths, descending from a notoriously low wage regime to a subsistence crisis caused by workers not getting paid for their labor.

If the Chinese government has seemingly ceded control over the workplace to foreign and domestic capital (while state-owned enterprises increasingly utilize capitalist-style managerial regimes), it has also presided over an empowerment process through the promulgation of laws that give workers new legal rights. These include: the National Labor Law (1995), the Trade Union Law (2001), the Labor Contract Law (2007), the Labor Mediation and Arbitration Law (2007), and the Employment Promotion Law (2007). Ironically, empowering workers as juridical individuals exercising contractual rights does not resolve the problem of workers' powerlessness in the labor process. Workers can only seek redress after the fact, and remain at the mercy of the capricious (in)efficiency and political will of the Labor Bureau and the courts.

Therefore, the increase in the amount of labor legislation seems to have coincided with higher numbers of labor violations, labor disputes referred for arbitration, and lawsuits, with little evidence that any of this is resulting in improved working conditions. The rise of rights consciousness is outgrowing institutional capacity to meet or contain workers' demands. Workers have more rights on paper—and are more aware of them—than ever before. But in reality they have little leverage in their places of employment, and the protection that their interests receive from the courts and the government is uneven at best. Not surprisingly, worker protests do not look as if they will disappear from Chinese life anytime soon.

One historical condition for the stunning success that China's version of authoritarian capitalism has registered over the past thirty years has been the growth of a global neoliberal regime of increasingly free trade and capital flows. This has created an influx of investment, insatiable demand for Chinese products, employment opportunities for Chinese workers, and room for the Chinese economy to grow by putting the squeeze on labor. But this way of doing things may be reaching a point of exhaustion. The global financial and economic crisis is pushing the fundamental problem—the dispossession of workers as direct producers—to the surface, testing the limits of the Chinese approach to development. If uneven decentralized accumulation has thus far kept labor unrest too spread out and particularized to pose a threat to the system as a whole, then massive and simultaneous factory closings triggered by the latest global downturn may foment qualitatively different kinds of labor activism.

Even before the crisis arrived in the second half of 2008, some grass-roots Chinese unions were finding themselves compelled by their members' wretched subjugation to devise new modes of organization and activism. There are now indications that some enterprise-level trade-union chairs are engaging in active, if still highly legalistic, defenses of their members' interests. Of particular note has been the serious effort of union chairs in Wal-Mart stores in both Nanchang and Shenzhen to press management through collective-bargaining tactics. Top officials of both the CCP and the ACFTU have expressed the wish that unions will pursue collective bargaining—the idea being that this will help to reduce pressure for more radical forms of activism. Yet both the Wal-Mart case and other examples from around China demonstrate that those higher up in the trade-unions' hierarchies are supportive of grassroots activism only to a point; enterprise-level labor leaders who push management too hard risk being seen as "unharmonious" and losing state backing.

In short, the question now is whether China can make the transition from a labor-squeezing strategy of development to a more expansive method that provides the benefits of rights, the rule of law, and basic protections for labor to all the country's workers. The strengthening and expansion of rationalized mechanisms of collective bargaining, and perhaps even some provision for lawful strikes, are options that the government—always anxious to prevent instability—is considering. But this would require giving up the belief that social conflict can be legislated or administered out of existence, and would also entail the emergence of the new working class as a far more organized political force than it is today—a prospect that terrifies most Communist Party leaders. In the long run, however, this type of rationalized contention could provide the foundation for a more stable and sustainable form of capitalism in China.

NOTES

1. Jude Howell, "Trade Unionism in China: Sinking or Swimming?" *Journal of Communist Studies and Transition Politics* 19 (March 2003): 102–22. Available at *www.ihlo. org/LRC/ACFTU/trade_unionism_in_china.pdf.*

2. State Council Research Office Team, *Research Report on China's Migrant Workers* (Beijing: Zhongguo Yanshi Publishing, 2006), 116.

17

THE NEW INEQUALITY

An Chen

An Chen, associate professor of political science at the National University of Singapore, was previously a research fellow at the Chinese Academy of Social Sciences. He received his doctorate from Yale University. He is the author of Restructuring Political Power in China: Alliances and Opposition, 1978–1998 *(1999). This essay appeared in the January 2003 issue of the* Journal of Democracy.

Capitalism has given rise to significant social stratification and rising class conflict in China. Will this push the country toward a Western-type democracy, at least in the near future? My answer is no. One major reason is that the development of capitalism and class politics in China is not likely to produce powerful prodemocracy social pressure or shape a pattern of class alliances in favor of democratization.

Many students of democratic transitions classify them according to two broad models. The first, which I will call the structural model, stresses the importance of broad socioeconomic conditions that favor democratization, or at least a shift away from full-blown authoritarianism. The second category is the "pact-based" or "negotiated" transition model, which focuses on the strategic choices and interactions of political elites in causing "authoritarian ruptures" and "democratic openings."

The latter model, which does not rule out structural pressures for democratic change, has been the most popular among scholars of post-1974 "third-wave" transitions. Yet this model seems hardly applicable to China. In most cases of negotiated transition, there was a tradition of civil society and organized political opposition that made it possible for elites (incumbents and opposition leaders alike) to play a bargaining game. But China's departure from authoritarianism, if it occurs, will not happen in such a context. In order to grasp the possible trajectories of a Chinese transition, then, we must turn to the structural model.

This model comes in several variants, a full account of which need not detain us here. Suffice it to say that the most significant in its appli-

cation to China is, in my view, the one that I call the classical structural
model. Derived mostly from European historical experience, this vari-
ant may shed light on crucial questions about China's future: Where
precisely are the agents of China's democratization to come from? And
what precisely will be the engine of democratization in a country that
has no democratic history, tradition, or culture? Recent decades of economic liberalization and consequent changes in the structure of Chinese
society have made the European experience relevant as never before.

The upshot is clear: China's political life is taking place within a
social and political context that is new *for China,* but which is also
familiar from a number of earlier historical cases, and which therefore should be fairly predictable, at least in outline, provided that
the basics of the classic structural model are intelligently revised in
light of the circumstance that sets the Chinese case—and indeed all
"recent" cases— apart from the older, "historical" cases.

So what divides "recent" from "historical" democratizers? Until
about a half-century ago, movement toward democracy was an incremental, long-haul process whose origins could be traced back to a tradition of political pluralism. Progress toward liberal democracy would
occur against a broad political background in which virtually all the
democratic components, such as the separation of powers, constitutional
rule, and parliamentary sovereignty, had been gradually instituted. Democracy became fuller as the right to vote was extended to ever wider
classes of people.

In most contemporary cases—China included—the antecedent regimes are autocracies that lack anything more than a semblance of minimal democratic mechanisms and that exclude nearly all social classes
from government. Yet even in these cases, democracy—including universal suffrage—is established in principle if defied in practice. So actual democratization, should it occur, will come in what Ruth Berins
Collier calls "a single reform episode of sweeping regime change," in
which all social groups are enfranchised.[1] What implications flow from
this? Partly because contemporary authoritarian regimes cannot be justified as such on ideological grounds, they are haunted by legitimation
problems. In China, where Marxist ideology has lost its grip on hearts
and minds and where the economy is increasingly integrated into an international community in which liberty and democracy prevail, the ideological or moral foundations of rule by the Chinese Communist Party
(CCP) have eroded considerably. And yet, except for a brief flirtation
with parliamentarism in the early twentieth century, authoritarianism
has invariably been the "normal" way of political life for the Chinese. In
the Chinese context, therefore, authoritarianism does not need to be justified in purely political terms. Its "legitimacy" may be well accounted
for by Max Weber's "authority of the 'eternal yesterday' . . . . of the mo-
res sanctified through unimaginably ancient recognition and the habitual

orientation to conform."[2] Other authoritarian regimes may have to rely to varying degrees upon the cooperation and support of private-sector actors for survival. In China, the relationship is reversed, despite the increasing economic importance and political influence of the private sector.

Despite the consensus in Western academic circles about the expansion of individual freedoms and socioeconomic pluralism in China recently, the communist party-state's ability to dominate Chinese society has not been significantly undermined. Insofar as the CCP regime has loosened its control over society or given up part of its institutional power, this has not been because of domestic or international pressure but largely according to the party-state's own agenda, an agenda that is partly—but only partly—dominated by the demands of a budding market economy.

How can democratization be jump-started under such a nearly almighty authoritarian state? Where will the basic dynamics or driving forces of democratization come from? And how powerful will they be? For a number of reasons, pressure from abroad is unlikely to play a major role in moving China toward democracy. On the contrary, democratization will require extraordinary pressure from within, pressure that can only be brought to bear by powerful social groups. But will such pressure be generated? It is on this last, key issue in particular that the classical structural model displays its explanatory power.

Social Stratification and Class Conflicts

At the model's core is the process of capitalist development. Capitalism entails the separation and mutual balancing of economic and political powers. It also causes social stratification and the diversification of class interests, transforming the state into an arena where interest conflicts are fought out. For these and other reasons, capitalism has a prodemocratic logic, and there is no special reason to believe that China is impervious to it. The market reforms of the last several decades have already produced economic forces independent of state control, and undermined the socioeconomic pillars of communist hegemony. Although still far more powerful than a traditional capitalist state, the Chinese government can no longer afford to be entirely unresponsive to society and indeed needs social support now more than ever in order to govern effectively. As Chinese society has continued to differentiate and stratify, class politics has become something with which the CCP must reckon.

Under Mao, there was no social class in the economic sense. Except for "class enemies," most Chinese citizens were either "workers" laboring in state-owned enterprises (SOEs) or "peasants" tilling the land in "people's [agricultural] communes." In the decades after Mao, it appears that about a third of all peasants left farming in order to seek nonagricultural employment.[3] Moreover, the "working class" whose ranks they swelled had split into upwardly mobile, solidly blue-collar, or downwardly mobile and even "underclass" groups.

In larger Chinese cities today, broadly speaking, one finds a four-class hierarchy. At the top is a tiny upper bourgeoisie comprising the most successful entrepreneurs. Then comes a middle class of smaller entrepreneurs, managers and other white-collar employees of foreign or large private companies, and professionals. These two better-off classes together account for probably no more than 13 percent of the urban population, making them about 5 percent of the country as a whole.[4]

Below the affluent classes stands a toiling class that includes the vast majority of the Chinese. At the bottom of society is an underclass with incomes below subsistence level. In recent years, massive joblessness among SOE workers has expanded the underclass to a politically significant size, perhaps approaching 50 million city-dwellers nationwide.[5]

In China, class politics are inflamed by a combination of intensifying socioeconomic polarization, rising dismay at the regime's failure to alleviate poverty, and growing anger over the corruption and gross disparities associated with state-led capitalist development. In 1998, the World Bank—using a method that did not take public officials' illegal income into account—estimated China's Gini coefficient at a worrisome 40.3 (where 0 represents perfect income equality and 100 represents perfect inequality).[6] This places China on a par with countries such as Bolivia (42.0, 1990), the Philippines (46.2, 1997), and Peru (46.2, 1996). An official report discloses that for all the efforts made to alleviate urban poverty, 30 million urbanites can still barely earn their subsistence.[7]

The widening income disparities among Chinese seem to many to have more to do with cheating and political corruption than with honest effort in the free market. Capitalists have typically made fortunes through collusion with dishonest bureaucrats or taken advantage of market chaos to get away with illegal or immoral maneuvers. As SOEs have been transformed into private, shareholding entities, for instance, many state-appointed managers have used their positions as "insiders" to become wealthy even as large numbers of "redundant" or "unproductive" SOE workers find themselves turned out on the streets.

The lack of institutionalized channels for the articulation of class interests or a legitimate political arena for class competition makes it impossible accurately to gauge the depth of social cleavages. But a recent report of the Chinese Academy of Social Sciences, part of which is based on surveys conducted in some "representative" industrial cities, provides some data verifying the escalation of class warfare. According to this report, only 10.6 percent of those surveyed found no "conflict of [social or class] interests," whereas 89.4 percent thought that "conflicts" existed among some or all social strata or classes. The social groups whose "class-struggle" consciousness was the strongest were private entrepreneurs (100 percent) and laid-off workers (90.5 percent). In the cities of Shenzhen and Zhenning, respectively, the percentages of surveyed industrial workers who complained about the "unequal" income distribution were 81 and 89, respectively.[8] There is mounting evidence that class antagonism no longer remains on paper, but has generated specific class-based demands upon the state. In the city of Hefei, about 85 percent of all industrial workers, whether employed or jobless, said that they wanted the government to tax the rich more heavily and increase welfare benefits for the poor; private entrepreneurs, by contrast, opposed both these ideas by 3-to-1 ratio. In the city of Hanchuan, 84.4 percent of the agricultural laborers appealed for more effective redistributive measures to address income inequality.[9]

Politics and the New Classes

Capitalist development, as history shows, can produce social groups that push for democracy. Democracy may also arise as a byproduct of the struggles among social groups when no single class can gain total power and all therefore agree on rules for competition. Does China have a prodemocratic class or classes? Is a democracy-fostering *modus vivendi* among classes a possibility? To answer these questions, we need to examine three related issues: 1) the nature of the contest among classes; 2) the relationship between each class and the state; and 3) how the various classes estimate the effects that will flow from such democratic staples as political pluralism, multipartism, free elections, and majority rule.

Unlike most of their counterparts elsewhere, China's newly affluent classes are unlikely to champion democracy. In the first place, economic vulnerability and political submission have always been their lot: Even those classes which are not direct appendages of corrupt political authorities must depend heavily on state-monopolized resources. Capitalism in China remains uniquely under CCP sponsorship and control, and middle-class Chinese who have done well by the market lack the autonomy from the state needed to translate their economic affluence into political influence.

What is more, intensifying class conflict and fear of the numerous poor are driving the rich from passive acquiescence toward active support for authoritarianism. Although such a dynamic is hardly unique to China, special circumstances tend to inflame and perpetuate China's class confrontation in such a way as to render a democratic conciliation among classes—let alone the formation of a multiclass, prodemocracy coalition against the state—very unlikely.

The Chinese case conforms to the classic class-struggle model of the few rich versus the many poor. Yet in China, the high concentration of wealth makes the rich disproportionately powerful in this struggle, even as their small numbers make them feel weak and vulnerable vis-à-vis the poor majority. In my interviews with better-off Chinese, they displayed considerable enthusiasm when democracy was equated with the rule of law. When democracy was defined more essentially as majority rule, their enthusiasm turned to suspicion. And when majority rule was further described as a simple numerical game in which the greatest number makes policy, most of them could not accept it.[10]

On the eve of democratization in Taiwan and South Korea, the wide diffusion of the benefits of economic growth had significantly enlarged the middle classes and shrunk both the traditional working class and the underclass. This new class structure favored democracy by: 1) moderating class antagonism and its attendant tendency toward political extremism; and 2) enabling the now very large middle class to picture itself as the likely overall winner under democratic conditions.

China's capitalist development will not produce such results any time soon. In all likelihood, the present generation of wealthier Chinese will continue to see the risks of democratization as outweighing its benefits. Everyone knows that the large, poorly educated majority of Chinese have little hope of making it into the middle class, and that the rich will keep looking to the authoritarian state to safeguard their property. To make state protection even more necessary, worsening socioeconomic polarization is radicalizing the poor, thereby heightening the panic of the rich.[11]

While the affluent classes back authoritarian stability, the lower classes seem to be moving to oppose the regime. But they are not calling for democracy so much as showing a revolutionary disposition in the form of street protests and riots that have recently become more violent and organized. This revolutionary thrust has in turn caused the worried affluent to draw together in opposition to mass empowerment and cemented the "pro-stability" alliance between the affluent and the regime.

In China, the radicalization of the poor may have deeper roots than material poverty. Income disparities are harder to justify in China, where traditions of egalitarianism run strong. If the animosity between rich and poor remains a matter between social classes, it need not escalate into violence or revolution, as has been confirmed by the experience of some capitalist societies where a key role of the (typically authoritarian) state has been to mediate between contending classes. But all this changes if the regime is taken to be the source of mass grievances and suffering. In China, bitterness over the income gap has stoked antiregime feeling because: 1) officials have failed to curb corruption, the source of so much illicit income; and 2) the regime has done little to alleviate mass poverty. In the Chinese context, the second failure is particularly damaging to the regime's legitimacy. With no democratic tradition, no legal means for the poor to organize and voice their grievances, and an imperial history of dynasties being over-turned by revolution, it is little wonder that China is witnessing some extreme actions by its discontented millions.

The Regime's Options

The CCP's leaders hold the key to China's political future. If they reject continued liberalization and democratic reform, it will be mainly out of fear that anarchy will ensue or that CCP rule will come to an end. Both fears are justified. Party leaders recognize the danger posed by the growing income gap, but they lack the capacity to provide a long-term solution. The regime cannot stop the decay of most state industries, nor does it have effective mechanisms to constrain the rent-seeking or predatory behavior of local cadres. Money-losing SOEs are further drains on the state budget. The new system of tax distribution favors the regions at the cost of the center, further hampering Beijing's ability to create a nationwide social safety net. Under such circumstances, if the state wants to slow or stop the intensification of income inequality, it will have to transfer the cost of alleviating poverty to the rich, thereby taking one side in the class conflict.

For the CCP, a self-proclaimed working-class party, "robbing the rich to pay the poor" *(jiefu jipin)* should be a logical option. But the leadership seems more or less to have ruled this out, not because the affluent classes have "bribed" the party leaders or otherwise achieved direct political influence, but because the private economy, which these classes run, has become China's only hope for sustainable growth. China currently owes more than half of its GDP to nonstate companies. In 1998, the private economy paid 46 percent of the total tax revenues nationwide.[12] In recent years, private capital has accounted for 35 percent of total investment but has contributed 60 percent to China's GDP growth.[13] It is estimated that by 2004, the private economy will make up more than 60 percent of the national economy and employ 75 percent of China's workforce.[14]

With the business class unwilling to hand over more of its wealth, the party-state will not be able to redistribute much income to the poor before growth suffers. To maintain the good performance of China's overall economy and enhance its competitive edge—a basic precondition for the regime's survival—the party-state must either align itself with private capital and pursue a trickle-down policy, or else try some-how to balance antagonistic class interests. At this point, it seems that sheer economic pragmatism is compelling the CCP regime to take the affluent classes as its main base of support, and to choose stability over further reform.

The shared interest of the party-state and the affluent classes aside, it may be premature to conclude that they have formed a solid alliance. In part this is because of tensions *within* the communist party-state between its center and its various local components. For the local CCP authorities, alignment with the rich has long been a reality: In labor disputes, for instance, local governments typically take the side of capital. In a hardly veiled symbiosis between local cadres and private business, the latter provides much of government revenue through tax payment and employment, contributing often decisively to local socioeconomic development, one of the key criteria for cadre promotion. In return, the cadres offer tax breaks and government contracts or loans, often deriving from them not only career boosts but actual shares of private profits.

For the central state, ties to rich capitalists must remain somewhat disguised. Signs suggest that the highest leadership has still not decided exactly how close and public those ties should be. Within the CCP's upper echelon exists a "leftist" (anticapitalist) group whose voice cannot be entirely ignored. To avoid further alienating the poorer majority, the current leaders have decided to keep the CCP's official commitment to socialism and "working-class–party" status, and have upped the amount set aside for poverty relief, although the increase is hardly enough to shrink or even freeze the widening income gap.

The CCP's lack of financial capacity and political will to diminish socioeconomic polarization has become one of the major reasons why China's capitalist development may not necessarily lead to democratization (at least through a top-down process in the near future). As poverty and income inequality continue to worsen, making the government a target of seething popular indignation, a revolutionary situation is looming. This situation terrifies the CCP leadership and the affluent classes alike, and hardens their antidemocratic tendencies. Since the CCP regime refuses to redirect state expenditure away from the military or other projects, it can redistribute income only by "soaking the rich." But the regime dare not go too far in that direction for fear that doing so may dampen the dynamics of China's sustainable economic growth. It is also because the rich, particularly at local levels, have achieved important influence over the policy-making process. The more developed the capitalism-oriented reform is, the greater wealth, influence, and power the rich will gain. Of course, the state would also benefit from the increased revenue that will flow in from rising tax payments. But simultaneously the state has to rely even more heavily upon the rich, making it even less likely that there will be any redistribution at their expense. As a consequence, China may be trapped in a vicious circle in which political repression and the revolutionary impulse reinforce each other in a deepening class conflict that precludes a peaceful political opening.

NOTES

1. Ruth Berins Collier, *Paths Toward Democracy: The Working Class and Elites in Western Europe and South America* (New York: Cambridge University Press, 1999), 188.

2. Weber referred to this authority as one of the "basic legitimations of domination." See H.H. Gerth and C. Wright Mills, eds., *From Max Weber: Essays in Sociology* (New York: Oxford University Press, 1946), 78–79. It seems safe to say that today this authority has been somewhat diluted, particularly among those segments of Chinese society that are more exposed to Western influence. But there is a countertendency. The authoritarian past and nearly everything associated with it keep being refreshed by a plethora of literary works, movies, and TV dramas drawing on ancient dynastic politics. The obsession of ordinary people with stories depicting the lives of Chinese emperors and palace conspiracies, among other things, suggests the real and omnipresent influence of China's political tradition and culture.

3. See Lu Xueyi, ed., *Dangdai Zhongguo Shehui Jieceng Yanjiu Baogao* (A research report on social strata in contemporary China) (Beijing: Shehui Kexue Wenxian Chubanshe, 2002), 160–98.

4. An Chen, "Capitalist Development, Entrepreneurial Class, and Democratization in China," *Political Science Quarterly* 117 (Fall 2002): 401–22. This estimate is based on my calculations from the relevant data as well as on official statistics.

5. See Long Hua, "Zhongguo Zhengzhi Fazhan Keneng Yinqi de Shehui Wenti" (The social problems that China's political development might bring about), *Xin Bao* (Hong Kong Economic Journal), 13 September 2000, 20; Chang Xinghua, *Jingji Biange Zhongde "Heixiang"* (The "black box" in the economic transformation), (Zhuhai, Guangdong: Zhuhai Chubanshe, 1998), 202.

6. World Bank, *World Development Indicators 2000* (Washington, D.C.), 66.

7. Xinhua News Agency, 11 March 2002.

8. Lu Xueyi, ed., *Dangdai Zhongguo*, 42–43, 80.

9. Lu Xueyi, ed., *Dangdai Zhongguo*, 115.

10. These interviews and surveys were conducted in China's five provinces between 1998 and 2000.

11. As Edward N. Muller observes, a high level of income inequality is bad for democratization because extreme inequality makes the working class "susceptible to the appeals of revolutionary socialism, which will inhibit the development of a broad pro-democratic coalition of the working class and middle class." See Edward N. Muller, "Economic Determinants of Democracy," in Manus I. Midlarsky, ed., *Inequality, Democracy, and Economic Development* (New York: Cambridge University Press, 1997), 133–55.

12. "Feigong Jingji Nashui zhan Zhongguo Banbi Jiangshan" (Tax payment by the nonpublic sector makes up half of China's total tax revenues), *Qian Shao* (Frontline) 104 (September 1999): 135.

13. Wang Jiahang, "Minying Qiye Chengwei Ziben Shichang Xinliangdian" (Private enterprises have become the new spotlight in the capital market), available online at *www. peoplesdaily.com.cn,* 10 September 2002.

14. Dexter Roberts et al., "China's New Capitalism," available online at *www.businessweek.com* (*BusinessWeek* Online), 27 September 1999.

18

THE TROUBLED PERIPHERY

Louisa Greve

Louisa Greve is vice-president for Asia, Middle East and North Africa, and Global Programs at the National Endowment for Democracy, where she served previously as director for East Asia. She managed NED's China grants program for fifteen years.

On balance, tensions and troubles in peripheral areas of the People's Republic of China (PRC)—especially the "autonomous regions" of Tibet and Xinjiang—strengthen rather than weaken the country's authoritarian regime. They buttress the Communist party-state's legitimating ideology and its bureaucratic systems of repression.

All-out crackdowns on dissent and religious freedom in Tibet and Xinjiang used to be cyclical affairs. Now the weight of the regime's heavy hand is felt more or less continuously. Since 9/11, the ruling Chinese Communist Party (CCP) has made its fight against the "three evil forces of separatism, terrorism, and religious extremism" a constant, unlike the episodic "Strike Hard" antiseparatism campaigns of the 1980s and 1990s. Tighter controls and more arbitrary arrests in Tibet and Xinjiang—especially since the 2008 disturbances in the former and the 2009 unrest in the latter—have thrown a blanket of repression over both regions as well as ethnic autonomous counties and townships in neighboring provinces. Life today in these areas includes wartime-style checkpoints, midnight sweeps of whole neighborhoods following any sort of public incident, and a sharp increase in forced disappearances of young Uyghur men. New tactics in response to the wave of self-immolations since 2009 of young Tibetans include collective punishment of their families and villages via the withholding of state benefits and the cancellation of public-works projects.

At the same time, coercive assimilation to Han Chinese culture has accelerated. Teaching in the Tibetan and Uyghur languages has been phased out over the past decade and a half in the schools, reaching elementary schools and now kindergartens. Children attending the five-days-per-week "boarding" day-care establishments may never fully master their parents' native languages. Not only are rebellious monasteries surrounded by armed security forces; even personal religious observances have been banned in the most severe totalitarian fashion. In Xinjiang, for instance, parents are forbidden to teach their religious beliefs to their children, and no one under eighteen may enter a mosque. Six teenaged Uyghur boys who were arrested in April 2010 for studying the Koran on their own after school are now serving sentences of eight to fourteen years in jail. Students, government employees, and nearly all others who are neither farmers nor itinerant peddlers are now prohibited from fasting during Ramadan. Workplaces and schools must appoint "Ramadan Stability Teams," and often provide daytime meals during Ramadan, with the understanding that anyone who refuses to eat will face punishment. Police also patrol the streets in the predawn hours; if lights show at apartment windows, officers demand entry to ascertain whether the family is eating a meal to prepare for the day's fast. If so, some or all family members will find themselves fined, demoted, or fired.

Islands of Misery

The regime's stated policy response to ethnic grievances is to promote economic development. This has brought the peripheral regions economic opportunities—for people with connections. It has also encouraged Han migration to these regions while fueling massive corruption and creating environmental problems that threaten the lives and livelihoods of many. In a cruel twist, some policies purportedly designed to protect the environment from overgrazing have in fact created islands of misery in Tibet and Inner Mongolia by forcing families of herdspeople to give up their animals and submit to being "villagized" into grim concrete housing blocks where only meager government handouts keep starvation from the door.

Programs to provide jobs to unemployed youth carry the effect, intended or not, of bringing large groups of young people to live in factory dorms thousands of miles from home. And while the same is true for millions of rural young Chinese who have left home to work in the export-production factories over the past two decades, the recruitment policy in Xinjiang has produced high anxiety among these teenagers' parents: Unlike in any other part of China, local officials are required to fill government-mandated quotas, using deception, pressure, and threats. Is it any wonder that Uyghurs would like to know why government policy is geared toward resettling young Uyghurs far from home in Han Chinese cities? In a similar vein, policies designed to provide greater educational opportunities for Tibetan and Uyghur youth steer young people away from their families and cultures—large numbers of the best and the brightest are now in programs where they spend their formative years at boarding schools in big eastern cities, a policy that puts tremendous pressure on intergenerational community ties.

Perhaps surprisingly to central-government policy makers—who may sincerely believe that such policies, if they succeed in bringing material improvement, will also lessen ethnic grievances—all these policies not only have fostered mounting discontent, but have undermined the regime's long-term goal of promoting stability by making social and cultural identity less tied to ethnicity. The March 2008 protests in the Tibet Autonomous Region and neighboring Tibetan areas are a case in point. News that police had detained a dozen monks for staging a peaceful, silent protest march in Lhasa spread within 48 hours to more than sixty other towns across the Tibetan plateau, in areas that are among the poorest, most remote, and least "wired" parts of the PRC. In parts of five provinces and autonomous regions, thousands of young people—some astonishingly brandishing the banned "snow lion" flag of Tibet—came out to register their discontent despite the certainty of violent police repression. In the event, this was but a foreshadowing of the post-2009 wave of young people who have sacrificed their lives by self-immolation for the sake of their ethnonational identity.

Could such episodes move China toward a "tipping point" that undoes the CCP regime? Might we see a replay of what happened two decades ago in the dying Soviet Union as central control unravels, weakened in part by the de facto secession of "captive nations"? In a word, this is unlikely. The share of China's population that is involved is too small—there are only about 6 million Tibetans, 9 million Uyghurs, and relative handfuls of other ethnic minorities in the PRC, a country of 1.3 billion people, more than 90 percent of whom are Han Chinese.

Moreover, the economic immiseration of the non-Han ethnic groups finds no general parallel in the populace at large. Residents of the PRC's Han Chinese heartland may be angry over inequality, gross corruption, and rampant injustice (all of which threaten the CCP's legitimacy), but there is a powerful constituency that derives significant economic benefits from the current system. Moreover, some defecting members of the Soviet *nomenklatura* were also attracted by the prospect of building their own crony-capitalist state. China's *apparatchiks* have already been enjoying life in just such a state for the past twenty or thirty years, and have no need to undo the current order in order to construct a cronyist realm.

In other words, there are few if any significant interest groups that would be tempted to take problems on the periphery as a signal to turn against the CCP regime. In fact, interest groups that would be harmed by a breakup, but thrive on the *threat* of breakup, are only growing stronger. To that sobering observation, others may be added. One is that the CCP regime's determination to maintain its grip on the periphery bodes ill for hopes that gradual promotion of the rule of law might show China a peaceful way out of its current quandaries. Another is that the "peripheral" experience depressingly demonstrates how readily and persistently the regime will fall back on the manipulation of Chinese-nationalist sentiment as a means of bolstering its doubtful legitimacy.

The Hollowness of "Autonomy"

The peripheral regions include not only Tibet, Xinjiang (literally "New Frontier," so coined by the Qing dynasty; Uyghur activists prefer "East Turkestan"), and Inner Mongolia, but hundreds of counties, prefectures, and townships in Sichuan, Qinghai, Yunnan, and other areas. By law they are "autonomous" and as such supposedly enjoy self-rule as well as a host of safeguards for their local languages, religions, ethnic traditions, and cultural expression. In reality, of course, the entire constitutional-legal edifice of "autonomy" is a giant fiction that Mao Zedong borrowed more or less whole from Joseph Stalin's trick of hiding the reality of centralized Soviet domination behind a paper façade of documents granting minorities self-government and an array of rights.

Mao made a number of fine-sounding promises as he pursued his project of extending complete Communist Party control over the whole territory of the former Qing Empire (1644–1912), but having served their purpose, those promises have not been kept. In the PRC, therefore, minorities have rights by law and all Chinese citizens have rights under the constitution, but the CCP and its security organs trample all such guarantees and other nominally democratic features of the system as often and as wantonly as they feel the need to.

China's doughty *weiquan* (rights-defense) lawyers, whose drive to use the existing legal system to enforce the rule of law has been blunted even in the big eastern cities, admit to complete helplessness when it comes to pursuing legal cases under what amounts to martial law on the periphery. When asked about his experience in trying to help a Han Chinese Christian arrested in the far west, one attorney privately declared, "Oh, there's really *no* law in Xinjiang."

It is becoming ever less likely that the rule of law, riding on a wave of desire for economic modernization, will re-emerge in the medium term as a common goal among powerful forces in the Chinese state and economy, or as a serious objective of would-be top-down Party reformers. Chinese who contemplate the experience of the periphery will only see confirmation, if more evidence is needed, of how far-fetched such hopes really are. There, the party-state has shown how willing it is to eviscerate anything resembling law-based rule when respect for law threatens its overriding concern with staying in power.

The buildup of an aggressive security state in the peripheral regions also holds grave implications for democratic prospects in China as a whole. First, the "stability-maintenance" agencies have seen their budgets—and the opportunities for graft available to their functionaries—grow astronomically. A not insignificant portion of this growth is a response to ethnic unrest. The security agencies' greater weight and independence (to the point where they now form a lobby of sorts that influences central policy) suggest a regime that will dig in and fight rather than embrace reformist accommodation in the face of discontent. Ethnic unrest, in other words, is feeding yet another antireform constituency.

Second, the reintroduction in Tibet and Xinjiang of totalitarian-style controls on ordinary personal freedoms (not targeted solely at people who specifically challenge abuses of power or speak out on political matters) is an ominous sign for all of China. Heartland Chinese overwhelmingly accept the state propaganda system's invocation of the "separatist" threat as justification for harsh policies toward the minorities. This attitude receives reinforcement from deep-seated racist attitudes that not only go unchallenged by civil society or state civic-education programs, but are embedded in the assumptions and rhetoric of the state's coercive assimilationist approach to dealing with Tibetans and Uyghurs. But the "national minorities" are not the only PRC citizens threatened by the heavy-handed state-security tactics now making a comeback on the ethnic periphery. To mention one dramatic example highlighted by China analyst Ethan Gutmann: Highly unethical practices occasioned by the shortage of transplantable organs—including what appears to be organ-harvesting from the bodies of live prisoners—are now a nationwide scourge (and, some say, a shoe waiting to drop in the Bo Xilai scandal). These practices were first tested on condemned prisoners in Xinjiang.

The CCP has learned from its study of the Soviet Union's demise not to underestimate the dangers of partial political reform. Because national minorities played such a conspicuous role in the USSR's unraveling, Chinese leaders feel especially anxious not to let restive minorities "get out of hand." This imperative fits in neatly with the Party's claim to have restored China to greatness after its "century of humiliation" between the First Opium War of 1839–42 and the Communists' victory over the Nationalists in 1949—a period, so the narrative goes, when China was invaded, divided, and dominated by foreigners. Tibet may be a high, forbidding plateau inhabited by only a few million residents, but it retains symbolic significance as a once-sovereign realm that is also the last territory to have put up armed resistance against forced incorporation into the PRC. The CCP regime has now declared it to be a "core interest" on the same level as Beijing's claims to sovereignty over Taiwan. While dissatisfaction with environmental disasters, widespread corruption, and abuse of power may be exposing the CCP to skeptical scrutiny, so far the appeal to Chinese nationalism has held fast. The vast bulk of Han Chinese seem to cheer their government's strong stance in defense of "territorial integrity" in disputes over various islands and in its Taiwan policy. They also embrace the internal, ethnic dimension of today's state-sponsored nationalism: Beijing's resolution in combating the "hostile forces" that are supposedly working to split Tibet and Xinjiang from the motherland. Moreover, Han Chinese almost universally seem to feel that their government is bringing civilization and development to what they see as backward minorities.

Overall, the response of the Chinese state—and of Chinese society at large—to the problems of the periphery is piling more tension and misery upon the populations there, but it is not undermining state power. If anything, the party-state seems to draw strength from peripheral troubles, and indeed these troubles continually undermine prospects for better governance under any future rulers, including those installed by the 2012 Eighteenth Party Congress.

So far, this brief essay has been a tale of woe. Is all the news bad? Will troubles on the ethnic and geographical periphery do nothing but undermine democracy's already tenuous prospects in China? Perhaps there is a glimmer of hope. Slowly but perceptibly, awareness of the rot at the PRC's edges seems to be growing. A small but rising number of Han intellectuals are showing a genuine interest in ethnic minorities' views, undaunted either by these views' lack of popularity or by the government's clear willingness to use ominous guilt-by-association tactics against anyone who even hints at sympathy for ethnic grievances.

Worthy of mention are several intellectual initiatives. One is Charter 08's inclusion of language about finding federalist solutions to China's problems. Another is the work of novelist and commentator Wang Lixiong, well known for championing the rights of Tibetans, and whose book *My West China, Your East Turkestan* is one of very few devoted to exploring the Uyghurs' perspective. The efforts of the now-shuttered Open Constitution Initiative (OCI) to analyze the reasons for Tibetans' sense of grievance and to propose policy alternatives was groundbreaking. Its May 2009 white paper challenged the official narrative on the causes of the unrest, and recommended that Chinese authorities do more to respect and protect the Tibetans' interests and rights, including their right to religious freedom. While the OCI fell short of demonstrating a full understanding of Tibetans' aspirations for democratic rights and cultural survival, it was nothing less than courageous in its attempt to undertake and disseminate independent research and analysis on an issue that is truly neuralgic for the Chinese state.

Finally, popular writers such as Yu Jie are breaking new ground by stating that Tibetans and Uyghurs deserve a say in their lives and the policies that affect them. Yet even Yu forthrightly admits that that he does not expect most Chinese to shed their deeply ingrained sense of racial and civilizational superiority. To his appeal is added that of 2010 Nobel Peace laureate Liu Xiaobo, who over the two decades before his imprisonment in 2009 wrote more than twenty essays touching on ethnic questions and problems. Yu and Liu may still be voices crying out in the wilderness, but it is encouraging that at least some Han Chinese are pointing out that the ethnic-nationality story has two sides, and that what the ethnic peoples have to say in their own cause deserves to be heard.

19

THE UPSURGE OF RELIGION IN CHINA

Richard Madsen

Richard Madsen *is Distinguished Professor of Sociology at the University of California, San Diego.* *His books include* Democracy's Dharma: Religious Renaissance and Political Development in Taiwan *(2007),* China's Catholics: Tragedy and Hope in an Emerging Civil Society *(1998), and* Popular China: Unofficial Culture in a Globalizing Society *(coedited with Perry Link and Paul Pickowicz, 2002). This essay originally appeared in the October 2010 issue of the* Journal of Democracy.

Over the years, these pages have featured many essays devoted to analyzing the prospects for democracy in China. Such analyses have focused on studying the resiliency (or fragility) of the current Chinese Communist Party (CCP) regime, and on weighing the significance of various protest movements or other actual and potential sources within China of pressure for democratic change. Among the latter, attention has been devoted to workers, rural dwellers, the middle classes, and online activists. But very little note has been taken of what may turn out to be the biggest threat of all to the CCP's ability to maintain its control—namely, the extraordinary growth of religious belief and religious movements in Chinese society.

Unlike liberal democracies, which generally accord their citizens the right to complete freedom of religious belief and practice, the People's Republic of China claims that it needs to control religion in order to preserve social harmony and economic modernization. The government has a bureau that is officially in charge of religious affairs—the State Administration for Religious Affairs (SARA). The state claims the prerogative of determining what counts as "true" and "false" religion, and uses its police power to attempt the eradication of "false" religion (often termed, in the parlance of Chinese officialdom, "evil cults" or "feudal superstition"). The state also chooses the leaders of approved religions and monitors many religious activities.

The Chinese government shares an assumption that is often encountered in liberal democracies—namely, that secularity is inseparable from modernity.[1] Liberal-democratic *governments* (as distinguished from various influential schools of thought found within liberal-democratic societies) are neutral on the matter, of course, and take no position on the question of whether religion has any future in the modern world. China's government is not neutral, but maintains instead that religion is destined to recede as modernization continues to proceed. Chinese officialdom derives its version of this "secularization thesis" from Marxism, and China's religious policy (like all government policy in that country) is set by the ruling CCP. The framework for religious policy comes from "Document 19," which the CCP's Central Committee promulgated in 1982 under the title "The Basic Viewpoint on the Religious Question During Our Country's Socialist Period."[2]

This document parallels the liberal-democratic handling of religious belief by relegating it to the private sphere of life: The "crux of the policy of freedom of religious belief is to make the question of religious belief a private matter, one of individual free choice for citizens." (Unlike liberal democracies, however, China has a constitution that offers no guarantee of freedom of association to complement freedom of belief.)

In a sharp contrast to the neutral, liberal-democratic approach to religious claims regarding what is true, however, Document 19 goes on to declare that religion is false, and makes government the active agent of a modernizing project that is meant to eventually eliminate religion altogether: "[W]e Communists are atheists and must unremittingly propagate atheism." In contrast to the "leftist" policies put in place during the Cultural Revolution that began in 1966—policies that tried forcibly to obliterate religion from public life—Document 19 is a product of the early Reform program of Deng Xiaoping, who was CCP leader from 1978 to 1992. Its approach toward religion is based on patiently waiting for scientific education, not political coercion, to spread atheism.

As suggested above, the notion that science and modernity will put an end to religion is not confined to Communist functionaries: It is in fact an assumption that elite social scientists in liberal democracies widely share. Until fairly recently, these social scientists would probably have overwhelmingly agreed with Document 19 that religion is a historical phenomenon whose demise will inevitably come with modernization, albeit probably not until a period of "cultural lag" has run its course: "Old thinking and habits," cautions Document 19, "cannot be thoroughly wiped out in a short period." Therefore, "Party members must have a sober-minded recognition of the protracted nature of the religious question under Socialist conditions. . . . Those who expect to rely on administrative decrees or other coercive measures to wipe out religious thinking and practices with one blow are even further from the basic viewpoint that Marxism takes toward the religious question. They are entirely wrong and will do no small harm."

The problem for the secularization thesis—and hence for the CCP—is that it appears to be wrong. Far from inexorably receding, religions all over the world are growing and seeking increasingly vigorous engagements with public affairs. Recognizing this, many Western social theorists (even confirmed agnostics such as Jürgen Habermas) are now searching for "postsecular" social theories.[3] Although there is great disagreement over the content of such theories, they all note that religions do not simply "rise and fall" according to a linear pattern. The theories also note that in modernized societies religion not only persists, but continues to evolve dynamically. Theorists now recognize that there are "multiple modernities," defined by different interactions between religious belief and practice on the one hand, and modern political and economic developments on the other.[4] It is generally conceded, moreover, that religion cannot typically be confined altogether to private life, but instead is (for better or worse) an active part of public life.[5] Finally, scholars are growing increasingly suspicious of definitions that conceive of religion in overly narrow, ethnocentric terms based on Western historical experience.[6]

There are heated arguments and unresolved issues concerning religion and its relation to public life in liberal democracies such as the United States, of course, but these are at least openly debated. In China, the secularist assumptions that underpin official religious policy are proving unworkable. The policies that Document 19 lays out are a complete failure, even in terms of their own goals of constraining the growth of religion, confining it to the private sphere, and keeping it out of politics and ethnic relations. Religion is growing rapidly, and has overwhelmed the CCP regime's systems of surveillance and control. Clumsy methods of suppressing unwanted forms of religion have backfired, raising rather than lowering the temperature of conflicts involving religion and the state. And attempts to decouple religion from the ethnic awareness of minority nationalities that might fuel opposition to the dominant Han nationality have failed as well. The policy debacle has become obvious enough that CCP leaders have begun to acknowledge it more or less openly, and some within the government are searching for a new approach to religious policy. But constraints on debate about sensitive religious matters are making it hard for the CCP and the state to move beyond the old policy, with its untenable assumptions; and when they do move, it is not in the direction of more liberal-democratic rights to religious freedom.

Official Policy and Social Reality

The problems with the official policy of containing religion, making it serve state aims, and keeping it within regime-approved channels start with the government's attempts to define religion itself. Official policy views religion in terms of private belief expressed through voluntary participation in congregations organized via institutions that have clearly delineated leaderships separated from the economy and polity. This fits the understanding of religion developed by nineteenth-century Western scholars who, consciously or not, were working from a secularized notion of Western Protestantism. Based on this definition, the Chinese government recognizes five (and only five) religions in China: Taoism, Buddhism, Islam, Catholicism, and Protestantism. At least some manifestations of all five are organized into distinctive institutions with recognized leaders, and are practiced through congregations of voluntarily associating believers.

The containment of religion is part of a policy that seeks to contain all the associations of a civil society. There is in principle no space in official Chinese policy for an independent civil society, and therefore no space for independent religious associations. The officially recognized institutions are thus placed under the supervision of "patriotic associations" that in turn are supervised by SARA, and above it the United Front Department of the CCP.

Yet SARA has no jurisdiction over any form of religion that has not received official recognition, even though such generally recognized world religions as Russian Orthodoxy, Judaism, Mormonism, and the Bahá'í Faith can all be found in China. Rural China, moreover, is home to millions of temples—many of them built in just the last decade—that serve as centers for local folk religions and their associated festivals. By no means do these temples and their liturgies represent a simple return to ancient traditions. Traditional rituals, myths, and practices are being enacted with modern technology such as video cameras and websites, and reconfigured to fit the sensibilities of villagers who are no longer farmers, but factory workers, entrepreneurs, and even professionals.[7] These folk religions are more a matter of public practice than private belief, and they are not organized into institutions clearly separate from local economic and political life. Such activities have been defined by the Chinese authorities as "feudal superstition," in contrast to real religion. But modern anthropologists would want to consider these activities, through which hundreds of millions of people in China seek fundamental meaning and celebrate community, as religious. In any case, none of these activities are under the purview of SARA, and there is confusion within the Chinese government about who should monitor them and what should be done about them. In fact, regulation of folk religion often depends on ad hoc arrangements by local officials, and different provinces follow different policies in handling its growth.

Even within the five officially recognized religions, moreover, most of the growth is taking place outside the state-supervised patriotic associations and hence not under the jurisdiction of SARA. For example, there is an extensive "underground" Catholic Church that is about three times larger than the officially recognized Chinese Patriotic Catholic Association. And even more amazing from a sociological point of view, there is an extremely wide array of rapidly growing unregistered Protestant "house churches."

When Mao Zedong and his Communists triumphed over the Nationalists and established the People's Republic in 1949, there were fewer than a million Protestants in all of China. Under Mao, who died in 1976, restrictions on religion and the religious were severe. Since 1979, however, the ranks of Chinese Protestants have grown exponentially. A conservative estimate favored by many leading scholars of religion within China puts their strength at around fifty million.[8] (Some Protestant leaders claim that there are really twice that number.) The vast bulk of this astounding growth has taken place outside the institutional bounds of the state-supervised Three-Self Patriotic Movement (TSPM). The fastest-growing sectors of all have been those dominated by evangelical and Pentecostal Christian assemblies that hew to a premillennial theology positing the imminent end of the world, the "rapture" of the faithful into heaven, and the arrival of global tribulations heralding the second coming of Christ.

Although most new Chinese Christians concern themselves with spiritual matters and have no interest in active efforts to bring on the apocalypse, some sects do see their faith as a mandate to bring about radical change in this world. The Chinese government's attitude toward unregistered Protestant "house churches" has been one of great suspicion, and it certainly does not like eschatological talk. It will also have noticed that a disproportionate number of those "rights lawyers" and other activists (including imprisoned dissident Liu Xiaobo) who have been pushing for political reforms are Christians associated with urban house churches or at least (like Liu) people known to be avowedly sympathetic to Christians and Christianity.[9]

The house churches have been growing so fast, however, that the government can neither stop them nor ignore them. Thus, parts of the government are trying to distinguish between those evangelical Protestants who take a relatively passive, spiritual stance toward their religious convictions and the minority with the potential for political confrontation. Since the Protestants outside the TSPM are not under the purview of SARA, however, other central-government agencies have been entering into discussions with those house-church leaders who seem to pose no danger to social stability and who want to distance themselves from the more militant religious activists. The Chinese State Council's Development Research Center held an important meeting for such leaders—its title was "Christianity and Social Harmony"—in the latter part of 2008. Meanwhile, however, agencies of repression such as the Public Security Bureau take a less conciliatory approach and have been increasingly prone to arrest house-church leaders since the first half of 2009. But since there are too many leaders in too many decentralized organizations for even China's security forces to arrest, the detentions seem arbitrary, with the great majority of house churches being unaffected.

Finally, there is the growth of new religious movements with flexible organizations that combine traditional social networks with sophisticated multimedia communications technologies. The best-known of these is the Falun Gong, which mixes Buddhist and Taoist ideas in a modernized form. Founded in 1992 as part of a wave of meditation practices for promoting spiritual harmony and physical health, the Falun Gong expanded rapidly to include perhaps ten-million followers by 1999.[10] In April of that year, in response to criticisms in the national media, the Falun Gong gathered ten thousand of its practitioners for a demonstration in front of the government headquarters in Beijing. Even though the demonstration was peaceful, CCP leaders considered it an illegal provocation and feared that it could set a precedent for more independent mass action.

Since the summer of 1999, the government has carried out a massive campaign to crush the movement, arresting and sometimes allegedly torturing and killing its leaders. Followers living abroad have organized their activities and publicized their plight through a newspaper (the *Epoch Times*), a television station (Tang Dynasty TV), and elaborate websites. Along with similar religious movements that have challenged the government's authority, the Falun Gong has been put into the category of "evil cults" that the state strives to crush by mobilizing new forms of police power on a vast scale, despite Document 19's warning that harsh coercive measures are "wrong and will do no small harm." The Falun Gong has been driven deep underground within China, yet at the same time it has become a force worldwide. Meanwhile, other "evil cults," including offshoots of Christianity, continue to spread.[11]

Back to the Future?

The first response to the breakdown of the old policies has been to tolerate different experimental, ad hoc responses to local religious developments, while officially maintaining the framework of Document 19. But in the absence of any unified theoretical approach to guide them, these responses produce an incoherent patchwork of disparate local policies. Moves to tolerate some religious activities are joined with new methods of repressing others. There does not seem to be much central coordination of these developments, and they proceed at their own respective paces according to the ambitions of the various bureaucratic units that initiate them. Recognizing the incoherence of its ad hoc policies, the Party is looking for a new understanding to guide its approach toward religion.

As with all "sensitive" issues in China, discussions about religious policy go forward not in public forums, but rather in closed-door meetings that bring together academic experts and political leaders. While spending a year at Fudan University in Shanghai not long ago, I myself was invited to give a lecture to one such group, the United Front Department of the Fudan University Communist Party Committee, which has been designated a "theoretical base" for developing policies toward religion.

My sense, from that experience and other interactions I had in China, is that leading Chinese experts agree on the unworkability of Document 19. Whether top CCP leaders will openly admit this is doubtful, given the Party's need to maintain an air of infallibility. But whether it is spelled out or not, the Party's strategy seems to be evolving along the lines suggested by leading experts such as Zhuo Xinping, the director of the Institute of World Religions at the Chinese Academy of Social Sciences.

Zhou's paper on "The Situation of Chinese Religion and Its Direction of Development" has been presented to the CCP Politburo. He begins with a long introduction on the place of religion in Chinese history and the relationship between religion and the state under the emperors. He discusses Marxism, but treats it as social science—subject to all the canons of empirical verification and so on—not as sacred dogma. When things are handled this way, it is the emperors and not Karl Marx who provide the touchstone for religious policy.

What is gradually emerging from all this is a somewhat more coherent policy that differs from Document 19 in being more accepting of many of the different forms of Chinese religiosity and more flexible in seeking to regulate them. But it is by no means a liberal-democratic policy. Instead, it is a back-to-the-future policy—a modern throwback to the viewpoint of the Ming (1368–1644) and Qing (1644–1912) imperial dynasties.

In Ming and then Qing China, the emperor was the "Son of Heaven." His main duty was to mediate between Heaven (considered a deity) and Earth. The legitimacy of his authority rested on this sacral role, which of course depended on a "Mandate of Heaven" that could be lost through imperial malfeasance. The emperor fulfilled his role by performing important rituals in the capital and elsewhere in order to secure Heaven's blessings for his subjects, and he had the ultimate authority to distinguish between "true teaching" *(zhengjiao)* and "deviant teaching" *(xiejiao)*. He thus combined the Western roles of king and pope.

Although the elites who furnished emperors with their chief advisors were schooled in a Confucian tradition that was skeptical about most forms of popular religious practice, the emperors often tolerated and even encouraged village cults, which usually drew on some mixture of Taoist, Buddhist, and Confucian traditions. Such rituals and myths would count as "true teachings" if they solidified the proper hierarchical relations within families, helped to build strong communities rooted in local agriculture, and thus bolstered social stability under imperial rule. As for large-scale Buddhist and Taoist monasteries, the emperors kept them in line through imperial patronage, which helped such institutions to thrive while ensuring that their leaders remained imperial loyalists.

By contrast, sectarian organizations that gathered people from different communities, contravened gender distinctions by allowing men and women to worship together as equals, preached an imminent end to the present era, and sometimes became the organizational basis for rebellion might be labeled heterodox (or in the English translation of the term *xiejiao* that is officially preferred today, "evil cults").[12] Their fate would be intense persecution.

Often the facts that might justify this distinction were ambiguous. When Jesuit missionaries such as Matteo Ricci brought Catholic Christianity to China in the sixteenth century, there was considerable debate within the imperial court about whether this "foreign teaching" should be considered orthodox or heterodox. The Jesuits eventually convinced the emperor that their teaching was compatible with the other teachings that sustained imperial rule, and the long-ruling Kangxi emperor declared in 1692 that Catholicism would count as an "orthodox teaching." But when, in what has become known as the "Chinese-rites controversy," Pope Clement XI ruled against the Jesuit missionaries' interpretation of what was acceptable for Chinese converts and thus contradicted the judgment of the emperor, Kangxi denounced Christianity as a heterodox teaching. Designations of orthodoxy and heterodoxy could change, but the infallible arbiter of such distinctions was always the emperor.[13] As Zhuo Xinping has noted, the basic imperial policy toward religion was that "the government is the master, religion is the follower" *(zhengzhu, jiaocong)*.

In 2008, Xi Jinping, the CCP leader who is the presumptive successor to current general-secretary Hu Jintao, declared that the Party was now a "ruling party" rather than a "revolutionary party."[14] The CCP will now justify itself by driving China's economic development, defending its territorial integrity, and promoting its rich cultural heritage. The regime's main slogan now lauds the "harmonious society," a notion with Confucian echoes. Harmony is said to depend above all on "social stability." In religious affairs, at least, it is imperial hierarchs and not Marx and Lenin who furnish the models to be followed.

The new line suggests that the state will tolerate a wide range of religious practices under the rubric of respecting "cultural pluralism." In line with official pronouncements, scholars such as Zhuo insist that the cornerstone of religious policy is the constitutional guarantee of religious freedom. But this is not freedom as understood in the Western liberal tradition. In some ways, the Chinese policy gives *more* support to religion than is the norm in countries such as the United States, where church and state are strictly separated and the latter may provide no direct economic support to the former.[15] In China, the government pays religious functionaries their salaries and funds the building of churches—provided that the functionaries and the churches alike belong to one of the officially accepted patriotic associations.

This government patronage is in line with the imperial state's custom of doling out patronage to temples. This is not a liberal toleration, based on an unalienable right to freedom of religious association. Rather, it is a modern manifestation of the old imperial principle that the state is the master, and religion is the follower. The state reserves for itself the prerogative of determining which practices make up orthodox "true religion" and which betoken a heterodox "evil cult." (In 2008, the Propaganda Department produced a video that made just this kind of distinction.) The state's chief criterion is the religion's practical effect: Does it or does it not contribute to a "harmonious society" under the direction of the party-state? In order to be fully legitimate, the official thinking goes, religions must work actively to build the harmonious society. If they are not working actively toward this end, the state must guide them so that they do fulfill their obligations. If they refuse to accept guidance, the state must crush them.

In its new incarnation, the supposedly secular CCP assumes a holy aura. It now presents itself as the carrier of a sacred national destiny. It carries out spectacular public rituals such as the opening ceremonies of the 2008 Beijing Olympics—ceremonies that powerfully evoked the glorious cultural heritage of Confucianism, Buddhism, and Taoism, but gave no mention at all to Mao Zedong or even to socialism.

This can lead to new patterns of religious tolerance and repression. Village temples and festivals that were once suppressed as examples of "feudal superstition" are now permitted and even encouraged, as long as they keep villagers happy and perhaps draw in some tourism. Like the imperial government of old, the CCP is partial to polytheism—a multitude of local cults keep rural society divided and incapable of mass action. Christianity is more problematic; it is a foreign religion, not part of the Chinese cultural heritage. But as long as Christian groups thoroughly indigenize—which in practice means that they accept the principle that the government is the master, religion the follower—they can be accepted. Even local house churches may be tolerated if they preach strong families and hard work and avoid challenging the police forces of the harmonious society. The encouragement of local folk religion seems to have slowed the recent growth of evangelical Christianity in the countryside. The Christian God then becomes one in a pantheon of local gods among whom the rural population divides its loyalties.

With the collapse of a religion policy based on the presumed inevitability of secularization, the CCP is thus falling back upon the old scripts of an enchanted imperial age. This may not work, however, because the Chinese state is ironically both too strong and too weak for it.

The modern state has the power to subject society to much more complete surveillance and control than did the imperial state. In order to fulfill its sacral ambition to exercise a modern Mandate of Heaven, the Communist party-state must attempt to exert that control. In imperial China, some religious practices gave people a chance to withdraw to spaces that were beyond the state's reach, but also so marginal as to be politically harmless.

Now, because of the very success of the Chinese state in extending its power, free space is so rare that even the attempt to retreat to it can seem like resistance. Moreover, events at the margins of society can now affect state power. Finally, because of the very communications technologies with which the modernizing government has criss-crossed China, marginalized groups can forge ties, exchange ideas, and influence one other. If these groups eventually end up undermining the CCP regime, that outcome will have come to pass at least in part because the regime had inadvertently laid down some of the conditions for its own destruction.

As the evolution of grassroots religion in China grows more dynamic, the government must now decide which of the churning changes in religious life are orthodox and which are not. Scholars and officials concerned with religious affairs are adopting the Chinese-American sociologist Fenggang Yang's idea that there are "red" (legitimate), "black" (illegitimate), and "grey" markets for religion.[16] The government's task is to sort the points of "grey" into clear-cut "red" and "black." Yet the "grey" market is so huge and diversified that this is very hard to do, and in any case it would require a degree of expertise that is in short supply in China.

The second problem stems from the Chinese government's inability to seal China off and completely control all its relationships with the outside world. The emperors could choose not to tolerate foreign faiths whose leaderships lay beyond imperial control. But in an age of globalization, the Chinese government cannot easily stop such faiths from influencing China.

Challenges of Religious Globalization

The Ming and Qing emperors had problems with universalist religions whose teachings transcended the boundaries of any particular empire and indeed could be invoked to call earthly rulers to account. Such religions could be tolerated only if thoroughly "indigenized"—that is, made supportive of established social order and imperial rule. Even religions that aspire to universalism can become all too easily absorbed into the immanent power structures of this world, of course. In the nineteenth century, both Catholic and Protestant Christianity came to China on the heels of Western imperialism and played a role in justifying colonialist projects that in Chinese eyes made the era a "century of shame" never to be permitted again. In the twenty-first century, by contrast, the flow of universalist religious movements into China—Christianity, Islam, and globalized forms of Buddhism—is mostly the result not of imperialist power politics but of the fluidity of networks and the porosity of borders in an age of global hypercommunication. Yet the Chinese government still worries—not without cause—that foreign governments might use the promotion of universal religions for the purpose of fomenting "color revolutions" that would undermine the party-state.[17]

As China rises to world-power status, its rulers seek to showcase its glory by exporting their country's "nonmaterial cultural heritage" around the globe. The government is establishing "Confucian institutes" to teach Chinese language and culture in Europe and the Americas. State-sponsored films, art troupes, and other efforts celebrate the Chinese past, including the legacies of Taoism, Buddhism, and Confucianism—all interpreted in ways that comport with the dominant Han Chinese culture and the state's preferred "government master, religion follower" formula. The regime appears to have few qualms about importing foreigners' "nonmaterial cultural heritage" in the form of globalized popular culture, but remains highly wary of absorbing global religious culture, especially to the degree that it may be influenced by authorities outside China.

Christianity, Islam, and Tibetan Buddhism all pose severe challenges to the CCP's neoimperial sacral hegemony. Although in many respects the Chinese Catholic Church has been indigenized, its theology still commits its leadership to be loyal to the pope. The Chinese government concedes that Catholics can accept Rome's "spiritual" authority, but it reserves the right to draw the exact line between spiritual and temporal. The pope, of course, thinks that Rome knows the proper boundary. For the state, global communications make the threat of foreign influence on the Catholic Church ever harder to eliminate. Negotiations between the Chinese government and the Vatican about normalizing diplomatic relations have been going on fitfully for more than two decades, but they are currently at an impasse. The main problem is that the Vatican seeks more religious freedom for Catholics than the government is willing to give. And the Chinese government is afraid that even if the Vatican formally agrees to its conditions, the pope has enough spiritual authority to influence Catholics in ways beyond the government's ability to control.

Protestant Christianity in China is much more decentralized, and does not pose the threat of a centralized ecclesiastical power attempting to impose its version of orthodoxy on Chinese believers. But as a global faith, it too is open to influence spread through modern media (and often carried directly by missionaries) from around the world. Thus, however indigenized Protestant Christianity becomes in China, it will remain in touch with spiritual movements from abroad. A completely secular liberal government would not have much problem with such cosmopolitan religious influence, but a government that claims a modern Mandate of Heaven cannot in principle tolerate it. The likeliest prospect is that the CCP will work on two fronts, trying to restrict Christianity's spread while also fostering indigenous folk religion as a rival. The restrictions, however, will most likely prove ineffective. Christianity will keep growing, China's ruling elite will keep arguing internally about how to respond, and the upshot will be a grab bag of seemingly arbitrary, incoherent policies toward Christianity.

From its beginnings, Buddhism transcended all boundaries of kinship and nation, but most of the Buddhism practiced by the Han Chinese in mainland China is closely identified with Han Chinese culture, and its leaders have been very willing to accept guidance from the state. The problem for the CCP is Tibetan Buddhism, which over the last fifty years has surged beyond the boundaries of Tibetan and Mongolian nationality and become a world religion, with enthusiastic devotees in the Americas, Europe, and elsewhere. Since his 1959 flight into exile, the Dalai Lama has become a global celebrity, welcomed and respected as a great spiritual leader by popes, kings, publics, and presidents. Both his office and his charisma bring him huge respect from most Tibetans, who already have plenty of nonreligious reasons to resist Han Chinese colonialism. But their allegiance to a faith whose most revered leader is beyond the control of the Chinese state makes their resistance even more threatening in the eyes of the Chinese government. According to the logic of sacral imperial rule, all lamas should accept the suzerainty of the Chinese emperor, even though in practice they might have wide leeway in their religious affairs. Following the logic of sacral emperorship, the CCP is not content merely to dispute the Dalai Lama's positions on Tibet, but seeks thoroughly to demonize the man. He is portrayed as equal in evil to Osama bin Laden, a person utterly devoid of any claim to spiritual leadership. Given the Dalai Lama's immense and far-flung popularity, such attacks are counterproductive. They merely alienate global public opinion and, if anything, increase the religious zeal of embattled Tibetans.[18]

A final challenge to the CCP's neoimperial sacral hegemony comes from Islam.[19] The Qing dynasty in the nineteenth century and the Republican government in the 1930s both faced uprisings from the Uyghur minority that inhabits China's far-western region of Xinjiang. The Uyghurs are Muslims, but the Islamic religion was not necessarily the major cause of previous rebellions among these Turkic people. Indeed, they practiced a variety of strands of Islam that divided rather than united them. But globalization has brought Uyghur Muslims into contact with worldwide Islamic movements.

There are pragmatic reasons for the Chinese government to worry about the radicalism that might come with such a religious revival, but the reaction against it seems so extreme as to be counterproductive. In the name of suppressing "separatism," some Chinese authorities have begun to attack Islamic practice itself. During Ramadan in 2008, for example, they forced Uyghur men to shave their beards, restricted access to mosques, and discouraged ritual fasting. This perhaps can only be explained in terms of the affront that a globalized Islam poses to neoimperial sacral hegemony. Such actions serve to add religious grievances to the many others that Uyghurs have against Han Chinese and could drive Uyghur movements closer to global movements of political Islam. It does not seem that such connections were made during the Uyghur uprisings of July 2009. But the Chinese government's general hostility to globalized Islam adds dangerous fuel to the fires of ethnic resentment.

With its "Great Firewall" of Internet filtering and massive surveillance resources, the Chinese party-state can inhibit the influence of universalizing religious movements, but it cannot block them completely. Moreover, even partial repression of such influences exposes China to censure from increasingly assertive global movements for religious freedom.

This will be confounding to a policy modeled on the sacral hegemony of premodern Chinese emperors. The one way to keep universalizing global religious movements from undermining that policy is for China to become so powerful that it can set the terms of its relationship with the rest of world. Then it can use its military and economic might to enforce its claim that universal standards of religious freedom do not apply to China and that universal religions can enter China only if they accept the "government master, religion follower" principle. Some political leaders think that they can accomplish this.

If they do completely succeed, they might one day come to regret it, because the accumulated pressure from frustrated religious believers could become explosive. The likelihood, however, is that China's political authorities will succeed only in part, and will experience ongoing frictions with global proponents of religious freedom. One can easily imagine grim scenarios of intensified conflict over religion's relationship to the state. In more auspicious scenarios, however, such international frictions will drive all sides to seek better ways of balancing the rights of increasingly assertive religions with the requirements of governance in a postsecular world.

NOTES

1. See Daniel Bell, "The Return of the Sacred: An Argument on the Future of Religion," in *The Winding Passage: Essays and Sociological Journeys, 1960–1980* (New York: Basic Books, 1981), 327.

2. Translated in Donald E. MacInnis, *Religion in China Today: Policy and Practice* (Maryknoll, N.Y.: Orbis, 1989), 8–26. In the nearly three decades since Document 19's promulgation, additional regulations regarding religion have supplemented it, but these have all been within the framework that Document 19 lays out.

3. See Jürgen Habermas, *Rationality and Religion: Essays on Reason, God, and Modernity* (Cambridge: MIT Press, 2002). See also the introduction to Craig Calhoun, Mark Juergensmeyer, and Jonathan VanAntwerpen, *Rethinking Secularism* (New York: Oxford University Press, 2010).

4. Shmuel Eisenstadt, ed., *Multiple Modernities* (New York: Transaction, 2002).

5. Jose Casanova, *Public Religions in the Modern World* (Chicago: University of Chicago Press, 1994).

6. Mayfair Mei-hui Yang, ed., *Chinese Religiosities: Afflictions of Modernity and State Formation* (Berkeley: University of California Press, 2008).

7. Kenneth Dean, "Local Communal Religion in South-east China," in Daniel L. Overmyer, ed., *Religion in China Today* (Cambridge: Cambridge University Press, 2003), 32–52.

8. Yu Jianrong (Institute of Rural Development, Chinese Academy of Social Sciences), "Religious Demography and House Churches, 2008," *Compass Direct News Service,* 3 July 2009.

9. Gerda Wielander, "Bridging the Gap? An Investigation of Beijing Intellectual House Church Activities and Their Implications for China's Democratization," *Journal of Contemporary China* 18 (November 2009): 849–64.

10. David A. Palmer, *Qigong Fever: Body, Science, and Utopia in China* (London: Hurst, 2007), 260–61.

11. The best-known "heterodox" Christian sect is the Eastern Lightening, which began in Henan Province, is quite strong in Shaanxi, and now seems to be spreading in Wenzhou. It has a female leader whose followers consider her a reincarnation of Jesus. There are at least ten other such quasi-Christian sects, with names like "The Established King," "The Lord God Sect," and "Three Ranks of Servants." See Richard Madsen, "Chinese Christianity: Indigenization and Conflict," in Elizabeth J. Perry and Mark Selden, eds., *Chinese Society: Change, Conflict, and Resistance,* 3rd ed. (London: Routledge, 2010), 246.

12. The term *xiejiao* has usually been translated in the English-language scholarly and historical literature as "heterodoxy." The phenomenon does not necessarily conform to the definition of a "cult" in a modern sociological sense. But official Chinese translations of the term into English render it as "evil cult," probably to intimate sinister connotations that would seem to justify crackdowns on such activities.

13. Richard Madsen, *China's Catholics: Tragedy and Hope in an Emerging Civil Society* (Berkeley: University of California Press, 1998). See also Richard Madsen, "Catholicism as Chinese Folk Religion," in Stephen Uhalley, Jr., and Xiaoxin Wu, eds., *China and Christianity: Burdened Past, Hopeful Future* (Armonk, N.Y.: M.E. Sharpe, 2001), 233–49.

14. He first made this statement in a speech at the Central Party School in Beijing on 1 September 2008. The speech was later reprinted in the school's official newspaper.

15. Zhuo Xinping, *Quanqiuhuade zongjiao yu Dangdai Zhongguo* (Global religions and contemporary China) (Beijing: Shehuikexue wenxian chubanshe, 2008), 30. A major mission of the Chinese Academy of Social Sciences is to give scholarship-based advice to China's central government.

16. Fenggang Yang, "Red, Black, and Grey Markets for Religion in China," *Sociological Quarterly* 47 (February 2006): 93–122.

17. Zhuo Xinping, *Quanqiuhuade,* 174.

18. Melvyn C. Goldstein, *The Snow Lion and the Dragon: China, Tibet, and the Dalai Lama* (Berkeley: University of California Press, 1999).

19. Dru Gladney, *Muslim Chinese: Ethnic Nationalism in the People's Republic,* 2nd ed. (Cambridge: Harvard East Asian Monographs, 1996).

20

CLASSICAL LIBERALISM CATCHES ON IN CHINA

Liu Junning

Liu Junning, *a former fellow at the Institute of Political Science of the Chinese Academy of Social Sciences, is an independent scholar and the editor of the journal* Res Publica *and a series of books on democratization. An earlier version of this essay was presented at a September 1999 conference, "Whither China? The PRC at 50," sponsored by the Cato Institute in Washington, D.C. It appears along with the other conference essays in* Ted Galen Carpenter and James A. Dorn, eds., China's Future: Constructive Partner or Emerging Threat? *(Cato Institute, 2000). This essay originally appeared in the July 2000 issue of the* Journal of Democracy.

The international press dubbed early 1998 as the "Beijing spring," noting that Chinese intellectuals, "emboldened by signs of tolerance," argued for political reform "more loudly than at any time since 1989."[1] Two different but closely associated voices were raised during those months: One called for political reform in China, while the other advocated classical liberalism as an alternative to established Marxist ideology. Although the latter voice received less attention from the outside world, it survived the former, which has been effectively silenced. This new school of thinkers, which calls itself *ziyou pai* ("the liberals"), made a formal appearance during the "Beijing spring" and declared that liberalism was making a comeback in China after an absence of almost 40 years.

The formal reappearance of liberalism indicates that a new stage has been reached in the intellectual odyssey of Chinese intellectuals. A leading figure in the liberal revival asserted in the preface to *Peking University and Liberalism in Modern China*, "After the largest-scale totalitarian experiment ever undertaken in human history . . . liberalism has convincingly been proved to be the most desirable and universal system of values."[2]

The resurgence of liberalism in China has not escaped the attention of the Western press. According to the *New York Times*, liberal political ideas and discussions are quietly making a comeback among Chinese intellectuals. More and more newspapers and journals are inviting frank talks about politics. Chinese leaders are learning that liberalism is a by-product of the market economy.[3] *Newsweek* reports that the "Chicago School economists," and especially the late Friedrich von Hayek, "are 'hot.'" Hayek's popularity is attributed to the fact that "he's the most anti-socialist economist around. Even Prime Minister Zhu Rongji has Hayek on his bookshelf."[4] Demand for his books is voracious. *Hayek Currents—Recent & Noteworthy,* an online bulletin, reports that "all 20,000 copies of the first printing of the new Beijing translation of Hayek's *The Constitution of Liberty* have sold out. Originally published in February, the book is currently in its second printing."[5] Commenting on the fact that Beijing's leading reformers and liberals got together on 27 February 1998 to discuss Hayek's *The Constitution of Liberty,* the *Far East Economic Review* noted: "This might sound arcane, but it is not. *The Constitution of Liberty* was banned in China when it was published in 1960."[6] According to one of its participants, the conference concluded that "the things Hayek talked about are exactly what China is going through now."[7]

The popularity of liberal ideas in China can also be gauged from the response of their adversaries. One neoleftist intellectual recently lamented, "It is natural for liberalism to be in the ascendant. And I deeply understand that its prosperity will endure for the long run. In this respect, I feel even more optimistic about the 'prospects' of liberalism than all the liberals. Therefore, I am more pessimistic about the future of [neoleftist] critical theory than . . . the liberals." While the "Beijing Spring" came to an end, the revival of liberalism that it inspired has survived and is thriving.

Background and Dynamics

This was not the first time that liberal ideas had come to China. Before the communists triumphed in 1949, there existed a group of liberal intellectuals who were squeezed from both sides by the authoritarian Kuomintang and the totalitarian Communist Party. These intellectuals and their ideas, along with what remained of private property rights and free enterprise, were completely eradicated by the 1957 Anti-Rightist Movement.

The recent resurgence of liberalism stems from the Chinese intelligentsia's longing for freedom in the post-Tiananmen era and from the profound transformation that China has undergone since the deaths of Mao Zedong and Deng Xiaoping. This period has witnessed the withering of communist ideology and totalitarianism, a process of social and cultural disintegration, and the emergence of a well-educated, active liberal intelligentsia. The latter includes both academic and public intellectuals who are dedicated to resistance to repression, respect for individual worth and freedom, and the promotion of liberal democratic institutions. China is shifting from a planned command economy to a heavily state-regulated market economy and from a Leninist political system to what may be called "one-party authoritarianism." Rapid economic growth has facilitated the development of a growing middle class, which is implicitly demanding that it be granted the right to participate in political decision-making and that limits be placed on government to protect its gains. The past decade has also witnessed the rapid growth of China's nascent civil society.

In spite or perhaps because of the fact that people in China today live in a spiritual vacuum and often succumb to crass materialism, Chinese intellectuals are demonstrating a growing interest in liberal values. The realm of government is shrinking and that of society and the market is expanding. Lifestyles, avocations, and aspirations are becoming increasingly diverse. The number of licensed nongovernmental organizations is growing rapidly, and people are also forming voluntary associations without first securing approval from the government. China's inhabitants clearly enjoy a broader range of choice in the cultural domain. The number of magazines, newspapers, and books being published is increasing dramatically.

The established ideology has been withering away both as an ideal and in practice, even though the regime that imposed it remains in place. Virtually no "true believers" are left in China. There is an unbridgeable chasm between the official ideology and the reality of the market economy. The two cannot coexist in harmony for long; one of them must give way.

This does not mean that the transition to liberal democracy has already been secured in China. Much effort is still required to steer China along a liberal course. Although the ruling ideology is collapsing because of the inner contradictions between China's political and economic systems, that does not mean that liberalism will automatically replace it.

Fortunately, however, the end of the totalitarian temptation has created room for liberalism to sprout and grow. Liberalism has now become a powerful intellectual movement, and China's political culture is shifting in a liberal direction. Today, almost all of those who shape public opinion and most of the "celebrities" in virtually all fields in China are liberals. Among Chinese intellecuals, pride in being a leftist has been replaced by pride in being a liberal.

The Intellectual Exodus

Before 1978, Chinese intellectuals had to operate in a totally closed society. China had been cut off from any ideas and theories other than the dominant ideology. It was only after China began to open up to the West in the late 1970s that intellectuals were gradually exposed to the outside world. At that time, due to decades of isolation and the apparent "vitality" of communist ideology, Chinese intellectuals were still preoccupied with finding a way to "perfect" the established system by initiating reform proposals that would make one-party rule more "democratic." Thus, while most Chinese intellectuals in the 1980s called themselves "democrats" and a few called themselves "humanist Marxists" (to distinguish themselves from "Stalinist Marxists"), none called themselves "liberals." These "democrats" put socialist democracy above individual liberty, and government planning and regulation above the mechanism of the free market. A number of them have been very critical of some of the regime's practices and policies, but not of the ideology behind them. Although "democrats" became disillusioned by this ideology, they could find no systematic alternative to it.

The 1989 Tiananmen Square Incident shocked and awakened these intellectuals. They gave up hope of "transforming the untransformable," decided to extricate themselves from the establishment, and began searching for a better, yet feasible, alternative. As a result of this intellectual exodus from the orthodox ideology, liberalism has come to be widely recognized by intellectuals as the only way out of China's present predicament. An eminent dissident reflected upon his intellectual odyssey in this way: "Before [the Tiananmen Square Incident], I was sympathetic only to some liberal ideas. The most important thing that I learned from the Incident is that I came to realize that I will not only stick to . . . liberalism as a theoretical value, but I will also put liberal values into practice."[8]

Another dissident, one of the founders of the China Democratic Party in 1998, explained why he viewed individual liberty and liberalism as the most effective weapons against tyranny: "Sometimes, democracy is not a sharp weapon in slashing tyranny; instead it sometimes becomes a slogan abused and paid lip service to by those tyrants. Only individual freedom and liberalism are the genuine antidotes against tyranny. What all the tyrants dread most is freedom, which is the cornerstone of all other human values and the real motivation that promotes the development of society, science and technology, culture, and commerce. Therefore, to cure the chronic and stubborn disease of tyranny in China, liberalism and individual worth are the most effective remedies."[9]

The post-1989 international environment has also been very favorable to the growth of liberalism in China. The "third wave" of worldwide democratization and liberalization and the collapse of the Berlin Wall have shocked, enlightened, and served as an example for Chinese intellectuals. After the demise of Soviet communism, liberalism is experiencing a worldwide renaissance, but once again, China has lagged behind. The history of China in this century is characterized by its belated efforts to "catch up" to world trends. (Unfortunately, in the first half of the twentieth century it caught the wave of communism, which was then on the rise worldwide.) In the late 1980s, it attempted in vain to catch the third wave of democratization. Since today's trend is the decline of totalitarianism and authoritarianism and the rebirth of liberalism throughout the world, it would be a tragedy if China once again missed the chance to join the mainstream of human civilization.

Domestically, the initial development of a market economy in China has laid a solid foundation for the development of liberal ideas and liberal social forces. Economic freedom and private property, although still very much limited, have given people an appetite for civil and political liberties. The case of China shows that a free market in commodities will ultimately result in a free market of ideas and a demand for liberal ideas. As long as people are free to choose, most people will choose liberty and liberalism.

People may ask how liberalism can take root and grow in a society like China. The answer may be found by looking more closely at the impact of the market economy, or what Adam Smith called "the system of natural liberty." The market mechanism in China promotes not only economic freedom but other freedoms as well. Take freedom of the press, for example. In the 1980s, the "democrats" argued that it should take precedence over economic freedom. Yet freedom of the press cannot be effectively exercised without economic freedom and private property. After implementing market-oriented reforms, the Chinese government stopped giving subsidies to most of the newspapers, magazines, publishers, and television stations. As a result, these media now have to interest their audience. Since more and more people in China are interested in liberal ideas, editors are enthusiastically publishing liberal articles, and even risking harassment from the official censors to meet the market's demand. And as I have learned, they do this not just for the sake of making a profit; an increasing number of them have developed their own interest in liberalism. As a matter of fact, these editors are pushing the intellectuals to produce liberal publications. In fact, the only way to stop the trend of liberalization today would be to resume full-scale media subsidies, which is beyond the government's capabilities.

A key factor facilitating the spread of liberal ideas in China today is the Internet. China is making a great leap forward into the "information age" and the "network society." Internet use is rapidly growing in China, particularly in universities and academic institutions. In 1997, there were about 640,000 Internet users in China; at the beginning of 1999, there were 2.1 million, and there are more than 4 million today. According to the latest report by the China Internet Information Center, it is estimated that, with falling prices for personal computers and Internet access, there will be 7 million Internet users by the end of 2000 and more than 33 million in 2003. E-mail is already the preferred mode of communication for Chinese intellectuals, both among themselves and with the West. The Internet could have a "revolutionary" impact on China, both economically and politically. The flow of economic information stimulated by the Internet is essential not only for attracting investment but also for creating an economic system that is fair, open, transparent, and competitive. Information flows have been loosened considerably in China over the last several years, due less to conscious government policy than to increased contact with the outside world and to the rise of electronic media, which are much harder to police than traditional "hard-copy" publications.[10]

The widespread use of the Internet makes it harder for the government to maintain a monopoly over information resources. The combination of the market and the Internet will promote the free flow of information into and out of China, making it easier for liberal intellectuals to use liberal resources outside of China, to communicate, and to spread liberal ideas more effectively. No library is bigger or handier than the Internet. It was from the Internet that I first learned about Western liberal think-tanks like the Cato Institute and read their online publications. In the middle of 1999, some websites on liberalism were set up in China. As Fidel Castro once said: "Socialism in Central Europe failed because people received more information than was necessary."[11] He understood very well the power of information. With the assistance of the Internet, information can become even more powerful.

The "Real McCoy"

Liberalism comes in many versions or "brands." Chinese liberals today must learn from the experience of the Chinese intellectual movement before the Communist takeover in 1949 and reflect on the causes of its failure in modern China. Hayek noted that, in the West, the label of liberalism was "hijacked" by liberal-minded democratic socialists. This also happened in China. Most modern Chinese liberals did not pursue their liberal pilgrimage all the way back to the fountainhead of classical liberalism; they stopped halfway and became either pragmatists in the mold of John Dewey or democratic socialists a la Harold Laski. These intellectuals shared an antipathy toward the market economy and private property rights and a preference for a centrally planned, heavily regulated, and egalitarian economic order. In their writings, they do not cite John Locke, David Hume, Adam Smith, Edmund Burke, Lord Acton, the *Federalist,* Montesquieu, Benjamin Constant, or Tocqueville; Rousseau's political writings were their main source of intellectual inspiration. Their favorite contemporary thinkers were John Dewey and Harold Laski, not Karl Popper and F.A. Hayek. They were collectivists, not individualists. They claimed descent from the French Enlightenment rather than the Scottish Enlightenment, and favored the French Revolution over Britain's Glorious Revolution and the American Revolution.

Thus modern Chinese liberalism was heavily stained by constructivist rationalism, perfectionism, and scientism, and therefore by socialism. As Hayek predicted, and as China's postwar history proved, the road that these earlier Chinese liberals thought would lead to freedom was in fact "the road to serfdom." That is the main reason why Hayek is probably more popular in China today than in the West. His judgment has proven sound in most aspects. His assessment—made in the 1930s—about the prospects of socialism and the command economy has proven to be absolutely correct. From Hayek and other contemporary classical liberals, Chinese liberals are learning about the crucial importance of economic freedom and private property rights, and about the link (and the often-ignored conceptual difference) between liberalism and democracy.

For this reason, most Chinese liberals today agree that the version of liberalism that is chosen matters a great deal; indeed, the fate of liberalism in China, and even of China itself, depends upon it. Thus today's Chinese liberals distinguish themselves from their counterparts in the 1930s and 1940s by going back to liberalism of the unadulterated, classical variety.

More and more classic liberal texts are being translated into Chinese, including the works of Wilhelm von Humboldt, Thomas Jefferson, Alexis de Tocqueville, Herbert Spencer, Frederic Bastiat, Ludwig von Mises, Karl Popper, F.A. Hayek, Milton Friedman, James Buchanan, Robert Nozick, Douglass C. North, Michael Novak, Isaiah Berlin, and Ayn Rand. Most of Hayek's important works have been translated into Chinese, including *The Road to Serfdom, Individualism and Economic Order, The Constitution of Liberty, The Fatal Conceit,* and *Law, Legislation, and Liberty.* Some informal reading groups have been established in China's universities to study the texts of classical liberalism. One of them is the Austrian Group at Peking University, composed of undergraduate, postgraduate, and Ph.D. students from the disciplines of politics, economics, law, sociology, and even the natural sciences. These publications have been widely and frequently quoted in graduate student dissertations, as well as in newspaper articles and academic papers. The demand for liberal ideas is so great that supply still lags behind.

Chinese liberalism today gives special attention to property rights, economic freedom, constitutionalism, the rule of law and limited government, individualism, toleration, pluralism, and the open society. The journal *Res Publica* (founded in 1994), the first Chinese academic journal since 1949 to concentrate on classical liberalism, has initiated a good deal of discussion about these topics.

Chinese Liberals and the Future

Classical liberalism now dominates China's intellectual landscape. No other school of political thought enjoys greater popularity in the Chinese intellectual community. Some skeptics, it is true, regard liberalism as premature and even superfluous, since China has existed for thousands of years without it. They regard liberalism as an alien doctrine, inasmuch as it originated in the West and has little in common with the Chinese cultural tradition. Nonetheless, I have confidence that liberalism will prevail in China, for it is an idea that is universal and grounded in human nature. If Chinese people hate having their property taken away by arbitrary government, if they want to enjoy the freedoms of speech and association without the fear of being thrown into prison, if they want to express their own views about public policy and policy makers without being accused of subversion, and if they want the freedom to choose which religion to believe in without fear of persecution, they have every reason to embrace liberal ideas. In the West, liberalism was the natural companion of the market economy. Now that the market economy has become the inevitable option for China, the gateway to liberalism can no longer be kept shut. Since the process of marketization in China is irrevocable, liberalism's triumph is inevitable.

In China today, there is considerable freedom to write on nonpolitical issues, and private discussion of political issues is far less controlled than before. An increasingly large range of activities is outside the reach of central and ideological control. People are no longer mobilized to participate in an endless series of political purges and campaigns, and they need not affirm communism as their ideal. They enjoy much greater occupational choice and geographic mobility. Individuals can withdraw from political life and pursue private interests, as long as they do not directly challenge the right of the country's leaders to rule.

Yet although the situation has improved greatly since the days of the Cultural Revolution, there are still substantial restraints on freedom in China. Chinese citizens are not yet free to express their political beliefs publicly, nor can they challenge the official ideology openly. Thus liberalism in China depends on its silent supporters. If they do not buy and read liberal publications, the supply of these publications will dry up. If editors do not risk their positions, their publishing houses, and their chances for promotion to publish liberal articles, liberalism's popularity will be short-lived. China's liberal intellectuals have also changed their strategy. They now look to the general public rather than to those in power, informing the Chinese people of the options that they may choose when a democratic breakthrough occurs. Their "platform" has been summarized as follows: "China's current government was designed to administer a command economy that no longer exists. Officialdom is too big and too corrupt, and must shrink. Officials must respond to the needs of citizens, not to orders from above. This will require elections, a strong legal system, and respect for individual rights."[12]

Although there is reason to be optimistic about liberalism's future in China, major obstacles remain. How will liberalism, which is defined in terms of individual freedom, overcome China's traditional ethos and communist legacy of collectivism? It is quite clear that the process will not be a smooth one, and its success cannot be taken for granted. In fact, China's liberal democrats are facing increasingly complex problems. For example, liberalism is now under attack not only from traditional leftists, but also from new young leftists trained in the West and armed with the weaponry of neo-Marxism, postmodernism, communitarianism, nationalism, populism, and many other "brave new" theories. Fortunately, it is much easier for the Chinese people to understand the value of property rights and economic freedom than it is for them to penetrate the obscurity of these high-minded leftist "discourses."

Today there is growing pressure not to confine liberalism to the intellectual sphere but to demand real change toward a society based on liberal principles. As Hayek said in *The Constitution of Liberty,* "Freedom of action, even in humble things, is as important as freedom of thought."[13] The task of liberal intellectuals in China is to do everything in their power to make the case for individual freedom. This new "bottom-up" strategy will eventually make a difference for China's future.

Liberals in China now are trying to build consensus and to shape the direction of political reform: to secure greater individual freedoms, to protect property rights, to strengthen legislative bodies, to place the military and the police more firmly under civilian control, to relax controls over nongovernmental organizations, to strengthen the judiciary, and to provide the populace with more meaningful avenues of political participation.

China finally has a good chance to get on the liberal democratic track. The opening up of China during the period of reform, the collapse of the communist regimes of the former Soviet bloc, and the great expansion of the global market all provide favorable conditions for democratization and liberalization in China.

What role is China likely to play on the international scene in the future? Will it be an emerging threat to the democracies or a constructive partner? To a very great extent, the answer depends on the fate of liberalism in China. A nationalistic and authoritarian China will be a threat. A liberal China, however, will be a constructive partner, since it is well known that liberal democracies do not fight one another. Thus it is in the best interests of the established democracies to encourage liberalism as the driving force for bringing democracy to China.

NOTES

1. Matt Forney, "Beijing Spring," *Far Eastern Economic Review* (Hong Kong), 2 April 1998, 20.

2. Liu Junning, ed., *Peking University and the Liberalism in Modern China* (Beijing: China Renshi Press, 1998), 4–5.

3. Elizabeth Rosenthal, "China's Leading University Celebrates and Ponders," *New York Times,* 5 May 1998.

4. Jonathan Alter, "On the Road in China," *Newsweek,* 29 June 1998.

5. "Hayek Currents—Recent & Noteworthy," available online at http://members.aol.com/ grgransom/hayekpage.htm.

6. Matt Forney, "Beijing Spring," 21.

7. Ibid.

8. Liu Xiaobo, cited from a report that appeared on Chinese electronic bulletin boards in early 1997.

9. Wang Youcai, cited from his article, "Liberalism, Constitutionalism and China's Democracy," which is posted on the Internet at www.asiademo.org/19980917b.htm.

10. John D. Sullivan, "Statement on How the Internet Promotes Free Market Philosophies and Democratic Principles Overseas before the House Committee on Commerce for the Center of International Private Enterprise," 29 July 1998, available online at www.cipe.org/events/press/jds7-98.htm.

11. Cited in Ibid.

12. Matt Forney, "Beijing Spring," 21.

13. F.A. Hayek, *The Constitution of Liberty* (Chicago: University of Chicago Press, 1976), 35.

21

CHINA'S CONSTITUTIONALIST OPTION

Andrew J. Nathan

*Andrew J. Nathan is Class of 1919 Professor of Political Science at Co-
lumbia University and a member of the Editorial Board of the Journal
of Democracy. His most recent book is* China's Search for Security *(coauthored with Andrew Scobell, 2012). This essay, which originally appeared in the October 1996 issue of the* Journal of Democracy, *is based
on a paper he presented at a conference on "Consolidating the Third
Wave Democracies: Trends and Challenges" held on 27–30 August
1995 in Taipei, Taiwan, under the auspices of the Institute for National
Policy Research of Taipei and the International Forum for Democratic
Studies of Washington, D.C.*

Of the plausible scenarios for China's future, the possibility of a new
constitutionalism has been taken seriously by only a few Western specialists.[1] Yet the constitutionalist scenario gains credibility from the
improbability of the alternatives. Civil disorder is the worst fear of
most Chinese, and few stand to gain from it. Local separatism would do
more economic harm than good to the southeastern coastal provinces
that are viewed as the most likely to secede, and would be opposed by
the Chinese army. Some in Tibet and Xinjiang would like independence, but they lack the military power to seize it. Coup plotters would
need broad support that would be difficult to marshal in the vast civil-
military command apparatus. No one in the new generation of leaders
seems to have strongman potential. And a factional stalemate would be
only an interim stage in the search for a solution to the problem of political authority. So the worst one can say against the constitutionalist
scenario is that it seems too sensible to be a genuine option.

Recent writings by Chinese scholars both within China and abroad suggest what the constitutionalist option might look like if it came to pass.[2]
Since Deng Xiaoping's reforms began, the authorities have licensed three
waves of discussion of constitutional issues. The first occurred during the
drafting of the new Constitution that was promulgated in 1982.[3] The sec-

ond took place during preparation for Zhao Ziyang's Political Report to the Thirteenth Party Congress in 1987. The third has consisted of a series of studies and conferences in academia and within the staff of the National People's Congress (NPC) since 1990, paralleled by work among members of the Chinese democracy movement now in exile.

The discussions are interesting as much for their diagnoses of what is wrong with the current system as for their proposals for reform. The diagnoses often carry implications too bold to be stated explicitly under today's political constraints. This essay details four sets of diagnoses and proposals on which the debate has focused, and which seem likely to be high on the agenda of post-Deng reformers whether the Chinese Communist Party (CCP) remains in power or not. The debates provide a script for reform efforts that are likely to be made in the coming years no matter who comes to power. For those interested in comparative constitutional design, the debates suggest how people living under a Soviet-style constitution see its possibilities for evolutionary reform.

Empowering the National People's Congress

The heart of most political-reform proposals is empowerment of the NPC.[4] Under the present Constitution the NPC is sovereign. There is no division of powers. The judicial and administrative branches report to the NPC. Either directly or through its Standing Committee, the NPC legislates; elects and recalls the top leaders of the other organs of state; supervises those officials' work, including the state budget and development plans; and interprets the Constitution and laws.

But the Constitution also acknowledges that the organs of the state operate under CCP leadership. In the NPC this leadership is exercised in a number of formal and informal ways. Party members make up from one-half to over three-fourths of the membership of the NPC, including the top layer of NPC officials and the majority of its Standing Committee, Secretariat, committee heads, and Presidium, as well as the bulk of its staff. Party cells guide the work of all these organs and staff. The central party organs instruct the NPC whom to elect to such posts as head of state, chair of the Military Affairs Commission, president of the Supreme People's Court, and procurator-general. The party center controls the NPC's budget, sets its long-term work plan, determines the agenda of its meetings, drafts much of the legislation that the NPC considers (although some drafting work is assigned by the party center to government agencies or NPC staff), and helps guide bills through committees to the final stage of passage by the NPC plenum.

The NPC's structure limits its ability to develop an autonomous ethos. It normally meets only once a year, usually in March, for 12 to 20 days; the Standing Committee (consisting of about 150 members) meets every two months for approximately one week. During NPC sessions, the huge membership of about three thousand convenes in full only to vote. Debate and discussion are limited to caucuses of provincial delegations.

Nonetheless, the legislature has shown a growing measure of assertiveness. In 1986, the Standing Committee refused to clear a draft of the Bankruptcy Law for presentation to the NPC plenum; it had to be returned to the relevant government agency for redrafting. In 1989, a substantial number of delegates opposed a State Council-drafted bill relating to the delegation of certain legislative powers to the Shenzhen Special Economic Zone, so the bill was postponed and later replaced by one that answered the members' objections. In 1992, only two-thirds of the deputies voted in favor of a proposal to build a huge dam on the Yangtze River at the Three Gorges; approval was postponed. In 1994, 337 votes were cast against the Budget Law, with another 274 abstentions and invalid ballots. In 1995, NPC delegates cast a total of 1,006 abstentions, spoiled ballots, and votes against the nomination of Jiang Chunyun as vice-premier, and many withheld support from the draft Central Bank and Education laws and from the work reports (reports of work performed over the past year and plans for future work) of the Supreme Procuratorate and the Supreme People's Court. In 1996, hundreds of delegates voted against or abstained from voting on the work reports of the procurator-general and the chief judge of the Supreme People's Court.

These events indicate that NPC members are taking their roles more seriously. The Congress passed 175 laws from 1982 to 1994 and is in the middle of a CCP-assigned five-year legislative plan to promulgate by the end of the century 152 additional laws deemed essential to China's economic and administrative modernization. NPC delegates and staffers have gained a greater sense of responsibility as their duties have expanded.

Freeing the NPC further from CCP control lies at the heart of the proposals for NPC reform, even though the proposals do not mention the problem explicitly. Proposals include the following:

Reducing the size of the NPC. Scholars argue that the large size of the NPC makes it unable to discuss proposals in plenary meetings, while discussion in small groups provides no efficient means of communication among members. Since the delegates' groups are divided mostly by territorial administrative unit, the discussion is dominated by high-ranking officials from the localities. To increase the ability to communicate and the efficiency of proceedings, scholars have proposed reducing the membership to between 700 and 2,000.

Lengthening sessions. Longer sessions would allow delegates to discuss proposed legislation more adequately.

Strengthening the committee and staff systems. The 1982 Constitution established a system of six committees for the NPC; two more were set up in 1988. The committees are supposed to help the Standing Committee with the study, review, and drafting of legislation and the supervision of other agencies of government. Scholars have proposed that the system be strengthened, though without suggesting specific methods of doing so. A related proposal is to establish (or strengthen, in the few cases where they exist) professional staff offices to help legislators at the national and provincial levels discharge their duties. The staff would consist of legal specialists working as full-time professionals.

Improving the qualifications of NPC members. Scholars have proposed that fewer officials and model workers be chosen for the NPC and that more professional politicians, legal specialists, and social activists be selected. Another proposal has been to establish a training school for NPC members.

Clarifying or improving the legislative process. Proposals include allowing NPC delegates to introduce legislation (they can do so in principle but never do in practice), ending CCP preview of legislation, allowing more time for NPC debate over legislative proposals, opening NPC sessions to the public and the press, and making a practice of voting on each part of a bill separately rather than on the bill as a whole. The idea behind these proposals is to center legislative action within rather than outside the NPC.

Increasing the NPC's role in rule-making. Scholars argue that the boundary between the legislative process and the process of framing administrative regulations is currently misplaced. Because the NPC meets so seldom, fewer rules are put through the legislative process than in most countries. Wide latitude is left for administrative agencies (the State Council, ministries and commissions, and others) to enact regulations that have the character of laws. This phenomenon is referred to as "administrative legislation" (*xingzheng lifa*). For example, the NPC has left the rule-making process pertaining to military affairs almost entirely to the Military Affairs Commission (nominally a state agency, but in actuality a party organ). Scholars have proposed a clarification of the division of rule-making powers between NPC and administrative organs in such a way as to give a larger role to the legislature.

Introducing two chambers. Some scholars argue that the NPC already has certain features of a two-chamber system and that these should be strengthened. Members of the Standing Committee are usually leaders of lower-level people's congresses or retired senior party, government, or military officials. Currently the Standing Committee exercises more power than the NPC itself because it meets more often and has more influential members. One proposal is to elect an upper chamber with three members from each province or provincial-level unit, with a lower chamber elected in proportion to population. The division of powers between the two houses is not generally specified.

Introducing the no-confidence vote. Scholars have proposed that if the work report of the government, Supreme People's Court, or Supreme Procuratorate is not approved by the NPC either initially or after one round of revision, the relevant official (premier, Supreme People's Court president, or procurator-general) should resign.

The common theme of these proposals is to increase the autonomy of the NPC and reduce the CCP's authority over it.

Invigorating Elections

Scholars have also put forward proposals to invigorate the process by which the NPC is elected. If implemented, they would also help make the legislature more autonomous.[5]

Of the four levels of people's congresses—national, provincial, county, and local—the two higher levels are indirectly elected, with NPC deputies elected by provincial congresses and provincial-congress deputies elected by county congresses. Local (village) people's congresses have been directly elected since the first elections in 1954. The Electoral Law of 1979 provided for direct election at the county level, as well as for multicandidate elections. With scattered exceptions in 1979-80, the county-level elections have not turned into competitive campaigns owing to tight party control through the local election committees.

The term "election" is a misnomer for the delegate-selection process, which is sometimes referred to more forthrightly as "production" (*chansheng*). At each level of people's congresses, the standing committee organizes the selection process for the level directly below. The standing committee supplies lists of persons who must be chosen in order to meet quotas of females, national minorities, "democratic personages," and other categories and to ensure that top party officials are included. It also supplies lists of other candidates from whom the remaining delegates must be selected. Few of the candidates are well known to the electors.

Reformers propose to free the elections from CCP control in several ways:

Improving the nomination process. Although ten citizens can join to nominate a candidate, this seldom happens. Even when it does, the final list of nominees is produced through a CCP-controlled consultative process. Rarely are there candidates not approved by the party. (These details pertain to county-level people's-congress elections, but the same types of procedures are used in elections at all levels, including the indirect elections to the NPC Standing Committee.) Reformers propose changes not in the rules but in their implementation, to allow genuine nominations from below with less party control over the process.

Reducing malapportionment. The Chinese system intentionally gives urban districts four times as many delegates per voter as rural districts in the county-level congresses; the imbalance is even worse at higher levels. This practice is justified by the Marxist theory that the urban proletariat is more progressive than rural peasants. Many reformers are nervous about granting too much power to rural people, whom they view as backward and pro-authoritarian. Political leaders fear that a farmer-dominated legislature would not support longstanding CCP policies unfavorable to rural residents. At least one scholar, however, has proposed reducing the rural-urban disparity to two-to-one. I am not aware of any proposal to move to a "one person, one vote" system.

Shifting to single-seat districts. At the county level, each district elects from one to three representatives to the people's congress. (Taiwan also has a multiseat-district system for its Legislative Yuan, but I have been unable to discover whether these two Chinese systems have a common historical origin.) Some writers have suggested moving to a single-seat system as a way of tightening representatives' links with their constituencies. This reform would force the CCP to work harder to ensure representation of its own cadres and protected categories such as women and national minorities. I do not know whether Chinese scholars have begun to look seriously at other institutional choices in the design of an electoral system, such as balloting rules, which could ultimately affect the party system and the stability of governments.

Direct elections. Scholars have refuted the idea that China is too backward or too large for direct elections to the NPC. They argue that the idea of direct elections is found in the Marxist classics, and that Chinese citizens who have been educated in advanced socialist ideas for more than 40 years must have as strong a democratic consciousness as did the citizens of capitalist systems when the direct election of parliaments began. As for constituency size as an obstacle to direct elections, they point out that each of the current NPC delegates represents a population of 360,000—fewer than the 510,000 represented by each U.S. congressman.

Competitive campaigns. Direct election would not be meaningful without reform of campaign procedures. The direct elections for local people's congresses feature an often perfunctory process of official "introductions" of candidates to voters, either on paper or at meetings. Reformers have suggested that the job be done better, that those who nominate candidates be allowed to speak for them, and that more time be spent on the process. The new procedures could build on the experience of competitive village-committee elections that have been going on since 1987, an experiment that some senior leaders see as a first step in training rural residents for a more democratic system.

Multipartism. Scholars have also proposed new legislation on parties that would allow multiparty competition, arguing that a party claiming to represent the people's interests should submit to the test of competitive elections. The CCP has advantages over other parties and could benefit from such elections, they contend. They argue that competition is a natural law and a dynamic of social development, not a monopoly of the bourgeoisie. Multiparty elections would keep the CCP on the right track and prevent the emergence of another Cultural Revolution.

Against the concern that electoral competition would create an out-of-control NPC, reformers argue that a more strenuous election process would be good for the CCP. Because the party faces no real competition and has most of the best potential candidates in its ranks, electoral reform would facilitate the advancement of the best CCP members as candidates. If campaigns are competitive, the CCP members closest to the people will win.

Constitutional Supervision

The Constitution gives the NPC the power to "supervise the enforcement of the Constitution" (Article 62) and empowers the NPC Standing Committee "to interpret the Constitution and supervise its enforcement" and "to interpret statutes" (Article 67).[6] These powers of supervision and interpretation are not equivalent to constitutional review in a system of divided powers. Since the NPC makes the laws, it could not very well declare one unconstitutional. Rather, "supervising enforcement" (*jiandu shishi*) means supervising the implementation or carrying out of the Constitution. Nominally, the NPC does this by hearing work reports from the other organs of government. It has seldom exercised its supervisory power in a more concrete way. A supervision law (*jiandu fa*), which would detail the means by which the NPC can exercise its supervisory power, exists in draft form, but its contents are not public.

Nor does the NPC Standing Committee often exercise its power of constitutional interpretation. It has responded occasionally to requests for interpretation from lower-level people's congresses. It has also issued a small number of "internal interpretations" (*neibu jieshi*) in response to requests from other government agencies. Such clarifications have the character of ad hoc problem solving, rather than formal constitutional interpretations.

Other agencies often substitute for the NPC Standing Committee in interpreting statutes. For example, the Supreme People's Court issued a brochure on how to understand the concept of marital breakdown under the 1980 Marriage Law. The Court has done similar work for the Civil Procedure Law of 1991, the Inheritance Law of 1985, and other laws. These activities seem to go beyond the constitutional authority of the Supreme People's Court to "supervise the administration of justice by the local people's courts" (Article 127); rather, the Court got involved because the NPC Standing Committee abdicated authority owing to a lack of time or expertise. The understaffed courts themselves often yield authority to administrative agencies, which have yet more personnel and expertise.

By making these diagnoses, scholars imply that the NPC's constitutional-supervision function should be strengthened. To this end, some have recommended the establishment of a specialized organ to exercise the powers of constitutional interpretation and supervision. Three proposals have been floated. The first is to establish a subsidiary committee under the Standing Committee to advise it in interpreting the Constitution.[7] The second is to establish a separate constitutional-supervision committee within the NPC, equal in rank to the Standing Committee and able to supervise all organs of state including the Standing Committee itself. The third is to establish a constitutional court with authority to reverse the actions even of the NPC, in effect creating a separation of powers and broadening the constitutional-supervision function to include constitutional review. Only the first of these proposals could be implemented without a constitutional amendment.

The discussion draws attention to the absence of a locus within the state apparatus where problems of jurisdiction and other intrastate issues can be solved. It also implicitly identifies the problem of CCP dominance as an obstacle to the lawlike functioning of the state. In addressing this issue, scholars have debated whether the CCP could be subjected to constitutional supervision. On the one hand, the party might be considered not subject to the Constitution, since CCP leadership is listed as a principle of state power in the Constitution's Preamble. On the other hand, the academic consensus is that the party is in principle subject to the Constitution, both because the Constitution lists political parties among the entities that it governs, and by virtue of the party's charter, which calls for it to obey the Constitution. But scholars recognize that it is impractical to exercise constitutional supervision over the party now. They envision a transitional stage during which the NPC might review selected CCP documents and notify the party of any contradictions with the Constitution so that the party can rectify them itself.

Judicial Independence

The Chinese Constitution states that people's courts "shall . . . exercise judicial power independently and are not subject to interference by administrative organs, public organizations or individuals" (Article 126).[8] This is not a provision for what those in the West understand by the term "judicial independence"—that is, the protection of each individual judge from interference in the lawful exercise of judicial authority. Literally, it holds that the courts should "independently carry out the judging power" (*duli xingshi shenpanquan*), meaning—as Chinese scholars interpret it—that the court as an organization should do its job exclusively, rather than having other organs share in the function, as occurred, for example, during the Cultural Revolution.

There is debate about the scope of the term "public organizations" (*shehui tuanti,* literally, "social groups") that appears in Article 126. The question is whether the CCP is included among these entities that constitutionally cannot interfere with the work of the courts. The dominant interpretation is that the category does not include the party. Scholars note that the 1982 phrasing is different from that of 1954, which stated, "People's courts independently carry out judgment, following only the law" (Article 76). In listing the entities that are prohibited from interfering in judicial processes, the 1982 Constitution seems to make room for groups that are not listed—namely, the CCP and the NPC—to get involved. In light of this reasoning and the fact that the Constitution mentions the principle of "Party leadership" in its Preamble, involvement of the CCP in the work of the courts is not deemed interference, but rather constitutionally sanctioned leadership.

Party "leadership" takes three forms. One is collective decision making. Under the "report and approval system," authority for court judgments is vested in a judicial committee of each court (*shenpan weiyuanhui*) that is led by the court president and vice-president, who are invariably also officials of that court's party group or cell. Thus judicial independence in China is not the independence of individual judges, but the independence of any given court as an organ. As one sitting judge told me, "If the [court] leaders want to change my decision, I have no power to interfere [*ganshe*]." In the Chinese judicial system, then, it is a judge's sticking to his own decision, rather than court authorities' changing it, that constitutes "interference."

The second form of CCP "leadership" is the "asking for instruction" system, by which lower courts are expected to bring important or complicated cases to higher courts to obtain instructions before handing down a judgment. Ostensibly aimed at avoiding the reversal of judgments, the process provides the opportunity for the party organs located in higher-level courts to decide the outcome of cases in lower courts.

Third, local CCP authorities (who are also administrative authorities) often issue directives to local courts on how to decide individual cases. The practice is of questionable constitutionality but is built into the system of party leadership. At each level of the administrative hierarchy (say, in a city), the local party committee has a subsidiary organ known as a political-legal committee (*zhengfa weiyuanhui*), which brings together the heads of the police, procuratorate, court, department of justice, state-security department, and civil-affairs department so that they can coordinate their work. As part of such coordination, the courts are required to seek the committee's guidance in deciding important or difficult cases (*zhongda fuza anjian*). If opinions are divided or the case is especially crucial, the political-legal committee may refer the issue to the full party committee at that level of the hierarchy.

The courts not only are led by the CCP but are constitutionally subordinate to the legislative branch. The Constitution says the courts are "responsible to" their respective people's congresses (Article 128). A people's congress cannot constitutionally interfere in a specific case, but it can require a report on a case, organize an investigation into the suspected mishandling of a case, or cashier and order the indictment of judicial officials who criminally mishandle a case. The frequency with which this happens is uncertain, but improper interference in court cases by people's congresses was sufficiently problematic that the NPC Standing Committee in 1989 issued a decision stressing the limits on such interference, presumably as a reminder to lower-level people's congresses.[9] Since local people's congresses are controlled by local CCP authorities, this seems to be a second channel for party control of the courts.

Judges and scholars have drawn attention to ways in which subordination to the CCP disrupts the courts' ability to perform their functions. Local courts often fail to enforce judgments in favor of out-of-town Chinese (or foreign) plaintiffs. Judges are reluctant to rule against local administrators in suits lodged by individual citizens under the Administrative Litigation Law of 1989 and the Compensation Law of 1994.

Proposals for improving the functioning of the courts are modest. Most involve improving the professional quality of judges and establishing better remuneration and more secure tenure. Judges in China, as in other civil-law jurisdictions, are civil servants. Their ranks are equivalent to those of various other bureaucrats across the system. Their incomes tend to be less than those of factory workers, educators, doctors, and government officials in many fields because of the lack of outside opportunities, bonuses, and supplements.

In 1995, the NPC adopted new legislation concerning judges.[10] The Judges Law mandates minimum qualifications for judges and specifies circumstances under which they can be removed from office. In these small ways it increases their independence. It states further that anyone who interferes with judges' exercise of their duties will be prosecuted according to law. But there is no law under which to prosecute such people, nor does the Judges Law define interference. The law does not solve the problem of inadequate remuneration; does not create a standard of judicial conduct; and supplies too many and too broadly stated causes for which judges can be dismissed. Some judicial reformers nonetheless see the Judges Law as the start of a trend toward independent individual judges who have job security, professional prestige, and adequate remuneration.

Other proposals relating to the judiciary include shifting more of the burden of evidence collection from judges to litigants, thus putting judges in a more neutral position; ending the system whereby judges get approval for their rulings from their administrative superiors; and reducing the practice of lower courts' seeking directives on specific cases from higher courts. A proposal has also been made to do away with the police power to sentence people under the "administrative punishment" system of labor reeducation. By moving many acts now deemed noncriminal into the criminal category, this would increase the number of cases that would have to be taken to court for judgment.

The central point of these reforms would be to strengthen the autonomy of individual judges in trying cases. More boldly, some Chinese legal workers view the arrangement by which people's congresses can intrude into judicial affairs as invasive, and have argued that the NPC's power over courts should be limited to reviewing their annual reports. This approaches advocacy of separation of powers.

Other Proposals

Aside from the proposals described so far, the constitutionalist debate has raised a number of other significant issues.[11]

The legal force of the Preamble to the Constitution. The debate over the legal force of the Preamble is in effect a debate over whether Deng Xiaoping's "four basic principles" (socialism, people's democratic dictatorship, Marxism-Leninism-Mao Zedong Thought, and Communist Party leadership), which are contained therein, are legally binding. Some scholars hold that the Preamble has legal force. A second view is that while the Preamble as a whole does not have legal power since parts of it are simply assertions of historical facts or goals, some stipulations in it have legal authority, including the four principles. A third view holds that the Preamble does not have legal authority because it is not written as a formal article. Rather, it is a statement of purposes and values, compliance with which is optional for law-abiding citizens who are not CCP members. Peking University professor Gong Xiangrui has gone so far as to argue, "The Constitution is, after all, not the Party's constitution. The spirit of the Preamble is in conflict with the principles of constitutionalism."[12]

Citizens' rights versus human rights.[13] Many scholars argue that the constitutional notion of citizens' rights should be changed to a notion of human rights as a way of symbolizing the importance of individual rights. Legal specialists have argued for years that certain laws—including the Public Demonstrations Law and the State Secrets Law, both passed in 1989—should be revised to protect such rights. The difficulty of finding the right balance between protecting and limiting rights has delayed the adoption of a press law that has been undergoing drafting on and off for more than a decade. A revision of the Criminal Procedure

Law in March 1996 increased the impartiality of judges, improved defense lawyers' access to clients and evidence, limited detention without charge to one month, and improved other procedural safeguards for defendants, at least on paper. Proposals have also been made to expunge crimes of counterrevolution from the criminal code and to eliminate the power of the police to imprison people for up to three years without trial ("administrative detention").

Separation of powers. Since the top leadership has ruled this subject out of bounds, it is seldom discussed explicitly. But some scholars privately favor greater separation of powers. They view the Paris Commune model of single-branch government (the historic root of the current system) as an immature one that was adopted under conditions of civil war in a single city and lasted only a few weeks. When implemented in a large country over an extended period of time, it confuses the division of labor between the legislative and executive branches, allows an unhealthy growth of executive powers, and undermines the ability of the legislature to supervise the executive. Some scholars see a germ of separation of powers in the provision in the current NPC Organic Law that states that members of the NPC Standing Committee cannot hold full-time offices in state administrative organs. A similar provision governs members of standing committees of local people's congresses.

Subjecting the Military Affairs Commission to the authority of the NPC. The Military Affairs Commission is a CCP organ, although it has a second, nominal, identity in the Constitution as a state organ. It promulgates its own laws and regulations without the involvement of the NPC. Some scholars argue that this exercise of legislative power violates the Constitution; some have suggested amending the Constitution to state more strongly that the Military Affairs Commission is subordinate to the NPC.[14] This would be a move toward shifting the military from party to state control, a process referred to in Chinese as "statization" (*guojiahua*) of the military. However, civilian control of the military through the Military Affairs Commission is already weak, and some scholars worry that it would be even weaker under the NPC unless the NPC were much more vigorous than it is now.

Federalism. China is a unitary state but has some quasi-federalist traditions. The Constitution and the Regional Autonomy Law for Minority Nationalities (1984) provide for the nominal autonomy of minority-inhabited areas. Deng Xiaoping's idea of "one country, two systems" for Hong Kong and Taiwan is reflected in the inclusion in the 1982 Constitution of Article 31, which provides for the establishment of Special Administrative Regions. Under the reforms, provinces have developed substantial economic, fiscal, and policy-making powers. Some Chinese scholars think that making the system more explicitly federal would help clarify Han-minority relations and center-province relations. Abroad, Yan Jiaqi has argued this position most strongly.[15]

Within China, scholars tend to avoid the term "federalism." Nevertheless, several have argued for new, clearer definitions of central and local powers, or for a "financial apportionment committee" under the State Council or the NPC Standing Committee to resolve issues of central-local revenue sharing and interprovincial financial transfers. Since the NPC is made up of local CCP elites, strengthening the role of the NPC would likely lead to increased articulation of provincial interests. In contrast to a national breakup, which would be inimical to constitutionalism, the lawful institutionalization of power-sharing between the center and the regions would be a move in the direction of a more constitutionalist regime.

Leninism and the Rule of Law

Although individually modest, the proposals reviewed here array themselves around the issue of the role of the CCP. The diagnoses of problems and proposals for change are cautious and technical, but they make clear that the authors see the Leninist one-party system as the main obstacle to the rule of law. In 15 years of legal reform, the Leninist core has developed mechanisms to bargain with, consult, and persuade other actors in an increasingly complex society. But power is neither grounded in popular consent nor limited by laws. As Carol Hamrin and Suisheng Zhao argue, China under Deng is a form of "bureaucratic authoritarianism."[16]

Legal scholars themselves are not a powerful constituency. Yet they possess expertise that the leaders need in order to fix problems in the system. As marketization erodes the old techniques of control, the leaders have turned to law to direct lower-level officials and constrain independent economic actors. Lawyers, judges, law professors, and NPC staff are pointing out that legal institutions cannot perform the tasks they are charged with unless they are given more autonomy. As one Chinese scholar put it, "When conditions are ripe, we should move from conceiving of [our government] as a 'people's democratic dictatorship' and start calling it a 'people's democratic constitutionalism' or a 'socialist constitutionalism.'"[17] Reliable and predictable processes of rule-making, adjudication, and enforcement will constrain the party leaders as well as other actors.

There are also more directly political reasons why some CCP leaders have promoted the discussion of constitutionalism. Politicians associated with the NPC (formerly Peng Zhen and Wan Li, now Qiao Shi) want to enlarge the NPC's power in order to increase their own influence. The regime is also influenced by foreign pressure and example with respect to investment law, tax law, contract law, court procedures, intellectual property rights, human rights law, and so on.

Constitutionalism also has opponents. If one faction would benefit from an increase in the NPC's strength, others would benefit from a continuation of the status quo. While law in some ways improves the functioning of the economy, many entrepreneurs and local communities have learned to profit through law evasion and personal connections. The experience of postcommunist Russia is often cited as evidence that China cannot afford to democratize. In its transition "from utopia to development," to use Richard Lowenthal's phrase, the regime has not found a way to replace revolutionary legitimacy with legal-democratic legitimacy. Constitutionalization would serve the CCP's interests in legitimation and stability. If the reform proposals reviewed in this essay were implemented, China would still be a dominant one-party system with weak separation of powers and weak federalism. To be sure, the process of transition to constitutionalism has been turbulent almost everywhere, and China's earlier history of failed experiments is not encouraging. But constitutionalism—which is not necessarily democracy American-style or Russian-style—is one of the most conservative options for change in a situation where stasis seems impossible.

NOTES

1. Besides some of my own writings, see Arthur Waldron, "China's ComingConstitutional Challenges," *Orbis* 39 (Winter 1995): 26. A longer and more fully referenced version of the present essay appears in Larry Diamond, Marc F. Plattner, Yun-han Chu, and Hung-mao Tien, eds., *Consolidating the Third Wave Democracies* (Baltimore: Johns Hopkins University Press, 1997).

2. Much of the information presented here was gleaned from seminar meetings and papers from a three-year study project on "China and Constitutionalism" conducted at Columbia University from 1992 to 1995. The project was supported by the Henry Luce Foundation, the National Endowment for Democracy, and the United Daily News Foundation. A series of papers from the project is being published over the course of several years in the *Journal of Asian Law* (formerly *Journal of Chinese Law*), starting with the Spring 1995 issue.

3. Official English translation published in *Beijing Review,* 27 December 1982, 10–29.

4. This section draws chiefly on Cai Dingjian, *Zhongguo renda zhidu* (The Chinese people's congress system) (Beijing: Shehui kexue wenxian chubanshe, 1992); Cang Lin, "Zhongguo lifa gaige de jige wenti" (Several issues in the reform of China's legislation), working paper, China and Constitutionalism Project, Columbia University, Spring 1995; Cao Siyuan, *Siyuan wenxuan* (Selected works of [Cao] Siyuan) (Beijing: Jingji ribao chubanshe, 1995); and Kevin J. O'Brien, *Reform Without Liberalization: China's National People's Congress and the Politics of Institutional Change* (New York: Cambridge University Press, 1990), ch. 7.

5. This section is based chiefly on Li Lin, "Zhongguo xianfa yanjiu de xianzhuang yu zhanwang" (The situation and prospects of constitutional research in China), working paper, China and Constitutionalism Project, Columbia University, April 1994, 12–16; Cang Lin, "Zhongguo lifa gaige," 21ff.; and Wang Liqun, "Zhongguo xuanju zhidu de juxian jiqi wanshan" (The limitations of China's electoral system and its improvement), *Renda yanjiu* (NPC studies) 11 (1992): 8–12.

6. This section draws chiefly on Tao Ren, "Zhongguo de xianfa jiandu he xianfa jieshi" (Constitutional supervision and interpretation in China), working paper, China and Constitutionalism Project, Columbia University, Spring 1994. See also Susan Finder, "The Supreme People's Court of the People's Republic of China," *Journal of Chinese Law* 7 (Fall 1993): 164–90; and Anthony R. Dicks, "Compartmentalized Law and Judicial Restraint: An Inductive View of Some Jurisdictional Barriers to Reform," *China Quarterly* 141 (March 1995): 82–109.

7. In 1989, some NPC deputies submitted a proposal to establish such a committee to help the Standing Committee review constitutional issues; it was never listed on the agenda of the session. *Renmin ribao* (People's daily), overseas edition, 30 October 1989, 1.

8. This section is based chiefly on Qiang Zhou, "Judicial Independence in China," working paper, China and Constitutionalism Project, Columbia University, Spring 1995. See also Shao-chuan Leng and Hungdah Chiu, *Criminal Justice in Post-Mao China: Analysis and Documents* (Albany: State University of New York Press, 1985); Donald C. Clarke, "The Execution of Civil Judgments in China," *China Quarterly* 141 (March 1995): 65–81; and Finder, "Supreme People's Court," 145–224.

9. Peng Chong, report on behalf of the NPC Standing Committee to the full NPC, 28 March 1989, in *Zhonghua renmin gongheguo quanguo renmin daibiao dahui changwu weiyuanhui gongbao* (Gazette of the Standing Committee of the PRC National People's Congress), 5 May 1989, 108.

10. "The PRC Law on Judges," Foreign Broadcast Information Service (FBIS), *Daily Report: China*, 21 March 1995, 32–37.

11. This section draws on interviews with participants in the Constitutionalism and China Project and on Li Lin, "Zhongguo xianfa yanjiu."

12. Gong Xiangrui, "Zhongguo xuyao shenme yang de xianfa lilun" (What kind of constitutional theory does China need?), *Faxue* (Law science monthly), 10 April 1989, 6.

13. Albert H.Y. Chen, "Developing Theories of Rights and Human Rights in China," in Raymond Wacks, ed., *Hong Kong, China and 1997: Essays in Legal Theory* (Hong Kong: Hong Kong University Press, 1993), 123–49.

14. See Jeremy T. Paltiel, "Civil-Military Relations in China: An Obstacle to Constitutionalism?" *Journal of Chinese Law* 9 (Spring 1995): 35–65.

15. Yan Jiaqi, *Lianbang Zhongguo gouxiang* (A conception for a federal China) (Hong Kong: Mingbao chuban she, 1992).

16. Carol Lee Hamrin and Suisheng Zhao, eds., *Decision-Making in Deng's China: Perspectives from Insiders* (Armonk, N.Y.: M.E. Sharpe, 1995), xxi–xlviii.

17. Du Gangjian, "Cong zhuanzheng dao xianzheng" (From dictatorship to constitutionalism), *Zhejiang xuekan* (Zhejiang journal) 3 (1992): 39.

22

THE MASSACRE'S LONG SHADOW

Jean-Philippe Béja

Jean-Philippe Béja, *a senior researcher at the Centre National de la Recherche Scientifique, is currently based at the French Centre for the Study of Contemporary China in Hong Kong. He is author of* A la recherche d'une ombre chinoise: Le mouvement pour la démocratie en Chine, 1919–2004 *(2004) and editor (with Fu Hualing and Eva Pils) of* Liu Xiaobo, Charter 08 and the Challenge of Political Reform in China. *This essay originally appeared in the July 2009 issue of the* Journal of Democracy.

"Kill two-hundred thousand to obtain twenty years of peace." Twenty years after the Tiananmen Square Massacre of 4 June 1989, this quote attributed to Deng Xiaoping appears to have been off by a great deal. It took only one-thousand to two-thousand dead for the Chinese Communist Party (CCP) to gain its wished-for two decades of quiet. Beneath the stable surface, however, the massacre still deeply affects the behavior of China's rulers and their opposition alike. The nervousness with which CCP leaders addressed the approach of Tiananmen's twentieth anniversary shows that, despite all efforts to erase this event from official histories and popular memory, the Party remains haunted by it.[1]

When tanks of the People's Liberation Army (PLA) rolled into downtown Beijing on June 4 to force out the students who—with help from citizens working to block troop movements—had been occupying Tiananmen Square since mid-May, the CCP and its top leader Deng Xiaoping were suddenly cast in a harsh new light. Since consolidating his power in the late 1980s, Deng had come to seem a hero to most Chinese. He had rehabilitated many of Mao's victims, allowed youths whom the late Chairman had consigned to the countryside to come back to the cities, relaxed controls over the rural economy and daily life, and thus earned much support from farmers, intellectuals, and young people. He was regarded as a pragmatist who stood up to the neo-Maoists and wanted to improve the average citizen's standard of living. His handpicked CCP secretary-general Zhao Ziyang had been talking about greater dialogue with society and even separating the Party from the government. Citizens at large were feeling freer to express discontent, while students and intellectuals were discussing prospects for increased democratization. Student demonstrations in 1986 had met with a mild official reaction that seemed one more piece of evidence for the notion that the Party had changed and was led by figures far less allergic to dissent than the Great Helmsman had been. The shootings of June 4 and the crackdown that followed shockingly reversed these impressions and expectations of regime leniency.

In the aftermath of the June 4 incident, Deng expressed grief only for the soldiers and police officers who had died,[2] while the students and local citizens who had resisted the PLA were condemned as "rioters." The contrast between this discourse and reality was so striking that it dealt a serious blow to the legitimacy of the CCP, whose basic nature seemed unchanged despite all the reforms of the 1980s. The long prison terms or death sentences meted out to the "rioters" and others who had dared to resist the army; the application of strict press controls; and the dissolution of all the civil society groups that had emerged during the 1980s showed the Party's willingness to impose its rule by force. Expression of dissent was out of the question, and the mere mention of the crackdown could land one in jail.

The main lesson that Deng drew from the "turmoil" or "storm" of 1989 was the need to reassert the so-called Four Cardinal Principles: socialism, Marxism–Leninism–Maozedong-thought, people's democratic dictatorship, and CCP leadership. For Deng, a Leninist, the breakup of the CCP had been and remained the gravest threat. Zhao Ziyang, in keeping with his belief in greater dialogue with society, had wanted to open talks with student demonstrators even after Deng had written in an April 26 *People's Daily* editorial that they were nothing more than "a handful of counter-revolutionaries."[3] When Deng decided to proclaim martial law on May 20, Zhao resigned in protest (two PLA marshals opposed martial law as well), causing Deng serious worry about a split in higher Party ranks. Zhao's refusal to engage in self-criticism over his actions led him to be placed under house arrest till his death in 2005.[4] His name has since been expunged from official media, including history texts.

Before Tiananmen, there was competition between the reformers who rallied around Deng and the Party conservatives headed by Chen Yun. Since then, the premium has been on maintaining unity within the CCP at all costs. Various senior leaders have obviously diverged over various policies, but matters have never been allowed to reach the point of a "struggle between two lines." The CCP's urge to close ranks and stay united is among the key legacies of 4 June 1989.

Legitimacy Through Elite Cooptation

Not long after Tiananmen, the breakup of the USSR and the economic woes that rocked its successor states gave the CCP's leaders a splendid chance to regain the initiative. Had not Mikhail Gorbachev's disastrous *glasnost* (openness) policy broken the once-mighty Soviet Union into shards and driven the Communist Party from power? Had the CCP done as Zhao wished and given in to the democracy movement, would not Tibet and Xinjiang have seceded, the Party fallen from power, and a dismembered China found itself sliding backward into dire poverty? Would not the dream of a China "strong and prosperous"—a dream shared not only by CCP leaders but by generations of Chinese intellectuals going back to the Opium Wars of the mid-nineteenth century—have been crushed? Had not Deng's resolve in the face of the dangerous prodemocracy agitation kept China united and saved it from dubious Western machinations?

Such rhetoric aside, Deng knew well that a major reason for the Soviet Union's collapse had been its economic failure, and that the redoubling of dictatorial controls would not by itself solve China's problems. Hence he overcame the reluctance of his conservative (orthodox Marxist) partners and launched a new wave of economic reforms in 1992.[5] Insisting that the CCP's main task was to make China strong and wealthy, he added that questions about whether a given policy was "capitalist" or "socialist" were beside the point, since "development is the most important thing." In order to achieve it, Deng stressed the importance of opening the economy, embracing globalization, and allowing entrepreneurs to get rich. To the intelligentsia, which had played such a large role in the 1989 protests, he offered what amounted to a new social contract. He may have morally rehabilitated intellectuals by declaring them part of the working class back in 1978, but this did nothing for them materially. After his southern tour in 1992, he allowed them to become entrepreneurs and to accumulate wealth. Many seized this opportunity and got busy creating high-tech and services enterprises. Those who remained in academia were allowed to join the international scientific community, and their pay, benefits, opportunities, and working conditions improved dramatically.

In short, the Party had decided to coopt the most problematic social categories, the ones that had been at the forefront of the democracy movement. Whereas in the 1980s students had been reluctant to join the Party, by the close of the 1990s more than 80 percent of them were applying for CCP membership. The Party, as Jiang Zemin put it, would, in addition to standing for China's vast masses, also represent its most advanced productive forces (entrepreneurs, engineers, and the like) and its most advanced cultural forces (intellectuals who would agree not to question CCP rule). The so-called Three Represents approach worked—in tandem with resolute efforts to prevent the emergence of any autonomous entities that might challenge Party rule—and the CCP gained support among the cognitive and economic elites who embraced what dissident and literary scholar Liu Xiaobo has called the "philosophy of the pig."[6]

As the new elite-friendly development policies were put in place, they began to irk workers in state-owned enterprises and peasants pinched by falling farm prices. In order to prevent the discontent that bubbled among these marginalized classes from crystallizing into a movement similar to the one that had spawned the 1989 ferment, Party leaders used carrots and sticks. Attempts to create autonomous unions or even discussion circles met with the latter in the form of instant suppression. Nothing like the salons, semiautonomous research centers, and semi-autonomous media that had flourished in the late 1980s was allowed to reemerge. When activists tried to found the China Democracy Party in 1998, Jiang Zemin gave the order to "nip [it] in the bud." Even innocuous "reflection circles" such as the New Youth Study Group, which had all of eight members, became targets of heavy repression.[7] Intellectuals who try to help workers and peasants articulate their grievances, always a nightmare for the Party, receive special attention from the internal-security apparat. The formation of unauthorized links or contacts between villages or work units is strongly forbidden.

Carrots have included concessions to the discontented. The stress placed on the "rule of law" as a safety valve since 2000 serves as a case in point. Victims of abusive officials are encouraged to press court cases against them. This allows the system to publicly redress grievances while atomizing citizens' claims and addressing them piecemeal, as individual complaints rather than as the stuff of social movements. The very recourse to courts involves acknowledgment of the regime's legitimacy.

When a protest erupts in a factory or village, the authorities may negotiate or they may send in the police (if not the *hei shehui,* local mafia thugs often linked to the local government). In no case, however, will officials do anything but strain mightily to prevent any protest from spreading. When workers at a plant in Liaoyang sought to recruit workers from the town's other factories for a demonstration in 2003, the protest organizers quickly found themselves in jail.[8] The absence over the last two decades of any large-scale social movement comparable to the democracy movement of the late 1980s is in no small part a testament to the effectiveness of the regime's dogged protest-containment efforts.

Exiles and Dissidents

For the opposition, one of the first consequences of the Tiananmen Massacre was the flight abroad of a large number of activists. In September 1989, for the first time since the foundation of the People's Republic forty years earlier, leaders of a Chinese mass movement gathered outside China. On this occasion they met in France, and their goal was to create an opposition organization in exile, the Federation for a Democratic China (FDC). The FDC was an attempt to gather various generations of oppositionists, some of whom had been abroad for a few years. Young students, former rightists, and Party cadres from Hu Yaobang's and Zhao Ziyang's networks met to design a strategy to fight the CCP. Finding a basis for cooperation proved difficult, however, and the FDC's status as an exile group unavoidably left it cut off from ground-level Chinese realities. Debates among its members were abstract and had no impact on developments in China. Competition for the support of foreign political forces provoked fierce inner struggles, and the dream of the emergence of a new Sun Yat-sen evaporated. After a few years, leading personalities began shunning the FDC and it slowly died out. The exiles' greatest achievements have been to help keep the memory of the 1989 movement alive and to inform foreign governments, publics, and media outlets about violations of human rights in China. In fact, organizations focused on the latter topic, such as Human Rights in China, Chinese Human Rights Defenders, and the China Labour Bulletin (which specializes in publicizing attacks on workers' rights), have been the most effective and enjoy significant influence in Western government circles.[9]

Yet for the exile community as a whole, the broadest avenue for affecting life in China is not a formal political organization or the attention of foreign governments, but rather person-to-person contacts with the numerous educated Chinese who, especially since the mid-1990s, have been going abroad to study, teach, conduct research, or take part in scholarly gatherings. As little as Beijing's state-security services may like it, these traveling Chinese intellectuals do meet their colleagues in exile, and they discuss the future of China with them.

After martial law was lifted in January 1990, and especially after Deng Xiaoping reaffirmed his commitment to economic reform during his 1992 swing through South China, the active ranks of the prodemocracy movement became much thinner. Yet a small minority of activists pushed on, despite an environment made hostile by more than just the omnipresence of the police. After Deng restated his commitment to capitalism, Chinese-style, a new mood of concern with moneymaking overtook all sectors of the populace. Demand for democracy and political reform fell, particularly among the city folk who had supported the student movement in 1989 and who were now busy trying to take advantage of the opportunities that Deng's new policy had opened up for them.

This is not to suggest that conditions were otherwise favorable when people became distracted by visions of personal enrichment. In the wake of Tiananmen, antigovernment demonstrations were strictly forbidden, the police were everywhere, and the fear of repression was overwhelming. Students were obliged to submit to military exercises under army supervision, and most of the leaders who embodied the spirit of '89 were in exile, in hiding, or in jail. Any push for democratization based on support among the elite was doomed because, after 4 June 1989, the leaders who had shielded and nurtured the democracy movement were purged from positions of power.

There was therefore almost no space for the expression of dissent. Nevertheless, some activists, especially those who had been sent to prison in the post-Tiananmen crackdown, refused to abandon the struggle for democracy. Once freed, they found themselves expelled from their respective work units (often universities or research institutes), banned by the police from starting private enterprises, under strict surveillance, and isolated from the rest of society. Their situation was reminiscent of what Czechoslovak dissidents had faced after Soviet tanks crushed the Prague Spring in 1968. So were their reactions. Like their Central European spiritual forebears, many of the Chinese dissidents resolved to "live in the truth" by speaking out against Communist Party abuses at every opportunity. They published political commentaries in the Hong Kong or international media, and later on the Internet. They tried to establish informal networks and protested in the foreign media (the only media open to them) when one of their number suffered police harassment or detention. They kept up demands for the reappraisal of June 4 by the authorities and called for the instauration of democracy.

The most active dissidents tended to be student leaders such as Wang Dan, or intellectuals such as Bao Zunxin and Liu Xiaobo, the latter of whom had left behind a teaching career in the United States in order to join the democracy movement in his homeland, and then did jail time after the Tiananmen Massacre. He and those like him refused to compromise with the government and acted as the conscience of society by reaffirming the principles that had been at the center of the democracy movement. They established good relations with the disaffected intellectuals and old Party cadres from Hu Yaobang's and Zhao Ziyang's networks who had become very hostile to the CCP leadership after the Massacre.[10]

Over the last two decades, they have written dozens of collective letters denouncing acts of repression against human-rights activists, defending workers victimized by heartless policies, demanding reversal of the official verdict on the events of June 4, and criticizing attacks on national minorities, especially Tibetans. Tight press controls have too often meant that these cries of protest have gone largely unheard within China, though the Internet has helped the "generation of '89" dissidents to reach a larger group of younger militants whose participation in democratic dissent dates from after 1989.

On the face-to-face level, older activists with roots in the 1989 democracy movement have been able to meet with younger people in private homes or, since the mid-1990s, in tea houses and bookstores opened by fellow activists of the '89 generation. The Wansheng bookstore in Beijing, founded by Gan Qi and Liu Suli, who himself spent a year in jail after the Massacre, was one of these places, and so has been the Sanwei bookstore, which continues to organize conferences on current affairs and on philosophical and legal subjects (known dissidents are not invited). The police watch such places, of course, and have often been known to ban Sanwei conferences. Yet personal gatherings continue to play an important role in the structuring of the would-be opposition.

Critiquing the System and Its Top Officials

Among the small minority of students and professional intellectuals who have continued to criticize the regime from a democratic point of view, several subgroups can be discerned. The first consists of professors or researchers who have expressed their doubts about some policies in public. Jiao Guobiao, a professor at Peking University, published an article denouncing the Central Propaganda Department. Subsequently barred from teaching and supervising doctoral students, he was later allowed to go abroad, and when he came home he drew closer to the dissident community.

The case of Li Datong is also of interest. A veteran journalist, he was the editor-in-chief of *Bingdian* (Freezing Point), a supplement to *Zhongguo Qingnian Bao* (China Youth Daily) and was dismissed for having published an article on the Boxer Uprising that differed from the official version. His firing provoked an uproar, and for the first time since 1949, journalists (in this case a hundred of them) publicly petitioned the authorities to reverse an official decision.[11] Li was kept on but in a lesser job, and banned from publishing in the *China Youth Daily*. He still places articles on the Internet and in Hong Kong papers, and he too has grown closer to the dissidents and signs their petitions.

Some Chinese too young to have taken part in the 1989 democracy movement have nonetheless drawn inspiration from the courage of their elders and shown themselves unafraid to criticize the regime's shortcomings. The CCP's grip on information in general and on teaching and research in the social sciences is among their prime targets. Yu Jie was a doctoral candidate in literature at Peking University when he began penning allegorical essays skewering the ethos that prevailed after 4 June 1989. Upon graduation, the Chinese Writers' Association withdrew its job offer, so Yu became an independent intellectual and a prominent dissident.

The expansion of the Internet has favored the emergence of a new generation of young oppositionists. Most start with online satire. This is how Liu Di, who used the pen name "Stainless Steel Rat," became famous. The authorities did not appreciate her humor, and she was imprisoned without trial. Dissidents launched petitions, and she was freed after almost a year in jail.[12] Upon her release, she too could find no job and grew closer to the dissident community.

These activists were pushed outside the system by the refusal of the authorities, acting on lessons drawn from June 4, to let them find or keep employment in a state-owned unit *(danwei)*, media outlet, or university. Therefore, ironically, it is the Party that appoints the members of the opposition. After the mid-1990s, some intellectuals could be openly critical of regime practices without losing their jobs, so long as they did not comment directly on taboo topics such as the Tiananmen Massacre. Even within these constraints, such critical intellectuals could still assist the dissident movement.

Those who gravitated toward the opposition after 4 June 1989 also included people who had lost relatives to the crackdown. Inspired by groups such as the Madres de Plaza de Mayo (a group of mothers of "the disappeared") in Argentina, a group of victims' family members founded the Mothers of Tiananmen (Tian'anmen muqin) under the leadership of Ding Zilin, a People's University professor whose 17-year-old son lost his life to official violence on June 4. The Mothers urged relatives of the dead to demand that the government acknowledge its responsibility for the Massacre. After June 4, the CCP had continued to exert pressure for continued silence, suggesting that those who were kin to Tiananmen protesters might even be seen as accomplices of "rioters."

Every year on June 4, the Tiananmen Mothers remind the authorities of their duty to accept responsibility and pay compensation. They try by all peaceful means to put an end to the cloak of official silence that to this day shrouds events which, for them, were of life-shattering import. Year by year, these ordinary and once politically quiescent citizens have grown in the conviction that they will never obtain satisfaction until the regime is reformed and guarantees citizens' rights. They now commonly join other dissidents in signing petitions demanding respect for human rights. In 1998, the Mothers wrote two open letters. One denounced human-rights violations, and the other condemned the corruption that accompanied the economic changes of that decade. The courage that the Mothers have shown in the face of police harassment is remarkable; they must be counted as one of the main currents of the opposition.

Convenient shorthand terms such as "the dissident community" or "the opposition" should not obscure the reality that we are dealing with a loose, unstructured movement that lacks a unified strategy and program. Since the Massacre and subsequent crackdown, the CCP has been careful to prevent the emergence of anything resembling an alternative political organization. On top of this, those who may rightly be called oppositionists display wide differences when it comes to their personal experiences, political views, and so on. This is not to say, however, that they cannot unite—as they did most recently in December 2008, when 303 signatories launched the nineteen-point manifesto known as Charter 08.[13] Its release (via the Internet) was timed to coincide with the sixtieth anniversary of the Universal Declaration of Human Rights.

Charter 08 has three parts. The first describes the failure to introduce democracy in China since the first attempt at constitutional monarchy in 1898. The second registers the signatories' agreement on the basic principles of liberalism—separation of powers; free, fair, and regular elections; official accountability; and the like. The final part is more concrete, and details the steps that must be taken if China is to become a democracy. All the signatories call for an end to the one-party system, the adoption of federalism, and the creation of a reconciliation committee (modeled on the South African Truth and Reconciliation Commission) with powers to award compensation to relatives of the victims of the various repression campaigns that the CCP has undertaken since coming to power in 1949.

A large number of drafts had circulated online for about three years before the Charter's signing and formal publication. The signatories come from several strata of Chinese society and various sectors of the opposition. Dissident intellectuals such as Liu Xiaobo (still subject to surveillance and detention at the time of this writing) may have been the prime movers, but everyone from established professors and researchers to peasant activists had a say in shaping the end product. The Charter's very existence is a sign that, despite CCP harassment, the opposition remains capable of forming and mobilizing networks.

The authorities have been trying to suppress the Charter, yet an additional eight-thousand people (and counting) from all walks of life have now added their names to it. That is a tiny number in a country of 1.2 billion, of course, but it remains the case that since Tiananmen, no principled, systematic call for deep transformation of the regime has obtained so much open public support.

The Civil-Rights Defense Movement

In 2004, when the CCP decided to add a human-rights amendment to China's constitution, many lawyers, legal scholars, and citizens became convinced that the new provision could be used to defend the rights of ordinary Chinese and that there was a duty to take part in this struggle. With the help of journalists, online activists, and an informal but widespread network of lawyers and legal experts, many victims of abusive officials began citing their rights under the constitution. Thanks to the

Internet and other new modes of communication, the so-called civil-rights defense movement *(weiquan yundong)* can be mobilized with relative ease by people who fall victim to official bullies. Its tools include demonstrations, petitions, collective letters, class-action suits on behalf of consumers, and suits by individuals.

The civil-rights legal network cuts across the class lines that divide intellectuals from workers and peasants. It differs from the organizations that intellectuals created in the 1980s.[14] At that time, criticism of the CCP came mostly from students and other educated types, and it focused on demands for the reform of the political system. The civil-rights defense movement, by contrast, originates with ordinary citizens who do not question the CCP's position or the nature of the regime, and who try to solve concrete problems by working through the system. These citizen-activists and the journalists and lawyers who help them are not asking for "freedom and democracy," nor are they even denouncing corruption in general. Instead, they are appealing to specific existing laws for the redress of specific grievances. This new attitude is certainly a result of the repression of the 1989 democracy movement.

The discontinuity should not be overstated, however. Many of today's civil-rights activists were very young in 1989, yet they know what the students did that year, are deeply impressed by it, and in private will readily acknowledge their debt to the generation of Tiananmen even while explaining how they differ from it. Xu Zhiyong sums it up this way:

> I have respect for those who raised human-rights issues in the past, but now we hope to work in a constructive way within the space afforded by the legal system. Concrete but gradual change—I think that's what most Chinese people want.[15]

Not all officials seem impressed by this stress on legality. In 2007, CCP Politburo member and chief of security affairs Luo Gan declared that the civil-rights movement was receiving support from the West and "harbored forces dedicated to overthrowing the Party's rule."[16] A year earlier, China's national legislature had passed new restrictions on lawyers' independence and their ability to act on behalf of abuse victims. Since every lawyer must renew his or her license every year, it is easy to put civil-rights specialists—who probably represent no more than 1 percent of the profession, if that—out of business. This happened to Gao Zhisheng in December 2005, to Li Jianqiang in Shandong in July 2007, and to other lawyers in Shaanxi.[17] And yet the civil-rights defense movement continues, while rights awareness among the citizenry grows.

Twenty years after the 4 June 1989 massacre, the CCP seems to have reinforced its legitimacy. It has not followed the communist regimes of

the Soviet bloc into oblivion. Its policies of elite cooptation, subtle response to social contradictions, and instrumental support for the "rule of
law" have become major complements to its continued control over the
press and the political system. It has made concessions to prevent discontent from crystallizing into social movements that might challenge its
rule, and it has sent in the police to silence dissidents. Over the course of
the same two decades, the opposition has had to wrestle with the trauma of
the June 4 Massacre and the huge difficulties that it has raised for anyone
who would challenge the CCP's primacy. The persistence of small groups
of dissidents, fed by a steady trickle of younger militants, shows that the
opposition represents a force and a set of ideas that cannot be neglected.
Yet the opposition is by no stretch anywhere near being able to mobilize
disgruntled citizens and to organize demonstrations like those of 1989. Instead, oppositionists act as their society's conscience, voices for the basic
principles of humanism in a society obsessed with materialism.

The emergence despite all obstacles of the civil-rights defense movement shows that ordinary citizens are increasingly aware of their rights
and are ready to take risks to defend them. China is doubtless a post-
totalitarian regime ruled by a ruthless Party. But there are signs suggesting that the Party's grip might not be as solid as it seems.

NOTES

1. Luo Bing, "Min'gan nian tishen jiebei bage yue" (Vigilance is heightened during eight months of the sensitive year), *Zhengming,* April 2009, 6–7.

2. Deng Xiaoping, "Address to Officers at the Rank of General and Above in Command of the Troops Enforcing Martial Law in Beijing, June 9, 1989." Available at *http://web.peopledaily.com.cn/english/dengxp/vol3/text/c1990.html.*

3. See "Overtly Oppose the Turmoil" (Qizhi xianmingde fandui dongluan), *People's Daily* (Beijing), 26 April 1989.

4. See Zhao Ziyang, *Prisoner of the State: The Secret Journal of Zhao Ziyang,* trans. and ed. Bao Pu, Renee Chiang, and Adi Ignatius (New York: Simon and Schuster, 2009), 29.

5. Suisheng Zhao, "Deng Xiaoping's Southern Tour: Elite Politics in Post-Tiananmen China," *Asian Survey* 33 (August 1993): 739–56.

6. Liu Xiaobo "Zhu de zhexue" (The philosophy of the pig), *Dongxiang,* September 2000, 29–36.

7. Philip P. Pan, "A Study Group Is Crushed in China's Grip," *Washington Post,* 23 April 2004; available at *www.washingtonpost.com/wp-dyn/content/article/2004/04/23/AR2005040206572.html.*

8. Philip P. Pan, "Three Chinese Workers: Jail, Betrayal and Fear; Government Stifles Labor Movement," *Washington Post,* 28 December 2002.
9. Jean-Philippe Béja, "The Fly in the Ointment? Chinese Dissent and U.S.-Chinese Relations," *Pacific Review* 16 (September 2003): 439–53.

10. These cadres express their criticism either through letters to the top leaders that are made public in Hong Kong, or in two journals that they are allowed to publish, the most influential being *Yanhuang Chunqiu.*

11. Joseph Kahn, "Ex-officials Protest Censorship by China," *International Herald Tribune,* 15 February 2006.

12. Chan Siu Sin, "Prison-Style Protest Aims to Free Student: Liu Di Has Spent 11 Months in Custody for Her Net Pro-Democracy Messages," *South China Morning Post* (Hong Kong), 3 October 2003.

13. Perry Link, trans., "China's Charter '08," *New York Review of Books,* 15 January 2009; available at *www.nybooks.com/articles/22210.* See also *Journal of Democracy* 20 (April 2009): 179–82.

14. On these organizations, see Jean-Philippe Béja, *A la recherche d'une ombre chinoise: Le mouvement pour la démocratie en Chine, 1919–2004* (Paris: Editions du Seuil, 2004).

15. Quoted in Erik Eckholm, "Petitioners Urge China to Enforce Legal Rights," *New York Times,* 2 June 2003; available at *www.nytimes.com/2003/06/02/international/asia/02CHIN.html.*

16. "Chinese Official Urges Local Handling of Unrest," *International Herald Tribune,* 8 January 2007.

17. For accounts of these episodes, see *http://crd-net.org/Article/Class9/Class10/Index.html.*

23

GOODBYE TO GRADUALISM

Tiancheng Wang

Tiancheng Wang is CEO of the National Committee of the Democratic Party of China. He has been a law lecturer at Peking University and spent five years in prison because of dissident activities. This essay draws from his book The Grand Transition: A Research Framework for the Strategy to Democratize China *(2012, in Chinese), written at Columbia, Northwestern, and New York universities with support from the Scholar Rescue Fund between 2008 and 2010. The essay originally appeared in the January 2013 issue of the* Journal of Democracy.

China is heading toward a tipping point, with two scenarios standing out as the most likely "scripts" for how a political opening will come about. Whichever scenario occurs, most Chinese intellectuals think they know the best course for the nation to follow. That course can be summed up in one word: gradualism. Since the Chinese Communist Party (CCP) regime's 1989 crackdown on the democracy movement, intellectuals have embraced the notion that only "slow and steady," step-by-step reform can offer China a safe and feasible path toward liberal democracy. But the intellectuals are wrong about that. Once a political opening starts, risks (including the threat of national disintegration) will continue to grow in number and severity the longer the transition process drags on. Instead of "taking it slow," China should shun gradualism and opt instead for a quick transition powered by early nationwide elections.

According to Robert A. Dahl, a democratic opening is most likely to occur when the costs of repression climb too high for the existing authoritarian regime to bear. Guillermo O'Donnell and Philippe Schmitter stress division within the ruling elite as an "almost necessary" condition for democratic transition. Barbara Geddes says that "single-party regimes are quite resilient and tend to be brought down by exogenous events."[1]

In my own view, based on close observation of Chinese politics, democratic transition will likely occur in China when either of two situations materializes. In the first, the Communist party-state finds that it can no longer bear the costs of controlling Chinese society. The CCP elite splits into hard-liner and soft-liner camps. If the latter gains the upper hand, it will begin a process of political opening. If the rulers stick together or if the soft-liners are weak, the second situation awaits. In this scenario, a triggering event exposes the weakness of the seemingly strong regime. The people, at once angry and confident, pour into the streets in vast numbers. The armed forces let it be known that they will not shoot citizens, the top leader falls, and an opening ensues.

"Stability maintenance" (*weiwen*) has been basic CCP policy since 1989. The moral and political costs (to human rights and dignity) of the complex and costly system that the regime has built to keep things on an even keel are real, if hard to quantify. Yet the system's sheer financial costs are massive, too, and they can be counted.

Public spending on domestic security—even going by official figures that almost certainly understate the true extent of such spending—has been the fastest-rising among all categories of public spending in China over the past two decades. It grew more than fourfold between 2002 and 2008, and in 2010 surpassed military spending. As of 2011, the PRC government was funneling more money toward the task of order-keeping at home than it spent on healthcare, foreign relations, and banking and securities regulation *combined*. This level of expenditure has been so stressful for local governments in poorer regions of the country that in 2009 Beijing had to adopt cost-sharing measures under which it pays up to 90 percent of the public-security tab in parts of central and western China.[2]

Behind the headlines about rapid economic growth that China presents to the world are sordid realities of official corruption, arbitrariness, and indifference to aggrieved persons. These, combined with the problems created by a distorted model of development that greatly favors some regions and classes over others, have bred considerable discontent. "Mass incidents," which are mainly protests against local governments, have increased rapidly, especially since the economy's pace of growth began to slow in 2008. They went up tenfold (to 87,000) between 1993 and 2005, and their numbers have continued to climb—in 2010, there were a reported 280,000 such events.[3]

That local protests have never snowballed into a national crisis is a tribute to the CCP regime's massive investment in domestic-order maintenance. But as we have seen, that investment is staggeringly expensive. How long can the regime keep it up? Since the unaccountable Communist party-state need not spend the bulk of its funds for public welfare,[4] it can divert as much as it thinks it needs toward order-keeping, as it has always done in the past. Yet even here there is a rough limit of sorts, since a populace whose needs are neglected will produce more "mass incidents," and these always have the potential to get out of hand.

I would not go so far as to say that political reform will occur simply because avoiding reform is costing the regime too much money, but at the same time there can be no doubt that the CCP is facing harsher challenges as the economy slows. The astonishing increase of mass incidents—they have tripled in number since 2007—means that the party-state is seeing its room to maneuver shrink. The CCP regime's legitimacy comes from rapid economic growth. As growth slows, the cost to the regime is not only financial but moral and political as well. Economists predict that China cannot maintain double-digit annual GDP growth any longer and will henceforth struggle to hit 7 percent. Some observers point to problems such as the housing bubble and local-government deficits and predict that China is heading for a full-blown economic crisis.[5]

Not only macroeconomic numbers but sentiments as well appear to be shifting in China. Intellectuals, most of whom seem to expect that democratic transition will flow from top-down reforms, are increasingly likely to say that reform must start soon or there will be a revolution. Friends of democracy are optimistic. Outgoing premier Wen Jiabao likes to talk about reforming the "mechanics" of the political system, but so far the ruling elite has shown no real signs of willingness to make serious changes. Unless that elite fails to get the economy back on track, its members will, I believe, stick together. This continued unity will at least keep open the possibility that the elite might devise a coherent top-down reform program. The biggest problem may not be preserving elite unity, but rather overcoming the effect of the sheer amount of corruption that is rampant among the rulers—any opening serious enough to threaten their grip on power will threaten their enormous ill-gotten wealth as well. And even a ruling elite desperate enough to consider political reform as a way out of its difficulties might still hold back if it lacks confidence that it can pull off reform successfully and keep things under its own control.

Gradual Reform or Quick Transition?

Since the 1989 crackdown, Chinese intellectuals have banked heavily on the idea that the safest and most feasible way to bring democracy to China's shores is gradual reform. To understand gradualism in this context, it helps to know that the typical Chinese intellectual works at a university or think tank that is under CCP control. In a highly repressive political climate such as China's, most will prefer advising or persuading the government to confronting it. Moreover, the kind of gradualism that these intellectuals have in mind differs from the concept of democratic transition familiar to Western academics.

By gradualism, the typical Chinese professor does not mean the processes of liberalization (or opening) and democratization that O'Donnell and Schmitter (or Juan Linz and Alfred Stepan) present as the two phases of democratic transition. The Chinese scholar is *not* proposing big steps such as the broad loosening of media censorship, the ending of the ban on parties other than the CCP, or free and direct national elections. Instead, the idea is to start political reform with minor changes that pose no threat to CCP control; to carry out such changes piecemeal rather than sweepingly; and above all to "go slow." The most important thing is to get reform rolling by raising only low-level concerns—the idea being that the rulers will instantly slap down any proposition that seems even a touch large or daring. The assumption is that small reforms will lead to larger ones, or that many minor reforms taken together will add up to a big change. Rapid and sweeping reform is to be feared anyway, for it holds too much potential for tumult and chaos. However well- or ill-grounded this anxiety, countless people share it, and they include not only academics but also high officials and businesspeople. It is arguably the single most formidable psychological obstacle to hopes for a democratic transition in China today.

Two proposals that have received wide notice within China help to illustrate the gradualism of which Chinese intellectuals are so enamored. Back in the late 1990s, prominent law professor Ji Weidong came up with what he called the "rule of law first" approach. "It is unlikely that a multiparty contest will occur in the near future," he wrote, "and [anyway] it will cause an extremely huge [amount of] chaos if direct election of members of the National People's Congress is granted."[6] Instead he recommended a focus on building respect for the rule of law by 1) encouraging the institutionalization of judicial independence, and 2) persuading the CCP to start abiding by the constitution. But what chance is there, absent democratization, that those in power will respect the constitution and guarantee the independence of the judiciary? As if oblivious to this problem, Ji added that he not only found a democratic transition an unlikely prospect for the near term, but would advocate postponing one in any case for fear that it would not go well.

A second influential proposal calls for making the internal procedures of the CCP itself more democratic. This idea, too, is based on the assumption that multiparty competition will not happen anytime soon and would be overly risky if it did. The most commonly recommended device for cultivating democratic methods within the CCP is to ensure that the number of candidates for various posts exceeds the number of those posts. One suggestion is to expand the number of those "running" for seats on the CCP Central Committee by 5 or 10 percent every five years.[7] Some scholars regard intra-CCP democracy as the best path to popular democracy.[8] Yet they do not explain how intra-Party democracy is possible without the existence of popular democracy. Why would a party running a single-party, nondemocratic system want to adopt free, regular, and open competition for its key offices as part of its way of doing business?

In short, the gradualism favored by Chinese academics puts the cart before the horse. Deliberately failing to voice crucial demands—for direct national elections to be held after ending the ban on independent parties, for instance—will not serve the cause of kick-starting political reform. On the contrary, it will more likely allow the ruling CCP elite to avoid making meaningful changes as it carries on instead with its decades-old effort to postpone indefinitely China's transition away from authoritarianism. Keeping quiet will only take pressure off the CCP and bolster the legitimacy of its single-party dictatorship. How, one wonders, can significant reforms occur if no one demands them?

Moreover, is slow and piecemeal reform really the least risky approach? The intention is clearly to keep the ruling elite feeling reassured that it can safely start a reform process. But what is the inducement for this elite to accept *any* of the risk that might come from making the political system more open? The elite's inclination—and surely it is not totally unreasonable—is to worry that any meaningful opening, even a minor one, may produce an avalanche effect that could leave the CCP stripped of its ability to control events.

To me, the case for a quick transition seems much stronger. It can be argued that once a political opening begins, the longer the span of time that elapses between liberalization and democratization—I call it the "L-D span"—the more risks and variables will come into play. This is especially so for a large country such as China, which has what Linz and Stepan call a "stateness problem."[9]

Most of the world's successful democratic transitions during recent decades have featured short L-D spans. Taiwan had a long transition to democracy (it lasted from 1986 to 1996), but almost all street protests took place after the key event, which was the ruling Nationalist Party's surprising decision to tolerate the creation of the opposition Democratic Progressive Party in 1986. In a classic case of nonviolent resistance, Chile saw peaceful mass protests against the military dictatorship of General Augusto Pinochet (1973–90) that stretched from 1980 all the way to 1989. Such protests are fine, but we should also bear in mind what is likely to happen over the course of a long transition. Based on his study of the transitions in Hungary, the Philippines, Poland, Portugal, South Korea, and Spain, Giuseppe Di Palma thinks that quick elections can curb chaos.[10] And Yossi Shain and Juan Linz note in discussing Brazil that "the gubernatorial elections which gave to the opposition control of eleven governorships in the most populated states did not lead to the collapse of the regime."[11] If elections in China go forward first at the provincial level, however, I predict a less happy result: The country will disintegrate much as did the Soviet Union and Yugoslavia two decades ago.

There is a great danger, in other words, lurking in the bottom-to-top sequencing of elections that Chinese gradualists favor. They want to start with township voting, then see elections held in the counties and cities, then the provinces, and only then at the national level. But given China's "stateness" issues—typified most starkly by the restive regions of Tibet and Xinjiang that Louisa Greve discusses in her contribution to this symposium—such an order of elections will confound the transition and could even lead to secession attempts by the northwestern and southwestern "peripheries." Linz and Stepan's observations regarding the effects of different election sequences in Spain, the USSR, and Yugoslavia are instructive.[12]

In view of these concerns, my suggestion is that the founding election be a national one. Let China as a whole vote freely first, and only then hold open contests at the provincial level (which is the true "problem" level; purely local races might be held without as much danger to national unity). Holding the founding election at the level of the provinces would invite a focus on emotional "stay or go" issues, and could undercut the national government's legitimacy and authority as well as wreck prospects for arriving at a "federalist" accommodation of the "ethnic" (non-Han) peripheries. Holding the first democratic election as a single event across all of China would, by contrast, offer a better chance to make citizens in every province feel that they have a stake in the country's future, foster the rise of nationwide parties, and enhance the legitimacy and authority of the new democratically constituted central government.

The Return of Revolutionary Culture

In 1995, the influential scholars Li Zehou and Liu Zaifu marked gradualism's rise to intellectual predominance by publishing a major book titled *Say Goodbye to Revolution*. But things change. A revolutionary culture has recently begun to reemerge. The gradualist school, though still potent, is losing followers. This change of sentiment and opinion has grown out of frustration at the absence of long hoped for top-down political reform, as well as feelings of dismay roused by the declining economy. Defections from gradualism also reflect a growing civil society consisting mainly of independent individuals who have come to form a network that does not automatically shy away from contention.[13] Then too, the upheavals that have rocked the Arab world and unseated several of its longtime dictators have set off intellectual shock waves among "netizens" and rights-defending activists in China. The rise of a new Chinese revolutionary culture could be seen in early 2012 when the popular young novelist Han Han blogged about his doubts as to whether democratizing China is an urgent necessity and received a rare (for him) storm of online criticism in return.

A critical question is how the ruling elite will respond as society grows less stable, desire for change becomes more fervent, and the economic growth that has long been the CCP's mainstay begins to slow. As I noted above, I do not currently rate the likelihood of an elite fracture as very high. Under pressure, China's rulers will pay more lip service to reform while seeking to avoid it in practice, preferring instead a "gradualism" that is so gradual it cannot be distinguished from stasis.

Only if the economy falls into a full-blown crisis will we be likely to see a split in ruling circles and the initiation of top-down political reforms. If this happens, I hope for a transition to democracy that is quick and decisive. If things move slowly, there could be an erosion of central-government authority that opens the door to national disintegration. Still another possibility is a limited tactical opening that could help the CCP to buy time and survive a crisis. In this case, China would end up still being ruled by an authoritarian regime, albeit a somewhat liberalized one. Gradualists, I believe, could well find reasons for supporting such a regime, and the gradualist school has many graduates that could lend a hand.

Perhaps China will be somewhat like Egypt under Mubarak, where the dictatorship experimented with limited openings during its early years (the 1980s), then brought these to a halt, lashed out at its opponents, "transitioned" to nowhere,[14] and finally had to be overthrown by crowds in Tahrir Square and a military that would not open fire upon them. You could call that the "revolution in the long term" scenario. Is a Chinese revolution in the nearer term a possibility? I believe that it is: Discontent is widespread, and there are no signs of any plan or even willingness to launch serious reforms from above. My hope in that case, of course, is that any revolution will turn out to be a gentle one, in which an authoritarian regime is toppled by massive popular protests that are as unstoppable as they are nonviolent.

NOTES

1. Robert A. Dahl, *Polyarchy: Participation and Opposition* (New Haven: Yale University Press, 1971), 15; Guillermo O'Donnell and Philippe C. Schmitter, *Transitions from Authoritarian Rule: Tentative Conclusions About Uncertain Democracies* (Baltimore: Johns Hopkins University Press, 1986), 15–16; Barbara Geddes, "What Do We Know About Democratization After Twenty Years?" *Annual Review of Political Science* 2 (June 1999): 115–44.

2. Xu Kai, Chen Xiaoshu, and Li Wei'ao, "Public Security Billing," *Journal of Finance and Economy* (Caijing), 8 May 2011, available at *http://misc.caijing.com.cn/chargeFullNews.jsp?id=110712639&time=2011-05-08&cl=106*.

3. See Yu Jianrong, "Social Conflict and Rigid Stability," *Strategy and Management,* merged version of issues 3 and 4, 2009), see *http://www.cssm.gov.cn/zazhi*; Tongda Huan, "The Emergency Brake at a Critical Point of Reform," *China Outlook,* 6 September 2011;

Simon Zhou, "The Leadership of the Fifth Generation of CCP Will Initiate Political Reform," *China Report Weekly,* 15 September 2010.

4. For instance, the government of Guangzhou City spent $70.4 million on stability maintenance but only U.S.$56.3 million on social security and unemployment insurance in 2007. Xiao Shu, "Why Is It Hard to Cut Down the High Cost of Keeping Stability?" *Oriental Morning Post,* 21 June 2009.

5. See Li Zuojun, "Chinese Economic Crisis Will Break Out in 2013," available at *www.21cbh.com.*

6. Ji Weidong, "China: Toward Democracy Through the Rule of Law," *Strategy and Management* 4 (August 1998): 1–10, see *http://www.cssm.gov.cn/zazhi.*

7. Hu Wei, "Intra-Party Democracy and Political Development," *Fudan Journal (Social Sciences)* 1 (February 1999): 1–11.

8. Cheng Li, "Intra-Party Democracy in China: Should We Take It Seriously?" Fall 2009, available at *www.brookings.edu/research/papers/2009/11/fall-china-democracy-li.*

9. See Juan J. Linz and Alfred Stepan, *Problems of Democratic Transition and Consolidation* (Baltimore: Johns Hopkins University Press, 1996), 16–37.

10. See Giuseppe Di Palma, *To Craft Democracies: An Essay on Democratic Transitions* (Berkeley: University of California Press, 1990).

11. Yossi Shain and Juan J. Linz, *Between States: Interim Governments and Democratic Transitions* (New York: Cambridge University Press, 1995), 83.

12. See Juan J. Linz and Alfred Stepan, "Political Identities and Electoral Sequences: Spain, the Soviet Union, and Yugoslavia," *Daedalus* 121 (Spring 1992): 123–39.

13. See the essay by Zhenhua Su, Hui Zhao, and Jingkai He in this cluster.

14. Daniel Brumberg, "Democratization in the Arab World? The Trap of Liberalized Autocracy," *Journal of Democracy* 13 (October 2002): 56–68.

24

THE BATTLE FOR
THE CHINESE INTERNET

Xiao Qiang

Xiao Qiang is adjunct professor at the School of Information of the University of California–Berkeley, and founder and chief editor of China Digital Times. *This essay originally appeared in the April 2011 issue of the* Journal of Democracy.

Scholars, journalists, and other commentators have extensively explored censorship in the People's Republic of China (PRC), but much remains to be learned. In particular, we need a better grasp of the "cyber-politics" of expanding online discourse and the capacity of the Internet to advance free speech, political participation, and social change. We also need to know more about the implications of (and limits on) the state's efforts to control what people can see, say, and do online. These issues are crucial to our understanding of China and Chinese society and the role of the Internet under an authoritarian, one-party regime.

It was in 2007—dubbed "Year One of Public Events *(Gonggong Shi-jian Yuannian)*" by one commentator[1]—that the Internet first helped to propel certain happenings into the official media despite resistance from censors. By doing so, Internet activity effectively set the agenda for public discourse. That year, stories about protests against the Xiamen chemical plant, slave labor at brick kilns, and the abuse of individual property rights spread rapidly online, generating so much public interest and debate that censors and the official media had little option but to report on them as well.

A look at the explosive growth of Internet access and use across China, the tools and methods used by the authorities to control the content and flow of information, and the emerging dynamics between Chinese Internet users, or "netizens," and censors shows that the expansion of the Internet and Web-based media is changing the rules of the game between state and society: Authorities are increasingly taking note and responding to public opinion as it expresses itself online. This trend will surely continue, with online public-opinion formation playing an important role in the future development of Chinese society.

Beginning in March 2007, blogger Lian Yue posted a series of articles warning the people in his hometown, Xiamen in Fujian Province, of the potentially disastrous environmental impact of a proposed paraxylene (PX) chemical factory in the city. He urged his fellow residents to speak out against the plant. Although provincial and city authorities vigorously deleted anti–PX factory messages on servers within their jurisdiction, the offending posts on Lian Yue's blog remained because its server was in another province. Word of the PX plant soon spread throughout the city via e-mail, instant messages (IMs), and text messages on mobile phones. A few months later, in defiance of warnings from local authorities, several thousand people showed up to protest in front of city hall. Participants reported the event live, uploading cellphone photos and texts directly to their blogs. Six months later, following two public hearings on the matter, city authorities decided to relocate the lucrative project. The official Xinhua News Agency praised the turnaround as indicating "a change in the weight given to the views of ordinary Chinese in recent years."[2]

The Xiamen story marks the rise of a remarkable new force in China's contemporary social and political life: popular opinion (communicated online) setting the public agenda together with liberal elements in the traditional media. According to the January 2008 blue book on social development produced by the Chinese Academy of Social Sciences, more than fifty-million Chinese read blogs regularly, making them "an important channel for people to voice their opinions about important events."

The government-run China Internet Network Information Center (CNNIC) found that by the end of 2009, the number of Internet users in China had skyrocketed to 384 million, with 53 million new users going online in the last half of that year alone.[3] CNNIC's 2010 statistics show that users are disproportionately young—more than 60 percent are under 25, and about 70 percent are under 30—and relatively well educated, with more than 40 percent holding postgraduate degrees.[4]

The rise of blogging, instant messaging, social-networking services such as QQ, and search-engine and RSS aggregation tools such as Baidu.com and Zhuaxia.com have given netizens an unprecedented capacity for communication. Internet bulletin-board systems (BBSs)—the primary way in which Chinese netizens access and transmit information online to a large number of people—play a vital role in Chinese online life. By early 2009, China had more than 13 million BBS users, with two-million posts published every day.[5] The Tianya Club *(www.tianya.cn)*, based in Hainan Province, has 33.4 million total registered accounts and between 100,000 and 500,000 users online at any one time. This online community has 200,000 daily online users, hundreds of thousands of new posts, and millions of commentaries a day. Another online forum that is popular among university students, Mop.com, is thought to be even larger, with more than fifty-million visits a day. Users discuss current events by posting comments on the bulletin boards of these major forums as well as in smaller virtual communities. Even when the subject is politically taboo or sensitive, under the cover of anonymity or using coded euphemisms, participants can express particular views—and in far bolder language than would be permitted in the official media.

The "blogosphere" has likewise expanded. Like BBSs, blogs exact only a very low cost of entry—anyone with Internet access can start a blog on a hosting service. According to CNNIC, the number of Chinese with blogs reached 221 million by the end of 2009. Of those, the number of active bloggers had risen to 145 million, a 37.9 percent increase from just six months before.[6]

Although most posts are personal in nature, more and more bloggers are writing about public affairs and becoming local opinion leaders. Blogs usually allow readers to comment, and because they often contain links to other blogs and sites, they act as units in a dynamic community. Together they form an interconnected whole—the blogosphere. While the popular BBSs often become forums where public opinion regarding various topics crystallizes, the redundancy of clusters and links in the blogosphere forms a networked information environment that makes absolute top-down control of content nearly impossible.

In addition to BBSs and blogs, chat rooms and IM services, such as those of QQ and MSN, are also popular channels of communication. On 5 March 2010, Tencent (owner of QQ) announced that the number of simultaneous online QQ users had reached 100 million.[7] These IM services play a crucial role in connecting Internet users, facilitating the spread of information, and coordinating actions through social networks. Finally, new photo- and video-sharing sites such as Youku and Tudou are the fastest-growing online applications. The richness of online images, video, and sound has created a powerful media space where millions of users can generate, distribute, and consume content.

Before the Internet, opportunities for unconstrained public self-expression and access to uncensored information were extremely limited. The new online freedoms have developed in spite of stringent government efforts at control and containment. Three Chinese characters may best describe the dynamic between authorities and netizens in Chinese cyberspace: *feng* ("block" or censor), *shai* ("place under the sun" or reveal), and *huo* ("set on fire" or rapidly spread).

Online Censorship

Since the PRC's 1949 founding, information control has been an essential component of the governing strategy of the Chinese Communist Party (CCP). The CCP has a monopoly on political power and has exerted firm control over all mass media, from newspapers and magazines to television channels and radio stations, making them mouthpieces for the Party line. As the reform-minded journalist Lu Yuegang once wrote, the CCP "must depend on two weapons: guns and pens. . . . The logic behind this philosophy is not only to control the pen but to have this control backed by the gun."[8]

Since the introduction of the Internet in China in 1987, the government has employed a multilayered strategy to control and monitor *(feng)* online content and activities. Authorities at various levels use a complex web of regulations, surveillance, imprisonment, propaganda, and the blockade of hundreds of thousands of international websites at the national-gateway level (the "Great Firewall of China").

Several offices govern Internet content—most notably, the CCP's Central Propaganda Department (CPD), which ensures that media and cultural content toe the party line, and the State Council Information Office (SCIO), which oversees all news-providing websites, both official and independent. Municipal, provincial, and county offices of the CPD and SCIO are responsible for overseeing all media published or hosted within their various jurisdictions. CPD officials frequently issue censorship directives to their local counterparts, who have some leeway to implement them as they see fit, and local officials sometimes issue their own censorship directives and fine, threaten, or shut down media outlets that report information which authorities would prefer to keep from the public.[9]

Officials use a number of tactics—keyword filtering, for example—to control online content. The Berkeley China Internet Project obtained a list of more than a thousand words that are automatically banned in China's online forums, including *dictatorship, truth,* and *riot police.* Censors customarily do not make clear exactly what content they intend to ban. The government's primary strategy for shaping content is to hold Internet service providers (ISPs) and access providers responsible for the behavior of their customers; thus business operators have little choice but to censor the content on their sites proactively. For example, regulations posted by the Guangdong Provincial Communications Administration state:

> The system operator will be responsible for the contents of his/her area, using technical means as well as human evaluation to filter, select, and monitor. If there should be any content in a BBS area that is against the regulations, the related supervisory department will hold the BBS as well as the individual operator responsible.[10]

Business owners must use a combination of their own judgment and direct instructions from propaganda officials to determine what content to ban. In an anonymous interview with this author, a senior manager at one of China's largest Internet portals acknowledged receiving instructions from either SCIO or other provincial-level propaganda officials at least three times a day.

Additionally, both the government and numerous websites employ people to read and censor content manually. Tens of thousands of websites hosted overseas are also blocked at the level of the nine national gateways that connect the Chinese Internet to the global network.[11] Websites hosted inside China can be warned or shut down if they violate rules of acceptable content, and individual Internet users who spread information that authorities deem harmful have been threatened, intimidated, or thrown in jail, most often on charges related to national security, such as "subversion." Speaking to the CCP Politburo in January 2007, President Hu Jintao called for improved technologies, content controls, and network security for monitoring the Internet, saying, "Whether we can cope with the Internet is a matter that affects the development of socialist culture, the security of information, and the stability of the state."[12]

Of course the government was already proving creative in its policing of the Internet. For example, since 2007 two cartoon characters, Jingjing and Chacha (from *jingcha,* the Chinese word for police), have popped up on Internet users' screens to provide links to the Internet Police section of the Public Security website, where readers can report illegal online information. A Shenzhen police officer explained: "This time we publish the image of Internet Police in the form of a cartoon, to let all Internet users know that the Internet is not a place beyond the law . . . The main function of Jingjing and Chacha is to intimidate, not to answer questions."[13]

Throughout 2008, Internet control was increasingly tightened in order to present a harmonious image to the world during the Beijing Olympics. Beginning in early 2009, the government further ratcheted up its efforts at control. The initiatives included a campaign against "vulgarity" (which encompasses not just pornography, but also dirty words, slang, and socially and politically unacceptable images) that aimed at search engines, Web-hosting services, and online communities.[14] According to official Chinese media reports, thousands of websites were closed as a result.

Likewise, as the twentieth anniversary of the Tiananmen Square massacre neared that year, the government temporarily shut down countless websites—including Facebook, Twitter, and Wikipedia— ostensibly for "technical maintenance." Then, right around the anniversary on June 4, the Ministry of Information Technology announced plans to require the preinstallation of a filtering software called Green Dam Youth Escort on all computers made or sold in China. After public outcry, however, these plans were scrapped. On July 5, in the aftermath of interethnic riots in Urumqi, Xinjiang Province—home to most of China's Uyghur population—the government again blocked Twitter and other microblogging sites.

Even with the censors' constant presence, the ephemeral, anonymous, and networked nature of Internet communication limits their impact. Moreover, a number of factors make the censors' work particularly daunting. First, the Internet is a many-to-many communication platform that has very low barriers to entry (and risks of use) for anyone who has an Internet connection. Second, with the complicated network topology—the blogosphere and the whole Internet with its redundant connections, millions of overlapping clusters, self-organized communities, and new nodes growing in an explosive fashion—traditional methods of content control such as putting pressure on a publisher to self-censor become nearly impossible.

The Chinese government's Internet-control system mainly aims to censor content that openly defies or attacks CCP rule or contradicts the official line on such taboo topics as the Tiananmen Square massacre or Tibet. Most important, however, is preventing the widespread distribution of information that could lead to collective action such as mass demonstrations or signature campaigns.

The Digital Resistance

The results of government censorship efforts are mixed at best. In early 2009, a creature named the "Grass Mud Horse" appeared in an online video that became an immediate Internet sensation.[15] Within weeks, the Grass Mud Horse—or *cao ni ma,* the homophone of a profane Chinese expression—became the de facto mascot of Chinese netizens fighting for free expression. It inspired poetry, videos, and clothing lines. As one blogger explained, the Grass Mud Horse represented information and ideas that could not be expressed in mainstream discourse.

The Grass Mud Horse was particularly suited to the contested space of the Chinese Internet. The government's pervasive and intrusive censorship has stirred resentment among Chinese netizens, sparking new forms of social resistance and demands for greater freedom of information and expression, often conveyed via coded language and metaphors adopted to avoid the most obvious forms of censorship. As a result, the Internet has become a quasi-public space where the CCP's dominance is exposed, ridiculed, and criticized, often by means of satire, jokes, songs, poems, and code words.

Such coded communication, once whispered in private, is not new to China. Now, however, it is publicly communicated rather than murmured behind the backs of the authorities. For example, since censorship is carried out under the official slogan of "constructing a harmonious society," netizens have begun to refer to the censoring of Internet content as "being harmonized." Furthermore, the word "to harmonize" in Chinese *(hexie)* is a homonym of the word for "river crab." In folk language, *crab* also refers to a bully who exerts power through violence.

Thus the image of a crab has become a new satirical, politically charged icon for netizens who are fed up with government censorship and who now call themselves the River Crab Society. Photos of a malicious crab travel through the blogosphere as a silent protest under the virtual noses of the cyber-police. Even on the most vigorously self-censored Chinese search engine, Baidu.com, a search of the phrase "River Crab Society" will yield more than 5.8 million results.

In China, the nebulous nature of the Internet allows information not easily accessible elsewhere to be revealed *(shai)*. Anyone who goes on-line will be exposed to multifarious sources of information and have unprecedented opportunities to exchange ideas and opinions on social, political, and personal issues. Simultaneously, the interaction between information and communications technology and the traditional media creates a dynamic that is challenging the boundaries of the existing censorship system and thereby the official media as well.

Netizens have launched endless so-called *shai* activities on bulletin boards, blogs, and video- and photo-sharing services: For "*shai* salaries," people post their own or others' salaries for comparison; for "*shai* vacations," users share vacation photos and experiences; and for "*shai* corruption," "*shai* bosses," and "*shai* riches," netizens publish information and opinions online about the elite that would otherwise go unsaid.

The *feng* and *shai* processes are constantly at odds with each other. Even when information is censored at a high level, it often makes its way through online cracks to spread among netizens. In addition, foreign websites and news media that provide Chinese-language services—including the BBC, Radio Free Asia (RFA), and newspapers based in Hong Kong and Taiwan—frequently publish information that is censored in China, which is then often redistributed inside the country by a small but active group of tech-savvy "information brokers" who know how to circumvent the Great Firewall and circulate the news via BBSs, mass e-mailings, and other online channels. Thus banned publications such as dissident newsletters and Voice of America updates can reach Chinese readers despite the government's use of advanced filtering technology.

The last character, *huo* ("fire" or information cascade), describes the phenomenon of news reports, comments, photos, or videos that spread through cyberspace like wildfire. The original item may appear on a bulletin board or blog post, or even in a local paper, and can generate thousands of subsequent comments and posts. Like water gushing through a hole in a dam, if the speed and volume of the dissemination is great enough, any attempt to stanch the flow will be in vain. Driven by dense clusters of interested netizens, the spread of controversial information can outpace the control of censors and quickly become public knowledge—a state of affairs that has huge political implications. When a *huo* phenomenon occurs, the Internet plays the role of a massive distribution platform that denies the government its agenda-setting power.

The *huo* process is especially potent when a local issue resonates with a broader audience and spreads beyond the limited jurisdiction of local officials, sometimes even making it into the national media. When corruption or environmental damage, for example, are exposed, local authorities implicated in the scandal often crack down on news websites hosted within their respective jurisdictions. But when such news finds its way to a website based outside the relevant local jurisdiction, the officials of that jurisdiction will have no means of directly suppressing it and no guarantee that their counterparts in other locales will choose to do so. Central authorities may likewise choose not to impose a blackout of online news about a problematic local issue or event. This gap in control between local authorities as well as between local and central authorities opens a space for netizens to transmit information.

For example, when drunken 22-year-old Li Qiming ran down two roller-blading college students on the campus of Hebei University—killing one and injuring the other—and was arrested after leaving the scene, he shouted: "Go ahead, sue me if you dare. My dad is Li Gang!" Li Gang was the deputy director of the local public-security bureau. Four days later, Mop.com ran an online contest asking entrants to incorporate the sentence "My father is Li Gang" into classical Chinese poems. The contest garnered more than six-thousand entries. A few days after that, the CPD issued a directive to prevent any further "hype regarding the disturbance over traffic at Hebei University." But the phrase "my father is Li Gang" has since become a popular Internet meme in China.[16]

The *huo* phenomenon also plays a critical role in the interplay between Internet expression and changes in the traditional media. Many Chinese journalists are leading double lives—reporters for the state-controlled media by day, bloggers by night. When covering touchy subjects—such as natural disasters, major industrial accidents, or official-corruption cases—print reporters must follow the lead of official sources before conducting interviews and publishing their findings. But journalists can now evade such guidelines by collecting and distributing information online, making it harder for censors to hush up sensitive stories. In fact, when such information becomes *huo* online, the traditional media have a legitimate reason to cover it. Some even follow breaking developments as these are reported in the online realm. *Southern Weekend,* for example, has an editorial section called Net Eye that picks up interesting online stories and publishes them in print.

An Avenue for Feedback and Accountability

In recent years, the processes of *feng, shai,* and *huo* have been at work, helping the Internet to drive public opinion. In early 2007, a netizen from Chongqing posted a photograph of a house, dubbed "China's Most Incredible Nail House," being threatened by a new development.[17] The image touched on problems of urban construction, property rights, and forced evictions, and the official media soon jumped on the story, which happened to break just as the National People's Congress was passing a new property-rights law that purported to protect individual homeowners.

Even as the official media began to carry the story, Sina.com (China's largest Internet portal) offered to pay for images and videos of the nail house, and Mop.com ran a real-time monitoring page. A local court ruled against the homeowners, but public opinion, swayed by poignant online images, heavily favored the nail-house owners. After they disobeyed the court order and refused to move, the central government issued orders to limit reporting, but the story lived on through photographs posted online by netizens. Ultimately, the developer bowed to public pressure, settling the case and compensating the couple for their property, which was eventually destroyed.

Sometimes the government has official reasons to acknowledge certain elements of a story while censoring others, as with news of the widespread use of slave labor at brick kilns in Shanxi Province in mid-2007. The story, which involved the kidnapping of children, slave labor, and the collusion of local police, party officials, and kiln owners, spread through the Chinese blogosphere and ignited national outrage. Reports in the official media followed, and soon top party officials—including Hu Jintao and Premier Wen Jiabao—publicly expressed concern over the issue. Details continued to emerge, and the story only got uglier, eventually spurring the Internet Bureau of the SCIO (also called the CCP External Communication Office) to instruct its subordinate offices and the main Internet news portals to stick to "positive propaganda," to emphasize the government's responsiveness in the brick-kiln matter, to ramp up the monitoring of websites, and to quickly delete information that could be harmful to the government.[18]

Although these cases show that official Internet censorship is not always automatically and fully employed nor always successful, in general the government is able to exert near-total control over information distributed online, particularly when officials make this control a priority. For example, when dissident writer Liu Xiaobo was awarded the 2010 Nobel Peace Prize, the CPD ordered all websites not to create or post stories about the prize and to delete any that already existed. The SCIO also issued a directive forbidding all interactive online forums, including blogs and microblogs, from transmitting prohibited words relating to the prize.[19] As a result, hardly any mention of last year's Nobel Peace Prize can be found on the Chinese Internet, let alone Liu Xiaobo's name or writings.

Nonetheless, there is a changing dynamic afoot: Some big stories are breaking online first only to be carried later by traditional media, thereby making bloggers and netizens information agenda setters. Moreover, despite government censorship efforts, the sheer speed and number of messages and Internet posts are making it ever harder, and in some cases impossible, for censors to stay ahead. The time lapse between the information cascade and top-down censorship instructions is critical, as is the gap in control between central and local authorities, which has allowed local events to become national news reported by the centrally controlled media. Once sensitive stories appear in the official media, the Internet amplifies and keeps them alive, preventing the government from ignoring or suppressing inconvenient news.

Since traditional media outlets still remain under CCP control, even the more progressive and outspoken publications such as *Southern Metropolis Daily* or *Southern Weekend* have only a very limited ability to push the envelope on political reporting. When mass protests, health epidemics, or official-corruption cases occur, the Internet is now the first place people go to find the latest news and to share experiences and opinions. For the first time, citizens are able to participate in a public dialogue about issues of crucial importance to their lives.

In 2007, Xinhuanet surveyed the most popular topics (not including those that had been deleted by monitors) in the three most influential online communities—Strong Country Forum *(bbs.people.com.cn)*, Tianya Club, and Kaidi *(club2.cat898.com)*.[20] In addition to the big stories that year, the study also found that other "sensitive social events" were popular, including those relating to governance, police violence, environmental protection, public health, judicial reform, and natural disasters. It also suggested that netizens' consciousness of rights is rising, as expressions such as "right to know," "right to express," and "right to monitor [the government]" are often used in connection with those large online public events. Furthermore, participants cited as concerns the credibility and responsiveness of various levels of government as well as issues of public morality and the crisis of values in society.

As Beijing-based Internet expert Hu Yong has written: "Since China never had mechanisms to accurately detect and reflect public opinion, blogs and BBS have become an effective route to form and communicate such public opinions of the society."[21] One of the direct impacts of this new information landscape is that negative reports and criticism of local officials—especially relating to corruption, social justice, or people's daily experiences—are now being exposed and nationally disseminated online and resonating across society. Sometimes such a process is tolerated by central authorities to keep lower officials in check and to allow the public to let off steam before it erupts uncontrollably, perhaps resulting in public protests. Such Internet-generated public opinion is sometimes the sole channel for providing feedback to officials.

Online oversight has an especially large impact on local officials in charge of administrative, legal, law-enforcement, and propaganda agencies. Once local officials lose control and information spreads beyond their jurisdiction, the vehemence of an aroused public may force them to change policies. In the words of a local propaganda official, for the government, "it was so much better when there was no Internet."[22]

Internet-driven public events have also helped to highlight issues that originate locally—or even abroad—but have wider implications for Chinese society. For individuals advocating political reform and social change, the Internet and the more reform-minded parts of the traditional media offer outlets to discuss topics that had before been taboo. For example, as prodemocracy protests erupted in Egypt in January 2011, Chinese authorities ordered that only Xinhua's account of events be disseminated. Yet even as Sina Weibo, China's version of Twitter, blocked the word "Egypt" from its search engine,[23] hundreds of thousands of posts on Sina Weibo remained available to savvy users, and netizens continued to spread the news from Egypt and discuss its implications for China's political reality. Eventually, in the wake of online calls for prodemocracy demonstrations inspired by events in Tunisia and Egypt, the word "Jasmine" was also barred from Sina Weibo.[24]

Citizen Mobilization

Often, the next step after public dialogue is collective mobilization and organization around issues of common concern. This is an area where Internet-based public opinion has the potential to make a powerful impact on Chinese society and politics. While authorities stifle civil society and independent social organizations, various grassroots groups that depart from the official line with regard to such social issues as the environment, women's rights, and homosexuality rely on the Internet to organize and distribute information. The expanded space for discussion of public affairs has allowed civil society to push the boundaries of associative and communicative freedoms.

The Xiamen anti-PX protests are now considered a milestone. One protester told a foreign reporter covering the story that at last, the people "can be heard." The city government, in return, listened to public opinion and adjusted its decision accordingly. This was a first in China and a very encouraging sign. The state-run Xinhua News Agency concluded, "The suspended controversial Xiamen city PX plant probably will not become a landmark wherever it finally stands, but it may have helped lay a cornerstone that boosts ordinary Chinese people's participation in policy making."[25] Of course the ruling CCP has not shown any sign of giving up its monopoly on political power and is still highly sensitive to the growing political impact of the Internet.

Online mobilization and protests have also made an impact beyond China's borders, becoming a significant factor influencing Chinese diplomacy and the country's image abroad. In November 2009, to commemorate the twentieth anniversary of the fall of the Berlin Wall, a German nonprofit created a virtual "Berlin Twitter Wall" where individuals could post their thoughts on the occasion through use of the Twitter hashtag "#FOTW." The site's introduction further invited participants to "let us know which walls still have to come down to make our world a better place!" In response, Chinese comments blasting the Great Firewall and Internet censorship dominated the virtual Berlin Wall for weeks. Alluding to Ronald Reagan's famous speech before Berlin's Brandenburg Gate, Chinese bloggers also waged a "Tear Down This Firewall!" campaign prior to U.S. president Barack Obama's visit to China in November 2009. Largely due to such efforts, President Obama addressed the issue of on-line freedom of speech at a town hall meeting with students in Shanghai.

Not all online mobilization is as spontaneous and anonymous as the campaign against the Great Firewall was. Influential bloggers may also mobilize their fellow netizens by acting as spokespersons for certain issue positions, or by giving personal authentication to messages that resonate with the people, or by articulating what others could not say in the face of political censorship. Bestselling author, race-car driver, and blogger Han Han is one such figure. Han is an outspoken critic of government censor-ship, and his blog posts are often deleted by censors. Nevertheless, his main blog received more than 300-million hits between 2006 and 2009. In April 2010, *Time* magazine listed Han Han as a candidate for the hundred "most globally influential people." Han Han subsequently wrote a blog post asking the Chinese government "to treat art, literature, and the news media better, not to impose too many restrictions and censorship, and not to use the power of the government or the name of the state to block or slander any artist or journalist."[26] This post generated some 25,000 com-ments from his readers and was viewed by more than 1.2 million people. The article has also been widely reposted online; in May 2010, a Google search found more than 45,000 links reposting all or part of the essay. Despite official efforts to use the Great Firewall to block Chinese netizens from voting for Han Han on *Time*'s website, he came in second in the final tally, showing the mobilizational power of his writing.

Government officials have begun to recognize that the Internet has set an irreversible trend toward a society that is more transparent, a citi-zenry that is more eager to participate in public life, and a public whose opinion carries more weight. Some officials advocate the need for po-litical reform to adapt to these forces. In a long 2007 article published in the official press, Xin Di, director of the Research Department of the Central Party School, listed five concrete examples to show the "incre-mental progress" taking place in China's political system.[27] Four of his five examples were not top-down efforts at political reform, but rather were related to official government reactions to Internet-driven public events. Although genuine political reform did not appear on the leader-ship's agenda at the CCP National Congress that year, some lower-level officials did recognize the important role of the Internet as a catalyst for political change in Chinese society.

These more forward-looking officials believe that the government should selectively tolerate or even welcome Internet expression as a barometer for public opinion. Permitting such expression allows the government to collect information about society, to be more responsive to citizens' concerns, and to provide a safety valve for the release of public anger. The Internet can also help to hold local officials more accountable—to the central authorities as well as to the public. In addition, the Internet plays a role in promoting political change when the interests and agendas of different government agencies or administrative levels do not align. In such a case, public opinion may help to bolster one side over the other.

A 2009 Chinese Academy of Social Sciences study on the Internet's impact on public opinion identifies netizens as a "new opinion class" that can swiftly influence society and describes the dual methods used by the government to cope with the growing challenge of online activism—clamping down on the Internet while also responding quickly to public opinion.[28] Indeed, this rising online public participation is an indicator that the rules of the political game in China may have started to change.

The CCP's censorship of both the traditional media and the Internet is certain to continue. Yet the increasing influence of online public opinion shows that the CCP and the government can no longer maintain absolute control over the spread of information. The Internet is already one of the most influential media spaces in China—no less so than traditional forms of print or broadcast media. Underlying ever-stronger measures aimed at bolstering state control is a rising level of public information and awareness in Chinese society. Furthermore, through online social networks and virtual communities, the Chinese Internet has become a substantial communications platform for aggregating information and coordinating collective action.

The conflicting forces of *feng, shai,* and *huo* will remain in tension with one another. The result is an emerging pattern of public opinion and citizen participation that represents a shift of power in Chinese society. The Internet allows citizens to comment on certain (albeit limited) topics, and to move them out of purely local arenas to the point where they can become national concerns. Moreover, these "public events" now play a role in promoting human rights, freedom of expression, the rule of law, and governmental accountability. An entire generation of online public agenda setters has emerged to become influential opinion leaders. Surely they will have an important role to play in China's future.

Furthermore, certain somewhat progressive media outlets such as *Southern Metropolis Daily* and *Southern Weekend* are also actively expressing more liberal political ideas and pushing the envelope whenever they can. Before the Internet, such reform-minded discourse could gain little ground against CCP propaganda. Now, as these liberal elements within the established media converge with independent, grassroots voices online, they are creating a substantial force that is slowly wearing away at the CCP's ideological and social control.

China is becoming an increasingly transparent and mobile society with more pluralistic values. The Internet has become a training ground for citizen participation in public affairs: It creates a better informed and more engaged public that is demanding more from its government. The CCP regime is learning to adapt to these new circumstances and becoming more responsive. Already we are starting to see compromise, negotiation, and rule-changing behavior in the regime's response to this challenge, indicating the possibility of better governance with greater citizen participation. From this perspective, the Internet is not just a contested space, but a catalyst for social and political transformation.

NOTES

1. "Xiao Shu: Hoping Xiamen PX Event Became the Milestone," *Nanfang Zhoumo* [Southern Weekend] (Guangzhou), 20 December 2007.

2. See Xinhuanet at *http://news.xinhuanet.com/comments/2007-12/23/content_7297065. htm.*

3. China Internet Network Information Center (CNNIC), "25th Statistical Report on the Development of China's Internet," January 2010.

4. CNNIC, "25th Statistical Report," and CNNIC, "20th Statistical Report on the Development of China's Internet," June 2007. Since July 2007, CNNIC has counted as "Internet users" anyone over six years old who visited the Internet from any terminal (including a mobile phone) at least once in six months. Before July 2007, an Internet user was defined as anyone who spent at least an hour a week online. As a result of this change, more low-income users, such as migrant workers and rural residents, who use mobile phones instead of personal computers as their main communications interface, are now being included as netizens.

5. "New Media Clash," Xinhua News Agency, 16 February 2009, available at *http:// news.xinhuanet.com/zgjx/2009-02/16/content_10825818.htm.*

6. CNNIC, "25th Statistical Report."

7. "Tencent Announces QQ Users Reached 100 Million," 5 March 2010, see *http:// tech.qq.com/a/20100305/000528.htm.*

8. "A Bold New Voice—Lu Yuegang's Extraordinary Open Letter to Authorities," *China Digital Times,* 20 July 2004.

9. U.S.-China Economic and Security Review Commission, Hearing on Access to Information in the People's Republic of China, testimony by Xiao Qiang, 31 July 2007.

10. U.S.-China Economic and Security Review Commission, Hearing on China's State Control Mechanisms and Methods, testimony by Xiao Qiang, 14 April 2005.

11. Jonathan Zittrain and Benjamin Edelman, "Empirical Analysis of Internet Filtering in China," working paper, Berkman Center for Internet and Society, Harvard Law School, 2003; available at *http://cyber.law.harvard.edu/filtering/china.*

12. "Hu Jintao Asks Chinese Officials to Better Cope with Internet," *People's Daily* (Beijing), 24 January 2007.

13. "Starting from September 1, New Virtual Cops Will 'Cruise' All Thirteen Internet Portals in Beijing," *Beijing News,* 22 August 2007.

14. The other agencies are the State Administration for Industry and Commerce (SAIC), State Administration of Radio, Film and Television (SARFT), and General Administration of Press and Publication (GAPP).

15. See *http://chinadigitaltimes.net/2009/02/music-video-the-song-of-the-grass-dirt-horse.*

16. Michael Wines, "China's Censors Misfire in Abuse-of-Power Case," *New York Times,* 17 November 2010, available at *www.nytimes.com/2010/11/18/world/asia/18li.html.*

17. See *www.flickr.com/photos/scorpico7/2765449045* for a photograph of the nail house.

18. "A Notice from the Central Government to Censor News Related to Shanxi Brick Kilns Event," *China Digital Times,* 15 June 2007, available at *http://chinadigitaltimes.net/2007/06/a-notice-from-the-central-government-to-censor-news-related-to-shanxi-brick-kilns-event.*

19. "New Directives from the Ministry of Truth (RE: Liu Xiaobo Wins Nobel Peace Prize)," *China Digital Times,* 8 October 2010, available at *http://chinadigitaltimes.net/2010/10/new-directives-from-the-ministry-of-truth-october-8-2010-re-liu-xiaobo-wins-nobel-peace-prize.*

20. "Study Report of Online Public Opinions in 2007," Xinhuanet, 5 February 2008.

21. Hu Yong, "Blogs in China," China Media Project Case Study (on file at the Journalism and Media Studies Centre, University of Hong Kong), 4 August 2005.

22. "Director of Propaganda Department of Shuide, Shanxi Province: Those Years Without Internet Were So Much Better!" *Southern News.net,* 30 January 2008, available at *http://news.qq.com/a/20080130/000639.htm.*

23. Pascal-Emmanuel Gobry, "China Blocks 'Egypt' on Sina Weibo, Its Twitter Clone," Business Insider SAI, 29 January 2011, available at *www.businessinsider.com/china-blocks-egypt-on-sina-weibo-its-twitter-clone-2011-1.*

24. Kathrin Hille, "China Authorities Block Democracy Campaigns," *Financial Times,* 25 February 2011.

25. "Common Chinese Have More Say in Policy-Making," Xinhuanet, 3 January 2008.

26. See "Han Han . . . Comes in at Number Two in Time 100 Poll: 'Let the Sunshine In,'" *China Digital Times,* 29 April 2010, available at *http://chinadigitaltimes.net/2010/04/han-han-let-the-sunshine-in.*

27. "Political Civilization in Detail," Xinhua News Agency, 4 February 2008.

28. Zhu Huaxin, Shan Xuegang, and Hu Jiangchun, "2009 China Internet Public Opinion Analysis Report," in Chinese Academy of Social Sciences, "2010 Society Blue Paper," 22 December 2009.

25

FROM "FART PEOPLE" TO CITIZENS

Perry Link and Xiao Qiang

Perry Link *is Distinguished Professor of Comparative Literature and Foreign Languages at the University of California–Riverside.* **Xiao Qiang** *is adjunct professor in the School of Information at the University of California–Berkeley, and founder and chief editor of* China Digital Times. *This article is based on Perry Link and Xiao Qiang, "From Grass-Mud Equestrians to Rights-Conscious Citizens: Language and Thought on the Chinese Internet," in* Restless China, *edited by Perry Link, Richard Madsen, and Paul G. Pickowicz (Rowman & Littlefield, 2013). This essay originally appeared in the January 2013 issue of the* Journal of Democracy.

Of all the transformations that Chinese society has undergone over the past fifteen years, the most dramatic has been the growth of the Internet. Information now circulates and public opinions are now expressed on electronic bulletin boards with nationwide reach such as Tianya Club (since 1999); blog-hosting portals such as Sina.com (since 2007); and microblogging services such as Sina Weibo (since 2010). According to a September 2012 report by the official China Internet Network Information Center, Internet users in the People's Republic of China (PRC) now number 538 million out of a total national population of about 1.3 billion. Sina Weibo has announced that its registered-user accounts reached 386 million in August 2012. The rise of such online platforms has given Chinese "netizens" an unprecedented capacity for self-publishing and communication, albeit within a heavily censored environment. The instantaneous, interactive, and relatively low-risk nature of blogging has empowered netizens to voice political opinions, form social connections, and coordinate online (and sometimes offline) collective actions.

Nevertheless, Chinese netizens are still speaking in a heavily monitored environment, and so their demands for greater freedom of information and expression often find voice through coded language and metaphors that allow them to avoid outright censorship. The government's pervasive and intrusive censorship system has generated equally massive resentment among Chinese netizens. The Internet has become a quasi-public space where the dominance of the Chinese Communist Party (CCP) is constantly being exposed, ridiculed, and criticized by waves of jokes, videos, songs, poems, jingles, fiction, sci-fi, code words, satire, and euphemisms. As a result, Chinese cyberspace has seen the emergence of a new political discourse.[1] Largely invented by young gadflies, a surprising number of these terms have begun to spread widely. Liberals, ultranationalists, and even the *People's Daily* (the CCP's official newspaper) have used them.

Will a new political discourse give birth to a new political identity? Old CCP assumptions about linguistic ritual as a tool to forge conformity remain in place. People are still trained to believe, for example, that *dang* (party) and *guo* (nation) are inseparable, or at least close enough that *aiguo* (patriotism) and *ai dang* (love of the party) need not be distinguished. In official language, *wodang* or "our party" implies "the party of everyone." This makes it especially significant that, in today's Internet lingo, terms such as *guidang* ([your] honorable party) are beginning to be used in ways that put sarcastic distance between the speaker and the Party. As this kind of usage spreads, it begins to raise questions of national identity. If netizens are rejecting "party equals country," what are they putting in its place? What does it mean today to be "Chinese"?

One reason why citizen inroads have reached further on the Internet than in other media is that linguistic innovations have helped the Internet to seem like a new, open realm. All human languages constantly evolve, of course, and in principle there is nothing "new" in having new terms appear on the Chinese Internet. But their production and spread there has been especially rapid. Some of the new terms grow from temporary code words that netizens have used in order to evade word filters. The term *zhengfu* (government), for example, counts as "sensitive," and efforts to skirt it have given rise to a number of new terms. One of these is *tianchao* (heavenly dynasty), which, besides avoiding filters, delivers the mischievous suggestion that the government is hardly modern. In a nod to George Orwell, the CCP's Department of Propaganda is referred to as the *zhenlibu* (Ministry of Truth).

One of the most famous Internet puns has to do with a character called the *cao ni ma* or Grass Mud Horse. The term literally contains those three words—there are Grass Mud Horse comics, videos, and stuffed animals that bring the character to life. The joke is that with only a shift of tone the words can easily be made to sound very much like a certain highly provocative and insulting profanity. Playful images of the Grass Mud Horse are novelties that circulate within the relatively small circles of people who enjoy such things. But the term *cao ni ma* as a spoken word has a much broader range and reaches many more people both on and off the Internet. In a famous photograph, the artist Ai Weiwei leaps into the air, naked except for a stuffed-animal Grass Mud Horse held over the middle of his body at crotch level in order to block his genitals from view. The photo is a jab at the CCP regime, for the expression "the Grass Mud Horse covers the middle" can mean, with a shift of tone, "f___ your mother, Communist Party Central Committee." The elegance of Ai's art is that he can induce viewers to think that second phrase without uttering a single syllable. To the regime's Internet police he can say, "You said it, not me!"

Another widespread term is *hexie,* which means "river crab" but is a near-homonym of the word for "harmony." The regime of recently retired PRC president Hu Jintao, in its public rhetoric, put great stress on the idea of a *hexie shehui* or "harmonious society." By recasting this official phrase to turn "harmonious society" into "river-crab society," netizens are evoking Chinese folklore, in which the crab appears as a bully known for scuttling sideways. Netizens also use *hexie* as a verb as well as a noun. When a website is shut down or a computer screen goes blank, the victims might say "We have been river-crabbed!" or, in other words, "harmonized" into silence.

Does New Language Lead to New Thought?

In recent years, Chinese netizens have shown that they possess boundless creativity and ingenuity in finding such ways to express themselves despite stifling government restrictions on online speech. Scholars and China watchers have argued about whether or not Internet repartee is a mere safety valve. By giving people a way to blow off steam, does it ultimately reinforce the status quo? Sometimes resistance does seem little more than a fun game: Reports from the official Xinhua News Agency will not say what really happened? Alright, we will. You close us down for doing so? No problem, we will jump around online and find another way. You keep doing it? Very well, we will lampoon you as a bunch of crotchety river crabs. The "safety-valve" theory holds that this kind of resistance, which is almost recreational, may be cathartic but hardly affects the way people think and behave in the offline world.

But others have argued that Internet sarcasm has deeper effects. Once it catches on, they say, it tends to spread. Satire of things such as bullying and corruption naturally extends just as far as the problems themselves extend—which is very far indeed, potentially into every corner of society. There, in those myriad corners, satire can begin to rot the foundation on which bullying and corruption rest, and "prepare the ground" for more significant change. One can even hope that regime change, when it eventually arrives, will be more likely to be peaceful than violent insofar as the ground for it has been softened.

An important shift takes place when sarcastic terms spread into general use: They come increasingly to lose their sarcastic bite and to seem just like normal terms. Talk of the CCP regime as the *tianchao* or "heavenly dynasty" began as barbed mockery, but once it spread and became standard, the sarcasm drained away and it turned simply into a way of saying "government." Similarly, the use of *pimin* (fart people) began as a bitter suggestion that powerholders see rank-and-file citizens as having no more value than digestive gas. Now it is just another way to say *laobaixing* (ordinary folks). But the seemingly innocuous process by which sarcastic terms are normalized can have profound consequences. It converts the terms from the relatively narrow role of expressing resistance to the much broader one of conceiving how the world normally is. When *tianchao* is used specifically as a jab at the regime, it is a tool with a purpose and can be countered with a return jab. But when it reflects and expresses normality, much more is at stake. The question of an alternative worldview and new political identity emerges.

Worldviews that differ from the official one are not new in the PRC. They certainly preceded the Internet. In the past, though, such views were almost entirely confined to private spaces—either to the privacy of individual minds or to small groups that were beyond public earshot. People who share alternative worldviews have not been allowed to hold public assemblies. Internet language, however, has nurtured new subcultures in which style and camaraderie have become values in their own right, and in which "cyber-assemblies" have emerged. Through online consultation, they can do many of the things that physical assemblies do in a free society: debate issues, argue over the wording of petitions and manifestoes, sign statements, vote in polls, and bring public pressure to bear on specific issues—all while each member sits separately in front of his or her computer screen.

Cyber-meetings resemble physical meetings in some ways that have politically important implications. They are, first of all, autonomous assemblies that usually originate from the bottom up. Consider an example. On 23 June 2011, netizens came across Weibo postings by an attractive twenty-year-old woman named Guo Meimei. Even as she flaunted her ownership of pricey handbags and cars (including a Lamborghini and a Maserati), Guo claimed to be a "commercial general manager" at the Red Cross Society of China (described by the *New York Times* on 3 July 2011 as "a government organization that is the country's largest charity"). After this netizen-discovered story went viral on the Internet, China's official media began to discuss it too, and eventually it reached even the international media. Netizens not only broke the story but drove the public's opinion of it. Online "assemblies" large and small denounced Guo, excoriated the Chinese Red Cross (which watched its donations plummet despite denying any link to her), raised suspicions about the entire world of philanthropy in China, and eventually decried the general decline in ethics across Chinese society as a whole.[2] The Guo Meimei case faded out almost as quickly as it flared up, so it is hard to say that it has left behind any enduring instance of "cyber-organization." In other cases, though, it is clear that online campaigns have indeed given birth to organizations. They have survived the issues that originally brought them together and have sometimes led to action "in real life" (or IRL, as the Internet acronym puts it).

In addition to forging some new group identities, Internet culture has subjected national identity to reimagination. What does it mean to be Chinese today, and how does netizen culture affect the question? The CCP has always offered a ready answer to the question of Chinese identity, and has stressed it in the schools and the media: To be Chinese is to stand with the Chinese Communist Party. To depart from the Party is to be not only politically incorrect but un-Chinese.

On the Internet, however, these axioms are being drawn into question, and alternative answers to the national-identity question are beginning to appear. A few years ago, a netizen with a sly sense of humor began using the terms *guidang* (your [honorable] party) and *guiguo* (your [honorable] state). *Gui* literally means "noble" or "expensive" and has long been placed before nouns as a polite way of saying "your": Thus *guixing* means "your honorable surname," and so on. *Guiguo* has also, for a long time, been an established way of saying "your country" when people from different countries are talking to each other in a formal way. But now, in some circles on the Internet, *guiguo* has taken on the sarcastic meaning of "*your* state"—in other words, the state that belongs to you rulers, not to me. The question "What is *guiguo*?" has popped up in Internet chat rooms. In one of these, in October 2010, a netizen wrote: "It turns out that this *guo* is not our *guo*, but the *guo* of a certain *dang* [that is, the Communist Party]. This fact makes the terms *guiguo* and *guidang* appropriate."

What Is It to Be Chinese?

But if netizens are putting ironic distance between themselves and "*your* state," the question arises of what *they* do identify with at the national level. What is it, in the new day, to be Chinese? This is a big question, and the answers that are beginning to appear are only tentative.

Consider *pimin* or "fart people," the playful tag that has come to stand in opposition to *guiguo*. The *pimin* usage originated from a notorious incident that took place on 29 October 2008, when Lin Jiaxiang, a 58-year-old Communist Party official, was eating and drinking at a seafood restaurant in Shenzhen City, near Hong Kong. He asked an 11-year-old girl for directions to the men's room, then told her to lead him to it personally. Once there, he grabbed her and tried to force her inside. She escaped and ran to her parents. Her father confronted the would-be molester and an argument ensued, during which Lin pointed at the father and yelled, "I was sent here by the Ministry of Transportation! My rank is the same as your mayor's! You people are farts to me! You wanna take me on?! You wanna test what I can do to you?!"

Unfortunately for Lin, the entire episode was captured by a security camera and leaked to the Internet, where it went viral.[3] Lin eventually was fired and "fart people" became a standard term. Gradually it morphed into a term of pride. Fart people came to mean "us" netizens and ordinary people, the ones on the receiving end of abuse, the ones who have no vote, the ones who empathize and identify with one another—the ones who, in short, form the polar opposite of *guiguo,* the country of Lin Jiaxiang and his entitled ilk.

The imbalance in power between *guiguo* and *pimin* is sometimes highlighted by the satiric use of *bei,* which originally meant "quilt" or, as a verb, "to cover," but about a century ago became a grammatical device used for translating the passive voice in Western languages. Using *bei,* an English phrase such as "my wallet has been stolen" can be rendered in Chinese as *wo de pibao bei tou le.* Now, *wo bei hexie le,* or "I have been harmonized," has become a standard quip when censors strike. The role of *bei* in this phrase is important. It signals that I *suffered* the action; it was done *to* me, and I in no way willed it. This "involuntarily passive" implication has led to a range of other sarcastic uses. One is *bei xingfu,* which literally means "happiness-ified." In the Mao era, it was said that the Great Leader *mou xingfu* (sought happiness) for the people; to be on the receiving end of this search, then as now, is to be *bei xingfu.* We look at the officials who "represent" us and see ourselves as *bei daibiao* or "undergoing representation." In each case, the point is that the "esteemed country" *acts upon* the "fart people," not the other way around.

Guiguo, pimin, bei hexie, and other terms of this kind have powerful implications. They imply that the twenty-first-century answer to the question "What is it to be Chinese?" does not have to be the formula "China equals the CCP," and that there is a terrain upon which people can explore alternative answers to questions of identity. Terms that suggest other ideas—ones that contain *min* or "people," for example—are becoming more salient. "Fart people" or *pimin* is sarcastic and as such provides no concept with which people will identify for long. But another word containing *min* is *gongmin* (citizen), and it too has been spreading on the Internet. *Gongmin* is dignified. Like *pimin* it establishes a distance between the citizen and the party-state; but unlike *pimin,* it can be the basis of a new concept of national identity. *Gongmin* are people who have *quan* (rights).

Talk on the Internet of rights of various kinds—the "right to know," the "right to express," the "right to monitor [officialdom]," and others—has been steadily increasing in recent years. In September 2011, a Tsinghua University law student named Li Yan—frustrated by the rejection of her repeated requests for research information on several government ministries—filed a lawsuit against the authorities on the basis of her "right to know."[4] For months after the July 2011 collision of two high-speed trains in Zhejiang Province, netizens citing the same "right to know" flooded the Railways Ministry with demands that it publicly list the victims. In October 2012, a Google search for the combination of the phrases "right to know" and "high-speed train" produced 13.5 million results (just a year ago, the same search had generated 3.75 million results). From such figures we can glean an indication of how many people were concerned by the issue and how fast such language spreads.

The opening of space on the Internet for expression of authentic public opinion along with the use of that opinion to bring pressure to bear on the state-run media and on decision makers, has already become an established pattern in China. It is unlikely that it can be dislodged. A number of events in 2011 alone—the Guo Meimei Red Cross scandal, the crushing to death of toddler Wang Yue,[5] waves of netizens making the journey to visit blind activist Chen Guangcheng at his home in Shandong Province,[6] and others—show how the mechanisms by which people can be heard and can exert pressure are not only in place but almost regular and predictable.

It is important to note as well that netizens who embrace the new online language also appear to embrace the political values of democracy, human rights, and freedom of expression. These netizens, with their growing numbers, expanding social networks, and increasing influence, seem to be evolving from "voices under domination" to "networked agents of change." The government's efforts to control online information, the implications and limitations of such control, and the capacity of Chinese netizens to advance free speech and facilitate political mobilization remain matters that are crucial to an adequate understanding of China. Are new forms of networked communication enhancing opportunities for social change and helping to move China toward a "threshold" for political transformation? Our study of the rise of a new Internet political discourse suggests that such possibilities are indeed increasing.

NOTES

1. "Grass-Mud Horse Lexicon," *China Digital Times*, *http://chinadigitaltimes.net/space/Grass-Mud_Horse_Lexicon*.

2. See Edward Wong, "An Online Scandal Underscores Chinese Distrust of State Charities," *New York Times*, 3 July 2011, available at *www.nytimes.com/2011/07/04/world/asia/04china.html?_r=1*.

3. "Lin Jiaxiang and the China Web Vigilantes," *China Digital Times*, 22 November 2008, available at *http://chinadigitaltimes.net/2008/11/lin-jiaxiang-and-the-china-web-vigilantes*.

4. "Qinghua xuesheng qisu sanbuwei xinxi gongkai yiweizhe gongmin jiandu zhengfu chao mai le yibu" [A Tsinghua University student's lawsuit against three ministries for information transparency marks a step forward in the trend toward citizens' monitoring of the government], *Chendi chuanmeiwang*, 16 September 2011.

5. "China: Two Arrested Over Hit-and-Run Toddler," *China Digital Times*, 23 October 2011, available at *http://chinadigitaltimes.net/2011/10/china-two-arrested-over-hit-and-run-toddler*.

6. Andrew Jacobs, "Chinese Persist in Bids to Visit a Dissident," *New York Times*, 24 October 2011, available at *www.nytimes.com/2011/10/25/world/asia/attempted-visits-to-chen-guangcheng-surge.html?_r=1*.

26

CHINA'S "NETWORKED AUTHORITARIANISM"

Rebecca MacKinnon

Rebecca MacKinnon is a Bernard L. Schwartz Senior Fellow at the New America Foundation. She is cofounder of Global Voices Online (www.globalvoicesonline.org), a global citizen-media network. This essay draws on testimony that she gave before the U.S. Congressional-Executive Commission on China (www.cecc.gov) on 24 March 2010. This essay originally appeared in the April 2011 issue of the Journal of Democracy.

To mark the twentieth anniversary of the fall of the Berlin Wall, a German arts organization launched a website called the "Berlin Twitter Wall." Anyone anywhere on the Internet could use Twitter to post a comment into one of the speech bubbles. Within a few days of its launch, the website was overrun by messages in Chinese. Instead of talking about the end of the Cold War and the fall of communism in Europe, Chinese Twitter users accessed the site to protest their own government's Internet censorship. One wrote: "My apologies to German people a million times [for taking over this site]. But I think if Germans learn about our situation, they would feel sorry for us a million times." Twitter is blocked in China. Still, a growing community is so determined to gain access to the widely used social-networking service and hold uncensored conversations with people around the world that these Chinese Internet users have acquired the technical skills to circumvent this censorship system—widely known as the "Great Firewall of China," a filtering system that blocks websites on domestic Internet connections.

In late January 2010, U.S. secretary of state Hillary Clinton—who two months earlier had stood at Berlin's Brandenburg Gate with other world leaders to celebrate the twentieth anniversary of the fall of the Wall—gave a 45-minute speech on "Internet Freedom." She spelled out how one single, free, and open global Internet is an essential prerequisite for freedom and democracy in the twenty-first century. "A new information curtain is descending across much of the world," she warned.

"And beyond this partition, viral videos and blog posts are becoming the *samizdat* of our day."[1]

But can we assume that Chinese authoritarianism will crumble just as the Iron Curtain crumbled two decades ago? It is unwise to make the assumption that the Internet will lead to rapid democratization in China or in other repressive regimes. There are difficult issues of government policy and corporate responsibility that must be resolved in order to ensure that the Internet and mobile technologies can fulfill their potential to support liberation and empowerment.

When an authoritarian regime embraces and adjusts to the inevitable changes brought by digital communications, the result is what I call "networked authoritarianism." In the networked authoritarian state, the single ruling party remains in control while a wide range of conversations about the country's problems nonetheless occurs on websites and social-networking services. The government follows this online chatter, and sometimes people are able to use the Internet to call attention to social problems or injustices and even manage to have an impact on government policies. As a result, the average person with Internet or mobile access has a much greater sense of freedom—and may feel that he has the ability to speak and be heard—in ways that were not possible under classic authoritarianism. At the same time, in the networked authoritarian state, there is no guarantee of individual rights and freedoms. Those whom the rulers see as threats are jailed; truly competitive, free, and fair elections are not held; and the courts and the legal system are tools of the ruling party.

As residents of a networked authoritarian society, China's more than 400-million Internet users are managing to have more fun, feel more free, and be less fearful of their government than was the case even a mere decade ago. At the same time, however, the government has continued to monitor its people and to censor and manipulate online conversations to such a degree that no one has been able to organize a viable opposition movement. According to the Dui Hua Foundation, a human-rights advocacy organization, arrests and indictments on charges of "endangering state security"—the most common charge used in cases of political, religious, or ethnic dissent—more than doubled in 2008 for the second time in three years.[2] Average Chinese citizens, however, rarely hear of such trends—an "information gap" which makes it much less likely that a critical mass of them will see the need for rapid political change. The system does not control all of the people all of the time, but it is effective enough that even most of China's best and brightest are not aware of the extent to which their understanding of their own country—let alone the broader world—is being blinkered and manipulated. All university students in China's capital now have high-speed Internet access. But when a documentary crew from U.S. public television recently went onto Beijing university campuses and showed students the iconic 1989 photograph of a man standing in front of a tank in Tiananmen Square, most did not recognize the picture at all.

The Chinese experience teaches us a globally applicable lesson: Independent activists and prodemocracy movements may have won some early skirmishes against censorship, but one cannot assume that their adversaries will remain weak and unskilled in the navigation and manipulation of digital communications networks. In fact, governments and others whose power is threatened by digital insurgencies are learning quickly and pouring unprecedented resources into building their capacity to influence and shape digital communications networks in direct and indirect ways. As Larry Diamond put it: "It is not technology, but people, organizations, and governments that will determine who prevails."[3]

In the public discourse about the Internet and repressive regimes, Western policy makers and activists frequently use Cold War–era metaphors in ways that are similar to Clinton's likening of blogs to Soviet-era *samizdat*. Such metaphors are strongest in the policy discourse about the Great Firewall of China. The Hong Kong–based communications scholar Lokman Tsui has criticized this "Iron Curtain 2.0" lens through which many in the West seek to understand the Chinese government's relationship with the Internet. "Strategies to break down the Great Firewall," he writes, "are based on the belief that the Internet is a Trojan Horse (another metaphor!) that eventually will disempower the Chinese state from within and topple the authoritarian government, as the barbarians in previous times have done for China, and as international broadcasting has done with regard to ending communism in the Cold War." Tsui argues that this framework for understanding the impact of the Internet on Chinese politics is not consistent with the growing body of empirical research and is therefore likely to result in failed policy and activism strategies.[4]

Guobin Yang, who began researching Chinese online discourse even before the Internet first became commercially available there in 1995, has concluded that in spite of China's increasingly sophisticated system of censorship and surveillance, the Chinese Internet is nonetheless a highly "contentious" place where debate is fierce, passionate, and also playful. After analyzing numerous cases in which Chinese Internet users succeeded in bringing injustices to national attention or managed to cause genuine changes in local-government policies or official behavior, Yang argues that the Internet has brought about a "social revolution, because the ordinary people assume an unprecedented role as agents of change and because new social formations are among its most profound outcomes."[5] Note that the revolution he describes is being waged mainly by Chinese people posting and accessing information on websites and services operated by Chinese companies—in other words, acting *inside* the Great Firewall.

In examining the use of information and communications technologies (ICTs) by China's "have-less" working classes, Jack Linchuan Qiu documents how Internet and mobile-phone use has spread down to the "lower strata" of Chinese society. This development has given birth to a new "working-class network society" that provides China's less fortunate people with tools for mobility, empowerment, and self-betterment. Yet he also describes how "working-class ICTs" provide new levers for government and corporations to organize and control a new class of "programmable labor." While Chinese workers have been able to use Internet and mobile technologies to organize strikes and share information about factory conditions in different parts of the country, Qiu concludes that "working-class ICTs by themselves do not constitute a sufficient condition for cultural and political empowerment."[6]

Can Online Activism Help Authoritarians?

In his book *Technological Empowerment: The Internet, State, and Society in China,* Yongnian Zheng points out that the success or failure of online activism in China depends on its scope and focus, and that some online activism—particularly that which is at the local level or targets specific policy issues over which there are divisions or turf wars between different parts of the government—can actually serve to bolster regime legitimacy. The least successful online movements tend to be those that advocate various forms of political "exit," including calls for an end to one-party rule by the Chinese Communist Party (CCP) and greater political autonomy or independence for particular ethnic or religious groups. "When the regime is threatened by challengers," Zheng writes, "the soft-liners and hard-liners are likely to stand on the same side and fight the challengers." On the other hand, successful online movements in China are usually characterized by what Zheng (following Albert O. Hirschman) calls the "voice" option, or what other political scientists call the "cooperation option." Such online insurgencies actually provide ammunition to reformist leaders or liberal local bureaucrats in their power struggles against hard-line conservative colleagues. Voice activism helps reduce political risks to reformist officials, who can point to online sentiment and argue that without action or policy change there will be more unrest and public unhappiness.[7]

Thus, rising levels of online activism in China cannot automatically be interpreted as a sign of impending democratization. One must examine what kind of online activism is succeeding and what kind is failing. If voice activism is for the most part succeeding while exit activism is systematically being stifled and crushed—thanks to high levels of systematic censorship and surveillance, in addition to the lack of an independent or impartial judiciary—one can conclude that the CCP has adapted to the Internet much more successfully than most Western observers realize. The Iron Curtain 2.0 mentality criticized by Tsui may indeed have blinded many Western policy makers, human-rights activists, and journalists to what is really happening in China. In 2005, *New York Times* columnist Nicholas Kristof wrote breathlessly: "It's the Chinese leadership itself that is digging the Communist Party's grave, by giving the Chinese people broadband."[8] Zheng's analysis, however, supports the opposite conclusion: The Internet may actually prolong the CCP's rule, bolstering its domestic power and legitimacy while the regime enacts no meaningful political or legal reforms.

Public-policy discourse and deliberation are not exclusive features of democracies. Political scientists have identified varying amounts of public discourse and deliberation in a range of authoritarian states. In 2008, Baogang He and Mark Warren coined the term "authoritarian deliberation" to explain how China's authoritarian regime uses "deliberative venues" to bolster regime legitimacy. While it is possible that the deliberation now taking place within Chinese authoritarianism might bring about eventual democratization, Baogang He and Warren believe that this is only one of two possibilities. The other is that the deliberative practices embraced by the state could stabilize and extend the CCP's authoritarian rule.[9]

Min Jiang applies the concept of authoritarian deliberation specifically to Chinese cyberspace, identifying four main deliberative spaces: 1) "central propaganda spaces," meaning websites and forums built and operated directly by the government; 2) "government-regulated commercial spaces," meaning websites and other digital platforms that are owned and operated by private companies but subject to government regulation, including elaborate requirements for content censorship and user surveillance; 3) "emergent civic spaces," meaning websites run by nongovernmental organizations and noncommercial individuals, which are censored less systematically than commercial spaces but are nonetheless subject to registration requirements as well as intimidation, shutdown, or arrest when authors cross the line or administrators fail to control community conversations; and 4) "international deliberative spaces," meaning websites and services that are hosted beyond Chinese-government jurisdiction—some of which are blocked and require circumvention tools to access—where content and conversations not permitted on domestic websites can be found, and where more internationally minded Chinese Internet users seek to conduct conversations with a broader global public.

It is important to note that the Great Firewall is meant to control only the fourth category of deliberative space, the one that is located outside China. Yet it is the first two categories, as Jiang points out, that have the greatest impact on Chinese public opinion. The state uses much more direct and proactive means to control the first three deliberative spaces, all of which operate within the jurisdiction of the Chinese government. Undesirable or "sensitive" content is either deleted from the Internet altogether or blocked from being published.[10]

The Web as Waterworks

Chinese scholar Li Yonggang has suggested that, instead of using a "firewall" metaphor, it is more helpful to think of Chinese Internet controls—which include not only censorship but surveillance and manipulation of information—as something like a hydroelectric water-management system. Managers have both routine and crisis-management goals: managing daily flows and distribution on the one hand and managing droughts and floods on the other. It is a huge, complex system with many moving parts, and running it requires flexibility. It is impossible for the central government to have total control over every detail of water level or pressure at any given time. The system's managers learn and innovate as they go along.[11]

Recent Chinese-government statements show that, like water, the Internet is viewed as simultaneously vital and dangerous. According to the 2010 government white paper "The Internet in China," rapid, nationwide expansion of Internet and mobile-device penetration is a strategic priority. The Internet is seen as indispensible for education, poverty alleviation, and the efficient conveyance of government information and services to the public. The development of a vibrant, indigenous Internet and telecommunications sector is also considered critical for China's long-term global economic competitiveness.[12] Globally, the Internet is rapidly evolving away from personal computers and toward mobile devices, appliances, and vehicles, with the most rapid rate of growth in Internet and mobile-phone use taking place in Africa and the Middle East. The Chinese government's strategy is for Chinese companies to be leaders in mobile Internet innovation, particularly in the developing world. Last year, Premier Wen Jiabao spoke on multiple occasions about the importance of "the Internet of things," encouraging breakthroughs by Chinese companies in what the government has designated as a strategic industry.[13]

Although the government has direct control over websites run by state-operated media as well as its own national- and provincial-level websites, by far the largest portion of the Chinese Internet is run by the private sector (or "government-regulated commercial spaces" according to Min Jiang's taxonomy of Chinese deliberative digital spaces). Chinese networked authoritarianism cannot work without the active cooperation of private companies—regardless of the origin of their financing or where they are headquartered. Every year a group of Chinese Internet executives is chosen to receive the government's "China Internet

Self-Discipline Award" for fostering "harmonious and healthy Internet development."

In Anglo-European legal parlance, the legal mechanism used to implement such a "self-discipline" system is "intermediary liability." It is the mechanism by which Google's Chinese search engine, Google. cn, was required to censor itself until Google redirected its simplified Chinese search engine offshore to Hong Kong. All Internet companies operating within Chinese jurisdiction—domestic or foreign—are held liable for everything appearing on their search engines, blogging platforms, and social-networking services. They are also legally responsible for everything their users discuss or organize through chat clients and messaging services. In this way, the government hands many censorship and surveillance tasks to private companies that face license revocations and forced shutdowns should they fail to comply. Every one of China's large Internet companies has a special department full of employees whose sole job is to police users and censor content.

In 2008, I conducted a comparative study examining how fifteen different Chinese blog-hosting services censored user-created content. The tests revealed that each company used slightly different methods and approaches in its censorship. The specific content censored also varied from service to service. In a number of tests, when I tried to post politically sensitive material such as an article about the parents of students killed in Tiananmen Square, or a recent clash in a remote town in Western China, internal site software would block publication of the post entirely. Other posts could be saved as drafts but were "held for moderation" until a company staffer could make a decision about whether they should be allowed. Other postings simply disappeared within hours of publication.

Lifting the Veil

In June 2010, a report giving Internet users a peek behind the veil of secrecy surrounding corporate complicity in Chinese Internet censorship appeared on the popular Chinese website Sina.com for a few hours before, ironically, being censored. It quoted Chen Tong, the editor of Sina's Twitter-like microblogging service, who described his company's censorship system in some detail: round-the-clock policing; constant coordination between the editorial department and the "monitoring department"; daily meetings to discuss the latest government orders listing new topics and sensitive keywords that must either be monitored or deleted depending on the level of sensitivity; and finally, systems through which both editors and users report problematic content and bring it to the attention of company censors.[14] In April 2009, an employee of Baidu, China's leading search engine, which also runs user-generated content services, leaked a set of detailed documents from Baidu's internal monitoring and censorship department confirming the company's longstanding reputation as an industry leader not only as a search engine and online-services company, but also in censoring both search-engine results and user-generated content. The documents included censorship guidelines; lists of specific topics and words to be censored; guidelines on how to search for information that needs to be deleted, blocked, or banned; and other internal information from November 2008 through March 2009.[15]

In its efforts to manage what the Chinese people can learn, discuss, and organize online, the government deploys a range of other tactics as well. They include:

Cyber-attacks: The sophisticated, military-grade cyber-attacks launched against Google in late 2009 were targeted specifically at the Gmail accounts of human-rights activists who are either from China or work on China-related issues. Websites run by Chinese exiles, dissidents, and human-rights defenders (most of whom lack the training or resources to protect themselves) have been the victims of increasingly aggressive cyber-attacks over the past few years—in some cases, compromising activists' computer networks and e-mail accounts. Domestic and foreign journalists who report on politically sensitive issues and academics whose research includes human-rights problems have also found themselves under aggressive attack in China, with efforts to expose their sources, making it much more risky to work on politically sensitive topics.

Device and network controls: In May 2009, the Ministry of Industry and Information Technology (MIIT) mandated that by July 1 of that year a specific software product called Green Dam Youth Escort was to be preinstalled on all computers sold in China. While Green Dam was ostensibly aimed at protecting children from inappropriate content, researchers outside and within China quickly discovered that it not only censored political and religious content but also logged user activity and sent this information back to a central computer server belonging to the software developer's company. The software had other problems that created opposition to it within U.S. companies. It contained serious programming flaws that increased the user's vulnerability to cyber-attack. It also violated the intellectual property rights of a U.S. company's filtering product. Faced with uniform opposition from the U.S. computer industry and strong protests from the U.S. government, the MIIT backed down on the eve of its deadline, making the installation of Green Dam voluntary instead of mandatory.

The defeat of Green Dam, however, did not diminish other efforts to control and track Internet-user behavior at more localized levels— schools, universities, apartment blocks, and citywide Internet Service Providers (ISPs). In September 2009, news reports circulated that local governments were mandating the use of censorship and surveillance products with names such as "Blue Shield" and "Huadun." The purpose of these products appeared similar to Green Dam's, though they involved neither the end user nor foreign companies.[16] Unlike Green Dam, the implementation of these systems has received little attention from foreign media, governments, or human-rights groups.

Domain-name controls: In December 2009, the government-affiliated China Internet Network Information Center (CNNIC) announced that it would no longer allow individuals to register Internet domain names ending in ".cn." Only companies or organizations would be able to use the .cn domain. While authorities explained that this measure was aimed at cleaning up pornography, fraud, and spam, a group of Chinese webmasters protested that it also violated individual rights. Authorities announced that more than 130,000 websites had been shut down in the cleanup. In January 2010, a Chinese newspaper reported that self-employed individuals and freelancers conducting online business had been badly hurt by the measure.[17] In February, CNNIC backtracked somewhat, announcing that individuals would once again be allowed to register .cn domains, but all applicants would have to appear in person to confirm their registration, show a government ID, and submit a photo of themselves with their application. This eliminated the possibility of anonymous domain-name registration under .cn and has made it easier for authorities to warn or intimidate website operators when "objectionable" content appears.

Localized disconnection and restriction: In times of crisis, when the government wants to ensure that people cannot use the Internet or mobile phones to organize protests, connections are shut down entirely or heavily restricted in specific locations. The most extreme case is in the far-northwestern province of Xinjiang, a traditionally Muslim region that borders Pakistan, Kazakhstan, and Afghanistan. After ethnic riots took place in July 2009, the Internet was cut off in the entire province for six months, along with most mobile text messaging and international phone service. No one in Xinjiang could send e-mail or access any website—domestic or foreign. Business people had to travel to the bordering province of Gansu to communicate with customers. Internet access and phone service have since been restored, but with severe limitations on the number of text messages that people can send on their mobile phones per day, no access to overseas websites, and very limited access even to domestic Chinese websites. Xinjiang-based Internet users can only access watered-down versions of official Chinese news and information sites, with many of the functions such as blogging or comments disabled.[18]

Surveillance: Surveillance of Internet and mobile users is conducted in a variety of ways, contributing to an atmosphere of self-censorship. Surveillance enables authorities to warn and harass Internet users either via electronic communications or in person when individuals are deemed to have transgressed certain standards. Detention, arrest, or imprisonment of selected individuals serves as an effective warning to others that they are being watched. Surveillance techniques include:

"Classic" monitoring: While surveillance measures are justified to the public as antiterrorism measures, they are also broadly used to identify and harass or imprison peaceful critics of the regime. Cybercafés—the cheap and popular option for students and the less affluent—are required to monitor users in multiple ways, including identity registration upon entry to the café or upon login, surveillance cameras, and monitoring software installed on computers.

"Law-enforcement compliance": In China, where "crime" is defined broadly to include political dissent, companies with in-country operations and user data stored locally can easily find themselves complicit in the surveillance and jailing of political dissidents. The most notorious example of law-enforcement compliance gone wrong was when Yahoo's local Beijing staff gave Chinese police account information of activist Wang Xiaoning in 2002 and journalist Shi Tao in 2004, leading to their imprisonment. In 2006, Skype partnered with a Chinese company to provide a localized version of its Internet-based phone-calling service, then found itself being used by Chinese authorities to track and log politically sensitive chat sessions by users inside China. Skype had delegated law-enforcement compliance to its local partner without sufficient attention to how the compliance was being carried out.[19]

"Astroturfing" and public outreach: The government increasingly combines censorship and surveillance measures with proactive efforts to steer online conversations. In 2008, the Hong Kong–based researcher David Bandurski determined that at least 280,000 people had been hired at various levels of government to work as "online commentators." Known derisively in the Chinese blogosphere as the "fifty-cent party," these people are paid to write posts that show their employers in a favorable light in online chatrooms, social-networking services, blogs, and comments sections of news websites.[20] Many more people do similar work as volunteers—recruited from the ranks of retired officials as well as college students in the Communist Youth League who aspire to become Party members. This approach is similar to a tactic known as "astroturfing" in U.S. parlance, now commonly used by commercial advertising firms, public-relations companies, and election campaigns around the world in order to simulate grassroots enthusiasm for a product or candidate. In many Chinese provinces, it is now also standard practice for government officials—particularly at the city and county

level—to coopt and influence independent online writers by inviting them to special conferences and press events.

The central government has also adopted a strategy of using official interactive portals and blogs, which are cited as evidence both at home and abroad that China is liberalizing. In September 2010, the CCP launched an online bulletin board called "Direct to Zhongnanhai," through which the public was invited to send messages to China's top leaders. Since 2008, President Hu Jintao and Premier Wen Jiabao have held annual "web chats" with China's "netizens." An official "E-Parliament" website, on which citizens are invited to post policy suggestions to the National People's Congress, was launched in 2009. The 2010 official government white paper lists a variety of ways in which the Chinese government solicits public feedback through the Internet. It states: "According to a sample survey, over 60 percent of netizens have a positive opinion of the fact that the government gives wide scope to the Internet's role in supervision, and consider it a manifestation of China's socialist democracy and progress."[21]

All of this is taking place in the context of the Chinese government's broader policies on information and news control. In December 2009, the Committee to Protect Journalists listed China as the world's worst jailer of journalists. In recent testimony before the U.S. Congress, Joshua Rosenzweig of the Dui Hua Foundation presented an array of statistics to support a grim conclusion:

> Over the past two-and-a-half years in particular, roughly since the beginning of 2008, there has been a palpable sense that earlier progress towards rule of law in China has stalled, or even suffered a reversal, and there is mounting evidence that a crackdown is underway, one particularly targeting members of ethnic minorities, government critics, and rights defenders.[22]

Thus online public discourse is indeed expanding—with government encouragement. The government is creating and promoting the impression both at home and abroad that China is moving in the direction of greater democracy. At the same time, the Chinese people's ability to engage in serious political dissent or to organize political movements that might effectively challenge the CCP's legitimacy has actually diminished, and the consequences for attempting such activities are more dire than they were ten years ago.

Networked Authoritarianism Beyond China

In their most recent book surveying Internet censorship and control around the world, Ronald Deibert and Rafal Rohozinski warn that "the center of gravity of practices aimed at managing cyberspace has shifted subtly from policies and practices aimed at denying access to content to methods that seek to normalize control and the exercise of power in cyberspace through a variety of means." This article has described a range of ways in which China is near the forefront of this trend. Deibert and Rohozinski divide the techniques used by governments for Internet censorship and control into three "generations": The "first generation" of techniques focuses on "Chinese-style" Internet filtering and Internet-café surveillance. "Second-generation" techniques include the construction of a legal environment legitimizing information control, authorities' informal requests to companies for removal of information, technical shutdowns of websites, and computer-network attacks. "Third-generation" techniques include warrantless surveillance, the creation of "national cyber-zones," state-sponsored information campaigns, and direct physical action to silence individuals or groups.[23]

While Deibert and Rohozinski characterize Chinese cyber-controls as being largely first generation, the Chinese government aggressively uses all the second- and third-generation techniques and has been doing so for quite some time. Indeed, the second- and third-generation techniques are essential because the Great Firewall alone is ineffective and permeable.

Deibert and Rohozinski point out that a number of governments, particularly those in Russia and several former Soviet republics, have bypassed the first-generation controls almost completely and instead are concentrating their energies on second- and third-generation controls, most of which (with the jarring exception of "direct physical action to silence individuals or groups") are more subtle, more difficult to detect, and more compatible with democratic or pseudodemocratic institutions. The Russian-language Internet, known by its denizens as "RUNET," is thus on the cutting edge of techniques aimed to control online speech with little or no direct filtering.[24]

Research in the Middle East and North Africa shows that while Internet filtering is more common and pervasive throughout that region, governments are increasing the use of second- and third-generation techniques. Many governments in the region have cracked down on online dissent through the skillful use of family-safety measures and antiterrorism laws. At the same time, they have made substantial investments in Internet and telecommunications infrastructure, recognizing that connectivity is essential for economic success.[25]

Some second- and third-generation controls are also used by democratically elected governments, including those of South Korea and India.[26] Intermediary censorship is deployed in a range of political systems to silence antiregime speech, fight crime, or protect children. The concept of holding service providers liable has become increasingly popular among lawmakers around the world, including in Western Europe—where the main goals are to combat intellectual-property theft and protect children. In the United States, activists are concerned about the weakening of due process, which has allowed government access to networks owned and run by corporations, all in the name of combating cyber-crime and cyber-warfare. Even the Chinese government has adopted a very similar language of cyber-security to justify its Internet-control structures and procedures. Deibert and Rohozinski are right to warn that "many of the legal mechanisms that legitimate control over cyberspace, and its militarization, are led by the advanced democratic countries of Europe and North America."[27]

Chinese authoritarianism has adapted to the Internet Age not merely through the deployment of Internet filtering, but also through the skilled use of second- and third-generation controls. China's brand of networked authoritarianism serves as a model for other regimes, such as the one in Iran, that seek to maintain power and legitimacy in the Internet Age. In Russia and elsewhere there is a further, disturbing trend: Strong governments in weak or new democracies are using second- and third-generation Internet controls in ways that contribute to the erosion of democracy and slippage back toward authoritarianism. This situation is enabled by a weak rule of law, lack of an independent judiciary, weak guarantees for freedom of speech and other human-rights protections, heavy or untransparent regulation of industry (particularly the telecommunications sector), and weak political opposition that is rendered even weaker by clever manipulation of the media, legal system, and commercial-regulatory system.

It is clear that simply helping activists to circumvent first-generation censorship and training them in the use of new technologies for digital activism without also addressing the second- and third-generation controls deployed by their governments is insufficient, sometimes counterproductive, and potentially dangerous for the individuals involved. Weak rule of law and lack of accountability and transparency in the regulation of privately owned and operated Internet platforms and telecommunications networks facilitate the use of second- and third-generation controls, which pose a great threat to activists. Therefore, strong advocacy work at the policy and legislative level aimed at improving rule of law, transparency, and accountability—in government as well as the private sector—is more important than ever.

The business and regulatory environment for telecommunications and Internet services must become a new and important focus of human-rights activism and policy. Free and democratic political discourse requires Internet and telecommunications regulation and policy making that are transparent, accountable, and open to reform both through independent courts and the political system. Without such baseline conditions, opposition, dissent, and reform movements will face an increasingly uphill battle against progressively more innovative forms of censorship and surveillance.

NOTES

1. Hillary Rodham Clinton, "Remarks on Internet Freedom," Washington, D.C., 21 January 2010; available at *www.state.gov/secretary/rm/2010/01/135519.htm.*

2. "Chinese State Security Arrests, Indictments Doubled in 2008," *Dui Hua Human Rights Journal,* 25 March 2009.

3. Larry Diamond, "Liberation Technology," *Journal of Democracy* 21 (July 2010): 82.

4. Lokman Tsui, "The Great Firewall as Iron Curtain 2.0: The Implications of China's Internet Most Dominant Metaphor for U.S. Foreign Policy," paper presented at the sixth annual Chinese Internet Research Conference, Hong Kong University, 13–14 June 2008.

5. Guobin Yang, *The Power of the Internet in China: Citizen Activism Online* (New York: Columbia University Press, 2009), 213.

6. Jack Linchuan Qiu, *Working-Class Network Society: Communication Technology and the Information Have-Less in Urban China* (Cambridge: MIT Press, 2009), 243.

7. Yongnian Zheng, *Technological Empowerment: The Internet, State, and Society in China* (Stanford: Stanford University Press, 2008), 164–65.

8. Nicholas D. Kristof, "Death by a Thousand Blogs," *New York Times,* 24 May 2005; available at *www.nytimes.com/2005/05/24/opinion/24kristoff.html.*

9. Baogang He and Mark Warren, "Authoritarian Deliberation: The Deliberative Turn in Chinese Political Development," *Perspectives on Politics* 9 (June 2011): 269–89.

10. Min Jiang, "Authoritarian Deliberation on Chinese Internet," *Electronic Journal of Communication* 20, nos. 3 and 4 (2010); available at *http://papers.ssrn.com/sol3/papers. cfm?abstract_id=1439354.*

11. Rebecca MacKinnon, "Chinese Internet Research Conference: Getting Beyond 'Iron Curtain 2.0,'" *RConversation,* 18 June 2008; available at *http://rconversation.blogs. com/rconversation/2008/06/chinese-inter-1.html.*

12. "The Internet in China," Information Office of the State Council of the People's Republic of China (SCIO), 8 June 2010; available at *http://china.org.cn/government/ whitepaper/node_7093508.htm.*

13. Robert McManus, "Chinese Premier Talks Up Internet of Things," *ReadWriteWeb,* 19 January 2010; available at *www.readwriteweb.com/archives/chinese_premier_inter- net_of_things.php.*

14. Jonathan Ansfield, "China Tests New Controls on Twitter-Style Services," *New York Times,* 16 July 2010; available at *www.nytimes.com/2010/07/17/world/asia/17beijing. html.* The full Chinese-language text of the report (which was deleted by censors from the original source) was reproduced by Radio France Internationale at *www.chinese.rfi.fr.*

15. Xiao Qiang, "Baidu's Internal Monitoring and Censorship Document Leaked," *China Digital Times,* 30 April 2009; available at *http://chinadigitaltimes.net/2009/04/ baidus-internal-monitoring-and-censorship-document-leaked/.*

16. Owen Fletcher, "China Clamps Down on Internet Ahead of 60th Anniversary," IDG News Service, 25 September 2009; available at *www.pcworld.com/article/172627/ china_clamps_down_on_internet_ahead_of_60th_anniversary.html*; and Oiwan Lam, "China: Blue Dam Activated," *Global Voices Advocacy,* 13 September 2009; available at *http://advocacy.globalvoicesonline.org/2009/09/13/china-blue-dam-activated.*

17. Oiwan Lam, "China: More than 100 Thousand Websites Shut Down," *Global Voices Advocacy,* 3 February 2010; available at *http://advocacy.globalvoicesonline.org/2010/02/03/china-more-than-100-thousand-websites-shut-down.*

18. Josh Karamay, "Blogger Describes Xinjiang as an 'Internet Prison,'" BBC News, 3 February 2010; available at *http://news.bbc.co.uk/2/hi/asia-pacific/8492224.stm.*

19. Nart Villeneuve, "Breaching Trust: An Analysis of Surveillance and Security Practices on China's TOM-Skype Platform," Open Net Initiative and Information Warfare Monitor, October 2008; available at: *www.nartv.org/mirror/breachingtrust.pdf.*

20. David Bandurski, "China's Guerilla War for the Web," *Far Eastern Economic Review,* July 2008.

21. SCIO, "The Internet in China."

22. Joshua Rosenzweig, "Political Prisoners in China: Trends and Implications for U.S. Policy," Testimony to the Congressional-Executive Committee on China, 3 August 2010; available at *www.cecc.gov/pages/hearings/2010/20100803/statement5.php.*

23. Ronald Deibert and Rafal Rohozinski, "Control and Subversion in Russian Cyberspace," in Ronald Deibert et al., eds., *Access Controlled: The Shaping of Power, Rights, and Rule in Cyberspace* (Cambridge: MIT Press, 2010), 23.

24. Deibert and Rohozinski, "Control and Subversion in Russian Cyberspace," in *Access Controlled,* 15–34.

25. "MENA Overview," *Access Controlled,* 523–35.

26. Michael Fitzpatrick, "South Korea Wants to Gag the Noisy Internet Rabble," *Guardian.co.uk,* 9 October 2008, available at *www.guardian.co.uk/technology/2008/oct/09/news.internet*; and John Ribeiro, "India's New IT Law Increases Surveillance Powers," IDG News Service, 27 October 2009, available at *www.networkworld.com/news/2009/102709-indias-new-it-law-increases.html.*

27. Deibert and Rohozinski, "Beyond Denial: Introducing Next-Generation Information Access Controls," 6.

27

THE TURN AGAINST LEGAL REFORM

Carl Minzner

Carl Minzner *is associate professor at Fordham Law School in New York, specializing in Chinese law and governance. He is the author of numerous works on judicial reform, citizen petitioning, and social unrest in China, including "China's Turn Against Law,"* American Journal of Comparative Law *(2011). This essay originally appeared in the January 2013 issue of the* Journal of Democracy.

What will be the future of China's authoritarian political system?

Many predicted that China's rapid development over the past several decades would inevitably lead to gradual liberalization. Economic growth was expected to generate a cascade of changes—first to society, then law, and eventually politics. Events appeared to confirm these projections. As Chinese authorities opened up the economy in the late twentieth century, they also launched sweeping reforms of the nation's legislative and judicial institutions.

The events of the past decade, however, have called these assumptions into question. From 2000 to 2011, per capita GDP in China more than quintupled, skyrocketing from US$949 to $5,445. But one-party rule remains intact under the Chinese Communist Party (CCP), and Chinese authorities have turned against many of the legal reforms that they themselves enacted back in the 1980s and 1990s. Lawyers have come under increased pressure. Political campaigns warning against rule-of-law norms have rippled through the courts. And under new policies making "stability maintenance" (*weiwen*) a top priority, central authorities have massively increased funding for extralegal institutions aimed at channeling, curtailing, and suppressing citizen discontent.

These shifts have choked off institutions for venting dissatisfaction and redressing ills that are key to the CCP's continued resilience as an authoritarian regime. The changes have fueled social unrest, funneling citizen grievances into a rising tide of street protests instead of institutionalized legal or political participation. And they have led to new worries at the center regarding the danger posed by individual CCP officials (such as disgraced Chongqing CCP boss Bo Xilai) seizing parts of the *weiwen* apparatus for their own ends. For precisely these reasons, an increasing number of officials, academics, and activists have called on central authorities to revive flagging legal reforms in the wake of the November 2012 leadership succession.

China may indeed be at a tipping point. But it is not clear which way it will tip. Authorities may restart legal reform as part of a comprehensive program of political and institutional transformation. Or they may refuse, risking an escalating spiral of social and political turmoil.[1]

Late Twentieth-Century Reforms

In the 1970s and 1980s, CCP authorities turned their backs on decades of political radicalism and socialist economic policies. They launched extensive legal reforms aimed at building new structures to govern China.

Officials reopened law schools shuttered during the turmoil of the Cultural Revolution (1966–76). They used academic and professional exchanges to aggressively import foreign legal concepts. They issued hundreds of new statutes and regulations, creating a comprehensive framework of civil, commercial, criminal, and administrative law. Authorities promoted court trials, conducted according to these newly promulgated laws, as the preferred venue for resolving ordinary civil or commercial grievances and disputes. In 1989, Chinese authorities even issued an administrative litigation law giving ordinary citizens limited rights to sue state authorities in court.

Reforms continued throughout the 1990s. Authorities professionalized the judiciary, moving away from the practice of staffing courts with former military officers. They removed definitions of lawyers as "state legal workers" and privatized the bar. By the early 2000s, the state-owned law firms of the 1980s had given way to an explosion of private firms, domestic and foreign alike. In 1997, central authorities adopted "rule according to law" (*yifa zhiguo*) as a core Party slogan. Parallel constitutional amendments followed two years later. Legal reform even emerged as a subject in China's foreign relations, with U.S. and Chinese diplomats agreeing to initiate cooperative exchanges on legal reform.

Naturally, Chinese leaders aimed to advance their own interests through these reforms. Ideologically, they wanted an alternative source of legitimacy to Maoist revolutionary principles on which to ground their rule. Practically, they desired new mechanisms to help resolve the mounting social conflicts created by rapid economic development and urbanization. Law, litigation, and courts seemed to be the solution. Administratively, central leaders sought new ways to monitor their local officials and better respond to pervasive principal-agent problems within the bureaucracy. They also wanted to gather better information on domestic problems facing China. Allowing citizens a limited ability to challenge local officials through court channels, or to offer opinions through legislative ones, promised to help address these concerns.

As Andrew Nathan noted in 2003, these reforms helped to strengthen the internal stability of the Chinese state.[2] They institutionalized CCP rule. They channeled popular discontent (regarding violations of citizens' rights or official abuses of power) into institutions *within* the existing political system, rather than radical underground organizations seeking to overturn the party-state. Legal reforms also played an important role in foreign policy. Rule-of-law discussions with foreign governments, for example, provided a politically more acceptable forum for discussing human rights in advance of China's 2001 entry into the World Trade Organization.

Central reforms emboldened bureaucrats farther down the ladder to push institutional change forward under the rule-of-law banner. By the late 1990s, Chinese legal academia was abuzz with discussions of constitutionalism and constitutional supremacy (*xianfa zhishang*). In 2001, the Supreme People's Court (China's highest judicial body) took the groundbreaking step of authorizing a provincial court to actually apply the (otherwise nonjusticiable) Chinese constitution in an individual case. Some local courts began to push the boundaries of their authority, independently proclaiming the invalidity of local rules and regulations that contradicted national law.[3]

Citizens used the new channels to protect their own interests. Civil and administrative cases multiplied. Farmers employed central authorities' rule-of-law rhetoric to challenge illegal local exactions and land seizures. By the early 2000s, a cadre of public-interest lawyers and legal activists (such as Chen Guangcheng) had emerged. They fused public-interest lawsuits and savvy media strategies to push for deeper reform, with some resounding successes. In 2003, after a migrant named Sun Zhigang died at the hands of city authorities in Guangzhou (Canton), three legal academics mounted a petition to the national legislature challenging the legality and constitutionality of the extrajudicial administrative system used to detain him. At the same time, extensive media coverage generated a public uproar regarding official abuses in Sun's case and similar ones. Remarkably, central authorities yielded—annulling the entire detention system nationwide.[4]

The Counterreaction

Despite the hopeful signs visible nearly a decade ago, officials have turned against their earlier reforms. Some concerns are practical. Late twentieth-century reforms were designed to steer civil and commercial disputes into trials before local courts. But rural China has limited legal resources. Trained judges and licensed lawyers are in short supply. Courts remain institutionally weak and commonly find it hard to enforce their verdicts. As China entered the twenty-first century, such problems led to violent showdowns between local courts and aggrieved citizens seeking justice, as well as surging numbers of extralegal petitions and protests to higher authorities regarding lower-court decisions.

Other concerns are explicitly political. State media have cautioned that "judicial concepts . . . not in accordance with [Chinese] national sentiment have 'blown into the East from the West.'"[5] Party authorities have warned that some judges have falsely used concepts such as "the supremacy of the law" as an excuse to avoid or oppose CCP leadership in judging cases.[6]

This has generated a backlash. Since the early 2000s, Chinese authorities have shifted citizen disputes away from court trials that are decided according to law. Judges face new pressures to resolve cases through closed-door mediation. Community mediation institutions dating from the era of Chairman Mao Zedong (d. 1976) have been dusted off and revived. New extralegal Party-led "coordination sessions" have been created, under the rubric of mediation, to handle those cases that officials fear are most likely to generate social protest.

In some areas, these efforts have permitted meaningful local experiments that may respond better to rural needs than the formal legal channels emphasized during the late twentieth century. In others, they have become convenient rationales for local authorities to abandon legal norms entirely as they seek to shore up social stability at all costs, whether by suppressing the legitimate grievances of individual petitioners or by caving in to mass complaints with no legal basis, but backed by many angry citizens.

Party authorities have also attempted to rein in politically wayward judges. In 2006, CCP officials launched new campaigns within the court system stressing loyalty to the Party and cautioning against Western rule-of-law norms. In 2008, central authorities installed a CCP functionary with no formal legal experience as head of the Supreme People's Court. There followed the so-called Three Supremes (*sange zhishang*) campaign—an effort to remind judges that CCP policies and "the people's will" are equal to (or above) the constitution. Lest anyone miss the message, both law-school curricula and the national bar examination were amended to include the content of these campaigns as mandatory subjects.

Lawyers have come under increased pressure. Party campaigns have labeled them "socialist legal workers" and pressed for creation of CCP cells within law firms. Loyalty oaths to the Party are now required to obtain a license to practice law. Authorities have escalated harassment and abuse of well-known public-interest lawyers and legal activists by shuttering the organizations of some and subjecting others to imprisonment, house arrest, and periodic disappearance or torture.

In short, CCP leaders are trying to neuter the very rule-of-law pressures that they themselves unleashed in the late twentieth century. They have sought to close down rhetoric (constitutionalism), channels (court trials), and social forces (lawyers) that activists had used to mobilize for greater change. And they have reasserted control over state actors (judges and courts) who might have been tempted to forget the realities of Communist Party control.

Where such concerns are absent, reforms have continued. In the area of criminal justice, for instance, Chinese authorities have developed noncustodial pilot programs for juvenile offenders. The 2012 Criminal Procedure Law creates additional protections for juveniles facing interrogation and trial. With regard to death-penalty cases, Chinese judicial authorities have made efforts to increase transparency and improve judicial review. As a result, foreign experts estimate that the number of executions in China has dropped by roughly half since 2007, to about four thousand in 2011.[7]

Tough central policies have generated a range of perverse effects. Ironically, they have heightened social unrest. Many citizens with environmental or land grievances against local authorities have concluded that the best chance for obtaining redress does not lie within state legal institutions that have been gradually undermined. Instead, they are increasingly resorting to direct (and sometimes violent) collective street actions, seeking to force central officials to intervene and local authorities to cave in. In response, central authorities have greatly increased the funding and influence of domestic-security organs. This has permitted some local governments to devolve into quasi-feudal satrapies in which officials use massive funds (and the politically correct justification of "maintaining social stability") to suppress legitimate citizen complaints, hide their own misdeeds, and enrich themselves through corruption.

Reform on the Rebound or Descent to Disorder?

The fall of rising Party star Bo Xilai in the first half of 2012 dramatically drew attention to these problems. Central leaders voiced concern about the ability of one of their own to amass huge, unchecked personal power and to challenge the low-key collective leadership norms that had prevailed since the beginning of the reform period two decades ago. Liberal scholars and officials used the Bo affair to criticize the CCP's turn against legal reform since the early 2000s.

Over the past year, indications have emerged that the counterreaction against legal reform may have now generated a backlash of its own. Central authorities have moved to downgrade the power of the CCP political-legal apparatus. The new CCP general secretary, Xi Jinping, has begun to revive language regarding law and legal reform that had gone into eclipse in recent years. Top Party leaders have issued new calls for applying rule-of-law principles to the task of upholding social stability. A new State Council white paper suggests that recent political campaigns in the judiciary may be wound down.

If implemented, such changes might represent a tipping point in Chinese legal reform. Central authorities may have recognized that if China is to solve its pressing problems, it will need meaningful institutions that can place independent checks on official power and provide bottom-up channels for citizen participation.

China today might be on the verge of a complex transition that parallels developments in South Korea and Taiwan during the 1970s and 1980s. In both cases, authoritarian powerholders pursued gradual political reform, opened the institutions of government to increasing levels of external civic pressure, and slowly but successfully shifted to more liberal systems of government. Today, both countries belong securely in the ranks of the world's developed democracies.

But it remains uncertain that China will steer such a hopeful course. The CCP's ruling elite could end up rejecting reform rather than embracing it. If so, China in the twenty-first century might resemble nineteenth-century Russia more than twentieth-century South Korea or Taiwan.

Like China today, late nineteenth-century Czarist Russia enjoyed decades of economic growth at rates that outpaced those of the United States and European nations, notwithstanding a bureaucratic-authoritarian political system that foreign observers saw as badly outdated. As the century drew to a close, speculation ran rampant as to when Russia might surpass Western powers in economic and military might.

Russia also found itself in the throes of massive domestic change. Military humiliation at the hands of Western powers in the first international war of the industrial age (the Crimean War of 1853–56) had exposed Russia's technological inferiority. As a result, the Russian imperial state initiated extensive economic and social reforms. Serfdom was abolished and peasants received more rights. Industrialization reworked the fabric of Russian life, bringing a tide of rural migrants to urban factories. Worker protests over conditions and pay began to erupt with increasing frequency. The new social media of the era—printed periodicals—permitted an educated elite to rapidly disseminate ideas throughout the country, often resorting to allusions or coded language to avoid imperial censors.

Czarist authorities launched sweeping legal reforms as well. They imported foreign legal institutions including models of legal education; a professional bar; Western-style courts and juries; and civil, commercial, and criminal codes. Excitement was palpable. "The slogans in the air in the 1860s were due process, open court proceedings, trial by jury, and irremovable judges."[8] Officials even established local representative assemblies with limited powers of self-government.

Citizens took eagerly to these new channels. Reformers sought to use local assemblies to gradually push the imperial regime in a more liberal direction. Radical activists took advantage of legal novelties such as open court proceedings and independent judges in order to turn trials into platforms calling for greater political change. In 1878, a young anarchist named Vera Zasulich became an instant media sensation when, after her arrest for trying to assassinate an imperial governor, the trial judge resisted government efforts to tamper with the case; her lawyer managed to turn the public proceedings into an indictment of police brutality; a jury of sympathetic citizens returned a verdict of "not guilty"; and crowds erupted into public demonstrations upon her release.

Such developments caused serious worry among political elites. As in China today, rule-of-law institutions came under increasing suspicion from an authoritarian regime dead set against fundamental political reform—particularly after anarchists assassinated the reformist Czar Alexander II in 1881. Under his successor, Russian authorities launched a two-decade–long rollback of liberal policies. They curtailed public trials, limited the rights of juries, asserted control over bar associations, removed political trials from the regular court system, and drastically reduced the powers of local assemblies.

Beginning in the late 1870s, imperial authorities also built up an extensive police state (one might call it "social-stability maintenance with Russian characteristics"). They increasingly took responsibility for upholding law and order out of the hands of judges and gave it to the police, including the Okhrana (the Czarist secret service). Agents of the latter enjoyed dramatically expanded powers that allowed them to detain and internally exile anyone even suspected of political crimes.

Of course, these measures did not succeed in stamping out all dissent. The existence of private property meant that there were limits on imperial power. Wealthy patrons continued to employ reformist intellectuals, despite state efforts to isolate them. Dissident authors continued to find markets for their works, notwithstanding state efforts to censor them.

The key result of Czarist counterreform in the late nineteenth century was to radicalize society. The imperial turn against law convinced moderates that gradual reform of the regime was impossible. Decades of indiscriminate state repression pushed together liberal constitutionalists, anarchist terrorists, religious nationalists, radical socialists, and ordinary citizens outraged by violations of their rights. And it drove all of them to adopt ever more extreme political positions.

Further, as imperial rule entered its waning years, hard-line policies helped to prevent the emergence of any organized and institutionalized political opposition. Like China today, imperial Russia had no Taiwanese *dangwai* (outside the party) movement, no South Korean opposition political parties, no Polish Solidarity trade union. It crushed any effort to organize these. This produced a surface veneer of political stability. But it also ensured that no coherent force existed to step into the void and pick up the power lying in the streets once the Czarist state finally crumbled. Instead, there was only a chaotic assortment of military strongmen, popular mobs, radicalized intellectuals, and—detraining ominously at the Finland Station—committed underground revolutionaries hardened by decades of repression.

Of course, China is not there . . . yet. Despite increasing domestic unrest, slowing economic growth, and rising tensions with neighbors, central leaders retain a firm grip on the levers of power. And despite the recent official turn against legal reforms, most activists still hope for (and seek) gradual reform of the Chinese state. They do not desire a radical upheaval that would shatter it. They want a soft rather than a hard landing.

But the risk of a hard landing is real. Pressures are building. Open legal and political channels are needed to funnel them in the direction of gradual change. If China does not build these now, it will not simply tip into transition, but rather plummet into cataclysm.

NOTES

1. Some content and language are adapted, with permission, from Carl Minzner, "China's Turn Against Law," *American Journal of Comparative Law* 59 (Fall 2011): 935–84.

2. Andrew J. Nathan, "China's Changing of the Guard: Authoritarian Resilience," *Journal of Democracy* 14 (January 2003): 13–15.

3. Keith J. Hand, "Understanding China's System for Addressing Legislative Conflicts," *Columbia Journal of Asian Law* (Spring 2013).

4. Keith J. Hand, "Using Law for a Righteous Purpose: The Sun Zhigang Incident and Evolving Forms of Citizen Action in the People's Republic of China," *Columbia Journal of Transnational Law* 45, no. 1 (2006): 127–31.

5. Wei Lihua and Jiang Xu, "Sifa shenpan zhong de renmin qinghuai yu qunzhong luxian" [Popular sentiment and the mass line in judicial trial work], *China Court Web*, 22 June 2011, available at *www.chinacourt.org/html/article/201106/22/455318.shtml*.

6. Minzner, "China's Turn Against Law," 947.

7. "Dui Hua Estimates 4,000 Executions in China, Welcomes Open Dialogue," Dui Hua website, 12 December 2011, available at *http://duihua.org/wp/?page_id=3874*.

8. Richard Pipes, *Russia Under the Old Regime* (London: Weidenfeld and Nicolson, 1974), 295.

28

THE RISING COST OF STABILITY

Xi Chen

Xi Chen is assistant professor of political science at the University of North Carolina, Chapel Hill. He has been a postdoctoral fellow at Harvard University and is the author of Social Protest and Contentious Authoritarianism in China *(2012). This essay originally appeared in the January 2013 issue of the* Journal of Democracy.

In the two decades since the Chinese Communist Party (CCP) put down the 1989 student protest movement, the People's Republic of China (PRC) has enjoyed not only stunning economic growth but impressive political stability as well. Political elites have maintained considerable solidarity, and at least until quite recently, power struggles and policy disputes at the CCP's top levels never posed any serious threat to the collective leadership or its succession arrangements. Chinese society was reasonably stable too. Social protests have risen dramatically in number since the early 1990s, but most have remained isolated and constrained. Rather than threatening the CCP regime's ability to survive, routinized popular contention has become a form of interest articulation, and as such has actually helped the political system to achieve a certain degree of responsiveness and accountability.[1]

No wonder, then, that starting about a decade ago the topic of "authoritarian resilience" became a feature in the field of China studies. In 2012, however, some evidence began to suggest that the CCP regime's stability may be more fragile than had been thought, and that even if a "tipping point" had not yet been reached, perhaps the system has begun teetering. The smooth process by which the so-called fifth generation of leaders was set to take over at the Eighteenth Party Congress was thrown into question when a massive scandal erupted around Bo Xilai, the CCP chief of Chongqing and a contender for the top ruling body, the Standing Committee of the CCP Politburo. Along with power struggles, debates over policy and ideology among Party leaders and intellectuals have been intensifying. President Hu Jintao's decade-old "no debates" policy seems as if it may be reaching the end of its shelf life.

In society at large, popular contention is nowhere close to getting out of control. Yet there remain reasons to wonder whether the current system of *weiwen* (stability maintenance) can continue. The CCP leadership is clearly anxious to keep it going, and *weiwen* has become a priority. Never before has the CCP devoted so many resources to this task. Almost the entire party-state apparatus is mobilized behind it, at a high and increasing cost that includes excessive and often illegitimate uses of force. What is worse, the system backfires regularly by inadvertently encouraging people to engage in "troublemaking" activities.

As many scholars have noted, the difficulties that the CCP is now experiencing can be partly explained by a variety of social changes that have posed new challenges to political authoritarianism. The information revolution, especially in the form of social media, has made collective action easier. The transition to a market economy has also released ordinary people from the *danwei* (work-unit) system and many other social-control mechanisms.

Ultimately, however, the difficulties that the stability-maintenance approach is now facing in China should be ascribed to institutional weakness. The all-encompassing *weiwen* system—which includes everything from secret-police agencies to courts and petition-receiving offices that can be used to press popular claims—is good at responding to challenges in the short term, but creates many serious long-term problems along the way.

In order to grasp the problematic nature of the *weiwen* system, it helps to know something about its source. It is the product of two competing forces: 1) the CCP's efforts to institutionalize its political structure, and 2) the influential legacy of Chairman Mao Zedong. Shortly after the turbulent Mao years, which concluded with the Cultural Revolution that raged from 1966 through his death in 1976, Deng Xiaoping and other leaders decided to overhaul the political system. Deng blamed the CCP's mistakes under Mao on a lack of good institutions.

The political reforms of the 1980s had two main aims: 1) to differentiate the CCP from the government, and 2) to establish formal rules and norms. Putting space between the Party and the state was thought essential to solving the problem of Party officials with too much power and responsibility.

Party officials were told to focus on "Party affairs" rather than the direct running of state agencies, mass organizations, media outlets, and state-owned enterprises. Deng and his fellow reformers took this step not to undermine the CCP's political monopoly, of course, but rather to make the Party more effective by relieving it of distracting administrative burdens. Similarly, the move toward formal rules and procedures—including an extensive legal-reform program that began in the late 1970s—was meant to promote long-term stability and the rational governance of a burgeoning market economy.

The reformers wanted to part with problematic Maoist politics, but Mao's legacies turned out to be very resilient.[2] Mao's resentment of differentiated and formal institutions and his romance with mass mobilization have continued to shape developments long after his death. Whenever reforms run into difficulties and the CCP seems threatened, its leaders tend to fall back on Maoist methods.

After the CCP regime's "close call" with the 1989 student movement, for example, almost all reforms aimed at separating the Communist Party from the government came to a halt. For Deng and his colleagues, the movement was a wake-up call. The willingness of so many party-state agencies to support the protesting students suggested that institutional differentiation and political liberalization would endanger the Party's grip on power. Then came the collapse of the Soviet and East European socialist regimes, underlining the danger that institutional reforms resembling Soviet leader Mikhail Gorbachev's *glasnost* (openness) and *perestroika* (restructuring) could lead to a loss of political control.

The CCP thus largely aborted reforms that encouraged relatively autonomous identities for public and semipublic agencies. Instead, it began to reassert direct control over the People's Congresses (China's many elected local legislatures), mass organizations such as labor unions, and the media. Of course, institutionalization in the classic style first described by Max Weber did not stop entirely after 1989. For instance, legal-system reforms continued into the 1990s and 2000s. As Andrew Nathan has observed, institutionalization also made great progress with respect to collective leadership, succession, and a variety of other areas, even though many new norms and procedures were informal.[3]

In the 2000s, when the CCP's leaders began to feel threatened by the rise of popular contention and moved to strengthen the *weiwen* system, they once again slipped into grooves that Mao had carved. In order to cope with rampant protests, riots, and other "emergency events," they looked for a system that could mobilize all kinds of resources and act quickly. For such a task, they concluded, relatively autonomous institutions that act according to their institutional interests and are constrained by rigid rules and procedures are not a good fit.

Paradoxically, China's market-based economic success and the recent financial difficulties of the West have furnished additional reasons for following the Maoist tradition. In Chinese leaders' eyes, the West's economic troubles discredit the "Western model" of democracy, the rule of law, separation of powers, and independent media. Has not China's recent success, they ask, proven the strengths of the CCP, especially its power to marshal resources in pursuit of key goals?

Given this thinking, it is no surprise that the *weiwen* system rests on a highly centralized power structure. Through it, Party leaders supervise and coordinate a bewildering and overlapping range of agencies—including police, surveillance, and propaganda organizations—dedicated to preserving social stability. The system's scope is remarkable. It includes not only state offices but also state-owned enterprises, semipublic bodies, and even private businesses. For example, many telecommunication companies and Internet service providers are required to conduct surveillance and censorship. At the same time, the system has a hierarchical structure that reaches from the central government all the way down to neighborhood and village committees throughout urban and rural areas alike. Such an all-embracing apparatus can usually identify and respond to any threats quickly and forcefully.

Yet the system does not rely solely on surveillance and repression. The CCP's leaders understand that they also need the means to address social conflicts and popular grievances. This is where the courts and the *xinfang* (petition) system come in.

The development of the judicial system illustrates very well the tension between institutionalization and the Maoist legacy. For thirty years, China has been undertaking legal reforms. Taken together, they form one of the best examples of the CCP's efforts to institutionalize the political structure. There have been great strides toward increased professionalism, more regular procedures, and the creation of a proper legal infrastructure. The courts have acquired a relatively distinctive institutional identity, and for a time even looked as if they were part of an evolution toward the rule of law.

About a decade ago, however, Party leaders began steering the court system toward Maoist populism. They took to warning against legal "Westernization" and insisted that Chinese courts should follow their own path. Adjudication and formality were downplayed in favor of mediation. Taking inspiration from the Maoist era, CCP higher-ups also warned judges and lawyers that they should take care to be responsive to "public views" and the "mass line." One of the Party's favorite methods for resolving legal disputes, known as "Ma Xiwu adjudication," stresses informality and morality over rules and laws. It stems from the revolutionary era.[4]

The development of the *xinfang* system also reveals Mao's continuing influence. It was Mao who first installed it as the channel through which Party leaders could receive complaints from ordinary people. Unlike most other authoritarian regimes, which go to considerable lengths to claim that they are liberal democracies, the PRC explicitly rejects liberal democracy and instead relies on the "mass line" as the main means of interest representation. According to this doctrine, CCP officials should hold extensive consultations with interested parties both before and after setting public policy. Petitions are important because they give "the masses" (to use Maoist jargon) an approved means for communicating with the Party elite.

But this system is inefficient at articulating interests and tends to encourage "troublemaking" petitioning tactics. In the highly centralized power structure, only leaders can effectively address popular claims. Inevitably, however, those with real power can only deal with a relative handful of petitions. In order to get attention, then, petitioners resort to disruptive tactics. At the same time, many local officials dislike petitions and may neglect or even obstruct them.

The CCP has tried to institutionalize *xinfang,* laying down rules and strengthening complaint-hearing bodies. Yet the system's combination of centralism and populism makes it resistant to institutional differentiation and formal procedures. No one takes the rules seriously. Petitioners often jump channels and try to go straight to higher-ups. A favorite means for this is to stage a large collective action. The rules say that no more than five people are supposed to deliver a petition, but it is well known that officials will take a petition with a crowd behind it more seriously than they will take an ordinary petition.

The story of the court and *xinfang* systems shows that when it comes to institutionalization, the CCP's leaders are of two minds. They know that it is useful for dealing with disputes and popular claims. Yet centralized power unconstrained by formal rules often seems to them just as needful, and even better at "solving problems."

An Unsustainable Model

How effective is the *weiwen* system? It is certainly good at removing "malicious" Internet posts and at bringing force to bear to suppress protests. The PRC party-state still commands vast resources and is capable of quick action. Yet three shortcomings of the system make it a poor bet for the long term.

First, its cost is enormous and rising. In 2011, the National People's Congress allocated the equivalent of US$95 billion to law and order. That staggering sum—it was slightly more than the PRC's military budget for that year—in fact paid for only a small part of the whole *weiwen* system. Much stability-related work is done "off-budget" by party-state agencies, state-owned enterprises, and private businesses. Then too, financial expenditures are not the only costs of the *weiwen* system, which also eats up less tangible public resources such as the time and attention of state officials.

The system is so costly in part because the party-state's sheer capacity for mobilizing resources breeds "overkill," especially when officials believe that the problem they are tackling is urgent. For example, local officials in Shandong Province reportedly spent close to $10 million over the past few years on efforts to control the well-known blind lawyer and rights activist Chen Guangcheng before his recent exile to the United States.[5] This may be an extreme case, but it is not uncommon for local governments to spend substantial sums on a single petitioner determined enough to spend years petitioning Beijing or a provincial capital.

The quest for stability, in a populist climate that does not value institutional boundaries and formal procedures, often spurs government functionaries to go way beyond their nominal roles in order to pacify protesters. When relatives of someone killed in a Hubei Province traffic incident failed to gain satisfactory compensation from the driver, they repeatedly staged disruptive protests in order to pressure the police. Although not legally bound to, stability-conscious police officials helped the family to find a lawyer and even went with them to court. When the lawsuit failed because the uninsured driver was poor, the police department paid the family from its own official funds and even took up a collection among its officers. This sort of thing of course encourages more protests—and more extraordinary actions to mollify protesters—in a cycle that threatens to drive *weiwen* costs up indefinitely.

The second problem of the *weiwen* system is that it tends to undermine the CCP regime's legitimacy by producing excessive and illegitimate uses of force. It is not surprising that such a formidable machine of social control can trigger excessive coercion. The system holds local officials strictly responsible; a single serious breakdown of order is enough to destroy careers. Internet surveillance and the security cameras that are now common in Chinese cities can provide nervous officials with targets for repression that they may go after rather than risk the "firing offense" of allowing a major disturbance to develop.

Here we see another of the system's contradictions: It tends to generate a high demand for force, but at the same time it needs and wants that force to be legitimate. Thus there exists a thicket of restrictions on how and when local authorities may use official force. But the restrictions serve all too often to drive coercion into the realm of informality and illegality. Officials following regular procedures may not be able to use force, but they can and do pay temporary staffers, private security firms, or even criminal gangs to do so. Such violence is frequently not only excessive but covert. Some local governments have used secret and substandard "black prisons" (*hei jianyu*) and even mental hospitals to deal with troublesome petitioners.[6] Many private security firms are abusive and poorly disciplined. One of the most notorious, Beijing's Anyuanding Security Company, hired out more than three-thousand guards to local governments looking for help in dealing with petitioners. Using force to excess and without legitimacy can hardly be good for regime stability. Here is another price of the *weiwen* system.

The *weiwen* system's final drawback is its perverse tendency to encourage unruly behavior. When the CCP's fondness for the "mass line" meets the instrumentalist attitude toward legality that is common within both officialdom and society at large, the result is contempt for rules and forms. Courts and agencies will bend the law to keep boisterous petitioners quiet, so ordinary Chinese citizens (provided they calculate that repression is not a major risk) have learned to "act out" in order to guard their interests or boost their bargaining power. Compensation for houses demolished under eminent domain is often minimal, but a few homeowners with the nerve to "make trouble" have received excessive payouts. Similarly, judges have received orders from on high to keep working with unhappy litigants even after their cases have been formally decided when the litigants resorted to "troublemaking" petitions. Following the principle of "the squeaky wheel gets the grease" in order to keep the peace certainly holds the danger of teaching people that disruptive tactics are a shortcut to special treatment.

The defects of the current *weiwen* system are no secret. During my recent field trips to Hunan and Hubei provinces, I heard judges and police officers ruefully say, "The more *weiwen,* the more instability." If even low-ranking officials know that the system has fundamental problems, why have CCP leaders not tried to change it?

The main answer, I believe, is that reforms are fraught with risk. If China's rulers want to maintain stability on a solid institutional base, they will need to initiate changes that will differentiate and liberalize the political system. From their experiences in the 1980s, however, they have taken away the lesson that such a move may ultimately endanger their monopoly on power. As long as the economy is growing rapidly and elites and ordinary people alike are mostly content with the status quo, putting off such a risky step will seem understandable and even sensible. If crisis or a sense of crisis supervenes, however, calculations may change. If rejecting reform seems likely to trigger a sudden regime collapse, embracing gradual political change may come to seem like a good way to gain a degree (perhaps even years) of breathing room.

The year 2012 was likely not a tipping point, but it was a year in which (to change the metaphor) many cracks in the façade of regime stability began to appear. From the standpoint of China's leaders, therefore, the year 2013 is probably a good time to begin a reckoning.

NOTES

1. Xi Chen, *Social Protest and Contentious Authoritarianism in China* (Cambridge: Cambridge University Press, 2012).

2. Sebastian Heilmann and Elizabeth Perry, eds., *Mao's Invisible Hand: The Political Foundations of Adaptive Governance in China* (Cambridge: Harvard University Asia Center, 2011).

3. Andrew J. Nathan, "China's Changing of the Guard: Authoritarian Resilience," *Journal of Democracy* 14 (January 2003): 6–17.

4. Benjamin Liebman, "A Return to Populist Legality? Historical Legacies and Legal Reform," in Heilmann and Perry, eds., *Mao's Invisible Hand,* 174. Ma Xiwu (1899–1962) was a Communist legal official who in the 1930s and 1940s stressed informality as a way of administering "socialist justice."

5. Voice of America, "Chen Guangcheng shijing zhongwai, weiwen yueweiyuebu-wen?" [Cheng Guangcheng incident shocks China and the world, stability maintenance leads to more instability], 29 April 2012, available at *www.voachinese.com/content/arti-cle-20120430-will-chinas-stability-prevervation-work-149545255/957538.html.*

6. Human Rights Watch, "China: Rampant Violence and Intimidation Against Pe-titioners—Officials and 'Retrievers' Block Citizens' Complaints," 9 December 2005, available at *www.hrw.org/en/news/2005/12/07/china-rampant-violence-and-intimidation-against-petitioners.*

Epilogue:
Two Essays by Liu Xiaobo

Two Essays on China's Quest for Democracy

The Nobel Peace Prize for 2010 was awarded to imprisoned Chinese writer and dissident Liu Xiaobo "for his long and nonviolent struggle for fundamental human rights in China." The author of eleven books and hundreds of essays, Liu has been a key figure in the Chinese democracy movement since the events leading up to the 1989 Tiananmen Square massacre. He was jailed in 1989–91 and again in 1996–99. His activities over the past decade included serving as president of the Independent Chinese PEN Center and as editor of *Democratic China* magazine. He was a principal drafter and a prominent signatory of Charter 08, a document—modeled on Czechoslovakia's Charter 77—calling for democracy and respect for human rights in China.

Shortly before the Charter was officially released in December 2008, Liu was detained by the Beijing Public Security Bureau. On 23 June 2009, he was formally arrested on charges of "inciting subversion of state power." Brought to trial in December, he was found guilty and sentenced to eleven years of imprisonment. He is currently serving his term at Jinzhou Prison in Liaoning Province, where his wife Liu Xia was able to visit him and to convey the news that he had won the Nobel Prize.

Two of Liu's most eloquent essays appear in the pages that follow. The first of these is entitled "Changing the Regime by Changing Society." The second, entitled "Can It Be That the Chinese People Deserve Only 'Party-Led Democracy'?" was written in response to the publication by the Information Office of the State Council on 19 October 2005 of "Building of Democratic Politics in China"—the first white paper on democracy-building ever issued by the Communist government of China.

Both of these essays were originally written in 2006 and posted in Chinese on the website *www.observechina.net*. They were translated into English by Human Rights in China and published in issue no. 1, 2010, of its quarterly journal *China Rights Forum*, along with other writings and statements by Liu and a great deal of useful information about him and his career. Interested readers can find this issue, entitled "Freedom of Expression on Trial in China," at *www.hrichina. org/public/contents/category?cid=173549*. We are most grateful to Human Rights in China for permission to reprint these essays, which appear here with very minor stylistic changes. These essays initially appeared in the January 2011 issue of the *Journal of Democracy*.

Changing the Regime by Changing Society

Liu Xiaobo

Translation by Human Rights in China

We have had over twenty years of reform, but due to the selfish ar-
rogation of political power by the Chinese Communist Party (CCP) and
the scattering of civic forces, in the short term I do not see any kind of
political force capable of changing the regime, or any liberal-minded
force within the circle of official authorities, like a Gorbachev[1] or a
Chiang Ching-kuo,[2] nor any way for civil society to build up political
power sufficient to rival official authorities. And so, China's course of
transformation into a modern, free society is bound to be gradual and
full of twists and turns. The length of time it will take may surpass even
the most conservative estimates.

At the same time, in terms of opposition to the might of the CCP
regime, civil society remains weak, civic courage inadequate, and civic
wisdom immature; civil society is still in the earliest stages of development, and consequently there is no way to cultivate in a short time a
political force adequate to the task of replacing the Communist regime.
In such a situation, change in China's political system and its current
regime—any plan, program or even action seeking instant success—can
be no more than castles in the air.

Yet this does not mean that there is absolutely no hope for a future
free China. The sky of Chinese politics in the post-Mao era can no longer be single-handedly obscured by a totalitarian ruler; rather, it has assumed two hues: darkness and light. Likewise, the relationship between
the officials and the people is no longer such that no one dares to speak
out, except to shout "Long live the emperor!" Rather, the political ri-
gidity of the authorities and the people's awakening to their rights, and
official suppression and civil resistance exist side-by-side at the same
time. The system is autocratic as before, but the society is no longer ignorant; the officials are tyrannical as before, but the civil-rights defense
movements continue to arise; the terror of literary inquisition is still
there, but it can no longer produce the deterrent of "killing one to scare
the rest"; the regime's "enemy awareness" is unchanged, but "politically
sensitive individuals" are no longer a terrifying "pestilence" shunned by
everyone.

In the Maoist era, for personal totalitarian control to be established,
four major conditions had to be met at the same time:

Comprehensive nationalization, leading to no personal economic autonomy whatsoever, turning the regime into an all-powerful nanny of
our countrymen, and making them economically dependent on the regime from cradle to grave;

All-pervasive organization, leading to the complete loss of personal freedom, turning the organization into the sole authenticator of legal status for our countrymen, who can hardly take a single step if they leave the organization, and making them personally dependent on the regime to the extent that without the shelter of the organization they have no social license;

Rigid tyranny of the machinery of violent dictatorship imposed on the entire social body; a dictatorial atmosphere created by an extreme rule of one man and by an "enemy" mentality, where every citizen is made a soldier; all-pervasive vigilance and ubiquitous monitoring, to the extent that every pair of eyes is turned into surveillance equipment and every person is under surveillance by his or her work unit, neighborhood [committee], neighbors, and even relatives and friends.

Mental tyranny imposed on the entire nation by an ideology of formidable cohesive power and power to inspire, and by large-scale mass movements, where the extreme personality cult and leadership authority create a kind of mind-control with one brain deciding what everybody thinks, and where artificially created "dissidents" are not just persecuted economically, politically, and in terms of social status, but are also made to suffer humiliation of character, dignity, and spirit—the so-called "criticism until they drop and stink," which is in fact a dual tyranny that is both physical and mental to the extent that the great majority of the victims succumbing to this mental tyranny engage in endless public self-humiliation.

Yet, in the post-Mao era, the society entirely based on official authority no longer exists. An enormous transformation toward pluralism in society has already taken place, and official authority is no longer able to fully control the whole society. The continuous growth of private capital is nibbling away at the regime's economic foundation, the increasingly disintegrated value system is challenging its ideology, persistently expanding civil-rights protections are increasing the challenges to the strength of the arbitrary authority of government officials, and steadily increasing civic courage is making the effectiveness of political terror wither by the day.

Since June Fourth [1989] especially, three of the four major pillars necessary for the establishment of personal totalitarian rule have been in various stages of decay and even collapse. Personal economic dependence [on the regime] has gradually been replaced by personal independence, and the living made through one's own efforts has given individuals the material base for autonomous choices, while bringing a plurality of interests to the society. Personal dependence on organizations has gradually been replaced by a smattering of personal freedom: The Chinese people need no longer live in organizations for lack of alternatives; the time when they could hardly take a step if they left the organization is gone, never to return. Chinese society is gradually moving toward freedom of movement, mobility, and career choice.

In the ideological sphere, the awakening of individual consciousness and awareness of one's rights have led to the collapse of the one great unified official ideology, and the diversification in the system of values is forcing the government to look for excuses for the passive adjustments of its ideology. A civic value system independent of the bureaucratic value system is gradually taking shape, and although indoctrination with lies and speech control continues, [the government's] persuasive power has significantly declined. The information revolution ushered in by the Internet in particular has multiplied and diversified the channels of information access and civic discourse, causing the fundamental failure of the means of control used by government authorities to block information and prohibit political discussion.

Of the four pillars of totalitarian rule, only political centralization and its blunt repression remain. However, because a social pattern where righteousness and justice reside with civil society while power resides with the authorities has gradually taken shape, the twofold tyranny of the Maoist era—persecution of the flesh and trampling of the spirit—is no more, and there has been a significant decline in the effectiveness of political terrorism. As for [the] government['s] persecution of its victims, it no longer has the twofold effect of using prison to deprive them of personal freedom and also using mass criticism to debase their integrity and dignity. Political persecution may cause its victims to suffer economic losses, may strip them of personal freedom, but it is unable to damage their social reputation, and even less able to place them under the siege of social isolation; and therefore it cannot destroy their integrity, dignity, or spirit. On the contrary, it has gradually turned into a vehicle for advancing the moral stature of its victims, garnering them honors for being the "civic conscience" or "heroes of truth," while the government's hired thugs have become instruments that "do the dirty work." Not only do the majority of those persecuted no longer beg forgiveness from the organization through endless self-criticism or undertake public self-humiliation; on the contrary, most are able to inspire reverence with their devotion to justice as they defend themselves in the dock under great organizational pressure, putting the Communist Party organization and courts into the moral position of defendants.

Meanwhile, following the collapse of the communist-totalitarian Soviet Union and Eastern bloc, the global trend toward liberalization and democratization has been gaining strength by the day. Pressure from the human-rights diplomacy of mainstream nations and from international human-rights organizations is making the cost of maintaining a system of dictatorship and terror politics increasingly high, while the effectiveness and the deterrent capacity of official persecution continue to decline, forcing the current Chinese Communist regime to put on a big "Human Rights Show" and "Democracy Show," both in its domestic governance and in its foreign response.

In other words, whether it is the everlasting practice of nonviolent resistance, or the prediction that the liberal system will be the "end of history,"[3] all these [theories] ultimately appeal to the spiritual aspect of human nature. Humans exist not only physically, but also spiritually, possessing a moral sense, the core of which is the dignity of being human. Our high regard for dignity is the natural source of our sense of justice. When a system or a country allows everyone to live with dignity, it can gain spontaneous approval from the people, which is how St. Thomas Aquinas understood political virtue: Virtuous good governance lies not only in maintaining order, but [even] more in establishing human dignity. [If it acts] otherwise, [a government] will provoke various forms of resistance, with conscientious objection among the principal forms. The reason why the liberal system can gradually replace dictatorship, and the end of the Cold War can be seen as the end of history, lies in the fact that the former [the liberal system] acknowledges and respects human dignity, while the latter [dictatorship] does not recognize human dignity and discredits it by dragging it in the dust.

The greatness of nonviolent resistance is that even as man is faced with forceful tyranny and the resulting suffering, the victim responds to hate with love, to prejudice with tolerance, to arrogance with humility, to humiliation with dignity, and to violence with reason. That is, the victim, with love that is humble and dignified, takes the initiative to invite the victimizer to return to the rules of reason, peace, and compassion, thereby transcending the vicious cycle of "replacing one tyranny with another."

Bottom-up reform requires self-consciousness among the people, and self-initiated, persistent, and continuously expanding civil-disobedience movements or rights-defense movements among the people.

In an unfree society ruled by a dictatorship, under the premise of a temporary absence of power that can change the dictatorial nature of the regime, the civic ways that I know of for promoting the transformation of Chinese society from the bottom up are as follows:

The nonviolent rights-defense movement does not aim to seize political power, but is committed to building a humane society wherein one can live with dignity. That is, it strives to expand an independent civil society by changing the way people live—the lifestyle of ignorance, cowardice, and willing enslavement—by first endeavoring to expand the space and resources for civil society in areas where the control by government authorities is weak. This is followed by sustained nonviolent resistance to compress the social space controlled by government authorities, and then by increasing the price the dictatorial government has to pay in order to control the civic sphere, shaping a pattern of gradual inch-by-inch progress of civil liberties at the expense of the contracting power of government authorities.

The nonviolent rights-defense movement need not pursue a grand goal of complete transformation. Instead, it is committed to putting freedom into practice in everyday life through initiation of ideas, expression of opinions, and rights-defense actions; particularly through the continuous accumulation of each and every rights-defense case, it accrues moral and justice resources, organizational resources, and maneuvering experience in the civic sector. When civic forces are not yet strong enough to change the macropolitical environment at large, they can at least rely on personal conscience and small-group cooperation to change the small, micropolitical environment within their reach. For instance, the fact that the rebellion of senior newsmen such as Lu Yuegang and Li Datong against the official news system achieved definite results was ultimately a function of the soundness of the small milieu within the *China Youth Daily*.

Regardless of how great the freedom-denying power of a regime and its institutions is, every individual should still fight to the best of his or her ability to live as a free person—that is, make every effort to live an honest life with dignity. In any society ruled by dictatorship, when those who pursue freedom publicly disclose it and practice what they preach, as long as they manage to be fearless in the small details of everyday life, what they say and do in everyday life will become the fundamental force that will topple the system of enslavement. If you believe that you possess a basic human conscience and if you heed its call, then display it and let it shine in the sunlight of public opinion, let the people see it and, especially, let the dictators see it.

One should unfailingly commit to liberal values, pursue the principle of tolerance, and promote multilateral dialogue, particularly when different voices and different choices arise among the people; and one should treat low-profile dealings as a supplement to high-profile resistance, rather than regarding oneself as an absolute hero and unreasonably assigning blame. Because even though enforced morality is different from enforced politics, it is still quite far from the tolerance that liberalism calls for. That a person is willing to pay a great price for the ideals he or she chooses does not constitute justification for forcing others to make comparable sacrifices for ideals.

Whether an insider or an outsider of the system, whether working from the top down or the bottom up, each should respect the other's right to speak. Even the statements and actions of people attached to the government, as long as they do not force constraints on independent discourse among the people and the rights-defense movement, should be regarded as a useful exploration of transformational strategies, and their right of speech should be fully respected. Those who advocate transformation from the top down should maintain adequate respect for the explorations of those working from the bottom up among the people. With the premise of mutual respect and equal treatment, the contention and dialogue between proponents of the top-down and the bottom-up positions will make a more useful contribution to shaping a popular consensus on the trajectory for transformation. This is the meaning of the saying, "All roads lead to Rome." Tolerance, however, does not mean tacit consent to tyranny, nor does it mean sinking into the quagmire of absolute relativism. The bottom line for the liberal nongovernmental position is, specifically, firm opposition by force of the words and deeds of the people to any government repression, whatever form this repression may take—intimidation, bribery, rectification, expulsion, prohibition, arrest, or legislation.

Institutional common sense on how to confront rather than evade an ever-present dictatorial power: [One must] take into one's own hands the initiative for improving the status of the population without rights, rather than pinning hope on the arrival of some enlightened master or benevolent ruler. In the strategic maneuvering between civil society and the government, regardless of how official policies may change, the most important thing is to encourage and assist the civil-rights defense movement and to hold fast to the independent position of civil society. Especially in a situation where one is alone in confronting bad governance amid a chorus of praise singers, one must be committed to the criticism of and opposition to the dictatorial regime from the position of an outsider. When the government's policy decisions are stiff, one must force them to become flexible; when the government's attitude loosens, one must take advantage of it to expand civic resources and space. While supporting enlightened policy making within the system, one must still hold fast to one's position as an outsider and persevere in one's criticism.

In sum, China's course toward [becoming] a free society will mainly rely on bottom-up gradual improvement and not on a top-down "Chiang Ching-kuo–style" revolution.[4] Bottom-up reform requires self-consciousness among the people, and self-initiated, persistent, and continuously expanding civil-disobedience movements or rights-defense movements among the people. In other words, pursue [the building of] free and democratic forces among the people; do not pursue the rebuilding of society through radical regime change, but instead use gradual social change to compel regime change. That is, rely on a continuously growing civil society to reform a regime that lacks legitimacy.

TRANSLATOR'S NOTES

1. Mikhail Sergeyevich Gorbachev (b. 1931) was the second-to-last general secretary of the Communist Party of the Soviet Union, serving from 1985 until 1991, and the last head of state of the USSR, serving from 1988 until its collapse in 1991.

2. Chiang Ching-kuo (1910–88) was the Kuomintang (Chinese Nationalist) politician and leader. The son of Chiang Kai-shek, he was first the premier (1972–78) of the Republic of China (ROC), and then its president from 1978 until his death in 1988. Under

his tenure, the ROC government, while authoritarian, became more open and tolerant of political dissent. Toward the end of his life, Chiang relaxed government controls on the media and speech.

3. See Francis Fukuyama, "The End of History?" *National Interest* 16 (Summer 1989): 3–18.

4. In 1987, President Chiang Ching-kuo ended martial law in Taiwan and began a gradual process of political liberalization, allowing opposition groups to form.

Can It Be That the Chinese People Deserve Only "Party-Led Democracy"?

Liu Xiaobo

Translation by Human Rights in China

On 19 October 2005, the Information Office of the State Council of the People's Republic of China released the white paper, "Building of Democratic Politics in China." Although this was the first white paper on democracy-building issued by the Communist government since it came to power, except for the fact that it was published, it broke no new ground in terms of content.

At the core of the white paper were arguments regarding the "theory of national conditions," "theory of [Chinese Communist] Party [(CCP)] authority," and "theory of the wisdom of the [CCP]."

The "theory of national conditions" in the white paper no longer stresses China's economic backwardness and the substandard quality of the population, but rather emphasizes that the central leadership position of the CCP was both a historical choice and the voluntary choice of the Chinese people—that is, it was created by history rather than the will imposed by the CCP on the people. Clearly, the purpose of the "theory of national conditions" is to refute the universal nature of democracy and to conceal the problems of legitimacy of the current CCP regime by invoking special national conditions.

The "theory of Party authority" publicly affirms China's current system of the supreme authority of the Party. Whether it is the abstract idea of democratic construction of popular sovereignty or the protection of human rights and specific human rights written into the Constitution, whether it is the institution of the National People's Congress (NPC) and the political consultative system or the so-called democratic central-ism with Chinese Communist characteristics, whether the grassroots de-mocracy process or rule by law—all of these must follow the guidance of the CCP authority and have nothing to do with popular sovereignty.

The purpose of the "theory of the wisdom of the CCP" is to declare that the credit for all of China's current achievements is due to the CCP, going as far as to defend a string of failures as great accomplishments. Similarly, whatever little democratic achievement there has been in China since the reforms is also all attributable to the wise leadership of the CCP and is most certainly not the result of spontaneous efforts of the people.

As a result, the white paper is tantamount to a declaration to the entire world: Above the democracy of people's sovereignty, the CCP authority is an even higher authority, and this Party authority is supreme, which is to say that "the Party is in charge of the people" and "the Party is in charge of democracy," and that the NPC is the puppet of the Party authority, the Chinese People's Political Consultative Conference (CP-PCC) is its ornament, the judiciary is its tool, and the vocabulary of human rights, democracy, and so on is just its window dressing. Like the white paper on human rights released by the CCP authorities, this white paper on democracy is full of lies. For example, the white paper states: "All power in the People's Republic of China belongs to the people." But China's 1.3 billion people are a flock of sheep herded by the Party authority and have no opportunity to participate in the election of the country's president. Another example is that the white paper proclaims "development of democracy within the Party." Yet the great majority of the 68 million Party members are no more than Party slaves and, likewise, have no opportunity to elect the Party boss.

This is the "Building of Democratic Politics in China" flaunted by the white paper!

So this white paper is not so much an announcement of the "Building of Democratic Politics in China" as it is a public defense of "protecting the dictatorial system of the supremacy of Party authority."

On 1 October 1949, after Mao Zedong ascended Tiananmen Gate, the chorus of "He is the great savior of the people" swept through the country—an enduring song that has to this day remained a nostalgic tool used by the people to vent their dissatisfaction. On 1 October 1984, after Deng Xiaoping descended from Tiananmen to review the troops and accepted the heartfelt support [expressed in the simple greeting of] "Hello Xiaoping," with one wave of his hand, the "chief architect" bestowed upon the little people the opportunity to make a dash for the small comforts of everyday life, to "let some people get rich first," and achieved limited economic emancipation. On 1 October 1999, after Jiang Zemin reviewed the troops, despite widespread attacks from all quarters, he was still secure in the key position as the "leading figure in inheriting the revolutionary cause and carrying it into the future." He embarked on yet another theoretical innovation of vast and mighty imperial largesse and let the capitalists who had amassed great fortunes join the CCP and be politically emancipated by royal decree, so that they were no longer just the United Front partners and political ornaments of the NPC and CPPCC but had become members of the ruling party. I do not know when the new Party boss Hu Jintao plans to ascend Tiananmen to review the troops and mold an image for his own "dear people."

I do not deny that within the CCP clique currently in power there could be high-ranking officials, such as Hu Yaobang and Zhao Ziyang, who treat the people well and possess an awareness of modern politics. When they were in office, they did make quite a few good policy decisions and took risks to advance political reform. But even when this was the case, people had to wait for their rights and benefits as if they were charities bestowed from above, not to mention that such good officials could not survive for long under the CCP system.

Let us take ten-thousand steps back: If our countrymen could come across an enlightened ruler often, or if the imperial bestowing of favors was not incidental behavior but, rather, occurred every now and then, then the national inertia of waiting for these favors, although an insult to human dignity, could be excused because of the tangible benefits received. Sadly, however, our countrymen endured great suffering and endless waiting only to encounter a wise sovereign by chance or an exceedingly miserly show of mercy. What they receive are always meager compensations and pathetic consolations that arrive too late, so why is it that they are still only capable of looking up to the crown? Moreover, throughout China's cyclical dynastic history, every act of the vast and mighty imperial benevolence has occurred either at the beginning of a new dynasty, when everything left undone by the previous regime is taken up, or during the crisis-ridden final years of a reign, and never for the well-being of the people but out of political necessity, to consolidate or maintain political power or save the regime. Our countrymen are still like infants who depend entirely on adult care and who know only how to wait for a wise ruler to appear. Can it be that Chinese people will never really grow up, that their character is forever deformed and weak, and that they are only fit, as if predestined by the stars, to pray for and accept imperial mercy on their knees?!

There is absolutely no doubt that on the post-Mao mainland, compared with the Mao era, our countrymen have gained tangible benefits in terms of food and shelter and an extremely limited space for personal choices. The pragmatic "cat theory" initiated by Deng Xiaoping,[1] compared with Mao's ideology, which stressed class struggle, had a nimble and soft flexibility. However, none of these changes have fundamentally altered the basic mode of existence of our countrymen; the relationship between the ruler and the ruled in this land has been the same throughout the ages, and has been handed down unchanged to this day. Namely, the power to initiate and make decisions about the rights and interests of the people, the fate of the country, any progress in society, and any improvements to the lives of the common people is firmly held in the hands of the dictators. [All improvements] are charity granted from above, requiring the subjects to shout the triple "Long live!" salute to show their loyalty and gratitude to the rulers, requiring famous public figures to play the part of critics who share their goals, and requiring hack writers with skillful pens to defend and praise them, in order to demonstrate the wisdom and virtues of the sovereign.

Even though there have been improvements in civil-rights defense movements in recent years, we must also look at the grim reality facing the cause of civil-rights defense. If not used by the treacherous dictators as a tool to seize power and establish a new dynasty, the bottom-up movement to win human dignity and personal rights and interests gets completely wiped out by the brutal autocratic machine, and there is no way that a succession of large-scale movements of popular disobedience, be they the traditional violent rebellions for dynastic change or the modern political opposition movements of peaceful resistance, can arise to shake the foundations of the authoritarian system and the slavish culture.

What is the reason for this?

Repression by the dictatorial authorities is, admittedly, one of the reasons, but the indifference of the populace is an even greater cause. In the minds of ignorant, cowardly, and blind people, being used is no different from being liberated and given a new life. As to the cowardly but smart cynics, being repressed means being subjugated, and thus becoming an accomplice, a lackey, or, at the very least, a silent, docile subject. When have our countrymen tasted the genuine liberation that comes with being the master of one's own affairs? When has China ever broken out of the vicious historical cycle of order and chaos under authoritarian dynastic rule?

For generations, up until this very day of CCP rule, expressions like "after liberation," "since the founding of the country," and "after the new China was established," and excuses such as "without the Communist Party there would be no new China," have become the most basic common understanding of history and a linguistic habit that has settled deeply into the nation's collective memory, universally used in people's speech and writing. Even the intellectuals and liberals within the Party who know the CCP's history like the back of their hands habitually use these terms for historical reference when exposing the countless crimes committed after the CCP took power.

Likewise, when common people today bring up the 1989 Movement and the June Fourth [Tiananmen] Massacre, the vast majority still casually toss around the words "turmoil" or "rebellion." Even the Beijing residents who personally experienced the great peaceful marches and the bloody massacre by and large use the vocabulary set by the government. And although the authorities have already quietly changed "turmoil" and "rebellion" to "political disturbances" in the public media, the people's language has not changed much accordingly. Since Jiang Zemin's regime persecuted the Falun Gong in 1999, the word "cult" has also entered the vernacular, spreading particularly fast among college, high-school, and elementary-school students. A few years ago, every time I heard acquaintances use the word "turmoil" to talk about the 1989 Movement, I wanted to refute it and correct them. These corrections were at first made angrily, then gravely, and, finally, with resignation. As time went on, I began to let them go. Forceful ideological indoctrination of minds that have been enslaved for a prolonged period inevitably hardens memory and language.

Linguistic philosophy's sacred monster Ludwig Wittgenstein maintained that language is not a tool of expression in the traditional sense but action itself, and that the way one chooses to express oneself linguistically is the way one chooses to think, [while] the way one chooses to think is the way one chooses to live. Therefore, by extension, if one habitually uses linguistic expressions of deep gratitude, one inevitably creates the savior mentality; the savior mentality inevitably leads to the slavish way of life of waiting for top-down charity and the fear that without the savior one will end up in a situation more desperate and pitiful than that of a homeless dog.

Time and time again, people have pinned their hopes for top-down political reform on those who have newly assumed office, but they end up disappointed each time. The most absurd part is that disappointment after disappointment still has not extinguished what little hope people have in the CCP-initiated reforms. Why? The usual response is that the national conditions make it so. Some people say that such a large country can only be controlled and governed by an authoritarian system. Others say that the CCP is too powerful and that it has too many monopolies on resources, so that unless it transforms itself no other force can challenge it. Some say that opposition groups in popular politics in many ways do not even measure up to the CCP, and that if they came to power they would be even worse than the CCP. Others say that economic development comes before political reform; to ensure high economic growth one must maintain social stability, and only with the CCP in power can stability be maintained. Still others say that the mainland population is too large, inferior, and ignorant, only fit to receive charitable guidance from the elites, and only capable of carrying out top-down reforms, et cetera. All of these arguments just go to prove: Without the CCP, or if the CCP were to step down, who could effectively rule China in its place? Do not democracy activists and people who hold divergent political views in China and abroad constantly run up against this question? And that is why waiting for the gift of happiness to be bestowed from above is the common people's only option.

At a time when our countrymen do not fight, not even preparing to

become their own masters, at a time when they have abandoned all efforts even before the struggle for their personal rights and interests has
started in earnest, people can universally concoct a subconscious assumption that without the current rulers the country would slide into
chaos. This type of assumption stems from the long-enforced ideological indoctrination of the CCP, as well as the slavish nature of our countrymen, which remains unchanged to this day. There is a reason why
dictators disregard historical facts and raise this type of assumption.
That is because every policy decision they make and everything they
say have only one ultimate purpose—maintaining absolute power. But
there is absolutely no reason for the people to believe in this assumption,
because the system that this assumption supports is precisely a system
that does not treat people as humans. Once our countrymen forget historical facts and believe in this assumption, they would have no qualms
in waiting for the pie to fall from the sky and would look for a wise
ruler or a virtuous master even if they have to die nine times looking for
one; they would view all bottom-up popular opposition movements and
those that fight for personal rights and interests as more of a hindrance
than help that only "add to chaos," and would defend those in power,
who have done one insignificant small good and 99 great ills, using that
one percent of good policy to defend that 99 percent of bad government.
Even when being massacred, starved, imprisoned, exiled, deprived, and
discriminated against, the little people still feel eternally indebted and
grateful and consider the dictators "great, honorable, and infallible."

A poem by Bai Juyi[2] says: "Wildfire never quite destroys them—They
grow again in the spring wind." In mainland China, this eternal, celebrated verse is decidedly not an apt description of people who have the
courage to stand up straight and tall, but rather an exquisite portrayal of
our countrymen accustomed to kneeling ever so gracefully. Under the
imperial throne, civil and military officials neatly fall to their knees as one
and shout the salute, "Long live! Long, long live!" three times. Atop Tiananmen, the dictator waves his hand and the largest square in the world
becomes a sea of subjects hailing their savior. Since the collapse of the
Qing Dynasty [in 1911] and especially since the CCP came to power, even
though our countrymen no longer kowtow physically like the people of
old, they kneel in their souls even more so than the ancients.

An admonition on how to be an upright person says: "Man is born free
and equal." Universal enslavement and inequality are never caused by
the ruler's excessive power or wisdom, but because those who are ruled
kneel down. Can it be that today, more than a hundred years after the
era of imperial power based on triple kowtowing and nine-fold kneeling
has been abolished, our countrymen are still humiliating themselves and
finding all sorts of justifications to defend their kneeling position? Can
it be that the mere favors of a good standard of living and allowing the
wealthy to join the Party have made our countrymen capable only of

falling to their knees and kowtowing in gratitude for the magnanimity and grace of the dictators?

For the emergence of a free China, placing hope in "new policies" of those in power is far worse than placing hope in the continuous expansion of the "new power" among the people. The day when the dignity of the people is conceptually and legally established is the day when the human rights of our countrymen will gain institutional protections.

TRANSLATOR'S NOTES

1. When Deng Xiaoping returned to power in the mid-1970s, after the Cultural Revolution, he famously declared, "I do not care whether a cat is black or white. As long as it catches mice, it is a good cat," to signal that he intended to put stress on pragmatism rather than ideology. This landed him in new trouble, and he was once again purged from all his official posts by Mao Zedong. However, after Mao's death Deng's position won the day, and set off decades of China's economic reform and opening to the outside world.

2. Bai Juyi (772–846 C.E.), one of the most celebrated Tang Dynasty poets, used elegantly simple verse to protest the social evils of his day, including corruption and militarism.

INDEX